REMEMBERING THE FUTURE
TOWARD AN ESCHATOLOGICAL ONTOLOGY

Metropolitan of Pergamon
JOHN D. ZIZIOULAS

Remembering the Future

Toward an Eschatological Ontology

Foreword by
Pope Francis

Edited by
Bishop Maxim Vasiljević

2023

Published by
St. Sebastian Press

Edited by
Bishop Maxim (Vasiljević)

Copyeditor
Sally Anna Boyle

Prepress & printing
Birograf COMP, Belgrade, Serbia

Contemporary Christian Thought Series, number 81

Copyright St. Sebastian Press & John Zizioulas Foundation © 2023

Address all correspondence to:
Sebastian Press
1621 West Garvey Avenue ⋰ Alhambra, California 91803
Email: westsrbdio@gmail.com ⋰ Website: www.westsrbdio.org

Publishers Cataloging in Publication

Names: Zizioulas, Jean, 1931–2023, author. | Francis, Pope, 1936– writer of preface. | Vasiljevic, Maksim, 1968– editor.

Title: Remembering the future : toward an eschatological ontology / Metropolitan of Pergamon John D. Zizioulas ; prefix by Pope Francis ; edited by Bishop Maxim Vasiljevic.

Description: [Alhambra, California] : St. Sebastian Orthodox Press, 2023. | Series: Contemporary Christian thought series ; no. 81. | Includes bibliographical references and index.

Identifiers: ISBN: 978-1-936773-95-4 (paperback) | 978-1-936773-96-1 (hardback)

Subjects: LCSH: Eschatology--Orthodox Eastern Church. | Theology, Doctrinal--Orthodox Eastern Church. | Ontology--Orthodox Eastern Church. | Fall of man--Orthodox Eastern Church. | Judgment Day--Orthodox Eastern Church. | Future, The--Orthodox Eastern Church. | Future life--Orthodox Eastern Church. | Orthodox Eastern Church--Doctrines.

Classification: LCC: BT823 .Z597 2023 | DDC: 236.088/2819--dc23

Contents

FOREWORD

by Pope Francis

To hold this book by John Zizioulas, Metropolitan of Pergamon, in my hands is for me still to clasp his hands in the friendship that bound us together. A posthumous book, as the title tells us, it comes to me as a sign springing from a past that has been liberated in the Future of God.

I first met John Zizioulas in 2013 when I welcomed the Delegation of the Ecumenical Patriarchate of Constantinople that came to Rome for the Feast of Saints Peter and Paul. It was a meeting that confirmed for me the conviction of how much we still have to learn from our Orthodox brothers and sisters with regard to episcopal collegiality and the tradition of synodicality.

In our conversations during successive meetings, he often brought up the topic of an eschatological theology that for years he had been hoping to turn into a book. When we prayed and reflected on the unity of Christians, he communicated his realism to me: this would only be achieved at the end of the ages. But in the meantime, we had the duty to do everything possible, *spes contra spem*, to continue to search for it together. The fact that it would be achieved only at the end should not feed complacency or find us idle: we had to believe that the Future was already in operation, "the cause of all being." A Future that comes *toward* history, that does not emerge *from* history. Not simply the end of the journey, but a companion in our life that is capable of "coloring" it with the colors of the Resurrection and with the voice of the Spirit that would have "remembered new things." He avoided the danger of our having our gaze fixed on a past able to make us prisoners, prisoners above all of old errors, of failed attempts, through accumulating negative junk, through encouraging the implanting of mistrust. We all suffer the negativity of looking backwards, and the sincere search for the unity of all Christians suffers from this in a particular way. The value of our traditions is to open up the path, and if instead they close it, if they hold us back, that means that we are mistaken in the way we interpret them, prisoners of our fear, attached to our sense of security, with the risk of transforming faith into ideology and mummifying the *truth* that in Christ is always *life* and *way* (John 14:6), path of peace, bread of communion, source of unity.

The *eschaton* knocks at the door of our daily life, seeks our collaboration, loosens the chains, liberates the transition to a good life. And it is at the heart of the eucharistic canon that for Zizioulas the Church "remembers the future," completing as he does in the chapters of this book a doxology to "Him who comes," a theology that he has written on his knees, in expectation.

I want to awake the dawn (Psalm 108:2). The psalm's verse calls on all the instruments and voices of humanity to cry out our need for God's Future. Let us awake the dawn within ourselves, let us awake hope. Indeed, "the substance of things hoped for" (Heb 11:1), the gesture that constitutes Christianity, is to give a sign, a tangible and daily sign, a humble and disarmed sign, of "Him who is and who was and who is to come" (Rev 1:8).

Vatican City, 15 October 2023

Francis

PREFACE

by Bishop Maxim Vasiljević

Typically, eminent authors, in the twilight of their careers, tend to produce final works that are not commensurate with the elevated standards their readership has come to expect. Contrary to this norm, John Zizioulas, at the culmination of his theological journey, has bestowed upon the academic world in this magnum opus, a work that surpasses all his previous endeavors in depth, insight, and scholarly rigor. The insights presented in his celebrated *Being as Communion* and *Communion and Otherness* provided the groundwork for the extensive exploration undertaken in this seminal piece that will likely be dissected and referenced even more extensively than the author's prior contributions.

Metropolitan John harbored a deep-seated aspiration to pen this masterpiece on eschatology, a desire that can be traced back to his lectures in the 1980s, where he reflects on the notion of the world as "creation." However, the journey to authorship of such a volume on the future was protracted. Frequently questioned about the anticipated publication date, the metropolitan would often respond with a touch of humor, remarking, "before the Second Coming, I hope." The publication, released posthumously a mere six months after his repose in Athens on February 2nd of this year, stands as both a fortuitous gift and a fulfilled commitment. It is thanks to his disciple, Andreas Goulas, to whom I express my warmest thanks, that five invaluable manuscripts have been bequeathed, culminating in this impressive volume.

The late Elder Metropolitan of Pergamon acknowledged the profound challenge of articulating the influence of the future on the present. In 1999, he remarked, "I realize that this concept is most difficult to grasp and to experience," attributing this difficulty to the fact that "we still live in a fallen world in which protological ontology is the dominant form of rationality." The future of things in this perspective is defined by its origins and the "given" or the "factum."

For the past decade, during my visits with colleagues to Metropolitan John in Athens, he would often divulge snippets from his forthcoming monograph with the intriguing title, "Remembering the Future." He would emphasize that his book is written for those who *have accepted* the fact of the Resurrection of Christ and are interested in *the "logical" consequences* that follow the acceptance of this fact: *credo ut intelligam*. Throughout many discussions, he urged us to examine critically both the foundations and ramifications of his groundbreaking assertion that "the future precedes the past" from both logical and ontological perspectives. He maintained that Christian theology represents a hermeneutics of Resurrection, a pivotal theme at the heart of this book's inquiry.

This work of Zizioulas presents a holistic Christian "Grand Unified Theory," as he underscores how eschatological ontology deeply influences the entirety of Christian doctrine. While the lengthy introduction and the first three parts of this book are being presented to the public for the first time in this compilation, some segments have been previously published in other contexts. Yet, each piece has been carefully revised and refined by the author specifically for this edition. Editing the manuscripts of the late Metropolitan John has been a journey marked by fervent passion and reverential trepidation. I was convinced unequivocally that I had been handed writings parallel in profundity to those of ancient philosophers and Church fathers. The confidence bestowed upon me by the John Zizioulas Foundation and Sebastian Press, served as an invaluable source of encouragement. Engaging in numerous discussions with patristic scholar Norman Russell about the entire manuscript, as we revised it together, and his assistance provided by the meticulous cross-referencing, expert advice on the relevant literature, and translation of patristic passages, together with his translation of Pope Francis's *Foreword*, has been both immense and gratifying.

The John Zizioulas Foundation expresses profound gratitude to Pope Francis for graciously providing the foreword to this book, imbuing it with his invaluable insights, heartfelt warmth, and straightforwardness. His enthusiasm and unwavering dedication to the theology of John Zizioulas shine through all that he says. I owe a special debt of gratitude also to Stavros Yangazoglou, George Papageorgiou, don Giuseppe Bonfrate, p. Pino di Luccio SJ, fr. Basil Gavrilović, Nikos Tzoitis, Dionysios Skliris, and Sally Anna Boyle.

Los Angeles, October 2023

INTRODUCTION

I. Between the "Already" and the "Not Yet"

E schatology is not simply a doctrine; it is an orientation, a perspective, a mode of existence. Eschatology does not concern only the future; it affects our past as well as our present. This is how the Church viewed and experienced the "last things" from the beginning. In the words of the late father Georges Florovsky:

> [For] indeed eschatology is not just one particular section of the Christian theological system, but rather its basis and foundation, its guiding and inspiring principle or, as it were, the climate of the whole of Christian thinking. Christianity is essentially eschatological ... The Christian perspective is intrinsically eschatological.[1]

This was precisely how the early Christians understood their very existence:

> The goal was indeed "beyond history," but history was inwardly regulated and organized precisely by this superhistorical and transcendent goal, by a watchful expectation of the Coming Lord. Only an ultimate and final "consummation," an ultimate and final reintegration or "recapitulation" could have given meaning to the flux of happenings and events, to the duration of time itself.[2]

This centrality of eschatology in Christian theology—acknowledged also by Karl Barth,[3] albeit without effect on his theological

---

[1] G. Florovsky, "Eschatology in the Patristic Age," in *The Patristic Witness of Georges Florovsky. Essential Theological Writings*, eds. B. Gallaher and P. Ladouceur (London: T&T Clark, 2019), p. 311.

[2] Ibid., p. 314.

[3] K. Barth, *The Epistle to the Romans*, trans. E. C. Hoskyn (Oxford: Oxford University Press, 1963), p. 314: "If Christianity be not altogether thoroughly eschatology, there remains in it no relationship whatever with Christ."

method—suffered a long eclipse in the Church's history. With the prolonged delay of the Parousia the Church began to settle herself in the world, building cathedrals that would last for centuries and making long-term plans for the future while often reconciling herself to social and secular influence and power. Eschatology was, thus, pushed to the end of history or, more commonly, to the end of the individual's life and the state of its future existence. As a result, Christian theology devoted to eschatology the last chapter of dogmatics (*de novissimis*) referring specifically to death, the state after death, the resurrection of the dead, the Last Judgment, the consummation of the world and life everlasting. The only relevance left to eschatology for history and the present life was the fear of God's final judgment and its ethical implications, or the desire for reward and "happiness" in the future state through the fulfilment of certain conditions in the present life (moral, ascetical, sacramental, etc.).

All this gradually led to the marginalization of eschatology in relation to the essence of the Gospel and of Christianity itself. Protestant liberal theology in the nineteenth century placed the "essence of Christianity" in the proclamation of ethical principles,[4] while theologians such as Friedrich Schleiermacher, following traditional lines, relativized the doctrine of the last things in comparison with other doctrines.[5] All this led Ernst Troeltsch to declare at the end of the nineteenth century that "today the bureau of eschatology is usually closed."[6]

Things, however, underwent a radical shift in the following century. As Hans Urs von Balthasar, writing in 1957, observed, "if Troeltsch's comment that 'the bureau of eschatology is generally closed these days' was true for the liberalism of the nineteenth century, it is on the other hand true that the same office has been working overtime since the turn of the century."[7] This historic shift had already begun around the end of the nineteenth century when the biblical

---

[4] Thus, e.g., Adolf von Harnack, *What is Christianity*, trans. T. B. Saunders (London: Ernest Benn, 1958,), *passim* and p. 54.

[5] F. Schleiermacher, *Christian Faith*, eds. H. R. Mackintosh and J. S. Stewart (Edinburgh: T&T Clark, 1928), p. 703.

[6] E. Troeltsch, *Glaubenslehre*, ed. M. Troeltsch (Munich and Leipzig: n.p., 1925), p. 36.

[7] H. Urs von Balthasar, "Eschatologie," in *Fragen der Theologie heute*, eds. J. Feiner, et al. (Einsiederln: Benziger, 1957), p. 403.

scholar Johannes Weiss brought to attention the central and crucial place of eschatology in the teaching of Christ in his work *Die Predigt Jesu vom Reiche Gottes*, published first in 1892.[8] This was followed by Albert Schweitzer's *Geschichte der Leben-Jesu-Forschung* in 1906 and his studies on the mysticism of St Paul.[9] Both Weiss and Schweitzer criticized the Protestant liberal theologians of the nineteenth century, endeavoring to show that Jesus was not interested in preaching a God who only reigns in the souls of human beings or in proposing ways by which society could improve morally, but rather in proclaiming the immediate intervention of God in history in accordance with the prophetic and apocalyptic tradition of Israel that expected the sudden coming of God's Kingdom in the days of the Son of Man or Messiah. The "essence of Christianity" was not, therefore, to be found in certain ethical principles, as Adolf von Harnack and other liberal theologians claimed, but in the coming of God's Kingdom. Whether this coming was imminent or delayed, future or "realized," was of secondary importance. The crucial thing was that eschatology constituted the heart of our Lord's teaching, and this in itself was a thesis of tremendous significance for all of theology.

The consequences of this thesis for systematic theology deserve special emphasis. Such consequences were brought out and underlined in the nineteen-sixties particularly by Karl Rahner, Johannes Metz, and Balthasar on the Roman Catholic side, and Jürgen Moltmann and Wolfhart Pannenberg on the Protestant side. Among these, it was mainly Pannenberg who worked out a complete *Systematic Theology* (in three volumes) on the basis of what might be called an "eschatological ontology."[10] Moltmann found a wide audience particularly among politically-concerned theologians, since his *Theology of Hope* appeared to be full of implications for social life, particularly in support of the victims of injustice and oppression in society.[11] Today, after a certain decline of interest in sociology and pol-

[8] Johannes Weiss, *Predigt Jesu vom Reiche Gottes* (Göttingen: Vandenhoeck & Ruprecht, 1892), especially in its second edition of 1900.

[9] Albert Schweitzer, *Eine Geschichte der Leben-Jesu-Forschung* (Tübingen: Mohr Siebeck, 1906).

[10] Wolfhart Pannenberg, *Systematic Theology*, 3 vols, trans. G. W. Bromiley (London and New York: T & T Clark International, 1991, 1996, 2000).

[11] Jürgen Moltmann, *Theology of Hope*, trans. J.W. Leitch (London: SCM Press, 1967).

itics, modern philosophers in Europe and in America keep alive in various ways the interest in eschatology, thus maintaining its centrality in contemporary thought.[12]

Orthodox academic theology, however, does not seem to have been affected by these developments. Its dogmatic manuals continue to treat eschatology as their last chapter covering subjects such as life after death, the final judgment, etc. The relation of eschatology to the other doctrines of the Church—or to the present life of the believer—is totally missing.

A different approach to dogmatics is to be found, as we have seen, in Florovsky and, in regard to the Liturgy, in the work of the late Alexander Schmemann. Both of them draw mainly from the liturgical experience of the Church, in which eschatology occupies a central place. For both of them, the *lex orandi* and the *lex credendi* must coincide and serve as the source and the foundation of dogmatic theology. Yet, in neither of them do we find a discussion of the implications that the integration of these two sources might have for systematic theology and Christian existence in its fundamental aspects. In the last century, an attempt to liberate Orthodox dogmatic theology from Western rationalism and lead it back to the patristic sources was made by the late Vladimir Lossky, who has exercised a strong influence on contemporary Orthodox thought, particularly with his book *The Mystical Theology of the Eastern Church*. Lossky did indeed lead Orthodox dogmatics away from western Scholasti-

---

[12] Emphasis on eschatology in modern philosophy could be traced back to Heidegger. The self-understanding of *Dasein* (hermeneutics of facticity) always projects itself toward the future and thereby becomes aware of its finitude ("Vorlaufen zum Tode"). See, especially, his *Ontology: The Hermeneutics of Facticity*, trans. J. van Buren (Bloomington, IN: Indiana University Press, 1999). The new generation of phenomenologists, such as Jean-Luc Marion, Jean-Yves Lacoste, and Richard Kearny, engage, each in different ways, some kind of eschatology in their phenomenological analysis. Marion in particular treats the relation between Eucharist and eschatology in his *Dieu sans l'être* (Paris: Presses Universitaires de France, 1991, pp. 197–222). The most interesting attempt to reconcile the phenomenological principle "back to the things-themselves" (Husserl) with eschatology ("the things-to-come") is made by J.P. Manoussakis with particular significance for theology. See his "The Anarchic Principle of Christian Eschatology in the Eucharistic Tradition of the Eastern Church," *Harvard Theological Review* 100:1 (2007) 29–46. Cf. more recently his *The Ethics of Time: A Phenomenology and Hermeneutics of Change* (London: Bloomsbury, 2017).

cism, yet in the direction suggested mainly by the thought of the Areopagetic writings in which eschatology is notoriously absent. Lossky did refer at several points in his work to the future eschatological state but he hastened to explain that this state is already present in the saints who, being already deified, enjoy the light of the Resurrection and have nothing *essential* to expect from Christ's second coming. Quoting St Symeon the New Theologian, he wrote that the Parousia will not occur for the saints: "for those who always walk in the light, the Day of the Lord will never come, for they are already with God and in God."[13]

This kind of eschatology leans too heavily on the side of the "already"—at least for a certain class of believers—taking away or marginalizing two basic aspects of Christian eschatological faith: the *eagerness* of the expectation of the Parousia, which marked so vividly the experience of the first ecclesial communities (Rev 6:1; 22:17, 20), and the longing for the resurrection of the *body* which will be granted *only in the future*. Laying too much stress on and contentment with the present state of the saints' union with God and their experience and manifestation of the divine light can lead to the position that the future Parousia will not affect the saints ontologically (that it will not add anything essential to them, but only to the rest of the world), and that their bodies *even in their present state of corruption and death* exist in perfection, not being in need of liberation from the bondage of death. In such a view of eschatology, corruption and death lose their tragic character and the future bodily resurrection is deprived of *ontological* significance for *all* human beings and creation.

This weakening of the longing for the Parousia has not been limited to theology; it has permeated also the religious life of the Christian communities, including the Orthodox Church. The widespread identification of the human being with its soul, which in the Platonic view prevailing among Christians is immortal, contributes to the diminution of the longing for the resurrection of our bodies and, thus, for the eschatological Parousia. The prayer *maranatha* (the

<hr />

[13] V. Lossky, *The Mystical Theology of the Eastern Church* (Cambridge: James Clarke & Co., 2005), p. 233. Cf. also his *Orthodox Theology: An Introduction* (Crestwood: St Vladimir's Seminary Press, 1978), p. 118.

Lord is coming, or Lord come) which dominated the worship of the early Christians has hardly any place in the petitions of Christian worshipers in our time. The salvation of the soul seems to have absorbed almost entirely the concern of the Christians, and this makes the coming of the Parousia and the resurrection *of the body* lose their existential urgency.

II. The Eucharistic Remembrance of the Future

The area of ecclesial life in which the eager expectation of the Parousia has survived, albeit without full consciousness of its significance, is that of worship and, in particular, the *Eucharist*. The *anamnesis*[14] of the events of the history of salvation for which the gifts of the Eucharist are offered to God in thanksgiving (εὐχαριστία) includes not only "the Cross, the Tomb, the Resurrection on the third day, the Ascension into heaven, the sitting at the right hand (of the Father)" but also "the Second and glorious Coming again (Παρουσίας)."[15] In the celebration of the Eucharist the ecclesial community remembers *not only the past but also the future.*

This remembrance of the future Coming of Christ is to be found in all the eucharistic canons of the East, but strikingly in *none* of the West.[16] It is notable that, as far as I know, this is true for all the extant eucharistic documents from the earliest times to the present. Such a consistent divergence cannot be without theological significance. It reveals the place eschatology occupies in the two great Christian traditions, confirming Yves Congar's pertinent observation that the East "suit beaucoup plus l'idée, très présent chez les Pères et dans la liturgie, d' une 'phanie,' d'une manifestation des réalités célestes, invisibles, sur la terre. Il s'ensuit une conception principalement sacramentelle et iconologique de l'Église" (the East "follows much more

---

[14] *Anamnesis* is is a Greek word that means the recollection or remembrance of the past. Anamnesis is a noun derived from the verb *anamimneskein*, which means "to be reminded."

[15] See the Liturgies bearing the names of St Basil and St John Chrysostom, which are in use in the Orthodox Church.

[16] See the texts of the eucharistic canons in A. Hänge and I. Pahl, *Prex Eucharistica* (Fribourg: Editions Universitaires, 1968).

the idea, very present in the Fathers and in the Liturgy, of a 'phanie,' of a manifestation of celestial, invisible realities on earth. This leads to a principally sacramental and iconological conception of the Church").[17]

The remembrance of the future Parousia in the eucharistic liturgy goes back to the earliest biblical sources. Paul already (1 Cor 11:26) sees the ἀνάμνησις (*anamnesis*) commandment for the celebration of the Eucharist as connected with the expectation of the Parousia: "For as often as you eat this bread and drink this cup, you proclaim the Lord's death until he comes." Joachim Jeremias after a detailed exegetical discussion concludes: "'Until he comes' apparently alludes to the *maranatha* of the liturgy with which the community prays for the eschatological coming of the Lord. This means that the death of the Lord is not proclaimed at every celebration of the meal as a past event but as an eschatological event, as the beginning of the New Covenant.... Paul has therefore understood the *Anamnesis* as eschatological remembrance of God that is to be realized in the *Parousia*."[18]

As the same biblical scholar observes,[19] Paul does not stand alone in this eschatological understanding of the *Anamnesis* commandment. In another primitive eucharistic text, the *Didache*, where eschatology dominates the entire eucharistic service, the remembrance of the Parousia also occupies a central place: "Remember, Lord, thy Church to deliver her from all evil and to perfect her in thy love, and gather her together from the four winds ... into thy Kingdom which thou hast prepared for her."[20] In each eucharistic celebration, the community not only asks for the coming of the future Kingdom but, at the same time, *anticipates* and *celebrates* its coming. God remembers the Church in his Kingdom and, at the same time, the community "remembers" the coming of the Lord in his Kingdom. The "not yet" is experienced and celebrated as an "already."

[17] Y. Congar, "Conclusions," in *Le Concile et les Conciles*, eds. B. Botte, et al. (Chevetogne and Paris: Éditions de Chevetogne, 1960), p. 287.
[18] Joachim Jeremias, *The Eucharistic Words of Jesus* (London: SCM Press, 1966), p. 235f.
[19] Ibid., p. 254.
[20] *Didache* 10.5, J.B. Lightfoot and J.R. Harmer, *The Apostolic Fathers* (London: Macmillan, 1926), p. 222. Trans. Lightfoot and Harmer, modified.

The Eucharist, therefore, was from the beginning a representation and celebration of the coming of the future Kingdom here and now (Jn 4:23; 12:31; 13:9). As Fr Florovsky remarks, "The Eucharist … is a hymn rather than a prayer. It is the service of triumphant joy, the continuous Easter … a sacramental anticipation, a foretaste of the Resurrection, an image of his Resurrection."[21] This is why it was from the beginning (Acts 2:46) celebrated "with gladness of heart." Vestiges of this understanding of the Eucharist are left in eucharistic services in the East as well as in the West, yet without a consciousness of the eschatological character of the sacrament any longer, as it is evident in the way the Eucharist is normally celebrated in the Church and treated in sacramental theology today.

Thus, in the way the Eucharist is celebrated today, the prevailing atmosphere lacks the joy and jubilation that characterized the primitive eucharistic liturgies. Exclamations such as "Hosanna" and "Blessed be the Coming One," which were originally in the liturgy used to greet the coming of the eschatological Lord, have survived in the liturgical texts as doxological remnants without raising in the hearts of the faithful the eager expectation and anticipation of the Parousia. In many cases, particularly among the Orthodox today, the Eucharist is celebrated in dark churches so as to create the atmosphere of "mysticism" or even contrition, while the splendor of iconography or of the clerical vestments inherited from Byzantium tends to be regarded as an offence to the humility displayed by Christ in his earthly life. What the Church "remembers" in the Eucharist today is no longer the glorious eschatological King but the humble and crucified Jesus. It is a remembrance of the past, not of the future.

This corresponds to the way the Eucharist is understood and presented in sacramental theology, particularly since the Middle Ages, in the West but also in the East. Maurice de la Taille expresses faithfully this theology when he writes that the *res tantum* (i.e., the ultimate meaning) of the Eucharist and all the sacraments is our union with *the sacrifice of Christ on the Cross*.[22] In the discussions

---

[21] George Florovsky, "Redemption," in *Collected Works,* vol. III (Belmont, MA: Nordland Publishing Company, 1976), p. 158.

[22] Maurice de la Taille, *Mysterium Fidei de Augustissimo Corporis et Sanguinis Christi Sacrificio atque Sacramento* (Paris: Beauchesne, 1921), p. 581.

about the Eucharist at the time of the Reformation, the prevailing question was in what way the Eucharist ought to be related to the sacrifice of Christ on Calvary. This has also been the dominant theme in all dogmatic manuals dealing with the Eucharist—Orthodox, Roman Catholic, and Protestant—ever since. The relation of the Eucharist with the eschatological Kingdom that we find in biblical and early liturgical eucharistic texts seems to have disappeared in the course of history. The Eucharist is, in the consciousness of contemporary believers, a remembrance of the past, not of the future.

III. God's Remembrance

What does "remembering" or *anamnesis* mean in a eucharistic context? In our common usage, remembering carries basically a psychological meaning: it signifies an act of our imagination, a mental recollection of a person, a thing, or an event. As such it bears no *ontological* meaning; it does not refer to a reality but to a personal thought or feeling. Remembering someone or something does not bring about their *presence*; it does not render them actual and truly existing.

Biblical research in our time has pointed out that the verb "to remember," which is used in the Bible frequently, indicated something more than a mental recollection of a person or an event; it was intended to *effect* something, to *create an event*.[23] This is particularly the case when the verb is used about God, but it applies also conversely to humans in their relation to God. The Old Testament, particularly the book of Deuteronomy (5:14; 7:18; 8:2; etc.), develops what may be called a theology of remembering,[24] and the same is true of the New Testament. God remembers his covenant (Lk 1:72) precisely in bringing about its fulfilment in Christ, and when he remembers the iniquities of Babylon (Rev 18:5) he applies his eschatological judgment. Christ's remembering of the thief on the Cross means no less than his entrance into the Kingdom (Lk 23:42). Equally, when God

---

[23] O. Michel, "μιμνήσκομαι," in G. Kittel, *Theological Dictionary of the New Testament*, vol. IV, trans. and ed. G. W. Bromiley (Grand Rapids, MI: Eerdmans, 1967), pp. 675–678.

[24] Michel, "μιμνήσκομαι," p. 675.

does not remember someone or something (for example, one's sins in Heb 8:12) he declares them nonexistent. God's remembrance always has an *ontological* meaning, not a psychological one (which, if applied in this case, would imply anthropomorphism).

The same ontological content must be given to remembering when the subject is human beings in their relation to God. The remembrance of the Passover ordered by God for his people (Ex 13:8) means that in remembering it each generation of Israel must consider itself as having been delivered from servitude.[25] In the same way, and even more dramatically, the celebration of the Christian Passover by the eucharistic community is not simply a psychological and mental act of its members but "an efficacious and creative event" in which a redemptive act of God is experienced by those who participate in it.[26] Whether we accept Joachim Jeremias's thesis that in the eucharistic *anamnesis* the subject doing the remembering is *God* (God remembers the Messiah Christ in his Kingdom),[27] or we understand the community as the subject who remembers (a remembrance of Christ's death, Resurrection, and Second Coming *by the Church*), we are talking of something that happens *here and now* and affects our existence ontologically. Remembering, in this case, can and does *create a reality that matters existentially.*

IV. The Light of the Post-Easter Experience

In the eucharistic *anamnesis*, remembering is not directed only to the past but also *to the future.* It is in fact a remembrance of the past *via* the remembrance of the future. This is crucial, and it seems to have been overlooked in theology. It constitutes a central point in the present study.

The Eucharist is undoubtedly an *anamnesis* of Christ's death, i.e., *of the past.* It is noteworthy, however, that it is *not celebrated on the day of the crucifixion but of the Resurrection.* And it was not an occasion of grief, as it befits a remembrance of someone's death, but

---

[25] See e.g., N. A. Dahl, "Anamnesis, mémoire et commémoration dans le Christianisme primitif," *Studia Theologica* 1 (1947) 83.

[26] Michel, "μιμνήσκομαι," p. 675.

[27] Jeremias, *The Eucharistic Words of Jesus,* p. 255.

one of "gladness of heart" (Acts 2:46). The fact that the death of Christ is regarded as a redemptive event is not enough to justify the absence of grief: on Good Friday, which is devoted exclusively to the commemoration of Christ's death, the prevailing feeling in the Church is that of mourning (and it is precisely for that reason that the Eucharist is *not* celebrated in the Orthodox Church on that day). The fact that the Eucharist was from the beginning celebrated on Sunday and with "gladness of heart" was due to its being a commemoration of the *Resurrection* and of the *Parousia*. The tone, therefore, in the event is set by *eschatology: it was the remembrance of the future that dominated the remembrance of the past. The past was remembered via the future.*

This raises a fundamental philosophical issue. If in the Eucharist we remember past events by placing them in the setting of the future, thus allowing the latter to provide the tone and ambiance in which they are recalled and experienced, this means that historical events acquire their significance for the present (they become "efficacious and creative events") only if they are understood and experienced as part of a future event that possesses finality and ultimacy. *The remembrance of the future serves, in this case, as a hermeneutical tool for understanding and appropriating the past.* Such a remembrance of the future does not undermine history but rather confirms and vivifies it. Eschatology and history are not two alternative or opposite ideas but united in the one and the same event.

This encounter of history and eschatology, in which the latter interprets and gives ontological significance to the former, constitutes the heart of Christian experience and, consequently, of theology. This is because in fact all of Christian life and thought is derived from one fundamental event: *the encounter of the risen Christ with his disciples in his appearances after the Resurrection.* Had it not been for these encounters we would have neither the historical Christ of the New Testament nor Christian worship as we know it.

It has been noted by modern biblical scholarship and must be constantly born in mind that in *all* four Gospels the historical life of Jesus, which is their subject, is presented, shaped and formulated *in the light of the post-Easter experience of the communities.* This does not necessarily mean that the historical facts of the life of Jesus are altered or distorted by the Gospels, but it does mean that they are *interpreted* and presented in the light of the encounter with the *risen* Christ. This applies also to St Paul: his Christology is based on his encounter with the risen Christ, an encounter which was a *sine qua non conditio* for genuine apostolicity and the apostolic *kerygma* (Acts 1:22; 1 Cor 9:11; 1 Jn 1:1; etc.).

Oscar Cullmann has pointed out and emphasized the importance of the post-Easter appearances of Christ for the emergence and formation of Christian worship.[28] We need not repeat here his arguments. Suffice to mention only the trivial use of the appellation "Lord" in our prayers to Christ or even in just our common references to him. It is normally forgotten that this term was originally used to indicate and proclaim the eschatological subjection of all things, including above all the power of death, to the risen Christ (Phil 2:14; 3:21; 1 Cor 15:2, 7). In other words *we worship the historical Christ only because he is the risen one, the eschatological Lord,* and we do so on the basis of the apostolic testimony that the risen Christ was encountered by the disciples who had seen, touched (1 Jn 1), and, above all, eaten with him (Acts 10:41; Lk 24:42; Jn 21:16) *within historical time.* It is this intrusion of the eschatological Christ into history that constitutes the source of worshiping him as the Lord to whom every knee shall bow (Phil 2:10), the Lord over evil and death itself. Take away these post-Easter encounters and the entire biblical Christology of Christ's divinity—indeed the whole content of the Gospels—collapses together with Christian worship as a whole.

Christianity, therefore, in all its basic claims and existential implications, depends entirely on the experience of the intrusion of the eschata into history and the interpretation and reception of the tradition *via* its encounter with the future. To employ Hans-Georg Gadamer's terminology, it is in the fusion of the "horizon" of the past with the "horizon" of the future that the past acquires its true meaning, its *hermeneutics.* For Christian theology, the past is not understood and interpreted by being placed in the horizon of the present, as it is for Gadamer, but in that *of the future.* The present emerges from this encounter of the past with the future either as a

---

[28] See Oscar Cullmann, *Early Christian Worship,* trans. A. S. Todd and J. B. Torrance (London: SCM Press, 1953), pp. 14–20.

dialectic, a "κρίσις" (judgment/crisis) in Johannine terms (Jn 2:19, 12:31), an either/or in the language of Soren Kierkegaard, or as a *conversion* of the past into an eschatological reality—a pure "Yes" without a "No," a eucharistic "Amen" (1 Cor 1:10) that equals a "sacrament." Time is "redeemed" neither through an escape into eternity in a Platonic manner, nor by a vertical "mystical" entrance of the eternal into the present, but by becoming "now" the bearer and the receptor *of its future*, its τέλος, the ultimate purpose for which it exists, as St Maximus would put it with reference to Christology and the eschatological Kingdom. The encounter of the risen (the eschatological) Christ with his disciples brought the end, in the sense of the purpose, of creation, into the present. It became in this way the "birthplace" of what we call "sacramental" reality in which events of the past and created realities become images of the Kingdom and carriers of the grace of immortality promised for the future, "antidotes to death" in the language of St Ignatius of Antioch, albeit, as yet only "in the Spirit," that is, as an "earnest" provoking thanksgiving and at the same time the eager longing for its future fullness and reality, the cry of "maranatha" of the first Christian communities.[29] The remembrance of the past *via* the remembrance of the future, which the disciples experienced in their encounters with the risen Lord (Lk 24:30–32), carried with it the giving of the Holy Spirit (Jn 20:22) that enabled them to "interpret" the Christ of the past (Lk 24:27; Jn 14:26) and to foretaste the gifts of the future Kingdom. When the Church celebrates the sacraments and particularly the Eucharist,[30] she prolongs the apostolic experience of the encounter with the risen Christ which included also "eating and drinking with him" (Acts 10:41) as an essential aspect of apostolicity. Through this experience, the future is fused with the past granting it its true meaning, its *hermeneutic*, in all its existential significance. This makes the Church "apostolic" in the deepest sense of this credal formulation, that is, a community which not only accepts and preaches the apostolic teaching but also *experiences* the grace and the gifts of the apos-

---

[29] Ignatius, *Ephesians* 20; *Didache* 10.6 (Lightfoot and Harmer, *Apostolic Fathers*, pp. 111, 222).

[30] The term used by the Greek Fathers for the Eucharist (and only for the Eucharist) was "Holy Mysteries."

tles' encounter and eating with the risen Lord, the entrance of the future Kingdom into time and history.

V. The "Earnest" of the Future Kingdom

All this calls for a deeper consideration of the role of *pneumatology* in theology. With the gradual weakening of the centrality of eschatology in theological discourse, it has been almost forgotten that the specific character of the activity of the Holy Spirit lies precisely in its connection with eschatology. This is apparent in the Bible and, quite interestingly, also in the Greek fathers. When the prophet Joel refers to the outpouring of the Holy Spirit "on all flesh" and the book of Acts applies this to Pentecost, the reference is clearly to "the last days" (Acts 2:18). The Spirit brings the eschata into history—this is his specific function and activity. For this reason, St Paul calls the Spirit the "earnest" (ἀρραβὼν) of the future Kingdom (2 Cor 1:22; Eph 1:14), the foretaste and experience in the present time of what is promised by God in the last days. The gifts of the Holy Spirit are all "fruits" and manifestations of the "new creation" (2 Cor 5:17; Gal 6:15), and the body of the future resurrection is filled with the Spirit (σῶμα πνευματικόν), as opposed to the "carnal" and "psychic" bodies which are subject to corruption and death (1 Cor 15:44). Christ's Resurrection itself involves the activity of the Spirit (Rom 8:11) and so does his birth as a human being (Mt 1:18; Lk 1:35) and, indeed, all of his earthly ministry with its teaching (Lk 4:18) and miracles (Mt 12:28). The Spirit makes Christ "the last Adam" (1 Cor 15:45), an eschatological being "dwelling" in history. Christology is either pneumatological, or it is no Christology at all. Pneumatology is not to be added to Christology; it is constitutive of it.

The connection of pneumatology with eschatology survives in the Greek fathers with St Irenaeus, the Cappadocian fathers, and finally St Maximus the Confessor, as notable examples. Irenaeus places in his anthropology the Spirit at the highest and final state of the human being in its growth from childhood to maturity, that is, its deification.[31] St Basil in distinguishing the specific activity of each

---

[31] Irenaeus, *Haer.* V. 6.1 (PG 7b:1137f)

person of the Holy Trinity in the economy, assigns to the Spirit the role of "perfecting" the work of the Father and the Son,[32] which is clearly a reference to eschatology. And finally, St Maximus in interpreting the "Our Father" quite bluntly identifies the Spirit with the Kingdom itself: "let thy Kingdom come, that is the Holy Spirit."[33]

Now, the role of the Holy Spirit in Christology is not only constitutive, it is also *interpretative*. The Spirit is the unique authority that tells us who Christ is and what he did and taught in his earthly life. The Gospels, which present to us the life and teaching of Christ, were written with the inspiration of the Holy Spirit (2 Pet 1:21). The disciples did not really know who Christ was; as it is stated in the Gospels, they often misunderstood him (Mk 6:52, 8:18, 9:32, 10:38, 14:40, 16:14). It was only the Holy Spirit that could teach them the truth (indeed, "the whole truth," in Jn 16:13) about Christ's identity and his teaching: "He [the Spirit] will teach you all and remind you [ὑπομνήσει: note the idea of remembering, again] of all the things I have told you" (Jn 14:26).

The Spirit, however, would not interpret Christ to the disciples by reminding them only of things of the past; he would also "announce [to them] *the things to come* (τὰ ἐρχόμενα)" (Jn 16:13). As we have already said, the Spirit's specific activity is to bring the eschata into history. In interpreting Christ, the Spirit places him in the "horizon" of the future—he presents the Jesus of history as the Christ risen from the dead and as the Lord to whom everything will be subjected. Only if the disciples understand the Jesus they had known in the past as the Christ of the future would they know the "whole truth" about him. This is what interpreting Christ in the Spirit means.

We are led, therefore, essentially back to the crucial significance for all of theology of the risen Christ's encounter with the disciples. The work of the Holy Spirit in history is to prolong into the ages of ages this encounter and, even more than that, to allow and enable the Christian community, those who would accept the apostolic testimony of his encounter, *to share themselves in it*, to have the same experience of seeing the risen one and dining with him in the ban-

[32] Basil, *De Spir.* 16.38 (PG 32:136B).
[33] Maximus, *Or. Dom.* (PG 90:885B).

quet of his Kingdom, in other words, to bring about and sustain the Church.

VI. The Reversal of the Direction of Time

If the subject of the risen Christ's discourses with his disciples during his post-Easter appearances was the Kingdom of God and if the Holy Spirit in interpreting Jesus brings into history the eschatological Christ and his Kingdom, the task of theology cannot but be an interpretation of the received faith, the apostolic *kerygma* and experience, in the light of eschatology. As the post-Easter encounters of the risen Christ with his disciples did not simply involve verbal conversation but also seeing, touching, and, above all, "breaking the bread" and eating with the risen Lord, theology cannot but draw in its interpretative task from the Church's liturgical experience in which the Holy Spirit prolongs in time and space those encounters. Theology must be an interpretation of the ecclesial (eucharistic in particular) experience in which the remembrance (in the sense explained above) of the future (Kingdom) acts as the hermeneutical "horizon" for the appropriation and proclamation of the apostolic *kerygma* at a particular time and situation.

The entrance of the eschata into history through the post-Resurrection appearances of the risen Lord and its prolongation into time and space by the Holy Spirit as a remembrance which brings about an "efficacious and creative event" implies a radical revision of our common conception of time. In Aristotle's definition of time as a movement from the earlier to the later, which is also basically our common conception of time, the "now" that stands between the past and the future is empty of ontological content, since, as Aristotle points out, there is "nothing"[34] (οὐθὲν) in it that can be measured and identified. This schema cannot accommodate the experience of time in the post-Easter encounters of Christ with his disciples. We need a new conception of time which would allow for the future to fill the "gap" of the "now," i.e., to give to time a content which would replace the Aristotelian οὐθὲν. There is of course a "mystical" approach to

[34] Aristotle, *Physics* IV 10–11, 218a 30ff.

this experience of time, according to which the "now" is filled with "eternity" in a kind of "eternal now," which is very often used to describe the experience that takes place in worship, quite frequently also by the Orthodox. In the case of the post-Easter experiences, however, the "now" is filled quite specifically not through simply a "mystical" experience but with the presence and experience of a *future* event, the second coming of Christ and the bringing of the Kingdom into history. This is a *reversal* of time, a movement not from the earlier to the later, as Aristotle sees it, but *from the end to the present* or even to *the beginning*, as St Maximus would describe it.[35]

It is obvious that our intellectual formation which is determined by protological thinking does not possess a concept to indicate this movement from the later to the earlier or to the "now." The concept of *prolepsis*, which is regularly used (particularly by Pannenberg) does not seem to be fully satisfactory, since it does not indicate that the initiation of the movement lies not with us but with the future kingdom which "visits" us. The same observation would apply also to the term *anticipation* which is preferred by others (e.g., Florovsky). We would need to employ a concept that would indicate the reversal of the direction of time from the end backwards, but this would require the development of an *eschatological ontology*—an ontology, that is, in which the truth of being lies at the end and not at the beginning.

The reversal of time from the future to the present does not apply only to the post-Easter encounters of Christ or to the liturgical experience of time. It permeates the entire biblical Christology—for example, the way Christ is presented in the Gospels and in the Pauline corpus. We normally describe the birth of Christ as "the miracle of Christmas," presenting it as a manifestation of God's *power*. This, however, is not how the authors of the Gospels speak of Christ. For them, Christ is the "Son of Man," or the "Messiah of *the last days*," the "last Adam" in Paul's Christological anthropology. The emphasis in the Synoptic Gospels (Matthew in particular) is placed on the fulfilment of the prophesies about the Messiah in the person of Jesus, that is, *on the coming of the last days which the prophets had foreseen.*

---

[35] Maximus, *QThal.* 59 (PG 90:613D–616A).

The Kingdom of God was expected in the future, but it was also present in Jesus' person (Lk 17:21).[36] In a typically Hebrew way of thinking, the "divinity" of Christ was implied in the authority to judge the world, to forgive sins, etc. (Mt 9:5)—all of these were eschatological and at the same time divine powers displayed *now* in Jesus of Nazareth. In Luke's Gospel, Symeon in holding Jesus in his hands asks God to dismiss him as he has seen and carried in his hands the Savior whom God had prepared for his people and all nations (Lk 2:29). And in the Fourth Gospel, with the exception perhaps of the Prologue, which is probably an independent piece of work, the eschatological Christ is present in the community, through the Spirit granting it the grace of communion with the eschatological Son of Man already now. Paul, on the other hand, speaks of the "Day of the Lord" as dawning already (Rom 13:13; 1 Thess 5:3, 5:8) and of union with the Coming Christ which is both eagerly awaited and experienced in his life (Gal 2:19; Phil 1:23, 3:7).

These are only a few examples of the crucial importance that the entrance of the eschata into history had for biblical Christology. This entrance cannot be conceived without the implication of a movement of time from the future to the present. But it is not only Christology and the liturgical experience of the Church, or indeed the Church herself, that must be understood in the light of this reversal of time. All the fundamental doctrines of the Christian faith must be viewed in this perspective. This would lead to a revision, sometimes a drastic one, of the way many of these doctrines have been usually presented in theology. The following may serve as representative examples.

The doctrine of *creation* is normally presented as an act of God completed in the past. Eschatology in this case does not affect the ontology, the *being* of creation but its *well-being*, its θέωσις as participation in the divine glory—an idea particularly familiar to Orthodox theology. If, however, we ground our doctrine of creation on

---

[36] The understanding of this verse as meaning that the Kingdom is present within the human being (in one's heart), which is common among Orthodox theologians, is a misunderstanding of the text. The phrase ἐντὸς ὑμῶν must be rendered as "in the midst of you" rather than "within you."

that of Christology,[37] as we find it in Pauline thought (Col 1:15) and in the cosmology of the Greek fathers, such as St Irenaeus, St Athanasius of Alexandria, and, particularly, St Maximus the Confessor, creation is conceivable only as incorporated and recapitulated in Christ, the Logos of God—that is, only when the economy of Christ is consummated. God is still working with Christ (Jn 5:17), and the Sabbath of his rest will come in the future.[38] This is how the Fathers, ever since the Epistle of Barnabas understood the Sabbath,[39] attaching to it an *eschatological* meaning, as we find it in St Maximus the Confessor's detailed and profound discussion of the term.[40]

God creates only complete and perfect entities. Creation is perfected only in the eschata—this is why its eschatological state is, according to the Fathers and against Origen's position, higher and better than the original one. In fact, as Maximus profoundly observes, it is only by looking at the eschatological state of creation that we can arrive at the knowledge of its beginning, its *raison d'être*.[41] Only through a movement from the end to the beginning, from the future to the past, can we "interpret," (i.e., understand) the mystery of why creation exists at all, of why it came into being in the first place, and why—this is important—it exists *in time* and has a *history*.

All this brings us back to what we already noted concerning the reversal of time from the future to the past brought about by Christ's appearances to his disciples after the Resurrection: only by the entrance of the eschata into history can the past be "interpreted" and understood. This hermeneutical principle which pertains to liturgical time and to Christology must be applied also to the doctrine of creation.

The same importance must be given to eschatology in dealing with the doctrine of the fall. We normally understand the fall as the loss of an original perfection owing to the disobedience of the first human beings to God's commandment, the cause of the appearance

---

[37] See on this Rowan Williams, *Christ the Heart of Creation* (London: Bloomsbury Continuum, 2018).

[38] Cullmann, *Early Christian Worship*, p. 88f.

[39] Barnabas, *Ep.* 15 (PG 2:772AB).

[40] Maximus, *Amb.* 65 (PG 91:1392f).

[41] Maximus, *QThal.* 59 (PG 90:613D–616A).

of all the evils in our existence, including corruption and death. Such an understanding of the fall is at odds with the scientifically established fact that corruption and death existed in creation long before the appearance of the human being and were not caused by human behavior. The idea of an originally perfect world was common to ancient mythology and religion, but, in spite of any *prima facie* evidence to the contrary, it was essentially foreign to both biblical and patristic thought. For both of these, creation and the human being were brought into existence with a call to *become* perfect, to grow into maturity, as Irenaeus would put it. For both the Bible and the Fathers, creation and the human being were called to a future state of existence much higher than the original one.

The fall, therefore, cannot consist in the loss of an original perfection; it must be seen rather as a refusal or a failure to obtain the perfection to which the human being (and creation) was called to arrive at in the end, a deviation from the movement toward the end and a subjection to what is already given as a *reality*. This is how the ingenuity of a thinker like St Maximus the Confessor perceives the fall: "The first human being," he writes, "having deprived (ἐλλείψας) the movement of its natural power of *the energy toward the end* (τῆς πρὸς τὸ τέλος ἐνεργείας) was diseased with the ignorance of its own cause." Evil, therefore, is nothing else but "the deprivation (ἔλλειψις) of the energy toward the end."[42] The human being has fallen not from its past but from its future; it refused to move to the end to which it was called, or for which it was created.

The deviation from the direction toward the future has automatically meant the subjection of humanity to what was already there, to *reality*. Since what was already there when the human being appeared was a state of corruption and death (the condition of animalhood from which humanity evolved), the fall "introduced" corruption and death by making it a *given* reality to which humanity was enslaved. The existential condition that resulted from this amounts, therefore, to *turning reality into a necessity* for the human being. Truth must now coincide with reality: *adequatio rei et intellectus*. Knowledge begins with the data provided by our senses and must

---

[42] Maximus, *QThal*. Prol. (PG 90:253AB).

not contradict them (Aristotle). Faith becomes a provocation to reason, and reality puts boundaries on human freedom. Humanity revolts and tries (unsuccessfully) either to free itself from its oppression in a Dostoevskyan reaction or to modify or improve reality (by successive reforms and revolutions), never being fully happy with it. The essence of the fall consists in humanity's enslavement to the past, its *exiling* of the future to the domain of the unreal and denial of it having an ontological effect on existence.

I have dealt elsewhere[43] with the importance of eschatology for the doctrine of *anthropology*, particularly if we approach the human being as a *person*. Only if we consider the human being from the point of view of its *telos*—not from what it actually is but from what it aspires to be—can we do justice to what it means to be human. The human being is distinguished from the other animals by its refusal to accept reality, including death itself (which it fights through creativity and art), faith in survival after death, and belief in immortality. In the words of St Gregory Nazianzen, the human being is ζῷον θεούμενον (an animal deified).

Eschatology is, thus, a constitutive element of Christian anthropology. The human being *par excellence* is Christ, the "last Adam" who has conquered death and deified humanity in himself. Take out this unity with God, this eschatological gift of the Holy Spirit, and the human being becomes an animal; it is no longer human, says St Irenaeus.[44] Humanity is not definable without its relationship with God, which makes Christian anthropology essentially a chapter or an aspect of *Christology*: the human being *par excellence* is *Christ*, a person united with God in the Holy Spirit. The human being as a person—not as an animal—is not truly human "until Christ is formed" (Gal 4:19) in it. Until that happens, humanity exists in a state of conflict between what it actually is and what it aspires to (cf. Rom 7–8), leading a life of tragic impasses, experiencing its freedom as a choice between given or imposed alternatives, between confirmation and negation, hope and despair. All this remains inexplicable without making eschatology a decisive constituent of the human

---

[43] See my *Being as Communion: Studies in Personhood and the Church* (Crestwood, NY: St Vladimir's Seminary Press, 1985), p. 57f.

[44] Irenaeus, *Haer.* V. 6.1 (PG 7b:1137f).

condition. For the Christian, unlike, for example, the hero of the ancient Greek tragedy who is bound by the past, human existence is inwardly regulated by the future, which in the person of the risen Christ enters history offering a revelation and a "taste" of what it means to be truly human.

VII. From the Omega to the Alpha

The claim of Christian doctrine and experience—liturgical, in particular—that the future enters into history (as it did with Christ's appearances and encounters with his disciples after the Resurrection) lending it meaning and exercising an existential impact on it, gives rise to questions of a philosophical nature: *credo ut intelligam.* The Church is not only apostolic; it is also *patristic.* The apostolic kerygma must be interpreted, that is, cast in the intellectual framework and culture of a particular time and place, and this is what the fathers of the Church did. Patristic theology is a work of *hermeneutics* in which the apostolic experience and faith is appropriated by being placed in the "horizon" of the way of thinking, of the Hellenic culture in which the Fathers were brought up and to which they were called as Christians to interpret the apostolic kerygma.

The intellectual framework in which the Fathers had to cast the apostolic faith was dominated and shaped by what we normally call *Greek* or *Hellenic* thought, in which we must include also *Latin* thinkers and authors of that time who, in spite of differences in approach and mentality, share essentially the same worldview with the Greeks. It was this worldview and intellectual framework that gave birth to and shaped also our own culture, which justifies the late Fr Florovsky's controversial statement that, "Hellenism is the common background and the basis of the whole Christian civilization. It is simply incorporated into our Christian existence."[45] In fact, it is the entire basis of our way of thinking in modern thought. This makes the fathers of the Church indispensable in any effort to interpret the apostolic kerygma even in our time.

---

[45] G. Florovsky, "Preface to *In Ligno Crucis*," in *The Patristic Witness of Georges Florovsky*, p. 67.

Now, "Hellenism means philosophy,"[46] and it was in this field that the hermeneutics of the apostolic faith had to be applied. This was a difficult task, particularly with regard to eschatology. Greek thought was intrinsically resistant to the idea that the future could enter into history and have an ontological impact on the past or the present. This is because Greek thought was *protological* in its ontology. Greek (and, for that matter, also Roman) thinking was past-oriented and placed perfection at the beginning of history, or even before it. Truth as ἀλήθεια was conceived as a recollection of what was already there and emerged from oblivion. Human destiny was already determined by the gods in the past, binding human beings forever. Philosophers and tragedians converged at this point: that there is no "substance" in the future and that hope is a concept irreconcilable with reason. (Friedrich Nietzsche was not exaggerating in his *Birth of Tragedy* in detecting a pervasive pessimism in later Hellenism.[47])

Now, probably under the influence of the Judeo-Christian tradition, later Western philosophy and theology did discover and emphasize the importance of the future. And yet, even in this case, the protological ontology of classical Greek thought has fully survived and made an indelible mark on our way of thinking. Thus, even in philosophies which have emphasized and made prominent the future, as, for example, in the various forms of social utopianism (Karl Marx, Ernst Bloch, etc.) or scientific evolutionary theories (Charles Darwin, Pierre Teilhard de Chardin, etc.), the end always evolves from the beginning in the form of a process or development, a teleology as Aristotle had conceived it, in which the Omega follows upon the Alpha, the future stemming from the past, eschatology emerging from protology. Any suggestion that the past derives from the future, or that the future makes the past, remains still a scandal and a paradox for our common-sense rationality.

[46] Ibid., p. 68.

[47] F. Nietzsche, *The Birth of Tragedy*, trans. S. Whiteside (London: Penguin Boooks, 1993) and *The Case of Wagner*, trans. W. Kaufmann (New York: Vintage Books, 1967), p. 97. In the literature of classical Greece, ἐλπίς is an ambivalent emotion meaning expectation yet also self-delusion. This exists, for example, in Hesiod's myth of Pandora, in Pindar's poetry, and in Euripides's dramas. In Stoicism, it becomes a rather vicious emotion. To the Romans, *Spes* was a much more benevolent deity. P. G. Walsh, "Spes Romana, Spes Christiana," *Prudentia,* VI (1974) 33–42.

This seems to also be the case with regard to theology. The revival of eschatology in the previous century brought up its significance in many respects (ethical, dogmatic, ecclesiological, socio-political, etc.)—we see this particularly strong and successful in the work of Moltmann—but threw little light on the subject of ontology and the possibility of working out an *eschatological ontology*. Process theology is based on the philosophy of Alfred North Whitehead whose concepts are largely derived from and modelled upon those of natural science and not of history.[48] Pannenberg was perhaps the only one to suggest an eschatological ontology by proposing and developing the principle that, "the future makes the past" and making resurrection the starting point and the focus of all of theology. Pannenberg's thought has, therefore, many affinities with what is being proposed in the present study. But, as the careful reader of this book will note, there are also certain divergences (probably due to the different Christian traditions from which the two authors draw) that affect eschatological ontology in a decisive way.

As we shall see in more detail, one of the most crucial questions concerns the role of *history* in eschatological ontology. In my view, the future of the eschata is not a prolongation of the historical future into eternity; it is rather a future that *visits* history from outside or beyond history. There cannot be in this case a "fore-conception" of the final future or a "development of the process of God's revelation and its coming to fruition."[49] The historical future does provide us with an *epistemological* tool with which to understand the past (the idea of destiny, finality, etc.), but it cannot provide the basis for an *ontology*; it may give *meaning* but not *being* to the past.[50] The historical future is itself subject to becoming "passed" standing itself in need of redemption by the final future. This cannot happen unless the eschatological future is of a metahistorical order, that is, free from the teleological predicament of the past which is *death*.

---

[48] Cf. A.N. Whitehead, *Process and Reality: An Essay in Cosmology* (first published in 1929). Corrected ed., eds. D.R. Griffin and D.W. Sherburne (New York: Free Press, 1978).

[49] W. Pannenberg, *Revelation as History* (with R. Rendtorff, *et. al.*) (London: Macmillan, 1969²), p. 451.

[50] Cf. T. Bradshaw's pertinent remark (*Pannenberg* [London: T&T Clark, 2009], p. 79) that for Pannenberg "meaning constitutes being."

Pannenberg lays stress—indeed he builds his entire system—on revelation as history, but revelation is not the same as ontology. Revelation appeals to knowledge, ontology to existence, to being or not being. It is, of course, true that for a great part of the history of Western philosophy going back to Aristotle, ontology is understood as metaphysics, ending up with notions such as substance, essence, etc.—*concepts* graspable by the mind. Ontology, however, as Martin Heidegger insightfully conceived it, cannot operate without reference to *death*. Being is ontologically tied up with death in historical existence, and this means that the historical future may give *meaning* to the past (Heidegger himself would admit that by his concept of anticipation) but not a *being free of death*.[51]

The Resurrection, however, is precisely not about knowledge but about the abolishment of death; it is not simply about revelation. As such, the resurrection does not bring a future which is "fore-conceived" or "anticipated" as a prolongation of the future of history, but grants *being*—not just meaning—to history as a whole, including what was once historical future. The future that the resurrection brings with it is a future that comes from "beyond" history; it grants history itself a true future, an end without end.

Eschatology, therefore, is about a future that *comes to* history and does not *come from* history. The risen Christ is ὁ ἐρχόμενος, "He that Cometh" in order to give *being* to history by liberating it from what negates being, death. History is "real"; it is not a phantom or a "vanity," but its being is not self-explainable. It does not come to it from the past; its beginning, like that of creation, is tied up with mortality. Unless there is resurrection, history is bound to collapse. If history's ontology is protological it cannot provide a future that grants it being. The eschatological future that will give being to history must not be regarded as an outcome of historical development—just as God himself cannot be the future of history—but as *grace*, as God's *visit* (cf. Lk 1:68, 78; Heb 2:6) to history, as a sharing in the life of God whose being is above history. Eschatology is in a sense a transcendence of history; it affirms history by liberating it from the mortal bondage of finitude.

[51] Cf. M. Heidegger, *Being and Time*, trans. J. Macquarrie and E. Robinson (Oxford: Blackwell, 1967), pp. 382–384 (German pagination).

All this finds its highest illustration in the case of Christ's death and its relation to his Resurrection. The death of Christ is not only for the remission of our sins; it is also, and perhaps above all, for "eternal life." With Christ's sacrifice on the Cross, not only sin is washed away but also human mortality. We have in this case an event not of juridical significance (as it is usually presented) but of *ontological* importance, a life-giving death.

This should not lead to an exaltation of Christ's sacrifice to the point of making it even an attribute of God's very being, as we find it, for example, in Moltmann's staurocentric perspective. As we have argued here, being and death cannot be reconciled ontologically. The death of Christ may display a loving God who shares the suffering and evil—even the mortality—that dominate history, but it cannot *qua death* liberate it from mortality granting it being. The Cross by itself cannot provide history with an ontology.

This was realized by the ontologically-minded Greek fathers. They believed in Christ's death as life-giving, and thus ontologically significant, *yet only on the condition that the Resurrection was already acting in it.* As Florovsky remarks in presenting the Church fathers' doctrine of Redemption,[52] the death of Christ on the Cross was not like our death; it was the death "of the Lord of glory" (1 Cor 2:8), i.e., of the one who rose from the dead. The three days in the tomb are the days of the Resurrection: Christ descended into hell raising the dead of the past, the dead of "history." It is not accidental that Byzantine iconography represents Christ's Resurrection as his descent into hades and the liberation of Adam from death. The Resurrection, therefore, was not a successive stage in Christ's life following upon his Cross and his burial; it was already present in Christ's death, as the factor that made this death ontologically significant. Had there not been the Resurrection, the death of Christ would prove that history is condemned to succumb to its finitude, to "being-unto-death."

---

[52] G. Florovsky, *"In Ligno Crucis:* The Church Fathers' Doctrine of Redemption," in *The Patristic Witness of Georges Florovsky,* pp. 71–79.

VIII. An Epiphanic Ontology

History needs the "breaking in" of the future into its course in order to acquire an ontological content, a being without death. This is not a "prolepsis" or even an "anticipation" of the future *by* history; it is an acting of the future *on* history, an impact *on* history coming from outside history. The future does not come into history "by observation" (cf. Lk 17:20) but as "a thief in the night" (1 Thess 5:2). It is, therefore, better to speak of an *epiphany* of the future (cf. Lk 1:79; 2 Thess 2:8; 1 Tim 6:14; 2 Tim 4:1, 8; Tit 2:13), in the sense in which the term was used in the Hellenistic world with reference to the appearance of a god or the solemn visit of a king.

Now, such a terminology to describe the relationship of history to eschatology would allude to *vision* rather than thought or mental impression of reality, and to symbolic representation, as in art. This would not necessarily lead us away from philosophical thought. In fact, vision was the source of classical Greek philosophy, as the origin of the term *idea* (ἰδέα) indicates. It was only later in Western philosophy that "idea" came to mean a product of intellectual action, usually strictly differentiated from artistic representation and vision. This has resulted in the dissociation also of ontology from categories of sight and image in our way of thinking.

The use of the notion of "image" (εἰκών) in the framework of a theology (and philosophy) of history appears explicitly in the thought of St Maximus the Confessor. In one of the *Scholia* attributed to him and confirmed in its content by the rest of his work, Maximus writes the following:

> The things of the Old Testament are shadow (σκιά); those of the New Testament are image (εἰκών); truth is the state of the things of the future.[53]

The philosophy of history that underlies this view of the *Heilsgeschichte* entails an understanding of history as a movement not from the past to the future but from the future to the past. The movement of history is neither circular leading history back to the beginning as in classical Greek thought, nor linear, driven and directed by the ne-

---

[53] Maximus, *Scholia eccl. hier.* 3.2 (PG 4:137D). Cf. *Amb.* 21 (PG 91:1253CD) and *Cap. theol.* 1.90 (PG 90:1120C).

cessity of a prescribed "entelecheia," as in utopian or evolutionary thinking. By being described with the use of a term such as *eikon*, history is presented as a tree which has its roots in the future and its branches in the present. We are confronted with an ontology of history which frees it not only from any natural necessity but also from human manipulation, while allowing it to be the realm of the exercise of human freedom. Like an icon in which the person is present in a way that transcends the material form in which it is presented,[54] history contains the future without engulfing it and turning it into a part or a phase of history. Such an *iconic ontology* serves a double function: it allows the human being to turn time into the realm of human creativity while subjecting this creativity to the truth of the future.

This "epiphanic" or "iconic" approach to the relation of eschatology to history makes history the ground of revelation without allowing truth to be "grasped" or "conceived" by the human mind, thus making room for the *apophatic* and the ineffable, and infusing into history the experience of *awaiting*, of eager expectation, of the *maranatha*, of prayer and *worship*. An iconic ontology keeps alive the "not yet" within the experience of the "already" of the Parousia.

IX. Eschatological Hermeneutics

The entrance of the future into the course of time affects our understanding of history in its relation to the notion of *being*, to what we call *ontology*. In what sense can we say that historical events have a true being, given the fact that historical time is in constant flux?

Classical Greek thought had to wrestle with this problem precisely because it attached to being a permanence and unchangeability that excludes uncertainty and doubt. Since history consists of events that undergo change and transience, attaching ontology to history would be absurd. And yet the ancient Greeks did develop historiography and were interested in the explanation of historical

---

[54] See Theodore the Studite, *Antirrheticus* 3.1 (PG 99:405A): "When anyone is depicted in an icon, it is not the nature but the hypostasis [the person] that is depicted."

events, in the "reason" why events happened the way they did. It is precisely at this point that ontology and history interact on each other in classical Greek thought.

Classical Greek historiography sought the "reason" (λόγος) or "cause" (αἰτία) of historical events, either in eternal laws governing the universe such as retribution (τίσις) and nemeses (as described by Herodotus), or in human reason, enabling us to foresee the outcome of a historical event, albeit often defeated and crushed by the forces of irrationality (as described by Thucydides); or in fortune (τύχη) (as described by Polybius). Personal history, as depicted vividly in classical tragedy, was also regarded as being ultimately governed by what the gods had decided for an individual in the past. In all these explanations of historical events, their reason (λόγος) *preceded* the events themselves. History had its *raison d'être* in the past; the present had its cause in the past, and it is the past that directs the present toward the future: the ontology of history is *protological*.

Judeo-Christian tradition had a different philosophy of history. The meaning of historical events, their "reason," ought to be sought not in the past, in preexisting causes, but in the *future*, in the end of history. Historical events have a *purpose* which lies at the end of history: it is the last act of God that reveals the meaning of the preceding events. The ontology of history in this case is *eschatological*.

This biblical view of history found its way into the patristic period not without difficulty. For those who were under the influence of Platonic thought, such as Origen and his followers, history had a movement toward the future, a teleology, but this movement was *cyclical*, with the end turning out to be a return to the beginning (περὶ ἀρχῶν). The underlying ontology of this view was *protological*. The first explicit and fully developed eschatological philosophy of history is to be found only in St Maximus the Confessor in the seventh century, who engaged in a refutation of the Origenist view and elaborated an understanding of history as having its "reason," its *logos*, in the end and not in the beginning. The seeds of this interpretation of history had been already sown by St Irenaeus in the second century—a deeply biblically-minded theologian—but it was in Maximus that it received an extensive philosophical elaboration. According to this interpretation, the beginning as well as the course of history could only be explained by looking at their end. We had, for the first time, a full-blown eschatological ontology.

This eschatological philosophy of history was not destined to last long. The interest in history was revived and received prominence in modern times, but, probably under the influence of the Enlightenment, the causes or reasons of the historical events were no longer sought in any metaphysical principle but *in the events themselves*. Historical events were *reified*, possessing a "substance" of their own, an ontology, being turned into "facts" which could not be undone. History became, thus, a sum of facts with their own ontology, which the historian had to discover and respect. Even in cases such as Utopianism, in which the facts and history as a whole possessed a teleology, a future, the ontological source of this teleology lay in the facts themselves, just as the branches of a tree owe their being to the roots or the seed from which they come. Just as in philosophy the truth, according to its medieval definition, consists in the *adequatio* of our mind with the objective reality (the *res*), in the same way the historian must discover and recognize the events of history as true in themselves.

This reification of historical events reached its peak with eighteenth-century historicism and has never abandoned our common-sense approach to historical truth: facts cannot be doubted nor undone; they possess being, an ontology of their own. An approach to history as consisting of *personal* (i.e., free and creative) human intercourse, developed particularly by Robin George Collingwood and Benedetto Croce in early twentieth century and continued later by G. Florovsky, has contributed to the liberation of history from reification without, however, leading it thereby to the direction of eschatology. It was mainly hermeneutics that opened the way to an eschatological perspective of history.

Hermeneutics emerged from the observation formulated by Wilhelm Dilthey (1833–1911) that, in order to understand historical life, we must understand its totality,[55] and this requires viewing the whole

[55] Just as an individual's or an institution's identity can be constructed only at the moment of its death, in the same way the history of the human race can be written only if viewed from its end. For an English translation of Dilthey's *Gesammelte Schriften,* see W. Dilthey, *Selected Writings,* ed. and trans. H. P. Rickman (Cambridge: Cambridge University Press, 1976), esp. p. 177f.

from the perspective of its end. This approach is used by Heidegger in his analysis of "being-unto-death," according to which there can be no understanding of our existence without the orientation toward the ultimate. There is, therefore, an essential relationship between the understanding of our finitude, our "being-unto-death," and our interpretation of our involvement in the world. As finite beings we require the mediation of hermeneutics to understand the world and ourselves. Thus, our origin (*Herkunft*) always comes to meet us from the future (*Zukunft*); hermeneutics presupposes a kind of eschatology in order to function. "The past as authentic history is grounded in the possibility ... to be futural. This is the first principle of all hermeneutics."[56]

From this perspective, historical events or facts do not possess a "being," an ontology of their own. Nietzsche's famous dictum, "there are no facts, there is only interpretation," may be made to apply to hermeneutics albeit with important qualifications. In eschatological hermeneutics, historical facts are not denied but acquire their truth, their meaning, their "wholeness," when viewed from the end of history instead of being conceived and "established" at a stage of incompleteness and fragmentation, in their past. (Only at the moment of one's death can we have the full and true picture of a person's, or an institution's, etc., historical identity, according to Dilthey.) Even in Heidegger's hermeneutics, the end does not negate the past, since our "being-unto-death," our futurity, throws us back to our heritage (our past, tradition, culture, etc.) so that we may, in an act of freedom, renounce its pastness through a productive response to previously unrealized possibilities. This idea of a "productive history" (*Wirkungsgeschichte*) serves as the basis of Gadamer's development of hermeneutics, although the eschatological foundation of hermeneutics is not as clear here as in the case of Heidegger. Yet, even for Gadamer, the future affects the past in a decisive way, as in every interpretation the already understood and the alien, the different or other and the new merge in hermeneutics offering endless interpretative, i.e., truth value, possibilities. Hermeneutics opens history to the future, to infinite possibilities.

[56] M. Heidegger, *Der Begriff der Zeit* (Frankfurt: Vittorio Klostermann, 2004), p. 123.

The affinities of philosophical hermeneutics with Christian theology are only slowly beginning to become apparent and affect theological methodology. Theology, on the whole, still operates with a view of tradition—be it Scripture, the Fathers, or doctrine—formed in the past and possessing an "ontology," a fixed identity and content. Eschatology as a hermeneutical tool is still awaiting its full application to systematic theology, and this need comes from the very center of the Christian faith.

It is a fundamental characteristic of the Judeo-Christian tradition to assume and operate with a view of history as a totality, a "whole" with a beginning and an end, and to assert that it is in the end that the meaning of history is disclosed. It is, therefore, through the end that we can understand the beginning and the past: eschatology interprets history. Up to this point, theological and philosophical hermeneutics concur.

When, however, we come to the Christian faith, we are faced with fundamental differences between theological and philosophical hermeneutics, at least regarding the way the latter has been presented by Heidegger and Gadamer. The first difference has to do with the way we understand the future as the basis for interpreting history. For Heidegger, the futurity of being is identical with *death*: it is our finitude that draws us back to the past in order to understand, or interpret, our historical existence (an infinite being does not need hermeneutics.) For the Christian faith, it is the *abolition of death* by the Resurrection that leads us back to the past in order to interpret history. The consequences are existentially important. In the case of Heidegger, the future brings us back to a state of existence in which we are still under the threat of death, struggling to overcome it, moving *toward* the end and never experiencing it as presence but always as a *possibility*. History is only an *anticipation* and not a real presence of the future, a "not yet" and never an "already." An "already" would threaten the temporal character of being, which is, for Heidegger, fundamental to ontology.

For Christian theology, time needs redemption. While being a relational and unitive factor in existence, time also separates beings in many ways, above all through death. For this reason history cannot acquire an ontology without the abolition of death, and this is precisely what the Resurrection offers to time: its redemption from death. By entering history, the Resurrection grants it *being-without-death*, thus providing hermeneutics with the "horizon" of *communion* between past and present persons and events, granting life and being to what death naturally divides, turning tradition from a museum relic into a living reality. It is by acquiring a future through the entrance of the Resurrection into history that the various generations and epochs meet one another, forming a common *culture*.

There is, thus, a difference between a "history of effects" (*Wirkungsgeschichte*) that emerges from "anticipation," as with Heidegger, and a culture and tradition that draw their existence from an entrance of the future resurrection into history. In the first case, history is, at best, a purely human achievement and, at worst, a "natural," ontological necessity (cf. evolutionary historicism). In the second case, that of the entering of the future resurrection into history, history and its creative effects are not simply human achievements subject to mortality but *gifts of God* coming to humanity (and creation) through the risen Christ, which are offered back to God in thankfulness and gratitude. The hermeneutical "horizon" becomes, in this way, *eucharistic* and history becomes *Christocentric* in its very being.

Such a "eucharistic" approach to hermeneutics means that cultural achievements *can* acquire eschatological significance provided that they are freed from mortality, from "being-unto-death." Eschatological hermeneutics involves the discernment of historical effects, since the coming of the eschaton comprises also the *judgment* of history, its purification from whatever smacks of death. Cultures and traditions are not sanctified automatically and generally; an acceptance of history *qua* history, as we find it in many contemporary theologians (Orthodox included), is incompatible with eschatological hermeneutics.

Since the entrance of the future into history through the Resurrection of Christ, this purified history has been sanctified, and it is no longer necessarily a carrier of mortality. Fr Florovsky is right in insisting (against existentialistic tendencies in modern theology) that "the *Heilsgeschichte* is still going on."[57] But this cannot be made to

---

[57] G. Florovsky, "The Predicament of the Christian Historian," in *The Patristic Witness of Georges Florovsky*, p. 217.

include all the historical events and historical products, and thus all of history *as such*. Florovsky himself recognizes the problem, as he refers to St Augustine's efforts to offer a survey of historical events in the story of the "two cities."[58] Is history to be divided into two compartments, as Augustine seems to suggest? Is there a "secular" and a "sacred" history living side by side, sometimes in agreement and sometimes in conflict? This seems to be the general assumption in most of modern Christian theology, but it has its problems, if placed in the light of eschatological hermeneutics. History is one, but it is, in its present state, ambiguous in its nature. Good and evil are still intermingled in it. The question whether history is "good" or "bad" is a false dilemma, because it is both; it contains being and nonbeing side by side. Viewed from the angle of eschatological ontology, which claims that being is true being only if it is ever-being, history possesses truth and being (an ontology) only, however, because of the entrance of the eschaton into its course.

We may conclude, therefore, that instead of the "two cities" image (of two histories running in parallel), we may conceive of history as a single entity, a tree whose fruits are fed by its roots which lie in the future, while its environment provides it with the ambiguous (positive as well as negative) conditions for its existence in time. The image of the "seed" to describe the presence of the Kingdom in history is biblical (Mk 4:26–32; Lk 8:5–11) and suggestive almost in every detail of the above description. The hostile environment (the "winds," the "hard rocks," etc.) is provided by history together with the fertile ground ("the good earth") for the seed of the Kingdom to grow and bear fruit. History is an ambiguous entity and does not lend itself to ontological or moral categorizing. It is through its relationship with the Kingdom that history acquires its ontological (and moral) status.

This leads to the significance of the *Church* in eschatological hermeneutics. If the Church is conceived as an eschatological community existing in history (*in* the world but not *of* the world: Jn 15:18; 17:6,14), and if history is "judged" and confirmed ontologically through the entrance of the Kingdom into its course, it follows that

---

[58] Cf. G. Florovsky, *Christianity and Culture*, vol. 2 of *The Collected Works of Georges Florovsky* (Vaduz: Buchervertriebsanstalt, 1974), pp. 26–30, 62.

the Church provides *by her very existence in history* a hermeneutical tool, a "horizon" in which historical events and actions are "received" and "transmitted" (by παράδοσις, that is, creatively interpreted) as events and actions of *communion*, not only among human beings (historical), but also with God and his Kingdom (eschatological). By placing the past in the "horizon" of the future, as happens in the Eucharist, the Church receives and incorporates all historical acts and effects *that can fit into this "horizon" of communion*, blesses and "sanctifies" them by incorporating them into herself as Christ's body, and thereby grants certain forms of culture not only moral quality and "value" but indeed life eternal,[59] which is true being.

X. Death and Resurrection

The employment of the notion of being and ontology with reference to history and to philosophy itself has been strongly attacked in our times, thus also putting into question the idea of eschatological ontology: what sense can the idea of being make in a philosophical context that has exorcised ontology? Since the notion of ontology occupies such a fundamental place in the present study, its rejection by modern thought cannot be bypassed.

This questioning of the idea of ontology is encountered, in our time, particularly among phenomenological philosophers and postmodern thinkers. Emmanuel Levinas regards the notion of being as implying a "totalization" that threatens otherness, while theologically inspired philosophers, such as Jean-Luc Marion, propose a "God without Being."[60] Post-modernism also in its various forms takes a negative stance against ontology trying to protect "difference" from the domination of "identity" and stability, and ultimately of truth.

---

[59] "What shall pass from history into eternity?" asked Fr Georges Florovsky. "The human person with all its relations, such as friendship and love. And in this sense, also culture, since a person without a concrete cultural face would be a mere fragment of humanity." This was quoted by the late Fr Matthew Baker. See the dedication of *The Patristic Witness of Georges Florovsky*, p. vii. This inspired statement by Florovsky would be modified by the present author so as to refer to the eschatological survival of culture *purified from the antinomies of history to which it is inevitably subject.*

[60] J.-L. Marion, *God Without Being*, trans. T. A. Carlson, 2nd edn (Chicago and London: University of Chicago Press, 2012).

The reasons given for this categorical rejection of ontology show that the only kind of ontology known to Western philosophy is the *protological* one. This kind of ontology does, indeed, involve some form of totalization that is detested by contemporary thinking, since it presents being in terms of "substance" and leaves otherness and particularity outside ontology, making it secondary and dependent upon the general and the "whole." Protological ontology *does* display this trait ever since Parmenides and the pre-Socratics, with classical Greek philosophy in its entirety sticking faithfully to it. Being in this case is a "given" to the particular human being, imposed on it and thus a threat to its freedom. No wonder, therefore, that a thinker such as Levinas would react strongly against Heidegger's *il y a* (there is) as an ontology implying generalization and a "tyranny" over the other, the particular, the "hypostatic." This leads this philosopher to the categorical rejection of ontology by seeking refuge in the Platonic "beyond substance" (ἐπέκεινα τῆς οὐσίας) combined with the Cartesian idea of the "infinite," which is presented as breaking into existence through the appearance of the "other."

Levinas's rejection of ontology is, thus, worked out with the help of protological ontological categories (the priority of the infinite over being). Eschatology does appear in his thought but it does not seem to determine his system. It is tied up with what he calls "the messianic time" in which "the perpetual is converted into the eternal,"[61] entering into the continuity of time through or in the form of the other who makes us his "hostage."[62] Eschatology, thus, does not refer to a "future." It is "either a new structure of time or an extreme vigilance of the messianic consciousness," which "forewarns against the revenge of evil which the infinite time does not prevent (*interdit*) from returning."[63]

This "breaking into" the course of time of what Levinas calls "the messianic time (or consciousness)" resembles the Christian idea of the entrance of the Resurrection into history. There are, however, fundamental points of difference which affect the concept of escha-

---

[61] E. Levinas, *Totalité et Infini* (The Hague: M. Nijhoff, 1971), p. 261.

[62] E. Levinas, *God, Death, and Time*, ed. by J. Rolland, trans. B. Bergo (Stanford, CA: Stanford University Press, 2000), p. 138.

[63] Levinas, *Totalité et Infini*, p. 261.

tological ontology. The first point was already mentioned and has to do with the idea of the future. For Levinas, the association of the idea of eternity with that of infinity manifests itself *within time*: "the infinite being is produced as time."[64] Against Heidegger, Levinas insists that, "it is not the finitude of being that makes the essence of time ... but its infinity."[65] Time is discontinued; there is no *ekstasis* of being in time. The infinite interrupts the course of time, and it is through its interruptions that time acquires infinity.

According to Levinas, this interruption of the course of time by the entrance of the infinite brings about a "nothing," a "dead time," which the infinite transforms into a "resurrection": "the nothing of the interval—a dead time—is the production of the infinite. The resurrection constitutes the principal event of time ... Death and resurrection constitute time."[66] Underlying this is Levinas's idea of *fecundity,* in which "the infinite being is produced as time, that is in a number of times through the dead time (*le temps mort*) which separates the father from the child."[67] In the father-son relationship "being is produced as multiple and as divided into Same and Other.... It is society (*société*) and, through that, time."[68]

Death, therefore, is not for Levinas an ontological problem; it must not be reduced to the scheme of "being versus nonbeing."[69] Death is the *non-response*: the separation from the other, *the death of the other*, which "individualizes me in my responsibility towards him"—"the culpability of the survivor."[70] Far from being an annihilation, as in the case of Heidegger, death gives birth in and through fecundity to my identity as I (*moi*) and, at the same time, to my responsibility for the other and, thereby, to *ethics*.

Resurrection, therefore, is not for Levinas something to be expected in the future; it occurs as part of the continuum of time that

---

[64] Ibid., p. 260.

[65] Ibid.

[66] Levinas, *Totalité et Infini*, p. 260f. Therefore, "time is not the limitation of being but its relationship with infinity. Death is not annihilation but the question that is necessary for this relationship with infinity, or time, to be produced," *God, Death and Time*, p. 19.

[67] Levinas, *Totalité et Infini*, p. 260.

[68] Ibid., p. 247.

[69] Levinas, *God, Death, and Time*, p. 8.

[70] Ibid., p. 12.

is interrupted by the entrance of the infinite. The "messianic time" is identical with this interruption, the entrance of the infinite bringing about the "messianic consciousness" as a "prewarning" against the revenge of evil, the return of which the infinite time cannot prohibit. Levinas dissociates death from being and the resurrection from the future, removing, thus, the ground for the construction of an eschatological ontology.

Christian theology takes a different view. Death is regarded by the Christian faith as an ontological problem because it turns "beings" into "nonbeings" (τὰ ὄντα into μὴ ὄντα: Rom 4:17). However, in the resurrection, God raises the dead (τοῦ ἐγείραντος τοὺς νεκρούς) and "calls nonbeings to be beings." As Marion notes,[71] the Bible does not know the concept of being in its metaphysical sense (τὸ εἶναι), while it does refer to "beings" (τὰ ὄντα) in their concrete particularity. This points to an ontology (the notion of "being" is ontological by definition) of *beings* rather than *being*. Death is not "annihilation" (as Heidegger conceives it), but this does not remove it from the scheme of "being versus nonbeing" (as Levinas suggests). We are rather faced with an ontology in which the particular being is *constitutive* of "being," a *hypostatic* rather than an *ousianic* ontology.

In previous writings[72] I have tried to show that for the Cappadocian fathers, for example, being is not, as it is for Thomas Aquinas, something that beings "have" (*ens dicitur quasi habens esse*), but rather something that beings "are," *a category that applies to particular beings by definition*. Ontology, according to the Cappadocian fathers, replies to two questions simultaneously: *what* (τί) someone or something is (the οὐσία or φύσις) and *how* (ὅπως or πῶς) someone or something is (ὑπόστασις).[73] The first of these two does not ontologically precede the second, and the second (the particular) does not derive from or "contain" the first. As St Basil explains in writing to Apollinarius (*Ep.* 361 and 362), the beginning or origin (ἀρχὴ) of the particular human beings is not to be found in human substance, either

---

[71] J.-L. Marion, *Dieu sans l'être* (Paris: Presses Universitaires de France, 2013), p. 128f.

[72] See my *Being as Communion* and *Communion and Otherness: Further Studies in Personhood and the Church*, ed. Paul McPartlan (New York: T&T Clark, 2006).

[73] Thus, Basil, *C. Eunom.* I, 14–15 (PG 29:545AB), and Gregory Naz., *Theol. Or.* III, 16 (PG 36:93AB).

"standing above" (Platonic) or "standing underneath" (Aristotelian), but *in a particular being, Adam*. It is the particular hypostasis that makes beings *be*.

This, not only does not allow us to give priority to the one God (*De Deo uno*) over against the Trinity—something that Scholastic theologians did not avoid[74]—but it also makes it unnecessary to speak of "God without being." The concept of being can be applied to God (as was in fact done by the Greek fathers) without introducing thereby the impersonal and totalizing *il y a* that rightly alarmed Levinas, while making it possible (contrary to Heidegger's objections) to employ ontology in theology.

All this affects the concept of eschatological ontology: in what sense is eschatology an ontology? If the central act of eschatology is the resurrection, in what sense can it be said that resurrection grants *being*? We have seen that Paul (Rom 4:17) speaks of God as giving life to the dead and thereby calling "nonbeings as beings (τὰ μὴ ὄντα ὡς ὄντα)." This means that death amounts to nonbeing and resurrection to granting being. Is Christian theology, therefore, closer to Heidegger who identifies death with nonbeing than to Levinas who dissociates death from the structure "being versus nonbeing"? To speak of death as annihilation would lead to understanding the resurrection as a sort of *creatio ex nihilo*. This would not do.[75] Christ's Resurrection itself retained, in a very real sense, some kind of continuity with his pre-Resurrection body (Lk 24:39; Jn 20:27). And the Creed speaks of the resurrection *of the body* or the "flesh." In what sense, then, is a dead being nonbeing and its resurrection an ontological fact?

Florovsky rejects the idea that the human soul can constitute the ontological ground of the human being. In death, he writes, "only the body can disintegrate. Yet it is not the body that dies but the whole man."[76] This means that the survival of the soul is not enough to allow us to speak of the survival of the human being. Death dis-

---

[74] See Karl Rahner, *The Trinity*, trans. J. Donceel (New York: Seabury, 1970), p. 58f.

[75] Cf. Gregory of Nyssa, *De an. et res.* (PG 46:76C): if in the resurrection the bodies were constructed entirely from new elements, that "would not be a resurrection but the creation of a new human being."

[76] Florovsky, "Redemption," p. 106.

turbs the ontology of the human being, and the resurrection of the body restores not just a part of human being, but its very being itself: *without eschatology the human being simply disappears.* Florovsky bases this on the evidence of early fathers, such as Irenaeus and Athenagoras of Athens for whom, "if there is no resurrection (of the body) human nature is no longer human."[77] This allows Florovsky to speak of death, "as a metaphysical catastrophe."[78]

But how can it be said that death is an ontological catastrophe if it is not, as we have seen, an annihilation? How can we associate death with nonbeing and resurrection with being if being somehow continues in spite of death? These questions arise inevitably only if being is conceived in itself apart from the *concrete mode* of its existence. Such an understanding of being as pure *esse* inevitably suggests nothingness as its opposite. Nihilism arose in Western philosophy precisely because of this kind of ontology. (Gottfried Leibnitz's question "why there is something rather than nothing?" leads directly to nihilism as the alternative to being.). If, however, we associate ontology with the idea of *beings*, of *hypostasis* as a primary ontological category, then the ontological question is not why there is something rather than nothing, but why something is *in this particular mode of being and not in another one.* If the mode of being (the *hypostasis*) is not a secondary and derivative ontological category but an ontologically constitutive one, death can be an ontological problem even if it does not involve annihilation. The "metaphysical catastrophe" would consist in this case in the loss of the *particular way of being*, the unique and uncommunicable identity of particular beings, their *hypostasis*.

The eschatological resurrection, therefore, must be seen as a resurrection not of being, but *of beings.* This does not make it less ontological in character, since, as we have argued, particularity or "mode of being," what the Cappadocian fathers called *hypostasis*, is a primary ontological category: its absence is tantamount to the status of a μὴ ὄν, a nonbeing. This witnesses to an ontology other than the substantialist one (which has nothingness as the alternative to being). Since a hypostasis is constituted through its relationships, death

---

[77] Athenagoras, *De res. mort.* 15 (PG 6:1003A).
[78] G. Florovsky, "*In Ligno Crucis*," p. 73.

and resurrection affect the *relationality* of being: they dissolve and restore respectively the *relations* that constitute the "mode" of a being. To put it briefly "no one lives to himself and no one dies to himself" (Rom 14:7). Life and death are not simply individual experiences; they affect the way beings relate to one another, their *hypostasis,* that is their very ontological ground (cf. Rom 5:12f.; 1 Cor 15:21f.).

The death (and the resurrection) *of the other* acquires this way a crucial significance. Levinas is right in pointing out that we have access to the reality of death only through the death of the other. His interest is, of course, in the quest of meaning rather than being (it is, in his view, meaning that leads to being and not the reverse),[79] and he sees in the death of the other an *ethical* rather than an ontological significance. Being for him is totally incommunicable from one being to another,[80] and the idea of communion carries for him no ontological import whatsoever.[81] In our perspective here, however, being not only is communicable but *depends* on communion. The death of the other causes the break of my relation with him, and it is in *this* sense that it is tantamount to my own death, to the removal of the ground of my own being, since as a being (a *hypostasis*) I acquire my being only through relationship with the other.

Eschatological ontology, therefore, presupposes as its basis the idea of "*being as communion.*" The resurrection is not, as we said, a *creatio ex nihilo*—the being it grants is not the opposite of nothingness. The resurrection is *a restoration of the relationships that constitute the "mode of beings" (their hypostasis),* which are broken by death. When Christ raises the dead young boy at Nain (Lk 7:11f.), the evangelist adds with meaning that after that "he gave him to his mother." The resurrection is a restoration of communion, not simply the revivification of a corpse. We miss its meaning entirely if we regard it as the raising of "individuals," of autonomous entities.

---

[79] "Meaning is not determined through the to-be or the not-to-be. It is being, on the contrary, that is determined on the basis of meaning." E. Levinas, *God, Death, and Time,* p. 184.

[80] E. Levinas, *Ethique et Infini* (Paris: Fayard, 1982), p. 58: "En réalité, le fait d'être est ce qu'il a de plus privé, l'existence est la seule chose que je ne puisse communiquer; je peux la raconter, mais je ne peux partager mon existence ... Le social est au-delà de l'ontologie."

[81] Cf. my critical remarks on Levinas' views in my *Communion and Otherness,* p.49f.

The eschatological resurrection is a resurrection *in Christ* (1 Cor 15:22f.). The life it offers is nothing else than the incorporation into the body of Christ. *Theosis* is essentially *incorporation into Christ* and only through its participation in the life of God as *filiation*. This Christological ground of *theosis*, which is often forgotten in theology, implies that the eschatological state of existence is a *corporate* way of being, a life of communion. It is for this reason that the Holy Spirit is operative in the resurrection both of Christ and of the eschata (Rom 8:11f.): by being life-giving (Jn 6:63; 2 Cor 3:6) and at the same time *communion* (2 Cor 13:13), the Spirit makes the being granted by the resurrection relational, a *communio sanctorum*.

The entrance, therefore, of the eschatological future into history through Christ's Resurrection brings with it the assurance that death does not break the relations that make up our "way of being" (our *hypostasis*) in an ultimate way but only temporarily (as a "sleep"—κοίμησις), and that at the present state of our historical existence the Holy Spirit keeps alive and "guarantees" (2 Cor 1:21) our relationship with those who have departed, by placing them in the *communio sanctorum*, in the body of the risen Lord. By being "remembered" in the context of the communion of the body of the risen Christ, those who have died maintain their "mode of existence," their *hypostasis*, through their communion with the living ones within the Body of Christ, in the Spirit. The survival after death granted by the entrance of the risen Christ into history is, thus, conceived in terms of an ontology of communion (the survival of each one's *hypostasis*) rather than of substance;[82] it is given as participation in Christ's body through the communion of the Spirit. The Church as the body of Christ and the *communio sanctorum*, particularly through its eucharistic *anam-*

---

[82] The immortality of the human being cannot be identified with the immortality of the soul but with the survival of the hypostasis—the person. Thus, G. Florovsky, "The Last Things and the Last Events," in *Collected Works*, vol. III, p. 259f: "The concept of the immortal soul may be a Platonic accretion, but the notion of an 'indestructible person' is an integral part of the Gospel.... Death is a catastrophe. But *persons* [my emphasis] survive and those in Christ are still alive—even at the state of death." It is clear that for Florovsky the survival of the human being in the so-called "middle state" between death and resurrection is to be understood not on the basis of the (Platonic) idea of the immortality of the soul but with the help of the notion of *personhood*, i.e., as a survival of the *hypostasis* established through *communion* in Christ's body, the Church.

nesis, emerges as the historical *locus* of the *proclamation* and the *experience* of this mystery and gift of God's love to the world—the gift of ever-being through Christ's Resurrection.

XI. Toward an Eschatological Ethics

The entrance of the eschaton into history through Christ's Resurrection and post-Easter appearances brings into time not only the *message* and the *hope* but also the *experience* of the future Kingdom. How is this experience manifested in historical existence? We have noted so far the importance of *worship* and, particularly, the *Eucharist* as ways of experiencing the entrance of the future into history: the eschaton is *remembered, celebrated,* and *participated in* as an "already" which is present and at the same time eagerly expected, as the assurance of the final victory over death, as the liberation of history from its antinomies, and as the transformation of being into *ever-being.* All this affects the human experience of time and history, as the past acquires ontological significance by being liberated from death and the historical "facts" or "events" cease to be "passed" by obtaining a future. In the same way, not only facts but also *beings* in general who exist in time under the domination of death are resurrected into the relations that constitute their particularity, their "hypostasis." Eschatology acquires in this way an ontological significance; *it becomes ontology.*

Now, how can the entrance of the last days into history be experienced in everyday life? How can eschatology *qua* ontology have any bearing on *ethics*? In what way can the "new being" granted by the resurrection as "ever-being" (i.e., true [ὄντως] being) affect our *decisions* and *actions,* not only in particular instances but also and primarily with reference to ethical principles, to what we call *moral theory*?

Founding ethics on ontology was common in classical Greek thought and continued to be so in patristic and medieval Scholasticism. Already Plato, in his dialogue known as the *Euthyphro* (12–13), places holiness and justice above the gods (or God), thereby founding justice and morality on the highest ontological level: the holy is loved by the gods because it is holy; it is not holy because it is loved by the gods. The Good is eternal, changeless, immovable—qualities applied to being by the Greek mind since Parmenides and the Presocratics. The ontological grounding of ethics is found also in Aristotle, with the difference that it is in his case *nature* that constitutes the basis of ethics, particularly in its teleology, in the idea of "man-as-he-could-be-if-he-realized-his-*telos*," as Alasdair MacIntyre puts it.[83] Stoicism follows the same line of grounding ethics on nature as an ontological category—as the ontological category, *par excellence*. The Greek fathers of the first centuries, being under the influence of Stoicism, adopt in many respects the idea of nature as normative for Christian ethics (e.g., St Basil)[84] with Thomas Aquinas in the Middle Ages elevating nature (combined with reason) to the highest criterion of morality through the idea of *natural law*. It was only in modern times, when nature began to lose its authority in philosophical thinking, that ethics ceased to be related to nature in order to become a matter either only of reason, as with Immanuel Kant and the Enlightenment, or simply of an individual's judgement, of what is socially beneficial or contributes to one's happiness. Hume's position that an "ought" cannot be deducted from an "is,"[85] although peculiar to his personal view, does indicate a broader trend in modern times to dissociate morality from ontology—a trend which, if placed in the context of the contemporary objections to ontology discussed in a previous section of this Introduction, shows how the original grounding of ethics on ontology has faded away in the course of time.

[83] A. MacIntyre, *After Virtue* (London: Duckworth, 1981), p. 52.

[84] See, among others, M. Spanneut, *Le Stoïcisme des Pères de l' Église, de Clément de Rome à Clément d' Alexandrie* (Paris: Le Seuil, 1957): "Très souvent les Pères ont établi en système des idées conformes à la Bible, mais qui ne s'y trouvent qu'implicitement ou passagèrement: la nécessité de l'apathie, la théorie de la liberté, de la loi naturelle, du cosmopolitisme.... Toutes semblent partir d'une même confiance dans les forces naturelles de l'homme. Souvent elles s'apparentent au stoïcisme essentiel et antique." St Basil's treatise *Ad adolescentes de legendis libris gentilium* confirms the "widespread willingness [of the Christians of that time] to admit unhesitatingly the identity of the highest pagan and Christian ideals of morality." J. Whittaker, "Christianity and Morality in the Roman Empire," *Vigiliae Christianae* 33 (1979) 213.

[85] A. MacIntyre, *A Short History of Ethics* (Notre Dame, IN: University of Notre Dame Press, 1998), p. 168.

The ontology on which ethics was founded in the past was exclusively a *protological* one. Whether we have in mind the idea of the Good or that of nature and reason as the basis of ethics, we mean certain *principles* or *models* and *criteria*, which *precede* our moral judgments and actions, given to us as *universal* values. Eschatology plays no role whatsoever in this connection of ethics with ontology: our moral values and principles do not come from the future; we do not draw our moral motivation from expectation but from conviction, not from what is coming but from what is given to us as true and, therefore, right.

This, however, was not how the first Christians were called and expected to live and behave. The ethics of the New Testament are thoroughly eschatological. The first Christians were asked not to care for the needs of tomorrow because the Kingdom was about to come at any time (Mt 6:25, 34; Lk 12:22). They were advised to sell their property and give it to the poor (Mt 13:44, 19:21), to avoid marrying (1 Cor 7:25–38) because in the coming Kingdom "they neither marry nor are given in marriage" (Mt 22:30), and to "walk in the light" avoiding all "the works of darkness," not because they are wrong in themselves but because "the day of the Lord has dawned" (Rom 13:12; 1 Cor 1:8) and every act done in the dark will be soon revealed and condemned. The commandments of God were to be kept not because of an intrinsic moral value they possessed but because of the immanent encounter with the coming Lord who would ask for an account of their fulfilment from his servants (Mt 18:23, 25:14). It is because of this eschatological outlook that ethical requirements such as those of the Sermon on the Mount, some of them contrary to reason or even to justice (turning the other cheek to be struck by your offender, loving your enemy, etc.) formed part of a "moral code" which could only make sense as an "interim ethic" (to use Albert Schweitzer's famous expression) that must surely be inapplicable after the long delay of the Parousia.

Ethics was, thus, for the first Christian communities, rooted in the Gospel of the entrance of the eschatological Kingdom into history through Christ's death and Resurrection. It was an ethics that sprang from the believer's participation in Christ's death and Resurrection through Baptism and the Eucharist; it was not a presupposition but a *consequence*, a "therefore," following upon the eschatological consciousness, the dawning of the day of the Lord:

> If therefore (οὖν) you have been raised with Christ, seek the things that are above where Christ is seated at the right hand of God ... For you have died and your life is hid with Christ in God. When Christ, who is your life, appears you, too, will appear with him in glory. Therefore (οὖν) put to death what is earthly in you, fornication, impurity, passion, evil desire and covetousness ... shake off from yourselves anger, wrath, malice, slander ... do not lie to one another (Col 3:1–9).

According to these ethics, sinful acts are sinful and ought to be avoided not because they are incompatible with a certain moral code but because they are irreconcilable with the "new creation," the eschatological state brought about by Christ's Resurrection and its existential significance.

All this, of course, made sense for as long as the expectation of the imminent coming of the Parousia lasted. As time went on and the Parousia was delayed, it was becoming apparent that these ethical precepts were difficult to apply in everyday life, and Christians had to accommodate themselves in their cultural milieu and its moral values. In this case, as MacIntyre observes, "it is not surprising that insofar as Christianity has proposed moral belief and elaborated moral concepts for ordinary human life, it has been content to accept conceptual frameworks from elsewhere."[86] Such frameworks were already present and available to the early Christians in the Hellenistic environment of late Judaism (see, e.g., Wisdom of Solomon 6:17–20) where ethical sorites were used to educate people morally, containing lists of virtues which the Christians adopted for their own use (see, e.g., 2 Pet 1:5–7; *Hermas* 5, 2–4). Thus, notions such as *virtue* (ἀρετή), which was part of the Greek ethical vocabulary since antiquity, were adopted and used frequently by the early Christians (see, e.g., Phil 4:8; 1 Pet 2:8; 2 Pet 1:3), becoming part of Christian morality throughout the centuries.

Eschatological ethics was, thus, fading into the background giving the impression that it was gradually succumbing to Hellenic mor-

---

[86] MacIntyre, *A Short History of Ethics*, p. 112.

al frameworks and values deprived of any reference to eschatology. Such was the case with the adoption of Stoic ethics by the early Christian writers, to which we have already referred, through the use of ideas like "nature" and "reason" to ground and justify ethical claims for Christianity itself. But, although this seems to have been the prevailing trend in the first centuries, a careful examination of the historical evidence shows that the original eschatological approach to Christian ethics did not entirely die out, surviving in forms which are worth noting, not only for historical reasons but also for the conception of Christian morality in our own time.

It is noteworthy that, in adopting the ethical sorites widely used in the Hellenistic culture, the early Christians modified them in such a way as to give them an eschatological orientation. These sorites often propose a scale of moral ideas, beginning with the less important and ending up with the highest ones as the epitome of ethical life. One such sorites converted into Christian use is found in the second epistle of Peter (dated from the end of the first to the beginning of the second century AD),[87] as follows:

> For this very reason make every effort, by your faith to produce virtue, by virtue knowledge, by knowledge self-control, by self-control steadfastness, by steadfastness godliness, by godliness brotherly affection, and by brotherly affection love (2 Pet 1:5–7).

As it is evident from the study of the literary sources of the time to which this epistle belongs, it appears to be common practice at that time for the Christians to adopt the form of ethical sorites used in the Hellenistic environment in which each virtue produces the next, with the addition of an eschatological climax at the end of the list. What is striking in this adoption is that, in the Christian use, the scale of virtues begins with *faith* (πίστις) and *knowledge* (γνῶσις) and ends up with *love* (ἀγάπη) to which often the inheritance of the Kingdom is added.[88] Ethical life, therefore, culminates with love as an eschatological "virtue," an idea going back to St Paul (1 Cor 13:8).

Let us take special note of this final point, as it will be of decisive importance when we come to the consideration of the forms in which

---

[87] See R. J. Bauckham, *Jude, 2 Peter,* Word Biblical Commentary, vol. 50 (Waco, TX: Word Books, Publisher, 1983), p. 157f.

[88] For references, see Bauckham, *Jude, 2 Peter,* p. 176.

the biblical eschatological ethics survived in the subsequent centuries. The second epistle of Peter also provides us with the first explicit reference to the delay of the Parousia and the problems it created for the early Christian communities. In chapter 3, the author of the letter makes clear reference to "scoffers" who will appear in the last days saying, "where is the promise of his coming? For since the fathers fell asleep, everything remains just as it has been since the beginning of the world" (2 Pet 3:3–4). It is clear that the ethics we encounter in this epistle reflects the answer of the early Church to the problems created by the delay of the Second Coming for the ordinary life of the faithful. The author of the letter tries to keep alive in the faithful the expectation of the Parousia while proposing ethical norms borrowed from the surrounding culture, modified in ways which would somehow preserve the importance of eschatology in ethical life.

The fate of this endeavor in the following centuries deserves particular notice. Already in the third century, a shift of values makes its appearance, which was to affect Christian ethics for the following centuries, particularly in the East. Clement of Alexandria knows the earlier sorites according to which to the Christian is added "to faith knowledge (γνῶσις), to knowledge love, to love the (heavenly) inheritance (κληρονομία),"[89] but he praises, in particular, knowledge (γνῶσις) as leading to perfection and as the necessary accompaniment of all virtues, including love itself: for "every act performed by one who has knowledge (ἐπιστήμονος) is a good act (εὐπραγία), while that of one who does not possess knowledge (ἀνεπιστήμονος) is a bad act (κακοπραγία)."[90] This makes knowledge a necessary condition of ethical life, paving the way to the trend that started with Origen and culminated in Evagrius, who would place the final goal of the Christian life and even the Kingdom of God in *gnosis*, the cultivation of one's mental activities to obtain union with God through *contemplation* (θεωρία).[91]

---

[89] Clement Alex., *Strom.* VII, 10 (PG 9:480A).
[90] Clement Alex., *Strom.* VII, 10 (PG 9:484B).
[91] Evagrius, *Cap. Pract.* 1.3 (PG 40:1221D): "The Kingdom of God is knowledge of the Holy Trinity, coextensive with the make up of the mind, and going beyond its incorruptibility."

In spite of the widespread influence that this trend exercised, particularly among monastic circles in the East, the earlier tradition which associated the eschata and the Kingdom with *love* rather than knowledge remained alive and was promoted by prominent theological and monastic leaders. Two figures stand out as the most representative of this tradition. One of them is St Macarius of Egypt, who lived in the late fourth century, and the other is the well-known St Maximus the Confessor of the seventh century.

Macarius is known for his stress on the *heart* (not on the mind, as Evagrius taught) as the center of the divine presence in the human being: "the heart is master and king of the whole body organization [...]; it rules over all its members and all its thought."[92] Salvation is, for Macarius, a matter of the transfiguration of the entire human person by the conversion of the heart through love, the heart being understood not as the place of feeling and emotion but as the center of the whole psychosomatic life of the human being.[93] The purification of the heart with the fire of love in the present life penetrates the whole body, and this love will reunite its members in the future resurrection.[94] The approach is anthropological, but it is nonetheless significant in that it recovers the original biblical connection of love with eschatology and, through that, with ethics.

It was St Maximus the Confessor, however, who for the first time elaborated a philosophically sound connection between eschatology and ethics through the notion of love. For this original and profound thinker, love is not only the summit and crown of all virtues but also the key to unlocking the Christological mystery in its entirety as it is experienced and lived by the human being. It is worth following his way of dealing with the traditional ethical concepts which he inherited from his predecessors and how he transformed their meaning by placing them in the context of eschatology.

Maximus inherited from his philosophical and theological predecessors two concepts which had always played a fundamental role in ethics since Aristotle and the Stoics: *nature* (φύσις) and *reason*

[92] Macarius Aeg., *Hom.* 15.20 (PG 34:589B).

[93] Cf. J. Meyendorff, *Byzantine Theology* (New York: Fordham University Press, 1979), p. 68.

[94] Macarius Aeg., *Hom.* 11.1 (PG 34:544D).

(λόγος). These were key terms also in Maximus' moral thought. Living according to nature (κατὰ φύσιν) as opposed to living against nature (παρὰ φύσιν) was for Maximus, as it was for Aristotle, the Stoics, and certain Greek fathers, a moral principle for the Christian. Reason (λόγος), on the other hand, was for him not only an anthropological but also a Christological principle which sustains the universe itself, uniting its parts and relating it to God's own Λόγος.

The remarkable thing about St Maximus is that he was the *first* one to eschatologize both *nature* and *reason* and, through that, *ethics itself.* According to Maximus, nature exists not for its own sake but in order to surpass itself in the future age and reach the state of "above nature" (ὑπὲρ φύσιν). In the same way, the "reasons" (λόγοι) of all beings are eschatologically oriented, driving toward the end (εἰς τέλος ἀπάγοντες). Living κατὰ φύσιν (according to nature) and κατὰ λόγον (according to reason) is no longer what Aristotle and the Stoics meant. Although nature and reason remain basic for ethics, they are so only through their *eschatological transcendence* which finally determines ethical action. According to Maximus, the human being was given by God in its very nature the desire for communion with its Creator and the freedom (the αὐτεξούσιον) to reach this goal for which it was created. All virtues, therefore, in moral life are part of this natural movement of humanity toward union with God and in this sense constitute living "according to nature" (κατὰ φύσιν). Up to this point, Maximus' ethics could be described as basically Stoic (or Aristotelian), but it would be misunderstanding him if we stopped at that (as some of his interpreters seem to do). Human nature, according to the Confessor, is not an end in itself; it contains a τέλος, a final destination, which is to go beyond or above itself, to the ὑπὲρ φύσιν. This teleology differs from that of Aristotle's concept of nature in that the end, for the Greek philosopher, is a *fulfilment* of nature, whereas for Maximus it is a *transcendence* of nature—union with God, that is, going beyond human nature.

For Maximus, the ὑπὲρ φύσιν points to the future age, the eschaton. To live ὑπὲρ φύσιν means to *live as if the eschaton has already come*, as if it can be foretasted and experienced in history (something similar to the eucharistic experience). Such a foretaste is what the Spirit brings into history with Christ's Resurrection, and, for this reason, this kind of ethics is a "therefore," a consequence, of dying and rising with Christ while the virtues cease to be mere human or natural achievements and become "fruits of the Spirit" (Gal 5:22). Christian ethics is, thus, eschatological in that it aims at making the human being a "being of the Spirit" (πνευματικός), foretasting the eschatological status of the "new creation."

Since it is, therefore, part of the human nature to move toward its own transcendence (to the ὑπὲρ φύσιν)—not to its fulfilment, which would be Aristotelian—living κατὰ φύσιν means for the human being (as distinct from the rest of creatures which are not endowed with this drive toward the ὑπὲρ φύσιν) an existence of struggling to live in a way that surpasses the natural state. The ὑπὲρ φύσιν, or the "supernatural," is not there as a "grace" to enable humans to fulfil the κατὰ φύσιν but as a way of life *to be lived and experienced already now, the eschatological state which the risen Christ has brought into history in the Spirit.*

All this is stated clearly by Maximus in *Epistle* 9 (a text which, strangely enough, has been almost neglected by eminent proponents of his thought) in which he presents a summary of his ethical teaching in a vivid way. In this letter, Maximus mentions three things which drive human will and action: God, nature, and the world (Θεός, φύσις, κόσμος), each of them trying to claim the human being's decisions and actions for itself. To those three correspond the following ways of living: the first one (God) drives the human being to the ὑπὲρ φύσιν; the second one (nature) leads it to act according to nature (κατὰ φύσιν), thus keeping a neutral position (οὐδετέρα) between God and the world; the third one (the world—κόσμος) leads it in the direction of animalhood (κτῆνος), which contradicts human nature (παρὰ φύσιν).[95] To these three forces driving human will and action correspond the three kinds of human existence, which Paul describes in his letters, in the following way:

σαρκικὸς = living παρὰ φύσιν
ψυχικὸς = living κατὰ φύσιν
πνευματικὸς = living ὑπὲρ φύσιν[96]

---

[95] Maximus, *Ep.* 9 (PG 91:445CD).
[96] Maximus, *Ep.* 9 (PG 91:448AB).

Maximus goes on to spell out these three categories by giving examples of the ethical behavior associated with each category. Thus, to the "fleshly (σαρκικὸς)" corresponds doing evil, to the "psychic (ψυχικὸς)" neither doing nor suffering willingly evil, and to the "spiritual (πνευματικὸς)" or "driven by the Spirit of God," who "cuts himself off from both world and nature," readiness not only to suffer willingly injustice and evil done to him but also to do good to those who do evil to him, following Christ's commandment—"if someone wants to sue you for your shirt give him your coat also" (Mt 5:40)— or applying the blessed Apostle's words, "being reviled we bless, being persecuted we suffer it" (1 Cor 4:12). And all of this is because "the purpose of the giver of the commandments is *to free man from world and nature.*"[97]

With such moral ideas, St Maximus not only departs radically from Aristotelian and Stoic ethics, but he, for the first time so clearly, *recovers the New Testament eschatological ethics* which had gradually eclipsed with the delay of the Parousia. This was, of course, not entirely his "invention," for it was already practiced and taught by the desert fathers, as we encounter it in the *Apophthegmata* of the fifth and sixth centuries. But it is in Maximus that this ethics receives philosophical as well as biblical foundation, placed in the framework of a radical revision of the idea of nature with the help of eschatology.

Now, the question that naturally arises is the following: can the ethics proposed by St Maximus be applied in circumstances other that those provided by the desert or the monastery? Can the Christian who lives in the world cut himself off from it or from nature and its demands? Does such an eschatological ethics have any meaning for the ordinary Christian in a secular society such as the one most of us live in today? And if the answer is that such an ethics is not applicable by Christians today, should we not deny any relationship of eschatology with ethics, as Christian theology has been doing for a long time now?

---

[97] Maximus, *Ep.* 9 (PG 91:448C). Here Maximus speaks clearly of nature as a necessity from which we are called to *free* ourselves—an idea that may upset some of his interpreters.

These questions confirm the problem of the relation of ethics to eschatology, which was already pointed out by Schweitzer when he declared the eschatologically inspired New Testament ethics as "interim," owing to the long delay of the Parousia, and decided to suggest an ethics based on the personality and life of Jesus.[98] Maximus believes, as we have seen, that this ethics can be always applied, albeit only by a few, but an ethics which does not claim universal validity would not be a satisfactory option for those who wish to lead a Christian life but must live in a modern world.

In view of this situation, a way must be found to identify some universal validity within eschatological ethics even if its application appears to be difficult in certain circumstances, particularly under the assumption of the nonimminence of the Parousia. My proposal in this case is the following: eschatological ethics can be *a source of inspiration* for Christian morality under all circumstances, even if its actual application is in some cases problematic. We can state here a few points that may help to deepen the discussion of the subject.

1. If we take the resurrection as the quintessence of eschatology, faith in it would affect morality in several ways. We may limit ourselves to the following:

a) As the abolishment of death, resurrection will confirm *being* as truly being (ὄντως) which can only be so if it is *ever-being*. Eschatology, therefore, is above all *ontology*; it is not about "well-being," but being itself, not about our *bene esse* but our *esse*. As such, ontology has the priority over ethics, which means that human beings must not be identified and treated ultimately by what they *do* but by what they *are*: morality must be subjected to ontology and not the reverse. The ethical consequences of this would appear to be extremely important, if we considered for example, a case like the following:

Someone committed murder this morning and, as we normally do, we will say that he *is* a "murderer." But the word "is" points to this person's being and in eschatological terms to his *ever-being*. This would imply that being a murderer is a permanent part of his iden-

---

[98] A. Schweitzer, *The Mystery of the Kingdom of God* (New York: Association Press, 1950), p. 174, and *The Quest of the Historical Jesus* (London: A. & C. Black, 1954), pp. 399–401.

tity that will follow him eternally: morality determines ontology. Such a position (which, alas, is the dominant one) not only makes *forgiveness*, which is part of the eschatological gift, incapable of erasing evil from one's being—thus allowing evil to be eternal—but it runs contrary to truth, since it implies that a murderer cannot but be such in everything he does, in every aspect of his personality—which, of course, cannot be true. Ontology in this case is subjected to morality, which annuls the very purpose of the resurrection as the restoration of being.

The implications of this are far-reaching, as they bring up one of the most crucial questions of ethics: *one's right to a future.* If ontology is subjected to morality and one's acts determine his or her being, *the past becomes dominant over the future*; not only can God not erase our sins but we are deprived of the possibility of an *ontological* change, of *metanoia,* that is, of having a future.

Here is, therefore, an ethical principle that emerges from Christian eschatology: *everyone is entitled to a future.* This principle becomes extremely significant in our time because of the rapid and wide spread of *technology,* especially in the form of digital communication, which encourages and allows unlimited access to information. "What happens to our lives," Stefano Rodotà asks, "in an age when 'Google remembers everything'?"[99] The collective memory of the internet which gathers every trace we leave behind us and stores it forever, not only exposes us to the danger of being used by others against our will and interest, but *it also enslaves us in our past* depriving us of the possibility to make a new beginning. In the name of every one's right to information and knowledge we are enslaved in our past. Technology takes away from us our future.

b) The resurrection does not affect only the human being but *the whole of creation.* The abolition of death for humans is tied up with the elimination of mortality in general. This is why the eschatological hope extends beyond humanity to all of creation which "waits with eager longing for the revealing of the sons of God ... because the creation itself will be set free from its bondage to decay and obtain the glorious liberty of the children of God" (Rom 8:19–20). Eschatol-

---

[99] S. Rodotà, *Il mondo nella rete* (Rome and Bari: Laterza, 2014).

ogy concerns the whole cosmos which, according to the Fathers, will also share in the future deification of the human being.

From a different angle, Oliver O'Donovan in his *Resurrection and Moral Order* convincingly argues the point that in the resurrection "creation and kingdom are linked in affirmation and fulfilment,"[100] since the resurrection both vindicates the created order and restores it by transforming it. O'Donovan argues that the whole of Christian morality depends on the reality of Christ's Resurrection, the only reliable basis for a serious personal or social ethics, including even political theory. From the perspective of the present study, too, which lays particular stress on the Eucharist, this would be fully acceptable. What emerges as a fundamental ethical consequence of the resurrection would thus relate to what is today called *ecology* or the relation of humanity to its natural environment.

Eschatology has often been presented in terms of the eternal life of human souls, a view shared also by St Augustine and much of the later Roman Catholic and Protestant tradition. This, as it has been shown by Lynn White Jr.,[101] was one of the factors that contributed to the appearance of the ecological crisis in modern times. The whole point of the resurrection is the raising of the *body* not as an immaterial entity, as Origen believed, but as a material one, as Methodius of Olympus argued in refuting him in the fourth century. The material creation participates in the Kingdom, as the Church from the earliest times (St Irenaeus) has believed and solemnly declared in the celebration of the Eucharist.

Eschatology, therefore, is a source of ecological ethics, so much needed in our time. Creation too has the right to a future—not just human beings. By depriving so many species of their future through direct or indirect extinction we negate the very purpose of Christ's Resurrection which includes the restoration of the created order in its entirety.

c) As we have already argued in a previous section, the future resurrection will not be a *creatio ex nihilo* but an affirmation of being

---

[100] O. O'Donovan, *Resurrection and Moral Order* (Grand Rapids, MI: Eerdmans Publishing, 1994), p. 184.

[101] L. White, Jr., "The Historical Roots of our Ecological Crisis," *Science* 155 (1967) 1203–7.

as *communion,* that is, the restoration of beings as unique identities established through their relationships which have been broken and destroyed by death. The resurrection, understood in this way, reveals the importance of *personhood* in eschatological ontology and by extension in any ethics inspired by it. Eschatologically inspired ethics is an ethics that gives ultimate value to the person.

In our Western culture today an ethics of the person would at first sight be most welcome and even exalted, but it would be so because in this tradition the person has been identified with the *individual personality,* i.e., an identity endowed with consciousness and reason and possessing a moral value by itself, regardless of its relationships.[102] Relationships, in this way of understanding personhood, do not *constitute* the person but are *chosen* (or rejected) by its free decision. Every "person" in this case possesses the right to a free choice of the way it relates to God, to nature (including its own body), and to the rest of human beings.

This individualistic approach has permeated ethics in all areas of life in our Western culture including the social and political sphere. The idea of *human rights* which is dominant in our time is normally understood as "the rights of *the individual*" (cf. the American Constitution). Ever since Thomas Hobbes and John Locke, political theory is based on the rights of the individuals who are called, in order to avoid "a war of all men against all men," to agree freely among themselves through a "social contract" how to organize their social life (the basis of modern democracy). This has not always proved to be easy, as the balance between society and individual is never achieved in a satisfactory way, leading to repeated revisions of the political systems (sometimes through bloody social upheavals and revolutions.)

Can eschatology contribute anything to social and political life? In the early twentieth century, theories of a *social gospel* (e.g., Reinhold Niebuhr and others) have suggested the possibility of sanctioning concrete social and political practices by seeking support in Christian theology. The discussion continues in our time between

[102] See the definition of "Person" by Boethius, *Contra Eutych. et Nest.,* 3: "naturae rationabilis individua substantia."

those who would regard Christian eschatology as contradicting and confronting the moral logic of the world with its humanistic values (John Howard Yoder, Stanley Hauerwas, etc.)[103] and others, including the Orthodox Aristotle Papanikolaou,[104] who supports the view that certain moral and political values, such as human rights, could be sustained by theological ideas like communion and personhood. In our approach here, which is built on the entrance of the eschaton into history through Christ's Resurrection and its foretaste and experience by the ecclesial community, eschatology seeks to *infuse* into social life certain ultimate values and, thus, cannot but endorse moral ideas and practices which are inspired by, or consonant with, these values. But it remains always true that the application of these values in history can never be satisfactory or unproblematic before the future resurrection purifies history from its antinomies.

2. A fundamental ingredient of eschatology in its relation to ethics is, as we have seen, the transcendence of nature by the demand to live ὑπὲρ φύσιν, an idea particularly stressed by St Maximus. How can this idea be applied to ethics in ordinary life as a general and universal moral rule and not simply as an exceptional behavior of a minority such as the monks and the ascetics?

Living ὑπὲρ φύσιν (i.e., as if the eschaton not only is imminent but is, in a sense, already here through the entrance of the risen Christ into history in the Holy Spirit) means that life κατὰ φύσιν does not fulfil itself if it obstructs, or does not lead to, living ὑπὲρ φύσιν. This can be illustrated with the case of *sexuality* and its relation to ethics.

Sexuality is part of human nature, of living κατὰ φύσιν. For the animals living κατὰ φύσιν is an end in itself, but for humans the end or goal of κατὰ φύσιν is the ὑπὲρ φύσιν. If nature is an end in itself, if it is not eschatologized by aiming at the ὑπὲρ φύσιν, as Maximus teaches, it does not fulfil itself; it deviates from its teleology and betrays itself. *The fulfilment of natural law is not a ground of morality for the human being* in Christian ethics. Thus, a male can bring forth

---

[103] J. H. Yoder, *The Politics of Jesus* (Grand Rapids, MI: Eerdmans Publishing, 1994). S. Hauerwas, *The Hauerwas Reader*, eds. J. Berkman and M. Cartwright (Durham, N.C: Duke University Press, 2001).

[104] See A. Papanikolaou, *The Mystical as Political: Democracy and Non-Radical Orthodoxy* (Notre Dame, IN: University of Notre Dame Press, 2012).

by nature a countless number of children, which would be "natural" for him if he were simply an animal, but it would be a betrayal of his *human* nature if this did not aim at or lead to the ὑπὲρ φύσιν (i.e., if sexuality [and nature] is not eschatologized). The same would apply also to *virginity*: the abstinence from sexual activity is a violation of living κατὰ φύσιν, if its aim is not the ὑπὲρ φύσιν. As the saying attributed to St Basil has it, "I have not known a woman, and yet a virgin I am not" (καὶ γυναῖκα οὐκ ἔγνων, καὶ παρθένος οὐκ εἰμί).

Now, what, in moral terms, is the ὑπὲρ φύσιν that eschatologizes the κατὰ φύσιν and makes nature fulfil its λόγος, its *raison d'être*? How do we ethically define the ὑπὲρ φύσιν in a way that would make it a universal moral principle applicable to all? The answer to this question was given by Paul in his first letter to the Corinthians and was faithfully followed by the patristic tradition that reached St Maximus—the only thing that will survive in the end is *love,* and it is this that expresses, in moral terms, the living ὑπὲρ φύσιν of which St Maximus speaks. Love is the climax of all virtues because all virtues find in it their fulfilment, their τέλος.[105] It is this that eschatology brings into morality as the ultimate aim of human life.

But why is love to be described as ὑπὲρ φύσιν? Is it not simply "natural" for human beings to love? Would it not suffice to keep the Aristotelian or Stoic ethics of living κατὰ φύσιν and still maintain love? The definition of love either as a feeling and inner disposition or as "doing good" is very common but would not fit the Christological and eschatological prerequisites of Christian morality. Simply "doing good" is, as we have seen, according to St Maximus, the characteristic of the "psychic" not of the "spiritual" human being; it is part of living κατὰ φύσιν. The love that Christ brought to the world and the Spirit grants by introducing the eschaton into history transcends nature by going beyond the instinct of self-preservation to the point of sacrificing one's rights for the sake of the other (1 Cor 6:7: "why not rather suffer wrong?"). Loving ὑπὲρ φύσιν goes beyond the idea of "human rights" in the direction of even renouncing one's rights (which means that "human rights" is for Christian morality an ethical principle that must be open to transcendence).

---

[105] Maximus, especially *Ep.* 2 (PG 91:396B-D).

Love, as the quintessence of eschatology and the ethical content of living ὑπὲρ φύσιν, permeates every area of life transcending what is natural into life "in the Spirit," which is the goal of Christian morality, a foretaste of the Kingdom. Sexuality is part of human nature but its end and λόγος is, for human beings, to lead to love, and the same is true for virginity even though it appears to deviate from nature. Marriage and family are not there in order to satisfy the demands of nature but to go beyond nature through love. Family is a workshop of love, and it is in this that its moral value lies. But if this love cannot exceed the limits of the family to reach the stranger or even the enemy, it is not the love that "never fails." Only when marriage and the family are open to reach beyond themselves, even to the point of renouncing their "rights," including their very existence (Mt 10:37; Lk 14:26), do they fulfil their τέλος. And this applies to all kinds of "rights" be it individual, social, national, or whatever; all these "rights" can be good, but their moral value is not intrinsic in their nature but in their openness to the immensity of love.

All this amounts to an ethics in which *virtues* do not possess a moral value individually and intrinsically, but only in so far as they culminate in love: they are "nothing" in themselves, as Paul declares in 1 Corinthians 13. Prophesy, faith, knowledge, self-sacrifice, almsgiving, etc., which are all regarded normally as possessing moral value, are "nothing" (οὐδὲν) unless they lead to love, and this is because love is the only "virtue" that will survive in the end. Love is not therefore one virtue among others; it grants eternal value to all virtues by liberating them from all exclusiveness and making them roads to the Kingdom, to the way the Trinitarian God exists.

Eschatological ethics with its maximalistic demands appears to be inapplicable and, thus, unrealistic, particularly at a time when the expectation of the Parousia is no longer vivid even among Christian believers themselves. This, however, does not render it meaningless. Its importance for all times lies not so much in the application of its concrete demands, which is difficult indeed, but in its infusing into moral life a perspective and a purpose that make it worth striving to achieve in spite of the limitations and antinomies of historical existence.

XII. *Toi, tu ne mourras pas*

"Aimer un être, c'est lui dire: *Toi, tu ne mourras pas*" (Gabriel Marcel)[106]

The moral essence of eschatology is *love,* because eschatology is about the resurrection, the *abolition of death.* Love cannot be content with anything less than the overcoming of death. Feeding the hungry is an act of love, but it is not true love if it stops at that. For the ultimate purpose of eating is to overcome death, and feeding the hungry can only postpone death. The answer to the statement above —"but this is the only thing I can offer my fellow human beings; I cannot give them immortality"—may sound reasonable, but it cannot satisfy love. Love cannot be content with what *can* be done; it seeks the impossible. It is, in this sense, inseparable from *faith* and *hope* (1 Cor 13:13). It is the "greatest" (μείζων) and yet one of the "these three things" (τὰ τρία ταῦτα) that remain—faith, hope, and love—as it is always accompanied by "the assurance of things hoped for, the conviction of things not seen" (Heb 11:1). Faith in and hope for the resurrection emerge as a demand of love.

Eschatology is about a life without death. It is also about a "re-membrance," an "experience," and a "taste" of such a life within a life contaminated by death. When the risen Christ encountered his disciples and dined with them, this "mystery" of a life without death present and operative within a life infected by death entered history and affected our present life. Those who have accepted the apostolic *kerygma* cannot but build their worldview and their lives on this "mystery."

In the present book, we are looking at this "mystery" in some of the basic areas of our existence. What does it mean to *be,* to exist, to *think,* to *believe,* to *worship,* and to *act* under the assumption that death does not have the last word in existence, that a life without death can be "tasted" and "experienced" in this life, albeit not as a permanent state, and that it is only on the basis of this assumption that existence can acquire meaning and value and not be "in vain"

---

[106] "To love a being is to say to him or her: You, you will not die." Gabriel Marcel, "*Tu ne mourras pas,*" *Textes choisis et présentés par Anne Marcel* (Paris: Éditions Arfuyen, 2012), p. 104.

(cf. 1 Cor 15:14)? For, if death has the last word in existence, all of God's creation is subject to disintegration and futility rendering, thus, invalid the apostolic *kerygma,* the very foundation of Christianity.

I have deliberately used the word "assumption" in referring to faith in the resurrection. This book is written for those who *have* accepted the fact of the Resurrection of Christ and, although there can be arguments to "prove" or support this fact objectively on rational or historical grounds,[107] this book is interested in the "logical" consequences that *follow* the acceptance of this fact: *credo ut intelligam.* The resurrection, in this case, is treated logically as a "hypothesis" (as in every science),[108] followed by the logical consequences it entails, tested and confirmed by the "law of non-contradiction": once we have accepted (by faith) the *kerygma* of the resurrection, what are the consequences that follow logically from this? It is very common among Christians to confess the article of the creed about faith in the resurrection but not follow this confession to its logical consequences in theology and life. As a matter of fact, many of the confessional differences among Christians fall under this category. This study aims at unveiling such logical consequences of the apostolic *kerygma* of the resurrection for those who have accepted it in the course of history, beginning with the first Christian communities.

The projection of the resurrection and the abolition of death as the key to unlocking the meaning and survival of existence may give the impression that other important and decisive events in the history of salvation are made redundant or meaningless. This would be a hasty conclusion. There are, of course, certain Christian traditions, which would stress the Cross as the center of salvation, placing the

---

[107] For rational arguments, see R. Swinburne, *The Resurrection of God Incarnate* (Oxford: Oxford University Press, 2003). On the historical question, see W. Pannenberg, *Jesus—God and Man* (Philadelphia: Westminster, 1977), p. 88ff.

[108] According to K. Popper, all sciences, natural as well as social, are expected to put forward hypotheses (*The Poverty of Historicism* [Boston: Beacon Press, 1967], p. 130f). Scientifically unwarranted assumptions are involved in all scientific enquiry (*The Logic of Scientific Discovery* [London: Hutchinson, 1968], p. 278). In the realm of theology, examples can be found in K. Barth for whom the World of God as revealed in Christ is a principle to be accepted as an axiom that needs no proof from which all dogmatic theology issues. Cf. W. W. Bartley, *The Retreat to Commitment* (London: Chatto & Windus, 1964), who would add P. Tillich as another example.

purpose of redemption in justification from sin rather than in the granting of immortality. (Admittedly, the present author operates under the influence of his own tradition.) But the projection of the resurrection as the central event in God's intervention in history aims precisely at validating ontologically the Incarnation and, particularly, the Cross, and not at undermining their importance for our salvation. The main thesis of this book is that all historical events (the Cross included) are subject to the law of mortality if they are left to themselves and are not vivified by the resurrection. It is here that eschatology emerges as a *sine qua non* condition of salvation. The Resurrection elevates the Cross to divine glory (Jn 13:31) because, without that, it would mean that even God is *definitively* under the power of death, with all the consequences that this would entail for existence (and, of course, salvation). Placing the Cross and all the salvation events (indeed, history as a whole) under the "grace" of the resurrection means liberating them from the law of mortality that has dominated all of existence since the human fall and granting them true and eternal not only meaning but *being*.

Implicit in this approach is, of course, the importance of *ontology* for theology. If salvation is a matter that concerns only the remission of our sins (and our subsequent justification by God), it is limited to anthropology (and with no regard for the problem of mortality). If, on the other hand, it aims to protect from the threat of disintegration which mortality poses to existence, salvation acquires *cosmic* dimensions: God saves in Christ not only humanity but creation as a whole, τὰ πάντα (Col 1:20). This makes ontology a fundamental dimension of theology and places eschatological ontology at the center of Christian faith.

Chapter One

ESCHATOLOGY AND ONTOLOGY

Introduction

1. Ontology and Theology

What does accepting the apostolic *kerygma* of Christ's Resurrection and the entrance of the "last days" into history mean for our *being*, our existence, and the existence of the world? The concept of being is not merely an academic subject; it does not refer to "metaphysics," a speculative description of the ultimate structure of reality, but to the most fundamental and *experienced* "fact" of existence in its universal and unshakeable inevitableness. The place that the verb "to be" occupies, since ancient times, in the structure of all our Western languages witnesses to the foundational character of being in the basic and commonest expressions of our culture. As Heidegger, in referring to the structure of our Western languages, has observed, "the little word 'is' which speaks everywhere in our language and tells of being, even when it does not appear expressly, contains the whole destiny of being—from the ἐστίν τε καὶ εἶναι of Parmenides" to our own time.[1] Our way of thinking in Western cul-

---

[1] M. Heidegger, *Identity and Difference*, trans. J. Stambaugh (New York: Harper & Row, 1969), p. 73. The fact that there have been different ways of understanding being from the classical times to the present, including recent attempts to reject ontology altogether in contemporary thinking (see the Introduction to this book), does not undermine or expunge the notion of being from our thought and language.

The "traditionalist" view which advocates a theology free from or uninterested in the concept of being overlooks the obvious omnipresence of the verb "to be," and thus of ontology, in every thought we make or sentence we compose. The idea of a "canon of faith" free from an explicit or implicit presence of ontology is a myth inspired and invented by anti-philosophical, confessionalist purism, totally unfounded in history. Already within the time range of the formation of the Bible and during the entire course of the patristic period, the "canon of faith" was constantly reinterpreted and cast in the philosophical idiom of each particular time, the concept of being always playing a key

ture is structured and revolves around the verb *to be,* and if Christian theology wishes to interpret the Gospel in this culture, it cannot but express itself in ontological terms.

The employment of ontological categories had become a hermeneutical necessity for theology already at the time of the encounter of Judaism with Hellenistic culture. Ontological terminology with reference to God appears clearly in the translation of the Bible in the Septuagint where the intentionally obscure self-designation of God in the book of Exodus (3:14) is translated into Greek as ἐγὼ εἰμὶ ὁ ὤν or ὁ ὤν ("I am the one who is" or "the Being One"). This way of referring to God established itself among the Greek-speaking Jews of the Hellenistic period when thinkers like Philo employed it with noticeable frequency.[2] Although this way of referring to God remained for the Jews a fixed formula which was repeated without a philosophical explanation, the exchange at times (e.g., by Philo) of ὁ ὤν with τὸ ὄν reveals a tendency, at least among the Jewish intelligentsia, to interpret the formula in a philosophical (Platonic) sense.[3]

The New Testament retains the Exodus formula undeclinable and without explanation in the book of Revelation (1:8, 4:8, 11:17)— ὁ ὤν καὶ ὁ ἦν καὶ ὁ ἐρχόμενος—sometimes combined with the word παντοκράτωρ as an expression of the supra-temporality and deity of God.[4] The ontological content of the formula becomes more evident when it is applied to Christ in the Gospel of St John in the form of ἐγὼ εἰμὶ as Jesus' self-designation (Jn 8:24, 28, 8:58, 13:19). In chapter 8 verse 58 in particular, the ontological sense of the formula is implied in the contrast between Christ and Abraham with the verb "to be" (εἰμὶ) applied to the former and "to become" (γενέσθαι) to the latter: πρὶν Ἀβραὰμ γενέσθαι ἐγὼ εἰμὶ. Similarly, in another passage

---

role in the process. This did not result in a "Hellenization of Christianity" but rather in the "Christianization of Hellenism" (Florovsky), thanks to the hermeneutical ingeniousness of patristic thought. To restrict the hermeneutics of the apostolic *kerygma* to the past would be tantamount to turning it into a venerable but dead relic. Hermeneutics is the task of Christian theology also in our own time, in the context of a culture which continues to structure its way of thinking and its language around the verb "to be."

    [2] F. Büschel, "εἰμὶ, ὁ ὤν," in G. Kittel, *Theological Dictionary of the New Testament,* II, (Michigan, MN: Eerdmans, 1964), p. 398.

    [3] M. Hengel, *Judaism and Hellenism,* II (London: SCM Press, 1974), p. 105, n. 372.

    [4] Büschel, "εἰμὶ, ὁ ὤν," p. 398.

(8:24) the ἐγὼ εἰμί is contrasted with ἀποθανεῖσθε: "if you do not believe that ἐγὼ εἰμί, you will die (ἀποθανεῖσθε) in your sins."

The designation of God in ontological terms with the ἐγὼ εἰμὶ ὁ ὤν formula is particularly used by the Greek fathers and in the Byzantine liturgy and art. Already in St Justin and the Apologists, the formula ὁ ὤν is not only present but often explicitly understood in a Platonic sense. In Justin, for example, God is described as "he who is always the same in himself and in relation to all things,"[5] which is a direct reference to Plato.[6] Origen continues in the same line,[7] while the Cappadocians unhesitatingly apply to the ὁ ὤν formula the idea of being in its philosophical content. Thus, Gregory of Nazianzus can write that the designation of God as ὁ ὤν (or τὸ ὄν) is "the more strictly appropriate name for him ... making everything contemplated therein always the same, neither growing nor being consumed."[8] "The ἀεὶ ὤν, as he [God] calls himself, ... [is appropriate] because he possesses in himself the whole being (ὅλον τὸ εἶναι)."[9] Similarly Gregory of Nyssa, in the same spirit, regards the notion of being as appropriate for God, because he contains the true being, and "it is not possible for anything to be unless it has its being (τὸ εἶναι) in the one that is (ἐν τῷ ὄντι)."[10] In the same line, Gregory Palamas in the fourteenth century will make use of the ὁ ὤν formula in order to clarify the notion of being by distinguishing it from that of essence: in the Exodus self-designation, God does not say "I am the essence" but "I am the who is," "the one who encompasses all being."[11] Theology has nothing to say about the *essence* of God, but this does not mean that it cannot refer to the being of God. The ἐγὼ εἰμὶ ὁ ὤν does not exclude ontology but its identification with ousiology.

All this is reflected in the liturgical life of the Church where the Exodus designation of God occupies a central place, at least in the East. This is evident in the eucharistic liturgies which bear the names of Basil the Great and John Chrysostom, both of them going back

⁵ Justin, *Dial.* 3.5 (PG 6:481B). Cf. Athenagoras, *Leg.* 4.2 (PG 6:900A).
⁶ Plato, *Republic* 6.484b.
⁷ Origen, *de princ.* I 3.5 (PG 11:150B).
⁸ Gregory Naz., *Or.* 30.18 (PG 36:128A).
⁹ Gregory Naz., *Or.* 45.3 (PG 36:635C).
¹⁰ Gregory Nys., *Or. cat.* 25 (PG 45:65D).
¹¹ Gregory Palamas, *Triads,* III, 2.12.

to the patristic period and still in use in the Orthodox Church. In the prayer of the Anaphora of these liturgies, God the Father is addressed as ὁ ὤν: thou who Art (Basil), "ineffable ... ever being, being always the same (ἀεὶ ὤν, ὡσαύτως ὤν)" (Chrysostom). Similarly, in Byzantine iconography, the capital letters Ο ΩΝ appear on the top of the figure of Christ (sometimes also of the Father whenever he is depicted) as an indication of his divinity. This is still found in the Greek Orthodox churches, usually on the three ends of the Cross where the three letters appear in the halo.

This consistent application of ontological categories to theology by the Greek fathers contained risks which ought to be avoided. The Parmenedian identification of being (εἶναι) with knowing (νοεῖν) could lead to the false conclusion that the human mind can grasp and conceive God in his essence. Ontology should be, therefore, distinguished from gnoseology, and the affirmation that God *is* should exclude the knowledge of *what* (τί) God is, his *nature* or *essence* (φύσις or οὐσία). Ontology, thus, acquires certain inner distinctions which the Cappadocian fathers, in particular, develop as a general rule: in speaking of being we must distinguish between *what* someone or something is and *how* one is[12] (i.e., the nature or *ousia* of being and the *mode* of being); substance ontology cannot state anything other than God simply *is*. However, being does not exclusively refer to *what* God is (his substance); it points also to *how* he is, to his *hypostases* or *persons* (Father, Son, and Spirit). God's substance is not accessible to us except through the *energies* it radiates by his creative and sanctifying love,[13] while his hypostases offer themselves to us for *communion* with divine being, above all in the Incarnation. *Ontology, therefore, can be applied to theology only in the form of being as communion.*[14]

The unknowableness of God's substance, therefore, does not annul the use of ontology in theology; it only calls for a rejection of substance ontology as a means of communion with God and knowledge of him and for a revision of ontology which would bring out the *mode of being* rather than its substance as the most appropriate ground

---

[12] Basil, *C. Eunom.* 14–15 (PG 29:545AB) and Gregory Naz., *Or.* 3.16 (PG 36:93AB).

[13] See J. Meyendorff, *Byzantine Theology* (New York: Fordham University Press, 1979), p. 186f, about the relevant patristic teaching.

[14] See my *Being as Communion*, pp. 15–48.

for an alliance between theology and ontological thought. The apophaticism of divine substance—indeed of any substance, according to the Cappadocians[15]—does not lead to a *negative* theology at the expense or the sacrifice of a *kataphatic* one, since this would make ontology, the employment of the notion of being in our reference to God, totally inadequate.

This observation would apply to all forms of apophatic theology in the patristic period in which the use of the term "being" for God appears to need qualification. A careful study of such apophatic statements reveals that the concern behind them is that an application of the term "being" to God (ὁ ὤν) may confuse God with his creatures which in our language are also called "beings" (τὰ ὄντα). The intention behind this hesitation to call God being is not to lead to a (Neo) Platonic "beyond substance" but, on the contrary, to affirm that *only God is the true being*. Thus, Dionysius the Areopagite would explain:

> Because God is ὁ ὤν and super-essentially grants being (τὸ εἶναι) to beings (τοῖς οὖσι) ... it is said that this one being (τὸ ἓν ὄν) by the production from it of the many beings ... is super-essentially exempted (ἐξῃρημένον) from all beings.[16]

And, the same author can write that:

> And not only the beings (τὰ ὄντα) but the very being (αὐτὸ τὸ εἶναι) of beings [come] from the pre-eternal being.[17]

In spite, therefore, of the limitations of the human mind and language (of which apophatic theology warns us), it appears that, at least in our Western culture, we do not possess a more appropriate concept to refer to God than that of *being*. As St Basil writes in defense of the pre-eternal existence and divinity of Christ, "no matter how far back you travel in thought you cannot get beyond the 'was' (ἦν)," because "nothing beyond the 'was' (ἦν) is conceivable."[18]

The use of the notion of being in our reference to God also occupied a central place in Western theology from the patristic period to the Middle Ages. In a way similar to that of the Greek fathers, St

---

[15] Gregory Naz., *Or.* 28.22–30 (PG 36:56f).

[16] Dionysius Areop., *De div. nom.* 2.11 (PG 3:649B).

[17] Dionysius Areop., *De div. nom.* 5.4 (PG 3:817CD). Cf. John Damascene, *De fide orth.* I, 4 (PG 94:8008).

[18] Basil, *De Spir.* 6.14 (PG 32:89A).

Augustine would state that being is the only name which God him-self has used in referring to himself: *non aliquo modo est, sed est, est.*[19] This would be repeated by Thomas Aquinas almost verbatim: "non enim significat formam aliquam, sed ipsum esse,"[20] while Duns Sco-tus would address God as "total being" and "true being" (*totum esse, verum esse*).[21]

Up to that point Western medieval theology would converge with Greek patristic thought: the Exodus self-designation of God can and, in the context of Greek culture, should be expressed in terms of being. Medieval theology, however, did not stop at that. It *raised the question of what this means for our understanding of being itself,* producing in this manner an ontology as a metaphysics of being, des-tined to affect Western philosophy for centuries. This was not the case with the Greek fathers who never embarked on an explicit and elaborate ontology. But it would be a mistake to conclude from this that the Greek fathers did not operate with ontology in their theol-ogy—they would not be Greek if they did not. Equally, those—and they are many—who maintain the position that the Greek fathers simply took over and used unchanged classical Greek philosophy overlook the fact that the Christian faith did exercise an essential impact on Greek culture and, of course, on philosophical thought in the patristic period. The difference between the Greek fathers and the medieval theologians is that the latter worked out explicitly and elaborately a metaphysics of being, whereas the former did not pres-ent their ontology as a system, transforming and converting it only *implicitly* to suit and serve the demands of their theology.

A comparison of Eastern and Western theology with regard to ontology deserves a special study and obviously cannot be attempted here. Certain points, however, must be mentioned, even briefly, as they bear on the present study.

A basic point of divergence between the Greek fathers and the medieval doctors on the subject of ontology concerns *the relation between being and beings.* Since according to the Scholastic theolo-gians God is, as we have seen, identifiable with the "total" and "true"

[19] Augustine, *Confess.* XIII, 31.46.
[20] Thomas Aquinas, *Sum. theol.* I, 13.11.
[21] Duns Scotus, *De prima rerum omn. princ.* I, 1.

being, transcending and "causing" all particular beings while remaining himself uncaused or the cause of himself (*causa sui*), *the question of unity and difference between being and beings*, becomes fundamental to metaphysics.[22] Being in this case precedes beings ontologically either as a "necessary" being contrasted with the "contingent" beings (Scholastics)[23] or as their "ground" (Heidegger). Beings are *contingent* on being, because they may or may not be (as they depend on being for their existence), while God as a *necessary being* (existentially and logically), becomes the highest "concept" or "idea."[24] The consequences of this ontology, which extend into our time, include such crucial subjects as the priority of *substance* in ontology, the accommodation of *freedom* in the idea of being, the relation of thought to being, and others.

There are several central aspects of this ontological system which would not be compatible with Greek patristic thought. The priority of being over beings is probably the most crucial one for theology, since it implies an ontology which, applied to God, leads to the view that the one God, or divine substance, precedes ontologically the Trinity, a position which in fact medieval theology had adopted and transmitted to Christian dogmatics. As Karl Rahner has observed, this position deviates from the biblical identification of God with *the Father*, an identification found also in the Trinitarian theology of Greek patristic thought.[25] The Greek fathers by identifying God

---

[22] M. Heidegger, *Identity and Difference*, p. 62. Heidegger finds the confusion of "being" with beings at the roots of Western metaphysics and insists on the need to disentangle the two by the differentiation of "being" from beings. He sees the history of Western philosophy as a history of the concealment of being, exemplified in what he calls *ontotheology*, a metaphysics "which thinks of beings ... with respect to the highest being which accounts for everything" (p. 70f), i.e., of "God" as a "cause" of beings and of himself (*causa sui*). The disentanglement of ontology from theology becomes for him imperative, and this sets the agenda for postmodern theologians engaging in an effort to propose a theology "above," "beyond," or even "without" being, by employing essentially a form of Christianized Neoplatonism. (Cf. W.J. Hankey, "*Theoria versus Poesis*: Neoplatonism and Trinitarian Difference in Aquinas, John Milbank, Jean-Luc Marion and John Zizioulas," *Modern Theology*, 15:4 [1999] 387–415).

[23] E. Gilson, *L'esprit de la philosophie médiévale* (Paris: J. Vrin, 1932), p. 63f.

[24] Gilson, *L'esprit de la philosophie médiévale*, p. 62: "Construire une métaphysique sur la présence en nous de l'idée de Dieu demeure donc une entreprise toujours légitime."

[25] K. Rahner, *The Trinity*, trans. Joseph Donceel (New York: Seabury Press, 1970), *passim* and esp. p. 15ff: "If, with Scripture and the Greeks we mean by ὁ Θεὸς in the first

with the Father as the "source" (πηγή), "principle" (ἀρχή), and even "cause" (αἰτία) of Trinitarian existence,²⁶ ignore the ontological priority of being and divine essence over beings (the *hypostases*). The Cappadocian fathers do not even hesitate to liken the persons of the Trinity to "three human beings,"²⁷ and their concept of being includes both the "what" (τί) someone or something is (nature/ousia) and the "how" (ὅπως or πῶς), i.e., the *mode* of existence, which they call *hypostasis* or *prosopon*.²⁸ The biblical ὁ ὤν points for them to a *concrete being*²⁹ and not to divine essence, to "deity" or "divinity." St Gregory Palamas sums up the entire patristic tradition when he writes that "God, when he was speaking to Moses, did not say 'I am the essence' but 'I am who I am'. It is therefore not 'He-Who-Is' who comes from the essence, but it is the essence which comes from 'He-Who-Is', for the 'He-Who-Is' embraces in himself all being (εἶναι)."³⁰ Hence he gives us the fundamental ontological principle which differentiates the Greek patristic from the medieval Latin ontology: *"the essence is necessarily being (ὄν), but being (τὸ ὄν) is not necessarily essence."*³¹

The liberation of ontology from ousiocracy through the elevation of *hypostasis* (the particular *being*) to a primary ontological status by Greek patristic thought opens the way to a revision of the metaphysics of being which had dominated philosophical thought for centuries. The alternative to being is not to be found in nonbeing in the sense of nothing (*nihil*); nonbeing does not mean annihilation.³²

place the Father [this] ... in line with Greek theology of the Trinity, would lead us to treat first of the Father." (p. 16)

²⁶ For a detailed discussion, see my *Communion and Otherness*, 2006, pp. 113ff. The identification of God with the Father is particularly clear in St Basil: "there are not two Gods, because there are not two Fathers" (*Hom.* 24, *C. Sabel.*, etc., [PG 31:605C]. "There is one God because he is the Father" (605A).

²⁷ Cf. J.N.D. Kelly, *Early Christian Doctrines* (London: A. & C. Black, 1958), p. 264.

²⁸ Basil, *C. Eunom.* 14–15 (PG 29:545AB) and Gregory Naz., *Or.* 3.16 (PG 36:93AB).

²⁹ Thus, St Basil, *Hom.* 24, *C. Sabel.* (PG 31:609C): "Should we ever link together the Trinity do not imagine the three as parts of an indivisible thing (for such a thought would be impious), but understand them as the unbreakable coexistence (συνουσία) of *three perfect things* (τριῶν τελείων)."

³⁰ Gregory Palamas, *Triads*, III, 2.12.

³¹ Gregory Palamas, *c. Akindynos*, III, 10. Cf. J. Meyendorff, *Byzantine Theology*, p. 188.

³² The Leibnizian question, "Why is there something rather than nothing?" which has dominated Western philosophy until our time (see J.-P. Sartre, *L'être et le néant* [Paris: Librairie Galimard, 1943]) and led to Nietzsche's nihilism, is a direct product of

Since being emerges not from essence but from a concrete being (a *hypostasis*) which, in Rahner's terms, "is not *positively* conceived as 'absolute' even before it is explicitly known as relative"[33] (i.e., from the communion of beings), *it is the breaking of this communion that constitutes nonbeing*. The nonbeings (τὰ μὴ ὄντα) of Romans 4:17 and 1 Corinthians 1:28 are nonexistent not because they are "nothing (*nihil*)" but because they have lost (through death) their specific "mode of being." Being in this case is only threatened by *death*, understood not as annihilation, as Heidegger conceived it, but as the destruction of the *mode* of beings, their relational existence which grants them their *hypostasis*, their *communion*. It is this kind of ontology that would make the understanding of the Exodus self-designation of God consonant with the theology of the Greek fathers: God, the ὁ ὤν, is not the divine ousia but the hypostasis of the Father whose being is constituted as Trinity, since being the Father implies his relationship with the Son and the Spirit, that is, an understanding of being as communion. The "death of God" that Nietzsche proclaimed and modern atheism professes is that of a "deity," a "substance." A Trinitarian God cannot die so long as he remains Trinitarian, for he is by definition *a "coinherence"* (περιχώρησις) *of beings* and, therefore, *life*. If death is conceived as the collapse of communion and the dissolution of beings into substances, the ὁ ὤν can never die, not because he is an eternal substance (substances are never "living" unless they relate), but because he is the Father, whose being is by definition relational.

It is this kind of ontology that is involved in Christian eschatology. Against such an ontological background, "the resurrection of the dead and the life everlasting," which the Christians "eagerly expect" (προσδοκῶ), acquire their proper meaning.

2. Ontology and Eschatology

The Bible's adoption of the concept of being to designate God brought Christian theology close to Greek philosophical thought in

---

this concept of being. Non-being in the sense of absolute *nihil* applies only to the origin of creation. By being related to God ever since, through his Logos, creation no longer experiences nonbeing as annihilation but only as a destruction of the *mode* of beings (death), not of their substance. (Cf. below, chapter two, "Eschatology and Creation").

[33] K. Rahner, *The Trinity*, p. 17.

many ways except in respect to the following condition: *for the Bible, the meaning of God's self-designation as being (ὁ ὤν) will be revealed only in the last days.* This is clearly stated in the book of Isaiah: "Therefore my people shall know my name; Therefore *in the last day* they shall know that it is I who speak; Here *am I*" (Is 52:6f).[34] Eschatology is the ground of theological ontology for biblical thought.

The use of the future tense of the verb "to be" is found in Greek literary sources as early as Homer, the Presocratics, Plato, the Hermetic writings, and other ancient Greek sources.[35] In all these cases, being is spoken of as past, present, and future: being "always was, is, and will be" (ἦν ἀεὶ καὶ ἔστιν καὶ ἔσται—Presocratics).[36] The intention behind this is to indicate the *eternity* of being, its unchangeableness and immutability. Time must be excluded from being: "The past and the future are parts of time ... which we wrongly apply to the eternal essence (ἀΐδιον οὐσίαν) ... to which in the true sense only the [tense] *is* is property applicable."[37]

The Bible, on the other hand, seems to have no difficulty in allowing being to be part of the course of time. The ὁ ὤν is for the Bible not only the one who "was" and "is" but also "He That Cometh (ὁ ἐρχόμενος)." We find this clearly expressed in the book of Revelation (1:4, 2:8, 4:8) which uses the three-tense formula in a way that calls for our attention: in what sense is "He That Cometh" part of God's self-designation as being (ὁ ὤν)? And how does the reference to God (and Christ) as the "One That Is" and at the same time the "Coming One" affect the notion of being itself, of ontology?

The designation of God as *being* and at the same time *coming* marks a radical departure from classical Greek ontology as expressed by Plato in the above-mentioned passage from the *Timaeus.* The identification of God, the *"One That Is,"* with the *"One That Comes"* implies a notion of being, which enters time and *becomes* history. The Incarnation is based on an ontology which allows being to become, since one of the Holy Trinity *became* human at a point in history, as

---

[34] Cf. E. Lohmeyer, *Our Father: An Introduction to the Lord's Prayer,* trans. J. Bowden, (London: Collins, 1965), p. 44.
[35] See F. Büschel, "εἰμί, ὁ ὤν," p. 399.
[36] F. Büschel, "εἰμί, ὁ ὤν," p. 399.
[37] Plato, *Tim.* 37df.

we confess in the Creed—a theological ontology which provoked the need for delicate distinctions and nuances in the patristic period. As far as the biblical thought is concerned, the crucial question to be considered is: *does the "One Who Is" as "He That Cometh" come from the past or from the future to the present?* When the author of Revelation calls God (or Christ) the "One That Comes," does he refer to the Incarnation or the Second Coming, that is, the Messiah who is expected to come?

A look at the Gospels shows that "He That Cometh" (ὁ ἐρχόμενος) is a *terminus technicus* denoting the Messiah or Son of Man who was expected to come in the last days: "are you he who is to come (ὁ ἐρχόμενος) or should we expect someone else?" (Mt 11:3; Lk 7:19, 20). Although the "Son of Man" idea in its nonbiblical origination must have been designating a preexisting figure, a primordial "Man," in the Judaism of Jesus' time, as Sigmund Mowinckel after a long discussion of the matter concludes, "the apocalyptics have, in fact, nothing to tell about the life and work of the Son of Man in his preexistence. All the emphasis is laid on his eschatological role.... Judaism, then, was unaware that the Son of Man was really the Primordial Man."[38] It is the future, eschatological coming of God that the expression "He That Cometh" indicates. Ο ἐρχόμενος does not come from the past but from the future.

Now, if the author of Revelation understood ὁ ἐρχόμενος in this way (and there is no reason to suppose that he did not; on the contrary, there are clear indications that he did),[39] his identification of ὁ ἐρχόμενος with the ὁ ἦν καὶ ὁ ὢν gives rise to questions of an *ontological* nature: can being (ὁ ὢν) be spoken of in terms of *time* and particularly of the *future*? Plato, as we have seen, would be horrified by an association of the notion of being (the ἀΐδιος οὐσία) with time, and so would ancient Greek thought in general. Biblical thought, on the other hand, in the words of Cullmann, "knows nothing of a timeless God,"[40] which makes Greek ontology totally incompatible

---

[38] S. Mowinckel, *He That Cometh: The Messiah Concept in the Old Testament and Later Judaism*, trans. G.W. Anderson (Oxford: B. Blackwell, 1956) (2005), p. 436.

[39] See Rev 1:5–7, 17; 2:8; 3:11.

[40] O. Cullmann, *Christ and Time*, trans. F.V. Filson (Philadelphia: The Westminster Press, 1950), p. 63.

with biblical thought. Cullmann himself in dialogue with Barth and others[41] tries to avoid the dilemma of "time or eternity" by suggesting the idea of an "endless duration of time" in the place of eternity. But the way he understands this duration is that of a *linear* history in which *the past events lead into the future ones*, exactly as Aristotle conceived time.[42] "All resurrection hope," Cullmann writes, "is founded upon faith in a *fact of the past* [my emphasis]; it is the fact of the mid-point of the redemptive line to which the apostles bear witness: that Christ is risen. *This hope is founded also upon a fact of the present which follows from that former fact* [my emphasis]: that in those who believe in the Risen One the resurrection power of the Spirit is already at work ... It is in that end time ... that the redemptive history finds its specifically future completion."[43]

The understanding of the *Heilsgeschichte* in terms of linear time, in which future events follow from former facts, makes eschatology ontologically dependent on history and eventually on protology. It is interesting that in establishing the link between the historical facts of the *Heilsgeschichte* and their "future completion" Cullmann introduces the presence and power of the Holy Spirit.[44] But he seems to overlook the truth that the Spirit does not simply assist in the process *toward* the eschatological completion of history; the Spirit also *brings the eschaton into history* (Acts 2:18). In the *Heilsgeschichte*, time paradoxically does not only move forward; it is made by the Spirit to move also *backward*. The last days are not only expected but also *experienced* in history *albeit while still being expected*. In history, eschatology is not only *promise* and *hope*; it is also, to some extent, *fulfillment*. The *Heilsgeschichte*, in order to be what it means (i.e., *Salvation History*), must involve a *redemption of historical time*, and this can

---

[41] Particularly with Barth's view that eschatology is a "state subsequent to time" (*Kirchliche Dogmatik*, II 1, [Zollikon: Verlag, 1940]), p. 709f.

[42] Cullmann, *Christ and Time*, p. 51f, in describing the Greek idea of time as "cyclical" seems to overlook Aristotle's definition of time as "the movement from the earlier to the later" (see note 40 above) which suggest a linear conception. J. McIntyre, *The Christian Doctrine of History* (Edinburgh: Oliver and Boyd, 1957), p. 42f., shows that Cullmann's interpretation of history as a linear "Heilsgeschichte" appears in the end as identical with the Greek idea of history.

[43] Cullmann, *Christ and Time*, p. 241f. Emphasis is mine.

[44] Ibid., p. 242.

only happen if the promise is somehow fulfilled *within the time's course*—otherwise history will either remain unredeemed or be made to possess in itself the central redemptive events, thus making eschatology secondary.[45] History itself stands in need of redemption, and this cannot happen unless "He That Cometh" (ὁ ἐρχόμενος) *visits* it and *dwells* in it bringing the future into the past and present of historical time.

The ontological consequences of such a movement of time from the future to the past come clearly to light when we try to interpret the biblical designation of God as ὁ ὤν, the "One Who Is." The identification of ὁ ὤν with ὁ ἐρχόμενος means that the Exodus self-designation of God is interpretable only by the "One Who Cometh": the meaning of ὁ ὤν is disclosed only in and by its identification with the ὁ ἐρχόμενος, in and by an eschatological event. This, as we have seen, is exactly what Isaiah 52:6 and beyond confirms when it says that the meaning of God's name the "One Who Is" will be revealed only in the last days.

The search for the truth of being *in the end of history* represents a radical departure not only from ancient Greek ontology, which would not tolerate an association of truth with history, but even from the established Christian conceptions of *Heilsgeschichte*, such as the one we find in Cullmann. Eschatological ontology seems to have vanished from our common-sense logic altogether and become a strange and paradoxical idea. This is why the survival of this biblically-rooted concept in the interpretation of the Gospel to the Hellenic culture by patristic thought proved to be one of the most difficult hermeneutical tasks of Christian theology. The Origenist tradition succumbed to the Platonic cyclical view of time, and a considerable part of patristic thought displayed a tendency to associate God's being with timeless eternity rather than speaking of it in eschatological terms. Nevertheless, the eschatological outlook was not entirely absent from patristic ontology. We can see it, for example, in the case

---

[45] It may be argued that the historical reasons for the weakening of eschatology in modern theology are to be found precisely in the prevalence of a linear view of the "Heilsgeschichte" in which it is in the historical facts (the Incarnation, Cross, etc.) themselves and not in their eschatological interpretation and conversion that the core of salvation lies.

of St Maximus the Confessor, to whom we shall be often referring in the present study. Following the path already paved by St Irenaeus in the second century, Maximus associates the revelation of God with the Incarnation of Christ (i.e., with the course of time and history) while recovering and supporting philosophically the biblical theology of history which locates the revelation of truth in the eschatological future: "the things of the Old Testament are shadow; those of the New Testament are image (εἰκών); truth is the state of the future (ἀλήθεια ἡ τῶν μελλόντων κατάστασις)."[46] We shall have to reflect again and again more deeply on this pregnant proposition, for it appears to provide a hermeneutical example of casting biblical eschatology in ontological terms without succumbing to Hellenic philosophy.

The association of the notion of being with history and time was not the only specific characteristic of the biblical conception of eschatological ontology. The application of the idea of being to God as he will reveal himself in the last days was accompanied in the Bible by a specific view of the *nature* and *kind* of being, and of its existential content. The way Christ himself interprets God's name in the Gospels is particularly instructive in this respect.

In the time of Jesus, the *Tetragrammaton* by which God's name was indicated had become a holy name which was spoken only in the Temple by the priests, while in everyday language the name used by the people to refer to God was "Adonai," or "Lord."[47] In a long discussion of the subject Ernst Lohmeyer shows that Christ replaced this designation for God with the name "Father" as an indication of his personal relationship—a very intimate one, indeed, as the aramaic *abba* indicates[48]—with God ("*my* Father"). This privilege was extended by Jesus also to his disciples and the community of believers as a special way of addressing God (as in the "*Our* Father"—the Lord's prayer).[49] The Isaiah prophesy that in the last days God will be revealed as ὁ ὤν of Exodus is now fulfilled in the person of Christ who, as the Son of God, reveals God's name as Father ("He who has

---

[46] Maximus, *Scholia. eccl. hier,* 3.2 (PG 4:137D).
[47] E. Lohmeyer, *Our Father,* p. 44.
[48] J. Jeremias, *New Testament Theology* (London: SCM Press, 1971), p. 62ff.
[49] E. Lohmeyer, *Our Father,* p. 47.

seen me has seen the Father." Jn 14:9). The last days are, thus, brought into history in the person of Christ who, precisely for that reason, can use for himself the "I am" (ἐγὼ εἰμὶ) name, as we have seen earlier. The Exodus designation of God, the meaning of which will be revealed in the last days, is now applied to Christ, precisely because he brings the eschatological time into history by being "one" with the Father (Jn 10:30)—a claim bequeathed to the patristic age for interpretation in the framework of Hellenic culture with all the well-known difficulties and controversies it produced.

The implications of this for ontology are significant. If the Exodus name of God, the ὁ ὤν, the meaning of which will be revealed only in the last days, is for the New Testament Christians to be interpreted as the "Father" of Jesus Christ, this means that God's designation as being must be understood as involving some form of *personal communion*. By identifying God (ὁ Θεὸς) with the Father, the Greek fathers not only, as Rahner has observed,[50] acted faithfully to the Bible, but at the same time they professed an ontology which, in its ultimate sense of God's self-revelation, involves personal *communion*. It was this relational ontology that provided the ground for the development of Trinitarian theology at a later stage.

The relational character of eschatological ontology, which has been overshadowed by the individualistic approach to religion in modern times, was fundamental in biblical and, even, in patristic thought. Not only does God's name (Father), as the Gospels interpret it, point to the relationality of being, but there is hardly any essential aspect of biblical eschatology which does not imply a relational ontology. The following points may serve as indicative examples.

a) The main figures related to eschatology in the Bible, which were applied to Christ in the Gospels, were understood as *collective* beings. This was a general characteristic of Jewish thought. As Cullman observes, "representation easily becomes identity in Judaism. According to the Jewish concept of representation, the representing can be identified with the group he represents."[51] This was the case

[50] K. Rahner, "Theos in the New Testament," *Theological Investigations*, vol. 1 (London: Darton, Longman and Todd; New York: The Seabury Press, 1974), pp. 125-130.
[51] O. Cullmann, *The Christology of New Testament*, trans. S.C. Guthrie and C.A.M. Hall (London: SCM Press, 1959), p. 140.

– 77 –

particularly with the figure of the *Son of Man* which in later Judaism was eschatological and, for this reason, came to be finally identical with the Messiah.[52] It was also true of the figure of the *Servant of God* (ebed-Jahwe) of the book of Isaiah, which Jesus applied to himself along with that of the Son of Man. In all these eschatological figures which became also Christological in the New Testament, a *community* was always presupposed as part of their identity, the one and the many forming an unbreakable unity. The eschatological figure of the Son of Man is accompanied by the "saints of the Most High" in the book of Daniel (7:13–27) and, quite significantly, reappears in the Gospels (Mt 25:31–46) as identifying himself with "these little brethren of mine" to the point of declaring that "truly, I say to you, as you did it to one of the least of my brethren, you did it to me" (Mt 25:40). The eschatological judgement is exercised by the Son of Man as a *corporate* being,[53] and it is not without reason that this figure has been regarded as the source of the idea of the Church.[54] In the words of Sigmund Mowinckel, "it is the eschatological *communio sanctorum*, the new, distinctive, eschatological people of God" that always exist with the Son of Man (even from the beginning).[55]

This is also true about the name or figure of the "Servant of God," which Christ adopted to indicate his mission, combining it, for the first time, with that of the Son of Man. Like the Son of Man, the Servant of God was understood in Judaism as a collective and at the same time individual figure, an idea which appears paradoxical to our Western mind but was typical of the Semitic thinking. "The *ebed Yahweth* figure ... is at the same time the whole people, the 'remnant,' and the One."[56] Although the specific characteristic of the

---

[52] Mowinckel, *He That Cometh,* p. 360.

[53] This is clear, for example, in the description of the last judgement in Mt 25:31–46. The idea behind the identification of the Son of Man with his "least brethren" reveals the collective character of this title in Dan 7:13f.: as the Son of Man, Jesus represents the "remnant of Israel" and through it all mankind. See T.W. Manson, *The Teaching of Jesus* (Cambridge: Cambridge University Press, 1955), pp. 227f and 265.

[54] F. Kattenbusch, "Der Quellort der Kirchenidee," in *Harnack—Festgabe* (Tubingen: J.C.B. Mohr, 1921), p. 143, and Y. Congar, *The Mystery of the Church* (Baltimore, MD: Helicon Press, 1960), p. 85f.

[55] Mowinckel, *He That Cometh,* p. 406.

[56] Cullmann, *The Christology of New Testament,* p. 55.

Servant of God figure is his vicarious suffering for the people of God, whereas that of the Messiah is his triumphant victory over its enemies, the two figures came to be regarded as one in late Judaism,[57] both of them, together with that of the Son of Man, constituting the eschatological figure which Christ assumed for himself in the Gospels.

Whether, therefore, as the vicariously suffering Servant of God or the triumphant and victorious Son of Man of the last days, "He that Cometh" was conceived in the Bible as being one with the community of the people of God, "the saints of the Most High" of the book of Daniel. In terms of Pauline theology, he was considered as the *head of a body* (1 Cor 12:12, 27; Eph 1:22, 4:15; Col 1:18), inconceivable apart from it, carrying with him and bringing into history, in the Spirit, the *communio sanctorum* of the eschatological Kingdom as *part of his own being*. The "ὁ ἦν καὶ ὁ ὢν καὶ ὁ ἐρχόμενος" of Revelation is a relational being, "recapitulating" in himself all beings (τὰ πάντα: Col 1:15–18), showing that the ontological quintessence of eschatology lies in communion.

b) The same relational ontology underlies the eschatological concept of *resurrection*. The association of the faith in the survival after death with the idea of *immortality* (usually of the soul) has radically changed the biblical concept of the resurrection. This has happened not only because of the prevalence of the Platonic idea of the immortality of the soul in Christian theology, or the weakening of the historical consciousness owing to the infiltration of the idea of eternity into Christian theology (to which Cullmann has drawn attention),[58] but also because the eschatological resurrection has been regarded as a matter of the fate of the *individual*. This is totally unbiblical and can lead, in fact, to the undermining of the very concept of the resurrection.

The individualistic conception of eschatology was characteristic of the Hellenistic religious thought, for which it was at death that the soul attained immortality through the escape from the material world of corruption and mortality to which the body belongs. The Hellenistic world, including most Hellenistic Judaism, knew noth-

[57] Ibid.
[58] Cullmann, *Christ and Time,* p. 232.

ing of a general resurrection at the end of history. Biblical thought and early Christianity, on the other hand, associated the hope of human immortality with the broader eschatological transformation of the world and the general resurrection of the dead. Immortality is inconceivable outside the general resurrection and a transformation of creation as a whole (2 Pet 3:10),[59] since corruption and mortality are a problem not only of the human individual but of all creatures in the present world.

Thus, the Christian concept of resurrection is both *corporal* and *corporate*. It is corporal in that it is the resurrection *of the body*, and it is corporate because it is *general* and concerns the entire human race and, by extension, creation as a whole. The being that resurrection restores is a *being of community and communion*, not of the individual. In the Old Testament, the corporate character of the resurrection is primally applied to the people of Israel. The prophesy of Ezekiel (37:1–14) which was regarded in the patristic period as a type of the eschatological bodily resurrection,[60] referred to the restoration of the people of Israel to their own land: "These bones are *the whole house of Israel....* Behold, I will open your graves and raise you from your graves, *O my people*" (11–12). This resurrection constitutes, at the same time, the healing of the division among the tribes of Israel and its future unity (15–22). The resurrection is not one of individuals but of a people, a community.

The New Testament continues and intensifies the understanding of the resurrection as both corporal and corporate. The scope is enlarged to include humanity as a whole with a redeeming effect on the whole creation. The axis and center is the Resurrection of Jesus Christ who is not understood as an individual but as the "head" and the "first fruits" (ἀπαρχὴ) of "those who belong to him" (οἱ τοῦ Χριστοῦ: 1 Cor 15:23). Pannenberg argues that the faith in the general resurrection preceded the faith of the Resurrection of Christ in

---

[59] Cf. Bauckham, *Jude, 2 Peter,* p. 182: the hope of human immortality really belongs in the broader context of the hope for a future cosmic eschatology.

[60] E.g. Methodius of Olympus, *De resur.* 14 and 18 (PG 18:235C and 324A). Also Origen, *Sel. in Psal.* 1.5 (PG 12:1091f), and John Chrysostom, *Expos. in Psal. CXV* (PG 55:321).

the minds of his contemporaries.[61] In any case, the two resurrections formed an unbreakable unity: just as the Son of Man or the Servant of God could not be conceived without the community surrounding him, in the same way the risen Christ is the "head of the body ... the first-born of the dead" (Col 1:17), the head of the eschatological community, the Church (Col 1:17, 24). This corporate character of Christ's risen body, which is so dominant in 1 Corinthians, is extended in Colossians from the realm of anthropology to that of ecclesiology and from that to cosmology, making the risen Christ's body inclusive of "all creation" (Col 1:15) by the abolition of death (1 Cor 15:25) so that in the end "God may be all in all" (1 Cor 15:28).

In the patristic period, both the corporal and the corporate character of the resurrection were challenged by the prevailing philosophical thought, but they finally survived in Orthodox theology. The idea of the resurrection *of the body* was defended by the Apologists of the second century with the argument that unless the body is raised there will no longer be a human being, because "God gave independent being and life neither to the nature of the soul itself, nor to the nature of the body separately, but rather to humanity composed of soul and body ... and if there is no resurrection (of the body) human nature is no longer human."[62] The same argument is used by Irenaeus,[63] but with the Platonic philosophical thought lingering over the spiritual atmosphere of their time, the Greek fathers could not help but proceed with explanations of the Christian faith in the resurrection that would somehow make sense to their intellectual environment. Thus, the Platonic idea of the immortality of the soul gradually established itself in patristic theology alongside that of the resurrection of the body, and the need appeared to explain the latter in a way that would make corporeality somehow compatible with the spiritual nature of the human being. Origen did this by distinguishing between the material elements composing the body and the

---

[61] W. Pannenberg, *Jesus—God and Man* (Philadelphia: Westminster, 1977), p. 79.

[62] Athenagoras, *De res. mort.* 13.1; 15.2, 6 (PG 6:1000B; 1004–5).

[63] Irenaeus, *Haer.* V, 6.1 (PG 7/2:1138A): "neque enim et anima ipsa secundum se horno, sed anima hominis et pars hominis" ("neither is the soul itself, considered apart by itself, the human being; it is only the soul of a human being and part of the human being"). Cf. G. Florovsky, "The Lamb of God," in *The Patristic Witness of G. Florovsky,* p. 89.

bodily *form* (εἶδος) which never loses its individuality and which survives in the resurrection.[64] This did not satisfy other patristic writers who thought that it did not do justice to the materiality of the human body and the full identification of the risen body with the one before death. The strong criticism of Origen's view and the defense of the full materiality of the risen body came first from Methodius of Olympus († c. 311) who insisted that the risen body was as material as the one before death with the only difference that it was filled with the Holy Spirit, Paul's description of it as σῶμα πνευματικὸν having nothing to do with immateriality.[65] Origen's argument of the distinction between the material body and its "form" (εἶδος) was taken up by Gregory of Nyssa in the fourth century and modified in order to allow for the material substance of the body to be united with its "form" through the *soul* as its "personal" center which draws the material elements decomposed by death to unity into one subject in the resurrection.[66] This theory preserved bodily materiality, albeit not exactly as it was before death but as it was created by God before the fall. Origen's views on the resurrected body were either openly rejected, as by Methodius and later on Jerome,[67] or modified, as by Gregory of Nyssa, Cyril of Jerusalem[68] and others, always with the intention of safeguarding the faith that the eschatological resurrection body is in some way identical to the natural and material body itself and not merely to its "form."

The insistence of patristic theology on the materiality of the risen body was intrinsically connected with the *universal* character of the future resurrection and, by implication, with its *corporateness*. Whereas the idea of immortality, which was borrowed from Hellenistic sources, could be applied to the *individual* (particularly in the form of the immortality of the soul), the resurrection was conceived only as a social and corporate event. None will be risen alone. Although there have been in the patristic period adherents to the belief that in

---

[64] Origen, *Sel. in psal.* 1.5 (PG 12:1092f).
[65] Methodius of Olympus, *De resur.* 3.13 (PG 18:317–28).
[66] Gregory Nys., *De anim. et resurr.* (PG 46:73–80; 145f).
[67] Jerome, *In Eph.* 5.29; *Adv. Iovin.* 1.36.
[68] Cyril Jerus., *Catech.* 18.187.

the eschata only the righteous will be risen, the prevailing view was that the resurrection will be universal, including both the wicked and the virtuous (cf. Jn 5:29).[69]

"Christian theology, which did so much to transform men's attitude to the after-life, speaks less of immortality than of resurrection."[70] The late Donald Mackinnon's observation is full of ontological implications. If the eschatological resurrection, rather than immortality, is regarded as the ultimate destiny of humanity (and through it of creation as a whole), the Christian gospel is not concerned so much with the salvation of the individual, as it has become customary for us to think, but with the restoration of the entire created order to its harmony and unity which corruption and death destroy. Pannenberg in a lengthy discussion of the question whether the resurrection can have any meaning for us today locates the significance of this idea in its importance for the individual seeking his destiny as different from that of the particular community and society in which he lives. But, interestingly enough, only a few pages later he has to correct (in fact, deny) this position by admitting that "the unity of human destiny for all individuals plays a role in regard to the universality of the resurrection. In spite of what has been said previously about the independence of the individual against his being absorbed into society, on the other hand, the unity of the humanity in terms of its destiny is still to be maintained."[71]

Indeed, if the resurrection can have any existential significance that would be relevant for us today, this would have to be attributed not so much to the undeniable existential dissatisfaction of the human being with its mortality and its constant struggle to overcome death[72]—this could be satisfied with the idea of the immortality of the soul—as to our belonging to a world which is dominated by cor-

---

[69] Origen, *Sel. in psal.* 1.5 (PG 12:1092A); John Chrys., *Hom.* 45.2 (PG 59:253).

[70] D.M. MacKinnon, "Death," in *New Essays in Philosophical Theology*, eds A. Flew and A. MacIntyre (New York: The Macmillan Co., 1955), p. 265.

[71] Pannenberg, *Jesus—God and Man*, p. 83–88. His remark "in Israel the idea of a future resurrection of the dead was not thought of as long as the individual was entirely absorbed in his people" does not appear to agree with the evidence (see our discussion of Ezekiel above).

[72] See the quotation from Ernst Bloch in Pannenberg, *Jesus—God and Man*, p. 84.

ruption and disintegration. The eschatological resurrection can have an existential meaning only if it is universal, that is, if it restores the relations that hold together the individual elements (or beings) that constitute creation (and humanity), which corruption and death disintegrate. Death is a universal problem affecting all creatures and their mode of being and can only be overcome by a general resurrection. The resurrection is the restoration of the particular beings as they are constituted by and emerge from their relations. This is the ontological significance of the resurrection.

The resurrection, placed in the light of this kind of ontology, is the quintessence of eschatology. The understanding of the resurrection as the *glorification of individuals*, which we encounter in Hellenistic Judaism[73] and find again in the patristic period[74] and in current conceptions of *theosis* in the theology of our time,[75] has overshadowed the corporate character it had in the Bible and in Pauline theology in particular, as well as in early patristic thought.[76] Viewed as the event of the recapitulation of all in Christ and as the *communio sanctorum*, the eschatological resurrection is above all an *incorporation* into the body of Christ and only secondarily the transformation, glorification, and beatitude of the individual. It is thus foretasted and experienced in history primarily *in the Eucharist* which,

---

[73] See Hengel, *Judaism and Hellenism*, I, p. 196f.

[74] See N. Russell, *The Doctrine of Deification in the Greek Patristic Tradition* (Oxford: Oxford University Press, 2004), pp. 131–2, 322, etc.

[75] Thus, glorification seems to be the quintessence of the eschatological Parousia in S. Bulgakov, *The Bride of the Lamb*, trans. B. Jakim (Grand Rapids, MI: Eerdmans, 2002), pp. 388, 394ff, 431, etc. The development of the theology of the Transfiguration in modern Orthodox thought, under the influence of the revival of the hesychastic tradition, must have played a crucial role in this respect. For example, Bulgakov, *The Bride of the Lamb*, pp. 399, 406, etc., and V. Lossky, *The Mystical Theology*, p. 220.

[76] This is particularly stressed by St Irenaeus. See, for example, *Haer.* I, 10.1 (PG 7: 549C) where the *anakephalaiosis* of all (τὰ πάντα) in Christ is presented as the essence of the eschatological resurrection. The Latin fathers of the fourth century display a tendency to stress more the aspect of the restoration of communion as the eschatological gift of the resurrection. Thus, Ambrose, while mentioning eternal light and glory as part of the eschatological state "his chief thought ... is of the blessed fellowship which the saints have with one another and with God.... The prospect of meeting and conversing with the saints in heaven played a great part in Western ideas about the future life at this epoch." In J.N.D. Kelly, *Early Christian Doctrines*, p. 488, references are made to other Latin fathers of that period.

as we have noted earlier, is celebrated "in gladness of heart" (Acts 2:46), constituting the eschatological event *par excellence* and the summit of ecclesial existence, incorporating us into the body of the risen Christ, as it will happen in the eschata.

All this leads to the conclusion that the being granted by God to his creation through the Resurrection of Christ and our resurrection in the Parousia is a being constituted in communion, exactly as God constitutes his own being as Trinity. *This* is the essence of *theosis*, to exist as God himself exists, by participating in *the way he exists*, by sharing by grace the way he is by nature. Theosis—and eschatology—is *incorporation into a body* (that of the risen Christ, the One of the Trinity), and thus an ontological matter which can only be expressed by an ontology of communion.

It is no wonder, therefore, that of all our human experiences, the one that will survive eschatologically is *love* (1 Cor 13:8). Love is not a moral but an ontological notion; it concerns the way we exist, our "mode of being" in our relation to the other. It makes us acquire our very being from our relationship with the other; it makes us exist as God, who *is* love (1 Jn 4:7), exists.

In employing the idea of being, biblical and patristic theology applied it above all to God. He is ὁ ὤν, the being *par excellence*, the giver of all being. Eschatology is not about our coming into being, as it happened in creation. In the act of creation, God *spoke* and being occurred. In his eschatological act, after having assumed our created being in the person of his Son, God reveals to us the true meaning of being, which is *his way of being* as Trinitarian communion and *love*, and invites us to partake of it through incorporation into Christ, with all that this implies for our existence. Thanks to this eschatological act, ontology acquires its full and true content and significance; it becomes a matter of "true being (ὄντως εἶναι)" and "ever-being (ἀεὶ εἶναι)."

In the lines that follow we shall attempt to unveil and discuss the main features of this ontology by considering its basic claims and its existential implications and contrasting them to conceptions of being in which eschatology plays no role.

The Birth of Eschatological Ontology

Eschatological ontology was the outcome of patristic hermeneutics, the attempt to express the biblical faith in a cultural milieu in which the notion of being served as the key to unlocking and interpreting the mystery of existence ever since the inception of philosophy with the Presocratics. Having accepted the Bible that knew nothing of being (the Hebrew language not even having a word for it),[77] the Greek fathers undertook the task of expressing in terms of being the biblical concern with *history*, which, although fundamental for the Hebrews, had no relation to being for the Greeks. This was a formidable task which only creative minds could bring to fulfilment.

The integration of the Greek concern for being into the eschatological outlook of the Bible required revisions of classical Greek ontology, which were in many respects revolutionary, radically different from ancient Greek thought and leading to a new ontology. What this essentially entailed was a *conversion* of the Greek mind from seeking being in the *past*, in the *beginning* of things, into looking for it in the *future*, in the *end*, in the *eschata*. This transition from protology to eschatology began with the questioning of cosmology in order to lead, through Christology, to an incorporation of history into ontology, and it had immense consequences for both theological and philosophical thought.

1. From "de principiis" to "ex nihilo": The Will as "Cause" of Being

a) Ancient Greek and Roman thought was markedly protological. The question pre-occupying the physicists and the philosophers of antiquity was, as Cicero expressed it, "quae sint initia rerum, ex quibus nascuntur omnia" (which are the beginnings of things, from which everything was born).[78] Theophrastus, who is regarded as the original source of ancient doxographical literature, presents Anaxagoras as the first one to modify the "opinions about the beginnings

---

[77] H. Arendt, *The Life of the Mind*, vol. II, *Willing* (New York: Harcourt Brace Jovanovich, 1978), p. 29.

[78] Cicero, *De divin.* II 4.11.

(τὰς περὶ τῶν ἀρχῶν δόξας),"[79] while Aetius in the second century, whose work contains invaluable information about the theories of the physiologists from Thales to Posidonius, devotes a chapter to the "Principles, what they are (Περὶ ἀρχῶν τί εἰσιν)."[80] This leads to a series of treatises entitled Περὶ ἀρχῶν, from Pseudo-Archytas down to Origen, Porphyry, Damascius, and others. Their basic premise is that everything that exists owes its being to a "beginning," i.e., to the *past*. The "principles" (ἀρχαὶ) are not simply the beginning of things; they are at the same time their *causes* (αἴτια).[81]

Plato appears to refuse to deal with "the principle or principles of all things" (τὴν περὶ πάντων εἴτε ἀρχὴν εἴτε ἀρχάς),[82] distancing himself from the physiologists, whom he fiercely opposed for not accepting a creator of the universe, providing for them in his *Laws*[83] severe penalties for their atheism. His insistence on the idea of god (θεός), the creator (δημιουργὸς) and "father" (πατὴρ) of the universe, which made the early Christians look sympathetically at his philosophy (the *Timaeus* was the most widely read and commented upon philosophical text in the first centuries of the Christian era), would appear at first sight to be congenial to biblical cosmology and, thus, welcomed by Christian thinkers. A closer look, however, into Plato's cosmology makes it clear that his creator god is subject to "principles" lying above him, binding and dictating his creative action and its results.

The Platonic creator was in fact nothing but an *artisan*, whose work consisted in making the universe a *kosmos*—an orderly and harmonious entity, as Heraclitus had conceived it.[84] Under Socratic influence, this *kosmos* would not be simply harmonious but also *beautiful* (καλὸς) and at the same time *good* (ἀγαθός); it would not be the result of a struggle between natural elements and forces, as the various theories of the physicists suggested, for there cannot be any "en-

---

[79] Theophrastus, *Physic. opinion.* frgm. 4 (H. Diels, *Doxogr.*, p. 478.18–20).
[80] H. Diels, *Doxogr.*, p. 276.3.
[81] Cf. Aristotle, *Metaph.* Δ 1,1013 a 17: πάντα γὰρ τὰ αἴτια ἀρχαί.
[82] Plato, *Tim.* 48c.
[83] Plato, *Laws* X, 908–909a.
[84] Cf. G.S. Kirk, *Heraclitus, the Cosmic Fragments* (Cambridge: Cambridge University Press, 1954).

vy" (φθόνος) in the good god, who "wanted (ἐβουλήθη) all of his creation to be like himself (παραπλήσια ἑαυτῷ)," that is, "good."[85]

The creator-god was, therefore, for Plato the "cause" (αἰτία)[86] of the world's order, beauty, and goodness but not of its *being* in an ultimate sense. This is because the creator-god had to operate on pre-existing ontological principles which accounted for the *being* of the universe. These conditions or principles, as described in the *Timaeus*, were *matter* (ὕλη), *ideas* (ἰδέαι), and *space* (χώρα, πανδοχές)—conditions applied to every artist and his work. The *being*, therefore, of the world has its ultimate beginning (ἀρχὴ) not in Plato's god but in pre-existing matter, space, and ideas, all of which restricted the creator's freedom, forcing him to struggle in order to produce the best possible result—a world which, in spite of any deficiencies, is the *best world we could ever expect or imagine*.

Such a view of the creator of the world was bound to create serious problems when Platonic philosophy encountered Christian thought, as we shall see below in some detail. For the moment, in considering the three mentioned ontological principles of Platonic cosmology, we must pay special attention to the predominant place occupied by one of these principles which played a decisive role in the encounter of Platonism with Christianity, namely the ideas: it was by fixing his eyes on the eternal and unchangeable ideas that the creator brought about the world, just as a carpenter in creating a bed or a table fixes his eyes on the idea of the objects he produces.[87] The ideas, therefore, precede the creator as an ἀρχὴ or αἴτιον of the world's being.[88] Beings are grounded on the eternal and true being, the ἀΐδιος οὐσία, which contains the ideas, and this makes the world eternal, beginning being in fact restricted to the orderly arrangement of its constituents and not related to its ultimate ontological emergence. An absolute and radical beginning of the universe would be an absurdity to the ancient Greeks.[89]

---

[85] Plato, *Tim.* 29c–30a.

[86] Plato, *Tim.* 29a: "the best of the causes" (ὁ ἄριστος τῶν αἰτίων).

[87] Plato, *Republic* X, 596b.

[88] There is discussion as to whether the ideas can be "causes," since they are not active. See R. Sorabji, *Time, Creation and the Continuum* (London: Duckworth, 1983), p. 308f.

[89] Sorabji, *Time, Creation and the Continuum*, p. 193.

We shall have to come back to the role of the ideas as "principles" (ἀρχαὶ) of the universe as we deal with the encounter of Platonism with patristic thought. In speaking of ontological principles in ancient Greek thought and their organic connection with protological ontology, we must also pay special attention to Aristotle, who not only deals extensively with the "causes" (αἴτια) of beings, but appears at first sight to do so in a way that might suggest some form of eschatological ontology.

Aristotle's doctrine of the "four causes" is well-known,[90] but it is mainly one of them, known as the "final cause" (τελικὸν αἴτιον), that appears to concern us here. We shall have an opportunity to discuss more extensively Aristotle's *teleology* which is often taken to be identical with eschatology. At the present stage, we limit ourselves to one fundamental observation, which is not always taken into consideration—namely that, although it appears at first sight that with this cause Aristotle moves in a direction where the future is decisive in ontology, a careful look shows that even in this case it is still the past that is, for him, the ground of causation. Thus, as Aristotle himself repeatedly explains, the final cause is not in fact but the *fulfilment of the preexisting nature of a thing* as, for example, the final cause of the birth of a man is in fact the fulfilment of man's essence. Thus, he can write that "that which something is and the end for which it is are one and the same thing" (τὸ μὲν γὰρ τί ἐστι καὶ τὸ οὗ ἕνεκα ἕν ἐστι).[91] His protological conception of causation is clearly expressed in *Metaphysics* book A when he writes that, "we insist (φαμὲν) that we know each thing only when we believe that we know its first cause (τὴν πρώτην αἰτίαν)."[92] The crucial question of metaphysics is for Aristotle, too, how we can arrive at the first principles of beings. As it is stated in book E of *Metaphysics*, the first philosophy does not simply study being as being but also "the principles (ἀρχαὶ) and the causes (αἴτια) of beings."[93]

This search for the beginning of things as an explanation and understanding of the world and all that exists or happens never

[90] See especially *Phys.* II. 3, 194b, 23–39.
[91] Aristotle, *Phys.* II. 7, 298a, 25–26. Cf. *Metaph.* A 3, 983a, 28.
[92] Aristotle, *Metaph.* A3, 983a, 25.
[93] Aristotle, *Metaph.* E 1, 1025 b3.

abandoned Greek philosophy in its successive stages through Middle to Neoplatonism and has formed decisively and irrevocably our Western culture to the present day. Not only does science operates by seeking the causes of things (i.e., by searching for what *precedes* a particular reality in order to understand and explain its present state), but also our common-sense logic in all its manifestations automatically and almost unconsciously raises the question of the "reason" accounting for everything that exists or happens. We are almost irrevocably formed by protological ontology.

b) Biblical thought appears to be radically different. Looking backwards is followed in the Bible by the well-known fate of Lot's wife (Gen 19:26), and Abraham, the founder and father of the people of God, is asked to seek its future in a totally unknown land. This future-oriented attitude is manifested vividly by the place of *prophesy* in the Bible. It is in the *last* acts of God that the past events receive their meaning. Even God's name will, as we have already noted, remain secret until its meaning is revealed "in the last day" (Is 52:64), and it is only in the eschata that we shall see God face to face (1 Cor 13:12). History receives its meaning only with its consummation.

This future-oriented attitude would have been limited in the Bible to history and its interpretation, but when the Gospel encountered the Greeks, the question of *cosmology* became inescapable: can this biblical orientation to the future explain how the universe came into being and is sustained in it? The question of *being* had preoccupied the Greek mind at least since Parmenides, and its application to cosmology had already taken the form we have just outlined. Everything in the universe has its "cause" in the past, rooted ultimately in eternal "principles" lying either in the nature of the universe itself or in eternally preexisting and unchangeable ideas, which dictate its direction in the course of time in such a way as to exclude any radically new beginning, any *future* which is not finally determined by the *past*.

The first difficulty, therefore, in any effort to convert Greek intellectual into biblical thought was bound to arise in relation to cosmology. In order to become a Christian, such a person would have to accept that the world was not always there but, instead, had a *radical* beginning. Such a view would be an absurdity in antiquity, and its intellectuals would be prepared to accept the idea of "beginning" only with regard to the arrangement of the various natural elements into an orderly *kosmos*—not of matter itself or of the ideas that give it "form" and make this *kosmos* "good" and "beautiful," an object of contemplation and knowledge.

A radical beginning of the universe was an absurdity to the Greeks because it challenged the assumption built deeply into their minds that everything that exists must have a "reason" which accounts for its existence. A radical beginning without a preexisting "cause" accounting for it would be inconceivable. The universe's being must be attributed to some "cause" if it were to satisfy the Greek mind. This was not necessary in the context of biblical thought, but it was inescapable for the Greek fathers, who were immersed in Greek culture.

The answer of a Christian to the question, "what accounts for the being of the universe?" would be simply, "God." This answer, however, would be given also by the Greeks without implying by it a radical beginning of creation. A radical beginning would require the negation or absence of any preexisting condition as a necessary ontological source and thus an *ontological derivation* of creation from something else, *including God*. If the being of the universe was an ontological derivation from God, its creation would cease to be a radical beginning, and God would be bound ontologically and necessarily with creation.

In searching for a connection of the universe's being with God in a way that would not make the being of the world an ontological derivation from God's being but a radically new being, the Greek fathers attributed creation to the Creator's *will*: the being of the universe did not derive from God's being but from God's will. This we find clearly expressed in patristic authors such as Theophilus of Antioch[94] (who explains *ex nihilo* as meaning that "God created whatever he willed, as he willed it") and especially in St Irenaeus[95] and later on in St Augustine.[96]

---

[94] Theophilus of Antioch, *Ad Autol.* 2.4 (PG 6:1053A).

[95] Irenaeus, *Haer.* II, 1.1; II 30.9; III 8.3.

[96] Augustine, *City* XI, 24; *Enarratio in Psalmum 134,* sermo 10. The view that creation derived its being from the will of God was strongly supported by John Philoponus in his work *De Aeternitata Mundi,* against Proclus. C Book 4-10.

But *can will bring about being*? Any relation of will with the notion of being would have been inconceivable in classical Greek
thought. The notion of will played no role in Greek philosophy.[97] In
Plato's *Timaeus* there is reference to the creator as having created
things "willing" (βουληθείς), but this refers not to the creation of
things as such but to their being "good" (ἀγαθὰ) as the creator himself is "good" (ἀγαθός).[98] In Aristotle, on the other hand, the closest
thing to the notion of will is that of προαίρεσις, which is a purely
moral concept having to do with preferring one action instead of
another.[99] It is with Neoplatonism that the concept of will *somehow*
enters the description of the emergence of the world,[100] but the strongly emanationist character of its ontology precludes any connection
of this concept with the emergence of an absolute beginning of any
being. As Richard Sorabji puts it: "The point [with regard to Ploti-
nus' use of the will] is not so much to deny that the One creates by
willing, as to *deny that what it wills is the existence of a creature.*"[101]
This is exactly, as we have noted, how Plato's reference to the creator's
will in the *Timaeus* ought to also be interpreted.

The attribution of the being of creation to the creator's will, the
emergence of being from will, was a novel, a revolutionary idea in the
history of thought, and it sprang from the Greek fathers' effort to
relate the being of the world to God without making it part of God's
being. This satisfied their Greek minds' search for causation in ontology, while maintaining the biblical faith in God's absolute freedom,
not only in its moral but also and mainly in its ontological sense. At
the same time, it led to a radical revision of Greek ontology and
opened the door to eschatology to become part of ontological thought.
The significance of this novel view of causation for eschatological
ontology will be discussed presently, but before we do that, it is necessary to make certain fundamental clarifications concerning the
content and meaning of the term "will."

---

[97] H. Arendt, *Willing*, p. 18.
[98] Plato, *Tim.* VI, 29e.
[99] Arendt, *Willing*, p. 15f.
[100] Sorabji, *Time, Creation and the Continuum*, p. 317.
[101] Ibid., p. 318. My emphasis.

In her magisterial work on "willing," Hannah Arendt makes the distinction between two different conceptions of will in the history of philosophy. One of them, known as the *liberum arbitrium*, understands will as the freedom of choice between two or more given possibilities. This conception, which has been the prevailing one in history and in our common references to freedom, bears no relationship with either ontology or eschatology, since the possibilities from which the will is called to choose are already *given* to it and, therefore, ontologically established beforehand, i.e., *in the past*. The framework of this kind of conception, on the other hand, is exclusively anthropological, leaving outside the being of creation, and, as it has eventually turned out to be in Western thought, basically *psychological* or having to do with the inner struggles within the human soul in its effort to arrive at the proper decisions and choices from the given possibilities.[102]

The other conception of the will, to which Arendt devotes a lengthy discussion, has an immediate bearing on both ontology and eschatology. Instead of denoting a choice between given and preexisting possibilities, this conception of the will indicates the *"power to begin something entirely new"* which "could not very well be preceded by any potentiality, which would then figure as one of the causes of the accomplished act."[103] This absolute newness is intrinsically connected with the *future*: what the will aims at in beginning something unprecedently new is to give being a future, to make the future ontologically significant.

This "novelty," which the Church fathers brought into philosophy, has never been easily absorbed by Western thought which has

---

[102] The understanding of will as fluctuations between equally desirable things, as a conflict between objects of willing may be traced to St Augustine's analysis of St Paul's letter to the Romans (chapter 7) where Paul's "two laws" are replaced by *two wills,* one carnal and the other spiritual, operating in conflict *within* the human being. The will is thus located within the *human soul.* Although this does not necessarily make Augustine responsible for the idea of *liberum arbitrium,* a line of continuity can be drawn between his analysis of the will and the modern representatives of voluntarism, including Descartes' discussion of the subject in his Fourth Meditation, and ending with modern psychoanalysis. This conception of the will does not concern us here, as it has no bearing on eschatological ontology.

[103] Arendt, *Willing,* p. 29. Emphasis added.

generally preferred to operate with the ancient view of "given" realities, logically and necessarily following one from the other, rather than admitting the "freedom" of the possibility of something absolutely new.[104] And yet, this seed sown by patristic thought bore fruit not only in the Middle Ages with Duns Scotus' defense of *contingency* as a positive and noble mode of being, but also in the modern times when, in addition to Nietzsche's preoccupation with the subject of will as the power to bring about something new, existentialist thinkers such as Jean-Paul Sartre apply this concept of will even to *ethics*,[105] while modern art in its most eminent representatives displays almost a tendency to *destroy* the given forms in order to bring about the *new* which the artist wills to create, a *creatio ex nihilo*.[106]

c) If the being of creation is derived from the will of the Creator, it means that it contains by definition a *future*, a *purpose*. Willing in

---

[104] It is worth quoting from Arendt (*Willing*, p. 32) about the preference deeply rooted in modern man for what is already given rather than the unpredictably new, for necessity rather than freedom, for the intellect rather than the will: "Religious and medieval as well as secular and modern philosophy found many difficult ways of assimilating the Will, the organ of freedom and the future, to the older order of things.... No doubt, even today if we listen to a dispute between two philosophers one of whom argues for determinism and the other for freedom it will always be the determinist who would appear to be right.... The audience will always agree that he is simple, clear and true" (p. 32). Arendt attributes this to the difficulty in accommodating will to the law of causality and to "our outward experience of the world of appearances, where as a matter of fact ... we seldom start a new series" (ibid.). From the viewpoint of theology, I would add, that the preference to ground our thought on the already given, on the past, rather than on the radically new and the future, derives from the fall and its consequences, which consist in our enslavement to *reality* (see chapter three, "Eschatology and the Fall").

[105] Thus J.-P. Sartre, *Essays in Existentialism,* ed. W. Baskin (London: Citadel, 1993), p. 55. I owe this remark to J.P. Manoussakis.

[106] Genuine art is not a copy of reality but the creation of an entirely new "being," "the beginning of a world" ("c'est le commencement d'un monde," in the words of Paul Valéry, *Oeuvres* I [Montpellier: Université Paul Valéry, 1957, p. 1327] with reference to music). The artist aims at *creatio ex nihilo* but stumbles on preexisting matter. This is why modern artists, such as Picasso, Lucian Freud, and others, alter the given forms, trying to create their own "world." The Aristotelian movement from potentiality to actuality is totally invalid in this case, since no one can maintain that, for example, the symphony produced by a composer was possible before it was actual (Arendt, *Willing,* p. 30). This illustrates the abysmal difference between Plato's conception of the Creator as an artisan and the Christian understanding of God as Creator. The *ex nihilo* rules out the "potentiality-actuality" principle both in the Christian doctrine of creation and in genuine art. Cf. H. Bergson, *The Creative Mind,* trans. M.L. Andison (New York: Philosophical Library, 1946), pp. 22 and 27.

the sense of bringing into being something utterly new is forward-looking, it is *willing to*, "the Will's forward thrust," as Nietzsche put it.[107] The will's projects always assume rectilinear time and a future associated with a purpose. Will is forward looking—it is essentially eschatological.

Precisely because the creation of the world was the product of the Creator's *will*, and because will is associated with the *future*, the beginning of creation coincided with the appearance of *time*.[108] *Creatio ex nihilo* and time are related to each other *via the concept of will*. Time, therefore, is in this case neither the Platonic moving image of eternity,[109] nor the Aristotelian movement "from the earlier to the later,"[110] a "coming-into-being [which] necessarily implies the preexistence of something which is potentially but is not actually,"[111] that is, a movement to a future which is in essence but a return to the past. By being the product of the will understood as the power to bring about something entirely new, time is a movement to an "end," a purpose higher than the beginning, an *eschaton* which is not the outcome of any *principium* and which grants ontological significance to the beginning.

All this makes history a *Heilsgeschichte*, an *economy*. By being the product of will, *creatio ex nihilo* initiates a movement toward the future which is not just a "natural" motion inherent in the beginning of time but an "intention," a "decision"—the *will* of someone. History lends time a *personal* "cause" for its movement; it makes it, as Collingwood, Croce, and Florovsky understood it, the field of personal creativity, of the emergence of novel will-products, anticipating (sometimes in agreement and sometimes in conflict) the ultimate will of the Creator, the future he has in his mind and intention in bringing about his creation.

It is precisely because *creatio ex nihilo* and time stem from the will that history is *economy*—a movement in time with a purpose set

---

[107] F. Nietzsche, *The Will to Power*, ed. W. Kaufmann (New York: Vintage Books, 1967), n. 698, p. 370.

[108] Basil, *C. Eunom.* 1.21 (PG 29:560B); Augustine, *Conf.* XI, 9–13 (H. Chadwick, *St. Augustine: Confessions* [Oxford: Oxford University Press, 1991], p. 227f).

[109] Plato, *Tim.* 37d.

[110] Aristotle, *Phys.* IV, 10–11, 218a.

[111] Aristotle, *De gener.* I, 3, 317b.

by Someone's will. The *economy* is, according to patristic thought, initiated by the "good pleasure" (εὐδοκία) of the Father[112] (i.e., rooted in a *personal* will), it is identified with history in the Son's will to "become human," and it is "perfected" acquiring its "end," its ultimate "purpose," by the will of the Holy Spirit—all three personal wills coinciding so as to form *one* ("natural") will. The ontology of the will runs throughout and philosophically sustains the biblical vision of existence as history moving to an ultimate consummation. *Eschatological ontology is, in this way, born, thanks to the hermeneutical ingenuity of patristic thought.*

Eschatological ontology reaches its maturity with the synthetic vision of St Maximus the Confessor in the seventh century. This vision comprises both the cosmological and the historical aspects of ontology with the anthropological consequences emerging as an integral part of the entire vision.

On the level of cosmology, Maximus inherits a history which goes back to Philo, the Middle Platonists, and the Stoics, who proposed revisions of Platonism that could be used to make it compatible with the biblical faith of the creation of the world by God in a way that would not subject the Creator to his creation. Such revisions particularly affected the idea of creation out of preexisting matter—a revision more notable in the Neoplatonists—but mainly the dependence of the Creator on preexisting *ideas* in creating the world. Using a text of Plato's *Republic* (597c) in which the philosopher refers to the ideas as created by God, and (wrongly) applying it also to the *Timaeus* which speaks clearly of the ideas as preexisting the creator, Philo came close to the interpretation, prevailing among the Middle Platonists, according to which the Platonic ideas are thoughts in the mind of God.[113] There is, thus, a firmly established vision of creation in the early centuries of the patristic period which speaks of an intelligible world (νοητὸς κόσμος) made by God to serve as a pattern (παραδείγματα) for making perceptive things.

In addition to Middle Platonism, Philo himself and the subsequent cosmological thought under the influence of Stoicism equated the ideas of the intelligible world with the "seminal reasons" (σπερ-

[112] Basil, *De Spir.* 16.38 (PG 32:136B).
[113] Sorabji, *Time, Creation and the Continuum*, p. 351.

ματικοὶ λόγοι) which were closely connected with the beginning of the universe. The identification of the Platonic ideas by Philo and the Middle Platonists with the thoughts of God and, eventually, with the Stoic *logoi* led to a cosmology in which everything that exists in the universe has its *logos* rooted in God making it intelligible and, at the same time, ontologically stable and secure, rooted in God himself and therefore *true*. Through the *logoi* of creation we can have access to God and at the same time to creation itself, making these *logoi* a key to unlocking the mystery of existence.

The history of this cosmological vision does not concern us here except in so far as it relates to the question of the world's beginning and the absolute freedom and independence of God from his creation—two fundamental demands of the biblical faith. It is precisely on this point that this vision of the world as connected with God via the intelligible *logoi* presented such serious difficulties that the use of the concept of *logoi* had, as Florovsky observed,[114] to be abandoned by the Church fathers until Maximus courageously recovered it, only in order to transform it in a way that could satisfy the demands of the Bible. This was done by a recovery and integration into cosmology of the notion of *will*, which provided at the same time the doctrine of creation with an eschatological dimension.

St Maximus begins by using the vocabulary, already established by Origen and the Alexandrian theologians, of the *logoi* of creation and their unity in the Logos-Wisdom of God: the *logoi* of creation are many in their specific individuality and at the same time one in their relation to the Logos of God in whom everything was created (Col 1:16; Rom 11:36).[115] These *logoi* were contained in God "from all eternity" and constitute the *origin* and *cause* (ἀρχὴ καὶ αἰτία) of everything that exists.[116] But they are neither part of God's being nor an emanation of divine essence in a Neoplatonic sense; they exist *in* God but also *toward* (πρὸς) God;[117] they are oriented toward a future

---

[114] G. Florovsky, *The Byzantine Fathers of the Sixth to Eighth Century, Collected Works*, vol. IX (Belmont, MA: Nordland Publishing Company, 1987), p. 216.

[115] Maximus, *Amb.* 7 (PG 91:1077C).

[116] Maximus, *Amb.* 7 (PG 91:1080C).

[117] Maximus, *Amb.* 7 (PG 91:1080BC). Cf. A. Riou, *Le monde et l'Église selon Maxime le Confesseur* (Paris: Beauchesne, 1973), p. 56f.

which is, in the first place, their coming into being through their creation at an appropriate time (τῷ ἐπιτηδείῳ καιρῷ) and, finally, their "recapitulation" (ἀνακεφαλαίωσις) in the Incarnate Logos and union with God.

There is, thus, built into St Maximus' use of the notion of the *logoi* the same quality we observed in discussing the idea of will above, namely the dynamism of a "purpose" (σκοπός), and it is this that distinguishes his use of the *logoi* from that of Philo, the Middle Platonists, the Stoics, and even Origen. This is why, in contrast to all these, Maximus borrows from Dionysius' vocabulary and calls the *logoi* of creation not *thoughts*, but *wills* (θελήματα) and "predestinations" (προορισμοί) of God, in the sense that they contain and lead to a *destination*, a purpose.

The universe, therefore, in being a product of the will is, according to St Maximus, not static. It is dynamic, but not in the Neoplatonic sense of an emanation from the higher to the lower state of being, which is a movement from "above" to "below." It is a movement *toward* an end, "the will's forward thrust." St Maximus expresses this in the most eloquent way in his famous response to question 60 of Thalassius: The eschatological recapitulation of all in Christ is "the great hidden mystery ... the blessed end for which everything has been constituted ... [and the end] for the sake of which everything exists but which does not owe its existence to anything else (οὗ ἕνεκα μὲν πάντα, αὐτὸ δὲ οὐδενὸς ἕνεκα)."[118]

Understood as "wills" leading to a purpose, the *logoi* of creation are no longer "eternal" in a way that could lead to the Origenist idea of an "eternal" creation[119] and do not contradict in anyway the *creatio ex nihilo* doctrine. God remains free from the world in bringing it into being but simultaneously retains through this will a relationship with it that allows him to enter into its *history*, the dynamic movement of his will toward a purpose. The *logoi* of creation by being God's "wills" are "leading to the end" (εἰς τέλος ἀπάγοντες);[120]

[118] Maximus, *QThal.* 60 (PG 90:621A). This is an allusion to Aristotle's "final cause" and, at the same time, its radical revision. See above, p. 89.
[119] Maximus rejects the Origenist view of an eternal creation explicitly in *QThal.* 60 (PG 90:625). Cf. Riou, *Le monde et l'Église*, p. 61 n. 52.
[120] Maximus, *QThal.* 59 (PG 90:616A).

that is, they are *eschatological* rather than protological. As Maximus would put it himself, it is only by looking at the end that we can know the beginning.[121] Creation is part of the economy and is inconceivable apart from its end. And the *logoi* of creation are not there for us to contemplate the beginning, but to move toward our final destination, our "end."

The conception of the *logoi* as divine wills rather than divine thoughts signifies the removal of theology from the realm of contemplation and knowledge to that of personal communion and *love*. The contemplative tradition, which had its roots in Origen, continued with Evagrius and his followers and was not unknown or entirely foreign to St Maximus. But, as Sherwood has shown,[122] the accent in St Maximus' teaching falls on *prayer and love*. With the association of the notion of the *logoi* with that of the *virtues* and ultimately with *love*, Maximus joins the tradition of St Macarius of Egypt who places the center of the human being in the *heart* rather than in the mind. His distinction between knowledge as ἐπίγνωσις (i.e., a mental function) and participation (μέθεξις) and his attachment of the latter to the eschata[123] move the center of gravity from epistemology to personal communion and love. Following St Paul's teaching that knowledge will be brought to an end in the eschata (1 Cor 13:8) while love will never fail (1 Cor 13:8), Maximus views the *logoi* of creation as leading ultimately to love. His vision coincides with that of St Gregory of Nyssa who declares that in the eschata *"knowledge will become love"* (ἡ γνῶσις ἀγάπη γενήσεται).[124] We are thus led miles away from classical Greek ontology, from the Parmenidian, "Being and thought are one," and from the quest of the origins of the world to the search of being in the end of history where being is transformed into love.

"Does God know beings according to their nature? No, he does not know them according to their nature; he knows them as his own wills, for he made them willing." This question was raised and an-

---

[121] Maximus, *QThal.* 59 (PG 90:613D–616A).

[122] P. Sherwood, *St. Maximus the Confessor. The Ascetic Life. The Four Centuries on Charity* (New York: Paulist Press, 1955), p. 87ff.

[123] Maximus, *QThal.* 60 (PG 90:621D).

[124] Gregory Nys., *De anim. et resur.* (PG 46:46C).

swered already in the beginning of the third century AD, attributed to Pantaenus, the founder of the Catechetical School of Alexandria. It is repeated by St Maximus and commented upon extensively.[125] Will does not only bring about being; it also affects *knowing*. If the concept of will is understood as the choice between given possibilities (the *liberum arbitrium*), this can lead to arbitrariness in knowledge—I know only what I choose to know, and I ignore what I do not like to know—a position displayed by certain literary forms of modern existentialism.[126] But if we understand will not as a choice of given possibilities but as the power to bring about something radically new (which is the only kind of will applicable to God and his relation to creation), the difference between knowledge of things according to their nature and knowledge of them as products of one's will lies in this point: in knowledge according to nature, we know what is given and is already there, while if nature itself is the product of the will (in which case its *logos* is a *thelema* and a *proorismos*, i.e., *eschatological*), we can only know something through its end, the reason *for* or *toward* which is made, the purpose that the willing subject had in mind in bringing it into being. It is only when its purpose is fulfilled that we can know what a being *is*. This is above all the case with the Being *par excellence*, the "One Who Is," whose identity the Bible, as we have seen, remains undisclosed till the "last day." But it applies also to the *logoi*, the "reason" of all beings. This is an ontological apophaticism which is not of the (Neo)platonic "beyond essence," *but of the eschatological "not yet."* Only in so far as the ultimate will of the Creator is revealed to us can we know the world. Knowing in this case is not answering the question of *de principiis*, "*quae sint initia rerum*" (which are the beginnings of things), but inquiring about the *purpose*, the *end* of what exists.

This kind of "epistemology" is based on *history* rather than *nature* (or on *nature as history*); it is a byproduct of biblical thought married with the ontological concern of Hellenism. It is an epistemology

---

[125] Maximus, *Amb.* 7 (PG 91:1085AB).

[126] One could give many examples from modern literature, such as Ionescu, Pirandello, etc. The wide-spread influence of social media in our time is contributing to the understanding of truth as a "personal" choice of the individual, with all the consequences this tendency may have for social life and a *common* conception of truth.

that strives to penetrate into modern physical science[127] having already conquered the historical sciences though the emergence of *hermeneutics.*[128] Orthodox theological epistemology remains on the whole unaffected by hermeneutics, oscillating between the traditionalist tendency to draw its content from a search of the *past* and the apophaticism of a "mystical theology" of a Dionysian type that is looking "above" rather than "forward" (i.e., in history and its ultimate purpose) in order to "know" beings and their meaning. Eschatology remains a foreigner to the prevailing theological epistemology.

2. From Teleology to Eschatology: The End as the Cause of Being

Christian eschatology is often, or rather normally, identified with *teleology.* There is a good reason for that in so far as both eschatology and teleology share the view that being is not static, that it moves toward a purpose, a future, an end (τέλος). We have seen in the previous section how central this is in Christian and patristic thought and how important it is for any attempt to integrate ontology into the demands of the Bible. This, however, does not exhaust the content of Christian eschatology. It is not enough to admit that being has an "end" (τέλος) toward which it moves. It is important to ask whether this "end" is an "outcome" of this movement of being or *its initiator,* its "cause." The following statement of St Maximus contains the problem in all its intensity: "This [the final incorporation of all beings into Christ] is the great hidden mystery ... [the end] *for the sake of which everything exists, but which exists on account of nothing else.*"[129]

If we take this statement as our guide, we come to the conclusion that in Christian eschatology it is not enough to confess that the things that exist move toward a purpose, a τέλος, as every teleology would claim; it must be added that: (a) the end accounts for and explains the being of everything that exists, and (b) the end is not the outcome, the result, of any preexisting cause; it is an *uncaused cause*

---

[127] This started with Einstein's understanding of being as *event* and continued with the development of Quantum Physics. See J. Polkinghorne (ed.), *The Trinity and an Entangled World* (Grand Rapids, MI: Eerdmans, 2010), *passim.*

[128] See the Introduction to the present book.

[129] Maximus, *QThal.* 60 (PG 90:621A). My emphasis.

(αὐτὸ δὲ οὐδενὸς ἕνεκα). This double claim of Christian eschatology makes it different from all teleologies known in philosophical and theological thought. It, in fact, runs counter to our common-sense logic and experience which demand that the future follow upon the past, the Alpha come before the Omega, the beginning of any movement precede its end.

In the lines that follow we shall consider briefly some of the most representative forms of teleology in philosophy as well as in theology, placing them under the judgment of the Maximian view of the "end" stated above. Having done that, we shall try to see how St Maximus' understanding of the "end" affects the content and structure of Christian eschatology in its very foundations.

a) The first philosopher that comes to mind when we speak of teleology is certainly *Aristotle*. He introduced movement into being and made the "end" a possession of being through the idea of *entelechy* (ἐντελέχεια). This was done as part of the movement from *potentiality* to *actuality*, which all beings undergo as they pass from genesis to corruption, in a way that safeguards the perseverance of being in spite of corruption and death. Entelechy (i.e., teleology) is an integral ingredient of ontology, at least with regard to the physical universe, to "nature." This allows nature not only to survive change and corruption but also to fulfil a *purpose*. "Nature does nothing in vain." "Nature as a good master of the house takes care that nothing will be lost which may be useful."[130] Nature always acts with regard to some object and always realizes the best. This guarantees the survival and the protection of the universe.

Related to teleology is also Aristotle's "final cause" to which we referred earlier. Everything in nature as well as in human activity aims at an "end" (e.g., health is the "final cause" of our walking just as the final cause of a seed is to produce a fruit or an offspring). Being is a constant movement from potentiality to actuality, to an "end."

Aristotle's teleology resembles Christian eschatology to a considerable degree, and it must have also influenced St Maximus' vision of the world. Judged, however, by the criteria which St Maximus attached to the notion of the "end," namely that the end should be the

---

[130] Aristotle, *De gen. anim.* III 2663b; *De caelo* 291 b13, a24; *De part. anim.* 686, a22, etc.

uncaused cause of everything that exists, Aristotelian teleology fails to satisfy them and thus be identified with Christian eschatology. For Aristotle, the end is not the cause of the beginning, but its outcome. The Maximian requirement that the end causes everything without being itself caused by anything cannot be applied to Aristotle's teleology. For the Greek philosopher, "a coming into being necessarily implies the preexistence of something which is potentially but is not actually."[131] Motion is the actualization of the potential.[132] The final cause is not always present; there are things which do not have a final cause,[133] and even if there is a final cause at work, its ultimate purpose is to realize what was already there from the beginning in potentiality. This applies not only to nature but also to human activity. The idea of a bed or of a sculpture is already present in the mind or soul of the artist and acts as the cause of the movement; the end simply confirms and realizes the beginning.[134]

b) Aristotle's teleology is basically naturalistic, inspired by and concerning the natural phenomena, and when it refers to human activity it does not involve *will* as a factor in the movement toward the end. The introduction of will into teleological thought happens for the first time in the modern era with the appearance of the idea of *progress*. This idea was entirely unknown in the ancient and medieval world. It seems to have appeared for the first time with Francis Bacon in connection with scientific knowledge (that is, the idea that each generation builds on the knowledge of the previous one)[135] and was extended to the realm of history, finding its apogee and support in the eighteenth century with the enthusiasm provoked by the French Revolution, and becoming ever since a leading force in political ideology up to our own time. Following Pascal's introduction of the idea that "not only each human being can daily advance in knowledge but that all men together progress continually,"[136] Progress became a quality of *humanity* as a whole, a faith in humankind's

[131] Aristotle, *De gen. et cor.* I, 3, 317b.
[132] W.D. Ross, *Aristotle* (London: Methuen, 1959), p. 84.
[133] Ross, *Aristotle,* p. 82.
[134] Ross, *Aristotle,* p. 77.
[135] See E. Zilsel, "The Genesis of the Concept of Scientific Progress," *Journal of the History of Ideas* 6 (1945) 3.
[136] B. Pascal, "Préface pour le Traité du Vide." Quoted by H. Arendt, *Willing,* p. 50.

movement toward a better future, a more or less "natural" characteristic of the human being which does not need any divine providence
in order to reach its fulfilment, its "end."

The history of the concept of progress does not concern us here
except in so far as it relates to the criteria of Christian eschatology
which we set by St Maximus' understanding of the "end" in ontology: *Is the "end" the "cause" of progress or its outcome? Is the future of
progress something that confronts us or something that we make, i.e., a
product of the past?* Moreover, does the "end" of progress have a content: *where does progress end?* Logically speaking, an end that does
not meet us but results from our action has no substance, and therefore, in fact, it does not exist, thus rendering progress itself meaningless. As Heidegger put it, "an infinite progress implicitly denies every
goal and admits ends only as means to outwit itself."[137] The idea of
progress, therefore, as it has been conceived in modern times, consists in a teleology in which the end not only does not cause the beginning but is in fact self-negating "by admitting ends only as means
to an end." The future, in this case, is an endless extension of the past
(or of a present which automatically becomes past) into an indefinite
destination in which the end ceases to possess an ontological content. We encounter here the same kind of teleology that we find in
postmodern philosophers for whom being or reality is a ceaseless
movement from signifier to signifier, bereft of origin and purpose.[138]
Such a teleology differs fundamentally from that of St Maximus for
whom the end is a "rest" (στάσις) and not an infinite *epektasis*.[139] The
idea of progress, as it has been understood in modern times, does not
allow for the ascription of a causative character to the end, not only
because the end is conceived in progress as an outcome and not as
the initiator of the movement toward the future, but also because it
lacks the ontological content or "identity" which would enable it to
attract and thus "cause" the teleological movement.

c) The attachment of a content to the end of teleology's movement, to the final destination of progress, appears to be found in the

---

[137] Quoted by H. Arendt, *Willing*, p. 50.
[138] See my *Communion and Otherness*, pp. 50–52.
[139] See A. Torrance, *Human Perfection in Byzantine Theology* (Oxford: Oxford University Press, 2020), pp. 40–81.

modern teleologies of *utopianism*. This is particularly the case with social utopianism, as we encounter it in Marx's vision of a classless society or more recently in the liberal theologians of the 1970s with their hopes for the overcoming of social evils and the establishment of the reign of God on earth in a way reminiscent of the nineteenth-century millenarianism, although in a less literal way. In all these, the content of the end is already present in human nature and is the outcome of the historical process in the struggles of the working class or of the liberation movements, etc. Even in the process theologians of the twentieth century, in whom the historical process is not a straight forward progressive movement but rather a continuous choice between more creative options in accord with God's initial aim and choices, the final outcome will be "The End of Evil," the incorporation of all in God, thanks to an ongoing harmonization of reality in God's primitive nature.[140] (It is only in Bloch that the future is declared to be prior to the past and the present but, as Moltmann has observed,[141] this stumbles on the problem of death which renders the future nonbeing, annihilating it ontologically.)

d) The same observations apply to scientific or naturalist teleologies such as those of Darwin, Teilhard de Chardin, and others. In Darwin, the progressive spirit of the nineteenth century is essentially focused on the present and attempts to delineate laws according to which the present emerges from the past. There are in Darwin no assertions about the end or about the laws and conditions of the future. And yet, Darwin does not avoid drawing conclusions about the future from his evolutionary theory when he writes, "and as the natural selection works solely by and for the good of each being, all corporal and mental endowments will tend to progress toward perfection."[142]

Darwin in his *Origin of Species* did not yet focus on humanity. It was Nietzsche with his idea of the *Superman* that spoke of human-

[140] See J.B. Cobb Jr., *Christ in a Pluralistic Age* (Philadelphia, PA: Westminster Press, 1975), *passim* and p. 257f.

[141] J. Moltmann, "Hope and Confidence: A Conversation with Ernst Bloch," *Dialog* 7 (1968) 49.

[142] C. Darwin, *The Origin of Species* (London: Encyclopedia Britannica, 1952), in the Conclusion.

ity as something to be overcome, albeit still within the state of finitude as part of this earth. It was mainly Pierre Teilhard de Chardin
that presented a teleology, based on scientific arguments, in which
not only the human race but the entire universe will be incorporated
into Christ through humanity. The entire universe moves forward
toward the future, from the Alpha to the Omega point, finding its
fulfilment in the Parousia of Christ, in the creation of a new heaven
and a new earth. This movement forward is so determined by natural forces that even the law of entropy may be tuned for inanimate
nature but not for life, which progresses toward a greater complexity
and diversity and by its very success counteracts physical entropy.[143]
The end is thus predetermined by the natural process itself; it does
not cause the past but is caused by it.

Teilhard's natural determinism in eschatology is shared by other physicists in our time, such as Frank Tipler, although cosmological
science today seems to hold a view of the end of the universe as heading for ultimate extinction of life (freeze or fry).[144] The threat of the
ecological crisis we are experiencing today shakes the very ground
of an optimistic natural teleology in a way similar to the collapse of
the expectations of social utopianism with the fall of the communist
state, or to the nineteenth-century hopes for the progress of the human race with the experience of the horrors of the Second World
War in the twentieth century. The overall conclusion is therefore
beyond any doubt: *all teleologies from the Aristotelian to the progressive and the utopian type conceive the end as an outcome of the past and
are incapable of securing an ontologically stable future. The past cannot
cause the being of the future.*

e) We shall discuss below the reasons for this as well as the alternative view of the end inherent in Christian eschatology, but before
we do that let us consider briefly the teleology offered by one of the
most eminent and representative Christian theologians of our time,
namely Jürgen Moltmann. Does the Maximian view of the end as
the uncaused cause of everything that exists fit into his eschatology?

---

[143] Pierre Teilhard de Chardin, *The Vision of the Past*, trans. J.M. Cohen (London:
Collins, 1966), p. 168.
[144] See below, chapter two, "Eschatology and Creation."

Moltmann places eschatology in the context of the idea of *promise*. He fervently objects to any notion of *epiphany* in eschatology, which he regards as unbiblical. "A promise is a declaration which amounts to the coming of a reality which does not yet exist."[145] Fulfilment does not replace what was promised with a new reality that possesses an ontology of its own but must be understood as "the eschatological setting-in-force (*In-kraft-setzung*) of God's promise to Abraham."[146] This would suggest that for Moltmann the "end," which in St Maximus' terms "causes" whatever exists or happens, is the outcome of a process that begins in the past and not one that enters from the future and "visits" it. The end cannot be "seen" (epiphany) or "experienced" in history; it can only be expected and *hoped for*.

This would apply also to the Resurrection, which for Moltmann too is the "end" *par excellence* of eschatology. The Resurrection sets in motion the eschatological process to which all of the world's history is finally subject,[147] but is not to be understood as something that enters into history and makes itself visible in its course. The post-Easter appearances to the disciples are "expounded in terms of the earlier promises and this exposition in turn takes place in the form of prophetic proclamation of, and eschatological outlook toward, the future of Christ which was spotlighted in those appearances."[148] All aspects of the post-Easter appearances take place as a waiting for, not as a foretaste. The "end" does not "cause" history by entering into it; it causes expectation rather than experience.

While the Resurrection appearances, according to Moltmann, do not provide us with an experience of the "end" but only with the hope for the final overcoming of death, God's love for the world is manifest and experienced in history *in the Cross*. While the overcoming of death remains a matter of promise and hope, the Cross is the place where Christ's Resurrection becomes significant *for us*: "through his suffering and death [Jesus becomes] the Christ *for*

---

[145] J. Moltmann, *Theology of Hope: On the Ground and Implications of a Christian Eschatology* (New York: Harper, 1967), p. 103.

[146] See C. Morse, *The Logic of Promise in Moltmann's Theology* (Philadelphia: Fortress Press, 1979), p. 35.

[147] Ibid., pp. 35–36.

[148] Moltmann, *Theology of Hope*, p. 191.

us."[149] We have here what Richard Bauckham called Moltmann's "dialectical Christology" according to which the identity of Christ is "sustained in contradiction."[150]

This, however, leaves us with a question: Is it the Cross or the Resurrection that finally (i.e., eschatologically) prevails? Moltmann is right in stressing that it is the same Christ that is crucified and risen. This is true concerning the personal identity of Christ, but if the Cross (and not the Resurrection) makes Christ existentially significant "for us," as Moltmann claims, we are left with death as our existential problem. The dialectical structure collapses existentially, and it becomes inevitable to ask which of the two states is the ultimate "end" that "causes" one's way of being (i.e., the *eschatological* state of existence). Does the overcoming of death (Resurrection) constitute the eschatological "end" of the economy or is it in a sort of combination of the abolition of death with the suffering of it that we should seek this "end"? Must we "eternalize" or "eschatologize" the Cross, that is, suffering and death, alongside the Resurrection, that is, the abolishment of suffering and death?

Moltmann's position is an inevitable outcome of his adoption of Karl Rahner's axiom that the immanent and the economic Trinity are to be fully identified. Applied to the subject of eschatology, this leads to the eschatologization of the Cross and by implication to the introduction of suffering and death not only into God's being (which Moltmann does explicitly in his *The Crucified God*) but also into the eschatological "end," "for the sake of which everything exists."

What is at stake, therefore, in this discussion is how *the future of which Christian eschatology speaks relates to the future of history: is the future of the resurrection bound up with the historical future* (like a "tomorrow" following upon a "today" and ultimately a "yesterday," i.e., *a past*), *or is it a future that "confronts" us as a "visitor" and—why not?—as an "epiphany"*? The question is crucial in any attempt to distinguish teleology from Christian eschatology, because in all teleologies the future is a *future of a past* (i.e., a historical future) while

[149] J. Moltmann, *The Crucified God: The Cross of Christ as the Foundation and Criticism of Christian Theology* (Minneapolis, MN: Fortress Press, 1993), p. 184.
[150] R. Bauckham, *The Theology of Jürgen Moltmann* (Edinburgh: T&T Clark, 1995), p. 93.

in Christian eschatology the future of the past, the historical future, leads ultimately to death (cf. Heidegger's famous dictum) and cannot produce an undying future (every historical future is bound to become past). Moltmann's building of eschatology on the ground of promise, in spite of his efforts to avoid entelechian conceptions of the historical process by employing the Blochian idea of the *novum* (stretching it even to the point of *ex nihilo*), does not allow him to conceive of a future that *comes to us from outside history*, a "metahistorical" future, which "causes" history without being "caused" by it.

All this is reflected also in Moltmann's treatment of ecclesiology. The Church lives essentially by the word of promise and of awakened hope. In the sacraments of Baptism and the Eucharist we have an "openness towards that which is as yet only on the way towards it," and in the Eucharist the Church "is not in possession of the sacral presence of the Absolute, but is a waiting, expectant congregation seeking communion with the coming Lord."[151] The eschaton has not entered into history except in order to awaken the *expectation* of the Kingdom, not its *experience*. The essence of eschatology is thus exhausted in *hope*.

The Eschatologization of History

All the teleologies that we have examined, whether secular or theological, operate with a future borrowed from history. While St Maximus conceives the "end" as causing everything that exists without being caused by anything, in these teleologies the historical future not only depends on the past but becomes itself past, that is, nonexistent—every historical "tomorrow" inevitably becomes a "yesterday", and a "tomorrow" which follows upon a "yesterday" is bound to become itself a "yesterday." A historical future not only cannot grant being but it ceases to exist itself, becoming a "fact," i.e., something that has "passed" and exists no longer.

History, as Collingwood and Florovsky conceived it, is a creative process: human being in its freedom creates events which make up the historical reality. In this sense, history is a positive thing, which

---

[151] Moltmann, *Theology of Hope,* p. 326.

in the case of the Incarnation acquires the character of *Heilsgeschichte* leading the economy to its consummation in the eschata.

In my personal view, this conception of history is not only one-sided but fails to see the problem inherent in the concept of futurity: the events created in history have a future that is bound to become past; they are facts and as such they have a "tomorrow" that becomes inevitably a "yesterday"—they are carriers of death. History in this case is a carrier of mortality.

Lacking, as they do, a future and being subject to the law of death, historical events or facts cannot be perpetuated in time or repeated. The only way for them to survive is by *memory*: psychology replaces in this case ontology, and "being" is identified with "remembering." This is exactly what we find in classical Greek philosophy: the essence of knowledge is the soul's capacity to remember. Plato's *Phaedo* is precisely about this, and Western thought in its entirety is, in final analysis, memory. The Battle of Marathon cannot be repeated, and this applies also to the events of the *Heilsgeschichte*; they can only be remembered; ontology is replaced by psychology.

Historical events, therefore, in order to survive (i.e., to overcome their "pastness" and acquire a future that does not become a "yesterday") need the "visit" or "intrusion" of the eschata, which would save them from falling into a mere psychological survival and, instead, grant them true *being*, "eternal life," a future that does not become past. This is why the eschata were called by the Fathers, "the eighth day" which knows no end. Without the interference of this day, historical events are subject to perdition by becoming "past."

Eschatology, therefore, saves history from being a matter of sheer memory. Yet, not all events of history need to be saved. There are historical events which by their very nature negate being, such as murder and all forms of hatred and destruction. Since the eschata aim at the affirmation of being, all historical events that deny being will have to disappear. Eschatology, therefore, acts as *a purification of history*. This is why the "Day of the Lord" has always been regarded as the Day of Judgement. It will be a judgement not on *moral* but *ontological* grounds, or on morals only as they stem from ontological demands (any act denying or obscuring the existence or affirmation of the other, etc. must disappear).

The purification of history has been assigned in the Gospels to the Messiah or the "Son of Man" who would do that by identifying himself with humanity in its historical existence. In the Incarnation, however, the future Messiah has already come, his futurity has been historicized: he was born at a certain period of time, grew up in the way all children do, and, above all, he was crucified and died at a certain historical time (under Pontius Pilate). This means that in Christology the future becomes a "tomorrow" like all historical "tomorrows," i.e., destined to be turned into a "yesterday" and die. By the very fact that ὁ ἐρχόμενος (in the future) is already here, Christ would then cease to bring the redemption of time that eschatology promises.

Christology, therefore, if it is "Christomonistic," does not carry with it the redemption of time that eschatology promises. Most Christologies are of this kind and, therefore, stand in need of correction. The crucial and decisive point lies in the role played by *pneumatology* in Christology. It is a role that is usually forgotten and must be brought up particularly in relation to eschatology.

In *Being as Communion*, I have stressed the fact that while Christ *becomes* history, the Spirit *transcends* it. The Spirit brings the last days into history (Acts 2:18), and this applies also to the Incarnation. Christ is born with the intervention of the Spirit (Mt 1:18), he performs his ministry always with the operation of the Spirit (Mt 12:28; Lk 4:18), and, most importantly, he is *risen* by the Spirit (Rom 11:13). The very term "Christ" signifies the one anointed by the Spirit.

The very identity of Christ, therefore, contains the Spirit. And, since the Spirit transcends history, the Incarnation itself transcends history—not, however, by and in itself, but because it is a pneumatological event.

All this means that our salvation is not due to the historization of the eschatological future in the Incarnation, but to the *eschatologization of history* through the Spirit. We are not saved because Christ became history, but because in Christ as the bearer of the Spirit history has been eschatologized. We must be careful not to give to history, as such, a positive status in existence. History cannot contain a future that is not turned into a "yesterday"—it would cease to be history if it did. The historization of eschatology through the various forms of Christology is a dangerous idea. Only the eschatologization of history can save it from death. Death is inevitably present in the historical notion of the "future," as there is no history in which the future is a "tomorrow" that does not become inevitably a "yesterday."

⁘

In conclusion, history creates events that can only be *remembered*, they can no longer *be*. Historical events lack ontology because they lack a future. It is the future that gives being: a futureless event is a dead "fact"; it is "past." Eschatology brings a future that is not of the same kind as that of the future given by history. It is an "end," i.e., the utmost of futurity, which, as St Maximus puts it, depends on no other end, an "eighth day" which is not following upon the "seventh" day but makes the seventh day acquire existence, a future. History, therefore, needs eschatology in order to survive; otherwise, it is condemned to death. Yet, not all historical events carry an ontological significance. Some of them, on the contrary, oppose being and cannot have a future, since in their very existence they deny future to other beings and eventually to themselves, as the demonic element in history demonstrates. Eschatology, as the affirmation of being and the granting of an endless future to beings automatically annihilates every historical event or act that deprives beings of a future, such as hatred and murder. Eschatology viewed in such an ontological light, brings with it *judgement*, the final judgement, which is not of a moral but of an ontological kind. The eschatologization of history means, therefore, its *purification* from everything that smacks of death and nonbeing. Christ, in his capacity of the conqueror of death through his Resurrection and the bearer of the Spirit will come to "judge the quick and the dead," as the Creed has it. The eschatologization of history is, thus, its *ontologization*, the only way for historical events to be creative and have a future.

Chapter Two

ESCHATOLOGY AND CREATION

Introduction: The Ontological Content of the Eschata

What does God promise to give us in his Kingdom? In the minds of most believers as well as in many strands of the theological traditions of both Eastern and Western Christianity, the ontological content of the eschata has been so weakened as to almost disappear. In the medieval Western tradition, the Kingdom of God has been identified mainly with participation in the bliss and beatitude of God,[1] while in the East, the dominant theme is the vision of God and participation in his glory.[2] In the Protestant tradition, the theme of justification dominated the scene for much of its history, while in more recent times, the emphasis has been put on the restoration of divine rule and justice in the world, which seems to preoccupy the Judeo-Christian literature of biblical times.[3]

In all of these cases, it is the *bene esse* and not the very *esse* that the eschatological state offers to humanity and the world. The *being* of creation is established protologically and is taken for granted in dealing with the Last Things. The eschata do not seem to concern the being but the well-being of creatures.

The reasons for such an unontological approach to eschatology are manifold. In the first place, the doctrine of creation seems to be exhausted in its consideration of the beginning of things in almost all manuals of Christian dogmatics. The world's being is securely established at the beginning when creation was declared by God to be

---

[1] For example, Dante's "beatific vision" and Pope Benedict XII in his constitution *Benedictus Deus* (1336) followed by the councils of Florence, Trent, etc.

[2] Cf. V. Lossky, *The Vision of God* (Leighton Buzzard, Bedfordshire: Faith Press, 1963). The theme of glory as the characteristic of the eschatological state of creation was already emphasized by S. Bulgakov, *The Bride of the Lamb*, pp. 401, 451, and elsewhere.

[3] See G. Sauter, "Protestant Theology," in *The Oxford Handbook of Eschatology*, ed. J.L. Walls (Oxford: Oxford University Press, 2008), pp. 248–262.

"good" or "very good," and whatever happened to it as a result of the fall of the human being does not affect its being but its well-being. In other words, the being of creation, once established, was not threatened by the nonbeing from which it came. The dialectic between created and uncreated existence ceased ontologically with the completion of the work of creation on the sixth day.

This approach to creation is accompanied by the view that creation was endowed with powers of survival, even beauty, in its nature. Some would call these powers divine/created "Wisdom" or "*Sophia*,"[4] while others would prefer the more patristic language of divine *energies*.[5] In both cases, the being of creation is regarded as having been well and firmly established protologically. Any reference to a threat of creation returning to nonbeing would be described as a "dualism."[6]

---

[4] Bulgakov, *The Bride of the Lamb*, p. 63: with creaturely Sophia "*uncreated* [his emphasis] forces and energies, submerged in nothing, receive a creaturely, relative, limited, multiple being and the universe comes into being. The world as the creaturely Sophia is uncreated—created. *That is the world's divine, uncreated ground in eternity* [my emphasis]." And further on p. 80: creaturely Sophia, who is the image of divine being, is "the world's soul and entelechy, who is being actualized or *becoming* (his emphasis) in the world. She is the life of the world." The eschatological resurrection is the manifestation in glory of what is "hitherto hidden and obscure" in creation (p. 451).

[5] Vladimir Lossky is the most famous exponent of the application of the concept of uncreated energies to the doctrine of creation. See his *The Mystical Theology of the Eastern Church* which has exercised an immense influence on contemporary Orthodox theology. An excellent discussion of Lossky's theology appears in A. Papanikolaou, *Being with God: Trinity, Apophaticism, and Divine-Human Communion* (Notre Dame, IN: University of Notre Dame Press, 2006). Lossky draws mainly from the doctrine of creation of Dionysius the Areopagite who sees creation as participating in God through the divine energies permeating the world. The appeal to St Maximus for support does not seem to be justified, since the location by Lossky of the *logoi* of creation, with which Maximus expresses the relation of creation to God, in the divine energies, appears to be questionable (see P. Sherwood, *The Earlier Ambigua of St. Maximus the Confessor* [Rome: Pontificium Institutum S. Anselmi, 1955], p. 179). Cf. the discussion of the relative texts by A. Riou, *Le monde et l'Église selon Maxime le Confesseur* (Paris: Beauchesne, 1973), p. 60 and L. Thunberg, *Man and the Cosmos: The Vision of St. Maximus the Confessor* (Crestwood, NY: St Vladimir's Seminary Press, 1985), p. 137ff. Maximus prefers a Christological approach to the God-world relation. As to St Gregory Palamas, who uses the language of divine energies extensively, his interest in applying this concept seems to lie more in anthropology than in cosmology.

[6] Thus, A. Papanikolaou, "Creation as Communion in Contemporary Orthodox Theology," in *Toward an Ecology of Transfiguration: Orthodox Christian Perspectives on Environment, Nature, and Creation*, eds. J. Chryssavgis and B.V. Foltz (Bronx, NY: Fordham University Press, 2013), p. 119, cf. pp. 106–120.

This protological approach to creation raises the question of the role of *Christ* in cosmology. If the being of creation is established, safeguarded, and guaranteed solely by uncreated/created Sophia or by the divine energies, which belong to divine *nature* and are common to *all three* persons of the Trinity, is there any reason to introduce Christology into our doctrine of creation? If the world's being is already firmly established at the beginning, what does the *incarnate* Christ contribute to creation other than the transmission of divine energies, which were already given to it by the three divine persons at the beginning? And what about the Resurrection and the Parousia? Do they have any significance for the being of creation?

At this point, another important aspect of the protological approach to creation arises concerning the being of creation, namely that of the cosmic significance of *death*. The Resurrection (both of Christ and the eschata) has to do with the defeat and the abolishment of death. In a protological approach, speaking of a cosmic death make no sense since the world's being is firmly established and guaranteed at the beginning. Death, in this case, appears to be an episode concerning exclusively the human being. Indeed, in the minds of most believers, death is thought of as a punishment inflicted only on humans for their disobedience to God—the death of non-humans or of creation itself counts little, if at all, in their consideration or concern. There is hardly any sense of *cosmic* death in most people's minds; death simply disturbs the well-being of humans. Death, in this case, is the "last enemy" (1 Cor 15:26), not of the world but only of humanity.

In the lines that follow, we shall consider the question of whether the being of creation was protologically established or whether it is dependent on the creation's eschatological state (whether being can make any sense without ever-being). How is the world sustained in existence until the coming of the last days, and in what way does the divine economy provide creation with the ever-being which it needs in order to overcome the danger of a return to nonbeing and thus truly be? We shall try to answer these questions primarily by drawing from biblical and patristic sources which will, finally, be considered in relation to other, non-theological approaches to the subject of creation.

I. The Mortality of Creation

Has the being of creation been fixed at the beginning, or will it be fixed in the end? If everything was ontologically perfect and firm at the beginning, the final destination of creation would have to be, ontologically speaking, a return to the beginning. Time and history would, in this case, form a circle, which would lead creation finally back to its original state.

Such a cyclical view of creation's history is to be found in ancient Greek thought and in certain non-Christian religions but, with the exception of Origen, is absent in biblical and patristic thought. The *telos* of all movement in creation is not potentially present from the beginning in the substance of things. The biblical and patristic view of creation conceived the world as created by God with a *telos*, a purpose, and a destiny, much higher ontologically than the beginning.

What does it mean to say that the final destiny of creation is higher than its beginning *ontologically*? It means that if this destiny is not fulfilled or realized, the being that was given to creation at the beginning will at some point cease and will become a "past," i.e., it will "die." Thus, there are only two ways of avoiding in our ontology of creation the possibility of its death: either by conceiving creation as having been endowed with ever-being or of creation as belonging to the end and not being present in the substance or nature of creation. In this latter case, what feeds creation with being is not the "fact" that it has been created but the purpose, the *telos*, for which it has been created and which is its ever-being. Creation is thus sustained in its being not by its past but by its future, since the ever-being (i.e., being not subject to the possibility of extinction and death) will be granted to creation only in the end and will not be part of creation's nature but a supernatural grace.

The Church father that has given us the most explicit expression of this eschatological ontology of creation is St Maximus the Confessor. Following the Irenaean view of humanity as having been created with a destiny, a purpose, higher than the beginning of its creation, Maximus extends the same view to creation as a whole.

Maximus' dealing with creation is deeply ontological. He repeatedly uses the triad "being—well-being—ever-being" to refer to creation, thus making ontology fundamental to theology, at least with regard to the doctrine of creation:

> There are, then, three utterly general modalities ... with which God has made everything: being (εἶναι), and well-being (εὖ εἶναι), and ever-being (ἀεὶ εἶναι). The first one was given by God in creation; the middle one depends on the exercise of our freedom (γνώμη), and the last one will be granted by God at the end in the general resurrection.[7]

Now, there are here two points of fundamental significance for our subject. The first is that "simply (ἁπλῶς) being," which was given by God to creation at the beginning, is to be called true being (ὄντως εἶναι) only when ever-being is added to it (προστεθὲν) in the future:[8] ὄντως εἶναι = ἀεὶ εἶναι. This confirms the point that it is only when ever-being is added to the original "simple being" that the latter acquires the status of true being. This gift of ever-being which is necessary for the protological being in order to be ὄντως εἶναι (true being) is an eschatological gift; it will be granted at the "great and common resurrection" which will give the grace of the incorruption of nature (τὸ κατ᾽ οὐσίαν μὴ φθείρεσθαι) to all creation together with the human being for whom it has been created.[9]

The second point is that "ever (or true) being" cannot in any way spring from created nature, since it is *totally inexistent in things even as a potential* (οὔτε φυσικῶς κατὰ δύναμιν τοῖς οὖσιν ἐνυπάρχει)[10]— another anti-Aristotelian hint. There is nothing in created nature that can guarantee its ever-being (which is truly—ὄντως—being). For this reason, Maximus categorically denies any power in nature that may make it capable of divinization:

> [Nature has] no [such] faculty, of any sort ... because then it [divinization] would no longer be grace but the revelation of an activity latent within the potentiality of nature. Further, divinization would then no longer be a paradox if it occurred as a result

---

[7] Maximus, *Amb.* 10 (PG 91:1116B) and 42 (PG 91:1352B).

[8] Maximus, *Amb.* 10 (PG 91:1116C).

[9] Maximus, *Amb.* 42 (PG 91:11348D–1349A).

[10] Maximus, *Amb.* 65 (PG 91:1392B). Cf. *Carit.* 3.27 (PG 90:1025A): "the ever-being or not [of creatures] belongs to the power (ἐξουσία) of the creator, while the participation in his goodness and wisdom lies in the will (βουλήσει) of the intelligent (λογικῶν) beings."

of natural capacity ... Divinization would be an achievement of nature, not a gift of God.[11]

"Nature is incapable of conceiving what lies above nature,"[12] Maximus would insist. And ever-being, or true (ὄντως) being, lies above nature, being totally a gift of eschatological grace.

Maximus connects all this with his understanding of *motion* in creation. Like Aristotle, he views creation as endowed with dynamism and movement, but unlike the Greek philosopher, he rejects any idea of motion or dynamism that comes from the nature of creation:

> All created things have their motion in a passive way, since it is not a motion or a dynamism that comes from the creature's own being (αὐτοκίνησις ἤ αὐτοδύναμις).[13]

The passive character of the motion and dynamism of creation implies that both the beginning and the end of motion lie outside creation, in God who is the cause of this motion in its beginning as well as in its end.[14] Motion in creation has an aitiology and a teleology, which lie outside creation in God, and this is why this motion is passive; with regard to its beginning, it is due to the Creator, and with regard to the end, it is directed again to God, in whom it will find its fulfillment and "rest" (στάσις).

Ever-being depends fully on God, and it is not secured by any natural powers inherent in creation.[15] Creation is endowed with certain natural qualities that can help it survive *up to a point* but not forever. This is because creation came out of nothing and is constantly threatened by nonbeing—Maximus cannot be more explicit on this point:

> The Greeks maintain that the nature (οὐσία) of beings coexists eternally with God, only their qualities being given to them by him, and that the nature of beings is not threatened by anything (οὐδὲν ἐναντίον); it is only in their qualities that contrariety exists. We, however, say that only divine nature has nothing oppos-

---

[11] Maximus, *Amb.* 20 (PG 91:1237AB).
[12] Maximus, *QThal.* 22 (PG 90:321A).
[13] Maximus, *Amb.* 7 (PG 91:1073B).
[14] Maximus, *Amb.* 22 (PG 91:1257CD).
[15] Maximus, *Carit.* 3.27 (PG 90:1025A).

ing it (μὴ ἔχειν τι ἐναντίον) since it is eternal and infinite and bestows eternity on others, but the nature of [created] beings has nonbeing as its opponent (τὸ μὴ ὂν ἐναντίον) ... since it has been produced from nonbeing into being.[16]

Thus, Maximus joins Athanasius of Alexandria in asserting the idea that having come out of nothing, created nature is constantly under threat of returning to nonbeing if left to itself. Athanasius would go as far as saying that *creation has nonbeing as its nature*,[17] and if "left to be carried and afflicted (χειμάζεσθαι) by its own nature," it "will risk [returning] again to nonbeing (κινδυνεύσει πάλιν εἰς τὸ μὴ εἶναι)."[18] Maximus uses similar language in speaking of the "risk" of created being "to withdraw to nonbeing (εἰς τὸ μὴ ὂν πάλιν κινδυνεύσας μεταχωρῆσαι)."[19]

The idea, therefore, that created nature is surrounded and constantly threatened by nonbeing is not foreign to the Fathers. That this does not necessarily imply an ontological dualism between created and uncreated being will be shown below. What we wish to stress at this stage is that the "fact" of creation, creation's "nature," does not guarantee or secure its being. In bringing about creation, God has not inserted *in its nature* a power of survival, of overcoming the nonbeing from which creation came. "Naturally," therefore, creation is mortal. There is no protological ontology possible in a Christian doctrine of creation.

This point bears particular significance when we come to discuss the relation of eschatology to scientific cosmology. Scientific cosmology in the twentieth century has pronounced itself not only on the beginning of the universe but also on its end. With regard to the beginning, the so-called "Big Bang" theory seems in many ways to point in the direction of the patristic *creatio ex nihilo*. But with reference to eschatology, the prevailing view seems to bring the Christian faith into conflict with science. Many theologians have noted

---

[16] Maximus, *Carit.* 3.28 (PG 90:1025B).

[17] Athanasius, *De inc.* 4 (PG 25:104B).

[18] Athanasius, *C. gent.* 41 (PG 25:81CD–84A): "the nature of creatures, having come from nothing, is fluid, weak, and mortal (ρευστή τις καὶ ἀσθενὴς καὶ θνητὴ) if left to itself."

[19] Maximus, *Amb.* 41 (PG 91:1308C).

this conflict,[20] and, as Pannenberg has advised, it is better to live with the conflict than seek an easy solution.[21]

In my view, scientific cosmology has done nothing but confirm the patristic view of creation, as it has just been expounded here. Scientists suggest that the universe "is heading for an all-enveloping death."[22] The final future of the universe, according to science, as forecasted by the combination of Big Bang cosmology and the Second Law of Thermodynamics, will be one of extinction ("freeze or fry"). In the face of this, theology is trying to preserve eschatological faith either by somehow dissociating humanity[23] and spiritual life or consciousness[24] from material creation, or by relying on the capacity of nature, shown by the billion years of cosmic evolution, to extend its survival into the future.[25] But neither of these two "escapes" can be satisfactory, at least from the patristic point of view, since the first one would imply that only humanity or the spiritual immaterial world has an eschatological destiny, while the second would make created nature capable of survival by itself.

From the perspective of the present study, what science seems to say about the final future of creation is in agreement with the Athanasian idea we stress here, namely that creation in its nature is mortal. Had science, which investigates exclusively the laws of nature, taken the view that the universe will not die, its conclusions would contradict the position presented here—that the being of creation is not guaranteed in any way by creation's nature (i.e., by its beginning)

---

[20] See R. Russell, "Cosmology and Eschatology," in *The Oxford Handbook of Eschatology*, pp. 563–580.

[21] W. Pannenberg, "Theological Questions to Scientists," in *The Sciences and Theology in the Twentieth Century*, ed. A.R. Peacock (Notre Dame, IN: University of Notre Dame Press, 1981), pp. 14–15.

[22] J. Macquarrie, *Principles of Christian Theology* (London: SCM Press, 1977), pp. 351--62. Cf. R. Russell, "Cosmology and Eschatology," p. 567 and G. Contopoulos and T. Cotsakis, *Cosmology: The Structure and Evolution of the Universe* (Berlin: Springer-Verlag, 1986), p. 186ff.

[23] In, for example, A.R. Peacock, *Creation and the World of Science* (Oxford: Clarendon Press, 1979), p. 353.

[24] In, for example, F.J. Tipler, *The Physics of Immortality: Modern Cosmology, God and the Resurrection of the Dead* (New York: Doubleday, 1994).

[25] Thus, J.F. Haught, *God after Darwin: A Theology of Evolution* (Boulder, CO: Westview Press, 2000), p. 123f.

but depends for its survival only on an eschatological future that bears no *natural* continuity with the past.[26] It is precisely this that makes creation's ever-being *grace*. And it is this that shows that protological ontology is valid as ontology only if subjected to eschatology, from which it draws its verification and confirmation. Creation without the eschata amounts to "being-unto-death" or rather being overcome (finally) by nonbeing, that is, to being an ontological absurdity.

II. The Sustainment of Creation

If created nature is in itself mortal and subject to corruptibility and, eventually, to the threat of a return to nonbeing (or, in the words of St Athanasius, has fluidity and nonbeing as its nature), how do we avoid a dualistic (or even a docetic) ontology of creation? If the being of creation depends on eschatological ever-being as the only "true" being (ὄντως εἶναι), how does it avoid a collapse into nonbeing until it is given ever-being in the future? We shall try to answer these questions with the help of patristic thought, while respecting the position of cosmological science concerning the mortality of created nature.

As we have just seen, according to both patristic and scientific cosmological thought, creation is in its nature mortal and, if left to itself, it is headed for eventual extinction. Unlike divine nature, created nature has had a beginning, and, for this reason, it is permeated by mutability (τροπή)[27] causing its decay and eventual death. It is, therefore, necessary for creation to be in communion with the uncreated God in order to avoid extinction.

---

[26] The eschatological state of creation is not, of course, *creatio ex nihilo* but *ex vetere* (Cf. J. Polkinghorne, "Eschatology: Some Questions and some Insights from Science," in *The End of the World and the Ends of God: Science and Theology on Eschatology*, eds. J. Polkinghorne and M. Welker [Harrisburg, PA: Trinity Press, 2000], pp. 29–30). It is true that in the Resurrection, Christ's risen body bears the scars of his passion (= the old creation), but this is not to be described as "natural continuity," since it is due to a personal intervention by God and not to a capacity of the old creation.

[27] Gregory of Nyssa, *Or. Catech.* 6 (PG 45:28CD): "The uncreated nature is insusceptible to the movement of mutability, change, and alteration, while everything that came into being by way of creation has an affinity with change, since the existence of creation itself started with change having come into being from nonbeing by the divine power."

Any divine-cosmic communion, however, must preserve the boundaries of each nature, created and uncreated. There can be no communion between God and the world, which would involve the transgression of the boundaries of their respective natures. This is so not only for theological but also for philosophical reasons: the concept of nature implies in its definition, in its *logos,* as Maximus would say, fixed boundaries that cannot be violated by any communion without leading to a collapse of the nature itself.[28]

Patristic thought was preoccupied early on with the subject of divine-cosmic communion as the only way of overcoming the natural mortality of creation. Yet, it is noteworthy that it never employed *natural* qualities to describe this communion.[29] It is the presence of a divine *person* in creation that guarantees and safeguards its protection from a return to nonbeing.

Athanasius of Alexandria makes this central to his cosmology in both his *Contra gentes* and *De incarnatione,* in which he deals extensively with this subject:

> Seeing that the entire created nature (τὴν γενητὴν πᾶσαν φύσιν) ... is mutable (ρευστὴν) and decaying (διαλυομένην), and in order that it may not suffer this and the whole [creation] be dissolved again into nonbeing (πάλιν εἰς τὸ μὴ εἶναι ἀναλυθῇ τὸ ὅλον) ... [God] has not left it [creation] to *be carried and afflicted by its own nature,* and in order that it may not run the risk of returning to nonbeing, being good he governs and ordains it *by his Logos* who is himself God,[30] so that creation being illumined by the sovereignty, the providence, and the ordering of the Logos, may be able to persevere securely, since it will partake of the Father's Logos who is the true being (τοῦ ὄντως ὄντος), being helped through him to [remain] in being (εἰς τὸ εἶναι) and not suffer what it would have suffered had the Logos not preserved it, I mean nonbeing (τὸ μὴ εἶναι).[31]

---

[28] Maximus, *Amb.* 42 (PG 91:1341D): "Every innovation, to speak generically, has naturally to do with the mode of the innovated thing but not with the logos of nature; because *a logos innovated corrupts the nature.*" Cf. ibid., (1329A; 1349B), etc.

[29] Chalcedon stands out as the normative position on this matter: in Christ divine nature and human nature united with each other "without confusion," i.e., without a transgression of their natural boundaries.

[30] The identification of the Logos with the second person of the Trinity is axiomatic in Athanasius' thought.

[31] Athanasius, *C. gent.* 41. Cf. ibid., 42.

The following points emerge clearly from this important passage:

a) Creation is constantly running the risk of a return to nonbeing. The reason is that it is created (γενητή) and, therefore, mutable and decaying in its very nature. What creation needs, therefore, is *being*, not simply well-being.

b) There is nothing in creation that can protect it from nonbeing; the only way for it to stay in being is communion with God. This communion is given to creation through the presence in it *of a divine Person*, the Logos.

It is evident from this last point that in the early centuries of patristic thought, divine-cosmic communion was conceived as realized *through personhood*. This remained the case throughout the patristic period, including in St Gregory Palamas.[32] It was only in modern times that this was overshadowed and replaced by ideas of divine-cosmic communion that employ natural rather than personal aspects of divine presence in creation.

The idea that God and the world are in communion through the Logos goes back to the prologue of the Fourth Gospel and reaches the Apologists and the early fathers probably through the influence of Philo. That the Logos is a *person*, distinct from the Father, although himself God, was already taught by Justin who identified him also with the only-begotten Son, who revealed himself in the Old Testament and "became man for our sakes."[33] Irenaeus followed the same line of reasoning adding to the role of the Logos in creation that of the Holy Spirit, reserving, however, for the former the *onto-*

---

[32] It is often overlooked that, according to St Gregory Palamas, the divine energies which are operative in creation are *enhypostatic* or "hypostasized" (see, for example, *The Defense of the Hesychasts* III, 1.18) and, therefore, personal. This is particularly underlined by O. Clément, *Orient—Occident: Deux passeurs, Vladimir Lossky et Paul Evdokimov* (Geneva: Labor et Fides, 1985), pp. 38–41, and in his *Byzance et le Christianisme* (Paris: Presses Universitaires de France, 1964), p. 46: "L'énergie n'est pas rayonnement impersonal subsistant de soi. Elle est comme l'expansion de la Trinité dont elle traduit *ad extra* la mystérieuse altérité dans l'unité." Cf. J. Lison, *L'Esprit répandu: La pneumatologie de Grégoire Palamas* (Paris: Cerf, 1994), pp. 85–91; 141ff. Also, S. Yangazoglou, *Communion of Theosis: The Synthesis of Christology and Pneumatology in the Work of St. Gregory Palamas* (Athens: Domos, 2001), p. 155ff. (in Greek).

[33] Justin, *Dial.* 128.4 (PG 6:776B; 105.1). Ibid., (720C–721A); *Apol.* I 63; Ibid., 425B; *Apol.* II 13; Ibid., (465C–468A).

logical significance of his presence for creation.[34] We shall discuss the significance of this below.

The Alexandrian theologians, therefore, and Athanasius in particular had inherited and further developed the faith that God and the world are in communion through the presence in creation of a divine *person*. The same faith is expressed by the Cappadocian fathers, who make frequent reference to the presence of divine energies in creation and yet reserve the role of bringing about and sustaining it for the person of the Son.[35] There is of course a cooperation of all three divine persons in the economy, but the Son has the specific mission of being the "creating cause" (δημιουργικὴ αἰτία).[36]

The divine energies in creation are always understood as energies of divine *persons,* and it is for this reason that each person of the Trinity has a specific mission in the economy.[37] This *personal* dimension in the divine-cosmic communion, with the exception perhaps of the Areopagite writings,[38] has been consistently observed throughout the patristic tradition, including, as we saw above, St Gregory Palamas.

When we come to St Maximus the Confessor, we encounter a developed cosmology centered on the person of the Logos. In faithfulness to the Bible and previous theological tradition, Maximus also regards the divine Logos as the person of the Holy Trinity in whom and for whom creation was brought into being and by whom it is sustained in existence.[39] But he develops this biblical and patristic idea in ways that are extremely significant for our subject.

In the first place, Maximus for the first time expands the idea of the presence of the Logos in creation to refer to the multiplicity of created essences and their unity: creation consists of a diversity and multiplicity of things that accounts for their otherness and uncon-

---

[34] Irenaeus, *Dem.* 5. *St. Irenaeus Proof of the Apostolic Preaching*, trans. and annotation J.P. Smith, *Ancient Christian Writers*, No. 16 (Westminster, MD: Newman Press, 1952), p. 50f.

[35] Basil, *De Spir.* 16 (PG 32:136B). Gregory Nys., *Or. Catech.* 5 (PG 45:21A;C). *C. Eunom.* 3, ibid., 481A-C.

[36] Basil, *De Spir.* 8.19 (PG 32:1000f).

[37] Basil, *De Spir.* 16.33 (PG 32:136BC).

[38] Dion. Areop., *De div. nom.* 4 (PG 3:693B). Cf. 2. Ibid., 637BC.

[39] Maximus, *Amb.* 7 (PG 91:1077C; 1085AC); *Amb.* 42 (PG 91:1329D).

fused individuality. This is expressed by Maximus with the use of the concept of the *logoi*:

> Of all things that do or will substantially exist ... the logoi, firmly fixed, preexist in God, in accordance with which all things are and have become and abide, ever drawing near through natural motion to their purposed logoi.[40]

The multiplicity and otherness of created things is rooted in the very pre-eternal intention of God and is not the result of some kind of "fall" (contra Origen). Maximus in this way roots otherness in creation in God's original and eternal will, not of course in his nature, for there is a difference between God's pre-eternal intention and its realization in time.[41] Thus, the *logoi* of created essences safeguard otherness and multiplicity as part not only of creation's being but also of its ever-being; otherness will be preserved eternally.

Now, the multiple *logoi* of created essences form at the same time a unity, and this takes place in *a person* of the Trinity, the divine Logos.[42] This point has to be emphasized because it indicates that the concept of *logoi* is not intended by Maximus to relate the world to God through divine natural qualities[43] but specifically through a person, the Logos of the Trinity. Maximus in this way joins with the Nicean and Alexandrian writers in affirming the divine-cosmic communion *through a person*.[44]

But Maximus does not stop there. He introduces into this personalist cosmology the dimension of the future and of the "end" (τέλος). The multiple *logoi* of creation are united in the person of the divine Logos, not just protologically (as pre-eternal wills of God) but also *eschatologically*. Maximus' protological ontology is polemical;

---

[40] Maximus, *Amb.* 42 (PG 91:1329AB).

[41] Maximus, *Amb.* 7 (PG 91:1081AB); *Amb.* 42 (1328B).

[42] Maximus, *Amb.* 7 (PG 91:1116BC).

[43] The *logoi* are not located in or identified with the divine energies (see note 5 above). For the *personal* character of the *logoi*, see D. Staniloae as presented by C. Berger, "A Contemporary Synthesis of St. Maximus' Theology: the Work of Fr Dumitru Staniloae," in *Knowing the Purpose of Creation through the Resurrection: Proceedings of the Symposium on St Maximus the Confessor*, ed. M. Vasiljević (Los Angeles: Sebastian Press, 2013), p. 400ff.

[44] P. Sherwood, *St. Maximus the Confessor: The Ascetic Life, The Four Centuries on Charity* (New York: Newman Press, 1955), p. 36.

his intention is to refute the Origenist *henad*. His own vision, which he states without a polemical motivation, is that of a creation in which the *logoi* find their fulfillment *in the future,* not in the past. This is why even in referring to the beginning of creation he hastens to relate the logoi to a *purpose* and a σκοπὸς hidden in them,[45] which is their "Sabbath," their final rest in God.[46] There is a "movement" in the *logoi* of creation, which is not a return to the past but a motion forward, to the "purpose" of creation, i.e., to the eschatological future. Maximus is explicit: you must not seek the beginning behind you but in the end!

> By seeking its end, the human being arrives at its beginning.... It is not proper to seek the beginning, as I said, as if it has been realized in the past (ὀπίσω γεγενημένην); but you must seek the end which lies ahead of you (τὸ τέλος ἔμπροσθεν ὑπάρχον); so that you know the beginning you left behind through the end, since you did not know the end from the beginning. And this is what the wise Solomon mystagogically says: *That which has happened, is that which will happen.* And, *that which has been made is that which will be made,* as if he was showing the beginning from the end. The end, therefore, is not, after the disobedience, shown from the beginning, but the beginning from the end. And one does not seek the *logoi* at the beginning but asks for the *logoi,* which move and lead to the end.[47]

Now, this movement forward is again a movement that unites creation in a person: *the incarnate Logos, Christ.* The end or purpose for which the world was created is a *person,* the incorporation of the *logoi* of creation *not in the divine Logos, as he was at the beginning, but in the Logos incarnate in time and history leading creation to its eschatological destiny.*

For Maximus, creation has a purpose, a destiny, toward the realization of which it moves. This is none other than its incorporation in Christ:

[45] Maximus, *Amb.* 7 (PG 91:1080C).
[46] Ibid., 1080D.
[47] Maximus, *QThal.* 59 (PG 90:613D-616A): One is reminded at this point of T. S. Elliot's famous verses: "in my beginning is my end ... In the end is my beginning ... The end is where we start from" (*Four Quartets,* [London: Faber and Faber, 1979], pp. 13, 20, 42).

This is the blessed end for which everything was created. This is the divine purpose pre-conceived at the beginning of things, which [purpose] we define by calling it a *preconceived end,* for the sake of which all things [were created] and which was [conceived] for the sake of nothing else. To this end was God looking in producing the essences.[48]

The definition of the "end" as something for the sake of which everything was created, an "end" moreover that was not created for the sake of any other "end," bears tremendous ontological significance; it suggests the idea that while the beginning depends on the end, the end does not depend on the beginning: the end is not derived from the beginning in the spirit of Teilhard de Chardin's movement of creation from the Alpha to the Omega point. The incorporation of created essences in the person of Christ is *the cause* for the sake of which they came into being originally, while itself remaining uncaused by the beginning. Thus, although creation appears to move *toward an end,* it is, in fact, being moved *by this end.*

Christ, the end of creation, causes creation to be. He does so not as the preexisting but as the *incarnate* Logos. Because being must be ever-being in order to be true being, creation's being must draw its being from the end, for the sake of which it was created, and this is none other than the incarnate Christ. The Incarnation, therefore, was the "end" of creation. We must now see how this relates to the ever-being of creatures.

III. The Ever-being of Creation

1. The Incarnation and the Eschata

The Incarnation is the end for which the world was created not simply because it brought about the unity of God with humanity, but because it *recapitulated all of creation in Christ.*[49] This recapitulation, however, is an *eschatological* event. It is rooted in the historical

[48] Maximus, *QThal.* 60 (PG 90:621A).
[49] Maximus, *Amb.* 7 (PG 91:1080B).

Incarnation of Christ, but it is fulfilled only when Christ will unite all in himself and establish his Kingdom (1 Cor 15:28; Eph 1:10).

The theme of the recapitulation of creation goes back to the New Testament (Rom 5:12–21; 1 Cor 15:22, 45; Eph 1:10) and is developed particularly by Sts Irenaeus and Maximus. It is a theme related to the *eschata via* the Incarnation. Its cosmological and ontological character is obvious: Christ is the head not only of humanity but of all creation, embodying it in his person and giving it eternal being. How does the Incarnation relate to recapitulation?

Two points seem to be of special importance for our subject. The first is that recapitulation is connected with anthropology, and the second is that it is Christ's *Resurrection* that constitutes the decisive "moment" of the Incarnation, in which the recapitulation of all is actualized in history. Let us consider these two points more closely.

Christ recapitulates creation and gives it true being *via humanity*. Irenaeus deals with this at length.[50] St Maximus, once more, undertakes the development of this idea in its cosmological implications. Humanity was created with a *cosmological mission*. Adam was created at the end precisely because he was called to unite in himself the whole creation and lead it to eternal life by uniting it with God.

> For this reason man is introduced as the last one into the existing things (τοῖς οὖσιν) as a natural link mediating between the extremes and bringing to unity into himself the things that are divided naturally by distance (τῷ διαστήματι)[51] in order that they may be united in God.[52]

This cosmic mission of humanity to recapitulate creation so that it may overcome divisions inherent in its nature[53] and accounting for its mortality means that the ever or true being of creation required the presence of a person in whom creation would be incorporated.

---

[50] Irenaeus, *Haer.* III, 16.6 (PG 7:925BC); III, 22.2–3. Ibid., 958; III, 23.1. Ibid., 960BC.

[51] Κατὰ τὴν φύσιν ἀλλήλων διεστηκότα τῷ διαστήματι. Note that the division refers to createdness itself and to *the nature* of created things. All five divisions mentioned by Maximus (created/uncreated, intelligent/sensible, heaven/earth, Paradise/oecumene, male/female) belong to the pre-fallen state and apply to the *nature* of creation (φυσικῶς διαιροῦσαν).

[52] Maximus, *Amb.* 41 (PG 91:1305BC).

[53] Maximus, *Amb.* 7 (PG 91:1092C): "the many [things] which are divided from one another *according to their nature* (τὰ πολλὰ ἀλλήλων κατὰ τὴν φύσιν διεστηκότα)."

The reason, according to St Maximus, is that the ever-being of creation would, in the eschata, take the form of *filiation* (we must remember that the world was created *by, in,* and *for a Person,* the only-begotten Son—Col 1:16), and this would require *freedom* on the part of creation,[54] something only the human being possesses having been created in the image of God and called to the "likeness."[55]

This cosmic mission of humanity the human being, in its freedom, refused to perform, and for this reason, God introduced a new and even "more paradoxical" mode[56] of saving creation from its mortality and leading it to the final purpose for which it was brought into being: the Incarnation confirms the crucial and decisive role of humanity for the survival of creation and draws its *raison d'être* from the eschatological purpose for which humanity and the world were created. The Incarnation, therefore, is not fully and properly understood until it is placed in its eschatological perspective. The Incarnation has a purpose, and this purpose goes beyond the *historical* event of the Incarnation, reaching the eschata. St Maximus expresses this clearly: the mystery of the Incarnation of the Logos reveals through the Cross and the burial of Christ the *logoi* of creation, but it is the Resurrection that realizes "the purpose for which God brought all things into being."[57]

---

[54] This is why Maximus, joining in this respect Irenaeus, stresses the role of the Holy Spirit (see below section 3) in divinization by attaching it to freedom: the human being was created at the beginning (κατ' ἀρχὰς) in the image of God in order to be born freely (κατὰ προαίρεσιν) in the Spirit and receive the "likeness" (τὸ καθ' ὁμοίωσιν) and become a creature of God according to nature and Son of God and God through the Spirit by grace (πλάσμα μὲν τοῦ Θεοῦ κατὰ φύσιν, Υἱὸς δὲ Θεοῦ καὶ Θεὸς κατὰ χάριν) (*Amb.* 42 (PG 91:1345D). It is noteworthy that becoming God (=divinization) and filiation are identical and refer not to the original creation but to the eschata. Consequently, the natural birth that followed the fall is "slavish subject to necessity (δούλην καὶ κατηναγκασμένην)," whereas birth in the Spirit is "a birth of freedom (ἐλευθερίας)." Ibid., 1348A. Cf. my distinction between "biological" and "ecclesial" existence in *Being as Communion*, pp. 49–65.

[55] Maximus, *Amb.* 42 (PG 91:1345D). See the preceding note.

[56] Maximus, *Amb.* 7 (PG 91:1097C). Cf. J.-M. Garrigues, "Le dessein d'adoption du Créateur dans son rapport au Fils d'après S. Maxime le Confesseur", in *Actes du Symposium sur Maxime le Confesseur, Fribourg, 2-5 Septembre 1980*, eds. F. Heinzer and C. Schönborn (Fribourg: Éditions Universitaires, 1982), pp. 173–192.

[57] Maximus, *Cap. theol.* I, 66 (PG 90:1108AB).

2. The Ontological Significance of the Resurrection

The Resurrection of Christ is the event that gives meaning not only to the act of creation but also to the entire Incarnation. Had there been no Resurrection, neither the birth nor the passion of Jesus, let alone his teaching, would have any ultimate significance; it was the Resurrection that confirmed the pre-Easter activity of Jesus.[58] The crucifixion had thrown wide open all of Jesus' claims to divine authority, and had it not been for his Resurrection, the apostolic *kerygma* would have no persuasive power at all. Indeed, as Paul puts it, "if Christ was not risen our faith is vain" (1 Cor 15:17).

But the Resurrection of Jesus could not be dissociated from the eschatological general resurrection (1 Cor 15:15–16).[59] The Resurrection of Jesus is a historical event containing in itself the future, the ultimate purpose of creation. Paul would go so far as to make *the Resurrection of Jesus depend on the future general resurrection*: "if there is no resurrection of the dead, then neither was Christ risen" (1 Cor 15:13). It is the eschata that give truth and "reality" to history.

Now, the Resurrection of Jesus had an ultimate ontological significance for only one reason: it brought about *the abolishment of death*. It is Paul again that expresses this position clearly in the fifteenth chapter of his first letter to the Corinthians. The Resurrection signifies the submission of all evil powers to Christ and God, that is, the establishment of divine rule in creation.[60] But this, according to Paul at least, will not be the *ultimate* eschatological act. The ultimate (ἔσχατος) enemy to be conquered is death, and it is in this rather than divine rule over the "principalities and powers" that we must seek the quintessence of eschatology. The abolishment of death is not simply an aspect of the divine rule; it is the ultimate of the ultimate, the very ἔσχατον of the ἔσχατα.

In order to appreciate this point fully, we must have an ontological understanding of death as a threat to creation's very being, otherwise it makes no sense to call death the *last* enemy to be de-

[58] Cf. Pannenberg, *Jesus—God and Man*, p. 7f.
[59] Cf. again Pannenberg who goes so far as to give priority to the faith in the general resurrection over Jesus' personal Resurrection. (*Jesus—God and Man*, p. 66f).
[60] This is a theme occupying a central place in Pannenberg's eschatology. See, among other places, his *Systematic Theology*, vol. 3 (Edinburgh: T&T Clark, 1998), p. 531.

feated in the Resurrection; there cannot be an eschatological ontology in its true sense without a conception of death as an ontological problem, as "a matter of life or death," of the being or not being of whatever in creation is regarded as possessing being and of creation in its totality. If death is regarded as an episode in the life of the human being and not as a matter that concerns all that makes up creation, including creation as a totality,[61] then the Resurrection has no ontological significance for the entire cosmos. Just as the death of a human person is not unrelated to the mortality which permeates creation in general (the human being dies because all creatures die—death is a "natural" phenomenon), in the same way there can be no resurrection of the human being without an abolishment of death in creation as a whole.[62] This interdependence between humanity and the rest of the material creation with regard to death and resurrection shows the ontological character of death and its cosmic significance.[63]

[61] In terms of scientific cosmology, this would mean that, according to the biblical and patristic view of creation, the "closed model" of the universe would be more compatible with the Christian faith than that of an infinite and imperishable world. Cf. Pannenberg, *Systematic Theology*, vol. 3, p. 589.

[62] The eschatological survival of the material creation was emphasized by Methodius of Olympus against Origen already in the fourth century: "If the nonbeing were better than the being of the world, why did God choose the worse in creating the world? But God made nothing in vain or worse. Therefore, God has brought about creation in order to be and remain" (*De resur.* XLVII, according to the edition by G.N. Bonwetsch, [Leipzig, 1917]). Athanasius would even speak of the "deification" of creation (*Ad Serap.* 1.25 (PG 26:589B).

[63] The ontological and cosmic significance of death is marginalized by K. Rahner, who seems to deal with death more as a "personal" act, i.e., as "dying." See his *On the Theology of Death* (New York: Herder and Herder, 1961). It is common in our time to speak of *Thanatology*, in which death is approached as a psychological experience focusing mainly on the problem of suffering. Pannenberg connects the resurrection of the dead with the universal resurrection allowing for a common destiny for all and for the idea of the wholeness of reality. Yet in reading him we miss the sense of tragedy of a creation longing for its liberation from the bondage of mortality (Rom 8:21)—a feeling we get, for example, from St Athanasius' vision of all creation threatened by nonbeing in its very nature. Pannenberg's ontology is heavily conditioned by the idea of *revelation* and the principle that meaning constitutes being (T. Bradshaw, *Pannenberg* [London: T&T Clark, 2009], p. 79), which leads him to develop a doctrine of creation conditioned by the idea of history and epistemological concerns. Moltmann, in his own way, tends to give priority to the tragic and "stauric" conditions of human history and whatever he has to say about the mortality which permeates created nature is resolved by a transfer of the threat of

Now, the abolishment of death and the granting of ever-being to creation in the Resurrection of Christ and the general resurrection will, again, require the recapitulation of all in a person, the last Adam, Christ. There cannot be ontological salvation of creation by means of natural qualities without the unity of created nature *in a person*. Paul is explicit on this matter in describing the eschatological event of the Resurrection (1 Cor 15:20–28). Christ's Resurrection is the "first-fruits" (ἀπαρχὴ)[64] of all the dead. Humanity must be involved in this last event and since the first Adam declined to serve this final purpose of creation, it will be through the last Adam (i.e., again through the involvement of humanity) that creation will acquire eternal being. Christ, as divine and human, will be the head of this eschatological mystery, creation will be incorporated in him, and it is only in this way that the whole of creation (τὰ πάντα) will enjoy eternal being, since "God will be all in all." We are again encountering the idea of *anakephalaiosis* (recapitulation) as the only way to the eternal being of creation.

3. The Holy Spirit and the Eschata

The coming and the giving of the Holy Spirit was associated with the "last days" from the beginning. Acts chapter 2 describes the event of Pentecost in eschatological terms by referring to the prophecy of Joel (Joel 3:1–5) and the outpouring of the Spirit in "all flesh" *at the last days,* while the Gospels associate the giving of the Spirit by Christ with his Resurrection (Jn 7:39, 20:22). In a similar manner, Paul speaks of the "earnest of the Spirit" (2 Cor 1:22; Eph 1:14) as a sure pledge of the inheritance of the Kingdom and regards the charisms of the Spirit given to the first communities of the Church as signs of the beginning (ἀπαρχὴ) of our future glory and filiation (Rom 8:23).

---

nothingness into God's very being and by making the Cross the place where God annihilates nothingness "in order to gather that Nothingness into his eternal being" (*God in Creation* [Minneapolis, MN: Fortress Press, 1993], p. 93).

[64] Ἀπαρχὴ could be rendered also with κεφαλὴ as in Eph 1:22; Col 1:18–20, etc. Cf. P. Lamarche, "Κεφαλή," in *Vocabulaire de Théologie Biblique*, ed. X. Leon-Dufour (Paris: Cerf, 1988).

This association of the Spirit with the eschata continues to mark the doctrine of creation in the patristic period. We encounter it in the Apologists of the second century, who connect the giving of the Spirit with the granting of immortality as an eschatological gift,[65] and later on, in St Basil, who assigns to the Holy Spirit the particular work of "perfecting" creation.[66] Perfecting can also be applied to the beginning and the present state of creation, and yet its full and proper meaning is to be found in the eschatological state when the Spirit liberates creation from its servitude to corruption[67] and when it is given as a reward to the righteous.[68] This finds its most explicit expression in St Maximus, who more clearly than any other of the Fathers identifies the Holy Spirit with the Kingdom of God: "Thy kingdom come, that is the Holy Spirit."[69] It is because of its eschatological association that the Spirit came to be specifically connected with *sanctification* (ἁγιασμὸς) in the patristic sources,[70] holiness being an attribute essentially only of God,[71] which will be granted to the saints as grace fully and permanently in his Kingdom as eternal "being together (communion) with God (Θεοῦ συνουσία)"[72] in God's "Sabbath rest," as St Maximus puts it.[73] Holiness is theosis itself, which will be no less than "indivisible identity" with God, stopping just short of the irreducible difference between created and uncreated natures.[74] This holiness is *only partially* (ἐκ μέρους) realized and experienced in this life; it is only the eschata that "will bring the fullness of grace by participation [in God]."[75] *All* forms of sanctification given to creation before the eschata, either in the case of individual saints or, above all, in the sacraments of the Church (Baptism, Chris-

---

[65] Thus, Tatian, *Or.* 13 (PG 6:833B); Irenaeus, *Haer.* III, 24.1 (PG 7:966B).

[66] Basil, *De Spir.* 16 (PG 32:136B). Cf. Cyril Alex., *Thes.* 34 (PG 75:584D).

[67] Basil, *De Spir.* 55 (PG 32:172B).

[68] Ibid., 40:144A.

[69] Maximus, *Or. Dom.* (PG 90:885B).

[70] Origen, *De princ.* 1.3.8 (PG 11:154B); Athanasius, *Ad Serap.* 1.23 (PG 26:584B); Basil, *De Spir.* 3.20 (PG 32:109C); *Epist.* 159; Ibid., 621A.

[71] Basil, *C. Eunom.* III, 2–3 (PG 29:660D).

[72] Gregory Naz., *Carm. moral.* 34 (PG 37:957A); Cf. Basil, *Reg. brev. tract.* 53 (PG 31:1117C).

[73] Maximus, *Cap. theol.* 1.47 (PG 90:1100BC).

[74] Maximus, *Myst.* 13 (PG 91:692CD) and *QThal.* 22 (PG 90:320A).

[75] Maximus, *Cap. theol.* 2 (PG 90:1165BC).

mation, Eucharist, etc.), are foretastes and anticipations of the eschatological state.

The Holy Spirit, therefore, is not absent at the beginning of creation or in the course of its history; he acts together with the Father
and the Son in all the events of the economy. In this respect, we can
talk about the divine energies as creating and sustaining creation.
But besides unity of operation, there is also *specificity* and particularity of mission in the economy, something the Cappadocian fathers
are, as we have seen, especially keen to stress, and this aspect is *not*
covered by a language of energies which are related to the divine essence and to all the persons of the Trinity. In ascribing, therefore, to
the Spirit the mission of perfecting creation, we must seek in it a *particularity, which we cannot find in the work of the other two divine
persons.* Just as we cannot say that the Son or the Spirit initiate the
economy, which is the particular work of the Father, or that the Father and the Spirit assume in themselves creation as the Son does, in
the same way we cannot confuse the Spirit's specific function in creation and the economy with that of the other Trinitarian persons.
The use of the concept of divine energies in the doctrine of creation
is important and necessary, to the extent that it serves the purpose
of indicating simultaneously God's immanence in creation and his
essential transcendence,[76] but if we exhaust our reference to God's
involvement in creation with the use of this concept, as most Orthodox theologians seem to do, we risk losing sight of the specificity of
each divine person's operation in the economy. It is not accidental
that the Cappadocian fathers were eager to speak of the particular
role of each divine person in the economy; they were sensitive to any
Sabellian undermining of personal particularity (just as it is not accidental that some Neo-Palamite theologians, not taking into account the specific context and intention of Palamas, tend to look
with suspicion on any use of personalist concepts in connection with
God's immanence in creation).

In describing the Holy Spirit's role in the economy as that of
perfecting or sanctifying creation or holding it together, we refer to

---

[76] This, and only this, was St Gregory Palamas' intention in using the language of energies. See J. Meyendorff, *The Byzantine Legacy in the Orthodox Church* (Crestwood: St
Vladimir Seminary Press, 1982), pp. 191 and 193.

something not to be applicable to either the Father or the Son. The Father creates the world with his two hands, the Son and the Spirit, to recall St Irenaeus' image. But as Irenaeus himself explains,[77] there is a particular work attached to the Spirit, distinguishable from that of the other two divine persons: the Son "establishes" and "consolidates the being of creation," "recapitulating it in the end of times" in order to "abolish death" and "bring about the communion of God and man"; the Spirit, on the other hand, "disposes and shapes the various powers" of created things, giving them "order" and "in the end of times renews man to God."[78]

It is evident from this that the distinctiveness of each divine person's work in the economy, which we encounter in St Basil, is an idea that goes back to St Irenaeus—and the Bible itself.[79] Applied to eschatology, this distinctiveness can be spelled out as follows:

Creation overcomes the mortality inherent in its nature, due to its having come into being *ex nihilo*, and enjoys ever-being in the eschata by being "recapitulated" in Christ. *Neither the Father nor the Spirit "recapitulate" creation*, because recapitulation involves the human being and, for that reason, requires *incarnation*. Incarnation is a *sine qua non* condition for the ever-being of creation. The entire economy from the beginning to the end is centered on the incarnate Son—this is particularly emphasized by St Maximus—and this means that there is only one economy, that of the Son to the very end. We cannot, therefore, conceive an eschatology in which the Holy Spirit operates in a way unrelated to the incarnate Son. Whatever the Spirit contributes to the eschatological state of creation *serves* the unique economy, that of the incarnate Son. (This is, in fact, the case in all stages of the economy, including the beginning of creation.)

In a cosmology based on or exhausted with the concept of divine energies, the Spirit grants to creatures divine natural qualities common to all three Trinitarian persons, and this is also applied to the eschatological *theosis*. If, however, we take into account the Christocentric character of the entire economy, we have to say no more than

---

[77] Irenaeus, *Dem.* 5–6, trans. J.P. Smith, pp. 50–51 with the important notes on p. 138f.

[78] Irenaeus, *Haer*, III, 24.2 (PG 7:967B). Cf. IV, 20.4. Ibid., 1034 A; IV, 33.15. Ibid., 1083A.

[79] 1 Cor 6:8; Eph 2:18. Cf. Rom 8:15 and Gal 4:6.

that θέωσις *is nothing but* χριστοποίησις; the Spirit does not divinize creatures by uniting them directly with divine *nature* (through the energies) but *by incorporating them into the incarnate Son*. It is not, therefore, sufficient, or even proper, to make the incarnate Son into an *instrument*, a means, through which creatures acquire divine qualities in theosis. Christ is not a means to an end; he is the end of theosis; he assumed creation not in order to inject into it divine qualities—this is the work of *all* the Persons of the Trinity—but to "enhypostasize" creation in his own hypostasis—something appropriate only to him.

The Spirit "perfects" the economy *of Christ*. St Athanasius expresses this in the following words:

> [T]he Spirit is the unction and seal with which the Word anoints and seals all things ... *[I]t pertains to the Word who anoints and seals*. For the unction has the fragrance and odor of him who anoints; and those who are anointed say when they receive thereof: "We are the fragrance of Christ." *The seal is the form of Christ* who seals, and those who are sealed partake of it, *being conformed to it*;[80] as the Apostle says: "My little children, for whom I am again in travail until Christ be formed in you." Being thus sealed, we are duly made, as Peter puts it, "sharers in divine nature"; and thus *all creation partakes of the Word* in the Spirit.[81]

Not only the specific activity of the Spirit (sanctification) but the very idea of theosis, as expressed in the key biblical text of 2 Pet 1:4, is understood by Athanasius as *partaking of the Word*: "sharers in divine nature" means, for St Athanasius, *partakers of Christ*.

The work of the Holy Spirit in theosis is, therefore, to incorporate creation into Christ, to build up the "body of Christ," to bring about the recapitulation of all things (ἡ ἀνακεφαλαίωσις τῶν πάντων) in Christ. This is the Spirit's specific contribution to the economy of Christ. The Spirit is the "power" (Lk 1:35, 4:14, 24:49; Acts 1:8, 10:38; Rom 15:13; Gal 3:5; 2 Tim 1:7) which opens up and transcends the limitations of the creation assumed by Christ, thus *liberating it* (2 Cor 3:17) from its natural boundaries so that it may enter into *com-*

---

[80] Χριστοποίησις.
[81] Athanasius, *Ad Serap.* I, 23 (PG 26:585A); *The Letters of St. Athanasius Concerning the Holy Spirit*, trans. C.R.B. Shaplan (New York: Philosophical Library, 1951), p. 124.

munion (2 Cor 13:13) with the uncreated God. This is the specific activity of the Holy Spirit in the Incarnation itself from the birth of Christ (Mt 1:18) to his earthly ministry (Mt 3:16, 4:1, 12:28; Lk 4:18) and his Resurrection (Rom 8:11). Unlike the Son, the Spirit did not assume the limitations of creation but "indwells" (Rom 8:4) in it always working supernatural events, never submitting himself to the human predicament or to the restrictions of creaturehood.[82] In this sense, it is said that the Spirit "perfects" Christ's economy, bringing the eschata into history and making the future Kingdom an already-foretasted experience.

The Spirit, therefore, cannot be spoken of unqualifiedly as being immanently present in creation; the Spirit *visits* creation whenever he wills (Jn 3:8); he does not "reside" in it as a "cosmic spirit," as Romanticism and German idealist philosophy would suggest. The Spirit is *invoked*; he is not assumed or taken for granted. Any notion of a "cosmic spirit" applied to the third person of the Trinity would put in doubt his personal freedom and lordship and would make a mockery of the *epiclesis*. If there is such a thing as a "cosmic spirit," this should not be identified with the third person of the Trinity. We have to find a way of talking about the Spirit's presence in creation without limiting his personal freedom and transcendence.[83]

An epicletic approach to the Spirit's presence in creation would require an eschatological ontology. Any protological ontology that would refer to the Spirit as being in creation "already" would have to

---

[82] In Moltmann's treatment of the Trinity's involvement in creation (*God in Creation*, pp. 94–103), the centrality of Christ is lost. The Spirit's operations in creation appears to be independent of Christ's work. This is why the *kenosis* of the Son is not sufficient to indicate God's economy in creation, and it becomes necessary to introduce (following Lossky and ultimately Bulgakov) also the *kenosis* of the Spirit (p. 102). But the Spirit *does not* empty himself, since he does not assume creation (without assumption there can be no emptying, in an ontological sense). The Spirit "indwells" in order to enable creation to transcend the limitations assumed by the kenosis of the Son (thus, the virgin birth, temptations, Resurrection, etc.). Had there been an ontological *kenosis* of the Spirit this would have had to involve also his death, as was the case with the Son.

[83] This is the problem with the idea of *panentheism* which is currently receiving attention also in Orthodox theology. A cosmology based exclusively on the doctrine of divine energies may offer support to such an idea, but a more personalist and "hypostatic" conception of creation would inevitably have to qualify any divine presence in the world with the notion of absence (or the paradox of presence-in-absence; cf. below) due to the freedom and transcendence which characterize personhood.

be qualified by the statement, "and not yet." The Spirit is present in history not as a given but as a foretaste of what *will be* given. Creation is not filled with the Spirit as *a fait accompli*, as a divine "immanence," but as an ἀρραβών, an assurance of a future outpouring and indwelling "on every flesh" (Acts 2:18). This "arrabonic"[84] presence of the Spirit in history rules out conceptions of divine immanence in creation that would take the Spirit's presence for granted. The expectation of the future outpouring of the Spirit in creation, the "substance of things not yet seen" (Heb 11:1), leaves room for the freedom of the Spirit and explains the epicletic character of Christian pneumatology.[85] In fact, it is the Spirit's specific function to make the entire economy oriented toward the future (Rev 22:17) and not toward the past, to turn the expectation of the future into the source of presence. It is because the Spirit brings the eschata into history, and not because of some other reason, that we are allowed to speak of his presence in creation. It is for the same reason that we invoke him to come again and again as if he were not here.[86] Without an eschatological ontology, such a paradox would be totally absurd.

4. Creation as Eucharist

The eschatological recapitulation of creation in the person of Christ, through which the universe is sustained in existence, is iconically manifested[87] and foretasted in the Eucharist. Celebrated originally on Sunday, the day of the Resurrection,[88] the Eucharist bore all the characteristics of the eschatological establishment of God's Kingdom: the gathering together of the dispersed people of God and by extension the unity of all creation in the person of Christ, the head of the Church (Col 1:18); the overcoming of all divisions caused by social and natural differences (Mt 19:13, 14:21; Gal 3:11; 1 Cor 11:21,

---

[84] We coin this adjective, borrowing it from Pauline vocabulary, as the best way of indicating the paradox of "already and not yet" implied in the epicletic character of pneumatology.

[85] More on this in chapter five, "Eschatology and Liturgical Time."

[86] See chapter five.

[87] On "iconic" ontology, see the *Introduction* of this book and *Excursus* to this chapter.

[88] See W. Rordorf, *Sunday: The History of the Day of Rest and Worship in the Early Centuries of the Christian Church* (London: SCM Press, 1968), esp. pp. 177ff and 238ff.

13);[89] the "antidote to death"[90] and the experience of immortality;[91] and the offering of all creation to the Father[92] so that he may be "all in all" (1 Cor 15:28).

Thus, there is no higher and fuller form of revelation and "experience" of the eschatological state of creation in history than the Eucharist. All other forms, such as the proclamation of the Kingdom by word or ethics and virtue, lack the presence of creation in the historical anticipation of the eschata, which we find in the Eucharist. This is why the Church, both in the East and in the West, has always regarded the Eucharist as the crowning and ultimate goal of the preaching of the Word[93] and the ascetic and virtuous life.[94]

The advantage of the Eucharist compared with other forms of anticipatory experience of the Kingdom in history lies in its catholicity which embraces the whole creation and not simply the human being. In the Eucharist, human word and deed are included, incorporated, and "recapitulated" in Christ together with the entire cosmos, acquiring in this way an ontological meaning in the fullest sense. The Eucharist in its catholic and cosmic dimension[95] reminds human beings that they are part of creation and that the eschatological Kingdom promised by God in Christ is not meant for humanity alone but for creation in its totality.

At the same time, the Eucharist reveals the central and decisive role the human being is called to play in the ever-being of creation.

---

[89] Cf. my *Being as Communion*, p. 149f.

[90] Ignatius, *Eph.* 20.2 (PG 5:661A).

[91] Irenaeus, *Haer.* III, 19.1 (PG 7:938f).

[92] Irenaeus, *Haer.* IV, 18.4–5 (PG 7:1026F). Cf. IV, 17.5 ibid., 1023C; V, 2.2 ibid., 1125A.

[93] With regard to the preaching of the Word, it is noteworthy that all liturgical traditions in the East as well as in the West, place it *before* the eucharistic service proper. St Maximus in his *Mystagogia* explains this by regarding the preaching of the Word as part of the historical reality which will be superseded by the arrival of the Kingdom signified and foretasted in the Eucharist.

[94] The ascetic life, too, was always regarded in the early Church as culminating in the Eucharist. A characteristic example is found in the life of St Mary of Egypt (fourth and fifth century) who ended a long period of severe ascesis by receiving holy communion. *Vita Mariae Aegyptiae*, attributed to Sophronius of Jerusalem (PG 87:3697–3725).

[95] See notes 89–92 above. Cf. G. Theokritoff, "The Cosmology of the Eucharist," in *Toward an Ecology of Transfiguration*, eds. J. Chryssavgis and B.V. Foltz (New York: Fordham University Press, 2013), pp. 131–135; E. Theokritoff, "Liturgy, Cosmic Worship and Christian Cosmology," ibid., pp. 295–323.

It is only through the human being that creation can be sanctified and anticipate its eschatological survival and glory (Rom 8:23). The human being is the "mouth" through which creation offers thanksgiving and glorification to the Creator.[96] Humanity assumes, in this way in a Christlike manner, the role of the *priest of creation*[97] whose ministry is to unite creation by healing its divisions,[98] which account for its natural decay and mortality, and by referring it back to its Creator as "his own"[99] property and gift which is called to be "divinized" by entering into communion with the Holy Trinity.

This Christological ministry of the human being takes place in the Eucharist epicletically—by the invocation of the Holy Spirit to bring the last days into history as an "already and not yet," a foretaste and an icon of the future Kingdom.[100] This makes the Eucharist the highest historical mode of the presence of all three persons of the Trinity in creation, not simply in the form of transmitting to it their common divine energies but in the distinctiveness of each divine person's activity in the economy. This personal or hypostatic dimension of the divine presence in creation through the Eucharist (the offering of creation to the Father by Christ in the Spirit)[101] is too important to be ignored, as is often the case, in an approach to the Eucharist (and creation) exclusively or primarily with the use of the concept of divine energies.

---

[96] It is the human being that "orders" nature to praise God in the psalms (e.g., Psalm 148. Cf. Daniel chapter 3). Cf. Leontius of Cyprus, *Sermo. c. Jud.* (PG 93:1604B): "Creation does not worship the Maker by itself directly, but through me the heavens declare the glory of God, through me the moon worships God, through me the stars glorify God." By a sort of "poetic license," the liturgical verse sometimes includes references to direct praise of God by nonhuman material creation, but in a strictly theological sense, it is the human being that mediates between material nature and God, acting as a "microcosm and mediator" (See Maximus, *Amb.* [PG 91:1305f]). It is significant that John of Damascus and the Seventh Ecumenical Council make use of Leontius' text.

[97] See my *The Eucharistic Communion and the World* (London: T&T Clark, 2011), pp. 133–141.

[98] Maximus, *Amb.* 41 (PG 91:1305f).

[99] "Thine own of thine own we offer unto Thee." Prayer of Anaphora, Liturgies of Sts Basil and John Chrysostom.

[100] See chapter five, "Eschatology and Liturgical Time."

[101] All ancient eucharistic liturgies are addressed to the Father. This does not mean, however, that the Son and the Spirit are not also recipients of the eucharistic offering. Cf. the twelfth century synodical decision following the theological position of Nicholas of Methone.

IV. Existential Consequences

1. Eschatology and Ecology

The implications of what has been said here for ecology are noteworthy. We can summarize them in the following observations:

a) Creation does not possess the power of eternal survival as part of its nature. Christian ecology cannot accept the view that if created nature is left to itself without human intervention its survival will be secured. The ecological problem cannot be solved with the adoption of some form of pagan naturalism.

b) Creation needs the human being just as much as the human being needs nature in order to survive. Any disjunction between nature and humanity is bound to be catastrophic for both of them.

In the biblical and patristic periods, nature and person formed an unbreakable unity.[102] It was only in certain trends of Greek patristic thought, such as those influenced by Origenism and Evagrianism,[103] that we encounter the view that the ultimate goal of Christian life is to make us "free from all matter." The main patristic tradition in the East, including Gregory Palamas and Hesychastic monasticism, insisted on the importance of the body and matter in our communion with God.

Although the East has never been totally free from Origenist and Evagrian influence, it was mainly in the West that a "denaturalization" of the human being acquired proportions leading to the present ecological crisis. Moltmann, after a detailed discussion of what he calls "the alienation of nature" in modern Western philosophy and science, pleads for the "naturalization of the human being" as the only way to overcome the ecological crisis. The human being "should not see himself initially as subject over against nature ... but

---

[102] Cf. my "Person and Nature in the Theology of St. Maximus the Confessor," in *Knowing the Purpose of Creation through the Resurrection: Proceedings of the Symposium on St Maximus the Confessor, Belgrade, October 18-21, 2012*, ed. M. Vasiljević (Los Angeles: Sebastian Press, 2013), pp. 85–113.

[103] E.g. Evagrius, *Praktikos, Chapters on Prayer*, 119, trans. R.E. Sinkewicz, *Evagrius of Pontus: The Greek Ascetic Corpus* (Oxford: Oxford University Press, 2003), p. 206. Cf. Meyendorff, *The Byzantine Legacy in the Orthodox Church*, p. 185.

he should first of all view himself as the product of nature."[104] Human beings do not *have* bodies; they *are* bodies.[105]

While Moltmann is right in pleading for the "naturalization" of the human being, his underestimation of the importance of humanity for the fulfillment of nature's eschatological destiny appears to be questionable.

We must distinguish between an *anthropocentric* and an *anthropomonistic* conception of creation. As I endeavor to show in this study, the biblical and patristic doctrine of creation reserves for humanity a crucial role in the world and its eschatological state. As it is stated by Paul in the letter to the Romans (8:20–23), creation was made subject to vanity and "groans and travails together" with us eagerly awaiting the revelation of the children of God so that it may be liberated from the servitude of corruption to the freedom of the glory of the children of God. The liberation of creation from corruption in its eschatological state is tied up with the glorious destiny of humanity. Moltmann's statement that "even without human beings, the heavens declare the glory of God"[106] contradicts the view encountered in Greek patristic literature that "creation does not venerate the Creator directly and by itself, but it is through me that the heavens declare the glory of God; through me the moon worships God, through me the stars glorify him, through me the waters and showers of rain, the dew, and all creation venerate God and give him glory."[107]

According to the Greek fathers, the human being is the "microcosm" or "macrocosm" and "mediator"[108] bringing the material world into communion with God, so that the whole creation may be deified in the eschata. It is precisely because the human being is part of nature that it can perform this function. Anthropocentrism is not to be confused with anthropomonism which is indeed unacceptable. The Christian doctrine of creation is better described not as

[104] Moltmann, *God in Creation*, pp. 49ff, esp. p. 51.

[105] Ibid., p. 52.

[106] Ibid., p. 31.

[107] See note 96 above.

[108] Maximus, *Amb.* 41 (PG 91:1305f). Cf. L. Thunberg, *Microcosm and Mediator: The Theological Anthropology of Maximus the Confessor* (Lund: C.W.K. Gleerup, 1965).

"theocentric"[109] but as *Christocentric*, which also implies the indispensable centrality of the human being in creation.

The Christocentric character of cosmology points to a conception of creation as an *open* system which transcends itself both in terms of space and of time. Creation cannot survive if it is closed to itself, without communion with what is not creation.[110] This is why an ontology of creation expressed in terms of nature is inadequate. The idea of "nature" or "substance" denotes a closed and "self-existing" reality, its λόγος being fixed and unchangeable.[111] Only when nature is *modified* can it transcend itself and enter into communion with another nature. This is a lesson from Chalcedonian Christology, as it is interpreted by St Maximus.[112] But this leads us to another ontological category, namely to that of *personhood*, for it is *only the person that can modify a nature*.

Creation needs personhood in order to transcend itself, to modify its nature and survive. Person denotes a τρόπος ὑπάρξεως, a mode of being, which renders nature modifiable and, therefore, relational and thus capable of transcending its limits. It is for this reason that the human being was introduced by God into creation as an *imago Dei*, so that creation may transcend the limits of its nature and reach beyond itself.[113] The human being is the only being in material creation which possesses personhood in the sense of the capacity to transcend the limits of nature and relate it to a reality beyond its boundaries. The refusal of the first Adam to perform this mission for the sake of creation would have condemned creation to succumb

[109] As it is by Moltmann, *God in Creation*, p. 31.
[110] Space and time are relational (see below), which means capable of transcendence, albeit *not by means of their nature*, which is subject to the condition of createdness.
[111] Cf. Maximus, *Amb.* 42 (PG 91:1345AB). Natures possess motion but "not in the sense that a nature could ever leave its own specified limits." H.U. von Balthasar, *Cosmic Liturgy*, trans. B.E. Daley (San Francisco: Ignatius Press, 2003), p. 157.
[112] Maximus, *Amb.* 42 (PG 91:1341D). "Every innovation, to speak generically, has naturally to do with the *mode* (τρόπος) of the innovated thing but not with the logos of nature; because a logos innovated corrupts the nature, as not retaining unadulterated the logos according to which it exists; but the mode innovated, the logos being preserved in its nature, manifests miraculous power." It is by means of this distinction that Maximus is able to interpret Chalcedon's Christology of unity of natures, divine and human, "without division" and yet also "without confusion."
[113] Maximus, *Amb.* 41 (PG 91:1305f).

to the limits and boundaries of its nature had it not been for the "new" or "second" Adam, Christ, who recapitulated creation in his person and led it through the Cross,[114] the death of self-sufficiency, to the Resurrection into new and everlasting life.

Creation, therefore, needs a *priest* who would refer it back to the Creator and make it possible for it to experience eternal life.[115] Christ as the human being *par excellence* acts as the priest of creation, and this is what humanity repeats every time the Church offers the Eucharist. The Eucharist creates, in a unique way, an *ecological ethos* by reminding the human being of its responsibility not only to protect and preserve the material world but also to open it up to eternal life and lead it to its eschatological destiny. Outside an eschatological perspective, however, ecology is meaningless.[116]

2. Eschatology and Natural Science

The personalistic approach employed in this study seems to bear no direct relationship with the interests of natural sciences. Science studies creation's nature and any use of personalistic categories appears to be irrelevant to its concerns. Yet, a more careful consideration of the way physical science approaches and conceives reality in our time reveals what may be described as an implicit use of personalist ideas in much of natural science. The following may serve as illustrations:

a) *The idea of relationality*

With the replacement of a mechanistic view of the world with the principles of modern physics, the idea of relationality has acquired a central place in physical science. As John Polkinghorne observes, "discoveries have been made and insights gained in physical science that have already indicated the need not to rely simply on atomistic accounts and reductive techniques of analysis, but to employ also a complementary approach characterized by holism and

---

[114] Hence creation itself, not just humanity, must go through the Cross. Maximus, *Cap. theol.* 67 (PG 90:1108B): τὰ φαινόμενα πάντα δεῖται σταυροῦ.

[115] See my *The Eucharistic Communion and the World*, pp. 133–141.

[116] Creation must be respected because it is endowed with a destiny that makes it worthy of ever-being.

intrinsic relationality."[117] This understanding of the universe has led to the formation of a truly scientific cosmology and to the possibility of some form of "Grand Unified Theory (GUT)," that is, to the intuitive conviction that there is a coherent structure expressed in the relationships of the physical world. Science now recognizes the substantial degree of relationality manifested, for example, in phenomena such as quantum entanglement[118] and the intimate linking of space, time, and matter (provided by Albert Einstein's theory of relativity) on the cosmic level, while a similar degree of relationality is also acknowledged in the realm of biology.

Relationality, however, is not simply an interesting phenomenon for the satisfaction of the scientist's curiosity; it is vital for the very being of creation and, therefore, of crucial *ontological* significance: if there is no relationality in creation, the unity of its constitutive elements collapses, and the universe ceases to exist. The physicist cannot turn a blind eye to ontology in referring to relationality.

Relationality has a meaning, a purpose, and this is to serve and secure the being of creation. If relationality disappears, the universe collapses. This purpose, however, is not fulfilled if relationality remains simply a *natural* phenomenon. As physical science itself observes, the natural law of entropy leads the universe to dissolution, destruction, and death. Here we see again that nature per se does not possess the means of true and ever-being, although it aims at that through relationality. Natural relationality is *ontologically deficient*; it aims at securing creation's being but, ultimately, lets it succumb to nonbeing.

Relationality is a concept borrowed from personalism. True relationality with an ontological meaning is to be found only in personhood understood not in its traditional Western sense as a center of consciousness but as an identity emerging from and sustained by relationships—a sense resulting from Greek patristic Trinitarian

---

[117] J. Polkinghorne, "The Demise of Democritus" in *The Trinity and an Entangled World*, ed. J. Polkinghorne (Grand Rapids, MI: Eerdmans, 2010), p. 2.

[118] See J. Bub, "The Entangled World: How can it be like that?" in *The Trinity and an Entangled World*, pp. 15–31; A. Zeilinger, "Quantum Physics: Ontology or Epistemology?" Ibid., pp. 32–40: Quantum entities can be found in states where effectively they behave as a single system, so that acting on one has an immediate effect on the others.

theology.[119] Only a person in this sense can express a relationality that gives being (ὑπόστασις) to nature.

If we turn once more to the thought of St Maximus the Confessor, nature is nonexistent if it is not "hypostasized": unhypostasized (ἀνυπόστατος) = nonexistent (ἀνύπαρκτος).[120] This is why everything in creation possesses a "hypostasis"—an identity distinguishing it from other identities without separating it from them, a relational identity.[121]

Hypostasis is a personal category, although not quite identical with that of person.[122] The difference lies in that a person is a hypostasis, an ἴδιον, which is not bound by necessity and can freely hypostasize nature.[123] It is only God and the human being that are hypostases in this personal sense, although the latter only in a "tragic" way, as it is conditioned by the limitations of createdness.[124]

In speaking, therefore, of relationality in creation, we speak of a *relational ontology*,[125] and, in so doing, we cannot help but employ, implicitly or explicitly, personalistic ideas. The relational structure of creation acknowledged by physical science today cannot maintain its ontological meaning if it remains a purely natural phenomenon subject as it is to the dissolution imposed on it by the laws of nature. If creation is to be truly and ontologically relational, it requires a hypostasization and "personalization" of its nature.

b) The Anthropic Cosmological Principle

Physicists John Barrow and Frank Tipler published in 1986 a book with the title *The Anthropic Cosmological Principle*. Although

[119] See my *Being as Communion* and *Communion and Otherness*.
[120] See my "Person and Nature in the Theology of St. Maximus the Confessor," in *Knowing the Purpose of Creation*, pp. 85–113.
[121] A fundamental idea in Maximus' ontology is the distinction between "difference" (διαφορὰ) and "division" (διαίρεσις): the former is constitutive of created relationality, while the latter destroys it. See Thunberg, *Microcosm and Mediator*, pp. 51ff.
[122] Cf. my "Person and Nature in the Theology of St. Maximus the Confessor," p. 91.
[123] Maximus gives the example of the person of Christ, who cannot be called "individual" (ἄτομον) precisely because, in him, "what is natural does not precede what is freely willed." *Pyr.* (PG 91:297D) and *Opusc. Theol.* Ibid., 201D.
[124] Cf. my *The Meaning of Being Human* (Los Angeles: Sebastian Press, 2021).
[125] It is noteworthy that theology and physical science can find a common language in the use of this concept. See Polkinghorne, *The Trinity and an Entangled World*.

the model proposed by the authors has been strongly debated by scientists,[126] certain of the underlying ideas in their proposition can be of significance to theology. In particular, it is important from the perspective of the present study that the human being is recognized as being crucial for the life of the universe. "It is not only that man is adapted to the universe. The universe is adapted to man ... According to this principle, a life-giving factor lies at the center of the whole machinery and design of the world."[127] Such a view of the universe would be basically consonant with Greek patristic cosmological thought.

As we have already noted, the Greek fathers regard the human being as a *sine qua non* condition for explaining the structure of the universe: creation was designed right from the beginning so that the human being might finally arrive to incorporate it in itself and lead it finally to communion with God.[128] The proponents of the Anthropic Principle undermined the dysteleology of previous cosmologists (e.g., Steven Weinberg),[129] and in the spirit of Teilhard de Chardin suggested a connection between physical cosmology and Christian eschatology, thus drawing the attention of Christian theologians, such as Pannenberg, who engaged in positive conversation with representatives of this cosmology.[130] In this way, a dialogue between science and theology seemed to bear promise in spite of strong reservations—even open opposition—from the theological side.[131]

It would be outside the scope of the present study to get involved in the debate concerning this subject. Looking at this discussion from the viewpoint of patristic thought, we cannot but welcome ideas of physical eschatology involving the recognition of a central place for humanity in creation. The way, however, in which the place of humanity in this eschatology is conceived by patristic thought dif-

---

[126] Cf. R. Russell, "Cosmology and Eschatology," p. 568.

[127] J.A. Wheeler, "Forward," in J.D. Barrow and F.J. Tipler, *The Anthropic Cosmological Principle* (Oxford: Oxford University Press, 1986), p. VII.

[128] Maximus, *Amb.* 41 (PG 91:1305f).

[129] Cf. R. Russell, "Cosmology and Eschatology," p. 567.

[130] W. Pannenberg, "Theological Appropriation of Scientific Understandings. Response to Hefner, Wicken, Eaves, and Tipler," *Zygon: Journal of Religion and Science* 24 (1989) 255–271.

[131] See R. Russell, "Cosmology and Eschatology," p. 568.

fers from that of the Anthropic Principle theory, as it does not share with it an understanding of life—and humanity—as *a storage of information*, a form of nonbiologically based memory, continuing into the eternal future.

Patristic eschatology is based on the resurrection of *the body* and of *the material creation*. Instead of placing the importance of humanity for the future of creation in the "intelligence" of the human being, patristic thought seeks it in the unifying of creation through its embodiment in personhood, that is, through the capacity to *transcend* the actual world by transforming without destroying its nature—a capacity to be found in personhood. The human being is a key figure in the passage from the old to the new creation, not because it possesses intelligence but, on the contrary, because it possesses *materiality*, which it is able to transcend and give things which are mortal by nature (ever-) lasting being. The eschatological transformation of creation, therefore, would probably be described more adequately in terms of art, rather than science.

3. Eschatology and Art

God creates like an artist rather than a scientist. The language which the Bible and the Fathers employ in describing the creation of the world by God seems to be borrowed from the building of an edifice (Heb 3:3–4), ordering and furnishing it, so that it may become κόσμος, a well-ordered, beautiful thing (καλόν, Gen 1:31). This was already the way creation was described by Plato in his *Timaeus*, and with the qualification of *creatio ex nihilo*, the same language continued to be used by the patristic authors.[132] It was only in modern times, under scientific influence,[133] that the world came to be conceived mainly as a well-organized and mathematically calculable machine reflecting God's wisdom, that is, the intelligence of the most reasonable of all beings.[134] God the creator came to be understood as a sort of "mathematician" in whose mind all the laws of nature are contained, and whosoever manages to grasp these laws not only knows

---

[132] The Greek fathers prefer the term *ktisis* to describe creation—a word pointing to art rather than science.

[133] Cf. J. Moltmann, *God in Creation*, p. 98.

[134] Ibid., p. 314.

the past and the present but can also foretell the future of creation with full certainty—an eschatology of absolute determinism.

Now, the image of the artist has to be interpreted before it can be used to describe God's creative activity. If we understand the world merely as something corresponding to human handicrafts, we do not necessarily avoid the deistic concept of creation as a machine. This is clearly the case with modern technology, in which the human mind produces machines to which it delegates its own physical activities— just as a deistic God would do with his creation.[135] We also have to exclude any conceptions of art as *aesthetical* achievements provoking pleasure and admiration without implying or expressing the emergence of new, unique identities, i.e., without an ontological significance. If we wish to describe the Christian Creator God as an artist, we have to think of art as, in Paul Valéry's profound observation with regard to music, "the beginning of a world."[136] The kind of artist that would suit the image of the Christian Creator would be neither the artist of the Romantic period, who seeks to elicit meaning, feeling, and "beauty" from a creative relationship between natural beauty and intelligence and understanding,[137] nor of one experimenting with the expression of subjective (or social) human experiences, the impasses and irrationalities of the human condition and life,[138] or the impossibility itself of attaining wholeness or "presence"[139] which have characterized so much of twentieth-century art. The Christian idea of creation can only be expressed by the image of an artist who aims at bringing about an entirely new world and not at eliciting meaning and beauty from what is already in existence.

---

[135] Ibid., p. 316.

[136] Paul Valéry, *Oeuvres*, I, 1957, p. 1327.

[137] Goethe's views on art are characteristic of this approach. Cf. his "Maxims and Reflections" (*Goethes Werke*, vol. XII, 1953, pp. 467–93).

[138] This is the case of the painter Francis Bacon, in our time. See D. Sylvester, *The Brutality of Fact: Interviews with Francis Bacon*, 1975 (reprinted 1987), pp. 8–29: "Man now realizes that he is an accident, that he is a completely futile being, that he has to play out the game without reason."

[139] This is the case of postmodernist art, as described by J.-F. Lyotard, "What is Postmodernism?" *The Postmodern Condition: A Report on Knowledge* (Minneapolis, MN: University of Minnesota Press, 1984), pp. 71–82: "Let us wage a war on totality; let us be witnesses to the unpresentable; let us activate the differences and save the honor of the name."

Although the above observations seem to put limits on the extent to which we can describe God's creative work using the concept of art, there are good reasons for the application of this image as perhaps the most adequate hermeneutical tool in the presentation of the Christian doctrine of creation and its eschatological ontology. Thus:

a) All genuine and really creative art presupposes and implies the intention to produce something new and unique. As Karl Mannheim describes what he calls the "aesthetic space,"[140] a work of art is determined neither by the space of the object ("this slab of marble") nor by the mere experience of the subject, but it has its own "objectivity." A machine or a technological product can be copied and multiplied, but a work of art must remain unique forever—any copy of it constitutes *another* "object," a different identity. God's creation is, in the same way, unique and irreplaceable, and any attempt to copy it is bound to fail.

b) The uniqueness of a work of art is inseparably linked with the uniqueness of the *person of* the artist. There is no art without personhood, without a person who freely creates it. God the Creator is personal, and his creation depends constantly on its personal relationship with him; it is *his*, or it is not at all, just as, for example, Mozart's music cannot be anyone else's work.

c) The most remarkable resemblance between God's creation and a work of art is the artist's *presence* in it in the form of his or her *absence*. This paradox marks every work of creation, whether it is the creation of God or of a human artist. The implications of this ontological paradox are of decisive significance for eschatological ontology.

In the first place, the presence-in-absence paradox confines the personal character of the creator's relation to the work of art. Had the creator been present in a way controllable by our senses, his or her freedom would disappear: "a person whose being we could survey and whose every moment we could anticipate would thereby cease to be a person for us, and where human beings are falsely taken to be existent beings and treated as such, then their personality is treated with contempt."[141] This would also apply to God's presence in cre-

[140] K. Mannheim, *Essays on the Sociology of Knowledge*, ed. P. Kecskemeti (London: Routledge and Kegan Paul, 1952), p. 50f.
[141] W. Pannenberg, *Basic Questions in Theology*, III (London: SCM Press, 1973), p. 112.

ation. There are many signs witnessing and pointing to God's presence in creation (Acts 14:17; Rom 1:20, for example), but none of them is controllable by our senses: the old "cosmological proof" of God's existence loses its weight when God's presence in creation is regarded as a personal presence. In the same way, divine energies and miraculous interventions by God in nature and history, being personal and "enhypostatic" cannot be objectifiable and controllable by human beings.[142]

This having been said, theology cannot be ultimately satisfied with the observation of antinomies.[143] God is at once present and absent in creation, and yet, if we think eschatologically, the future must finally lean on the side of *presence*, for this is required by the nature of revelation as *life* and *love*. God reveals himself in creation clothed in a "cloud of ignorance"; his ultimate will, however, is that we see him "face to face" (1 Cor 13:12), and although this eschatological vision will never reach a satiety and an end, it will nonetheless be a clear *Parousia*, without *apousia*—a presence without absence.[144]

The absence, therefore, of God in creation now is a presence in the sense of the anticipation and foretaste of the eschatological presence, the *Parousia*. All signs indicating God's presence in creation now (divine operations, charisms, holiness, miracles, etc.) are *signs of the Kingdom to come*. We now walk by faith, not by sight (2 Cor 5:7), faith being the "substance of things hoped for" (Heb 11:1). God's presence in creation now is a presence as an "already" and an absence as a "not yet." It is the eschatological Parousia that allows presence to be what it means—a presence without absence, a pure "yes" and not

---

[142] If the divine energies in creation were not personal but simply natural, they would be detectable by science and, in the end, controllable by our wills. It is because of the personal character of the divine presence in creation that the divine energies operate *freely* and not as "a matter of course" (e.g., the miracles of holy relics do not occur automatically but only when God—a Person—freely wills).

[143] The language of antinomies, employed by certain trends in modern Orthodox theology, is helpful in describing historical revelation but ceases to work in an eschatological perspective in which only God's "yes" prevails and God is seen "as he is" (1 Jn 3:2).

[144] Gregory of Nyssa, *Vita Moys.* (PG 44:405BC). As it is pointed out by N. Eubank ("Ineffably Effable: The Pinnacle of Mystical Ascent in Gregory of Nyssa's *De Vita Moysis*," in *International Journal of Systematic Theology*, 16 [2014] 25–41.), the ascent of the soul does not end up in darkness (γνόφῳ) but in the vision of the Tabernacle, which is Christ holding τὰ πάντα together (Col 1:16).

an antinomical "yes and no." "For the Son of God Jesus Christ ... is not one who is Yes and No, but in him is Yes. For all the promises of God in him are Yes, and in him Amen unto the glory of God through us" (2 Cor 1:18–20).[145]

Human creativity is also oriented toward the future from which it receives the confirmation of its ontological uniqueness. A work of art may not be immediately recognized as such, and it may take a long time until it is validated and confirmed as an achievement worthy of eternal survival and "immortality." And like all historical events and human activities, it will be subject to a future hermeneutic and finally to the *last judgment*, which will give it its ultimate ontological confirmation, the eternal survival of itself and its creator (cf. 1 Cor 3:13).[146]

d) Finally, a striking resemblance between God's creation and a work of art is to be found in their transformation from an "old" to a "new" creation. God creates *ex nihilo*, whereas the artist can only create *ex vetere*, i.e., from preexisting matter. When, however, we come to the transition from the original to the eschatological state of God's creation, God, too, renews creation without destroying the old. And yet the passage from the old to the new creation has to go through the Cross,[147] i.e., some kind of death. Creation is "enslaved" to corruption (Rom 8:19–21) and needs to be liberated from its continual process of annihilation inherent in its natural mortality.[148] This "suffering" is creation's passage to eternal life, to its "resurrection," and it is a "suffering" *because* of the eschatological longing (ἀποκαραδοκία) for ever-being, a "cross" that implies already the resurrection and makes sense only because there will be a "resurrection," a future. It is because of this longing for ever-being that was implanted as a τέλος,

---

[145] The context is eschatological, as it is evident from the verses that follow immediately (22–23), speaking of "the earnest of the spirit."

[146] It is important to include in the eschatological destiny of a work of art, not only the work itself but *the person of the artist*, as well. For example, the survival of Mozart's music without the survival of Mozart himself would not be satisfactory ontologically. *Being* (the artist's personal identity, including his or her body) is not exhausted by, or identical with, meaning.

[147] Cf. Maximus, *Cap. theol.* I, 67 (PG 90:1108B).

[148] Moltmann devotes some beautiful pages to this subject in his *God in Creation* (pp. 38–39).

a "purpose," in the original creation and is expressed by the human being that creation presents itself as "material" open to transformation both by God (in his "new creation") and by the artist who creates from it a "new world," in the expression of Paul Valéry. Had it not been for the eschatological orientation of creation, no artistic work claiming eternal meaning would be possible.

Creation *ex vetere*, therefore, must be itself understood eschatologically: it is because the "old" was created with an inherent "longing" for ever-being that the new creation is not a creation *ex nihilo* but *ex vetere*. Both God and the artist create *ex vetere*, drawing from the ἀποκαραδοκία of the future state of creation. Instead of eliciting capacities of nature as in Romantic art (and its Aristotelian ontological background), drawing from the past, art grasps and applies creation longing for a state of existence (the ever-being) that lies *beyond and above its nature*, a supernatural χάρις. Eschatology is the source of creativity. All genuine art, consciously or unconsciously, draws from the faith that "what is corruptible will clothe itself with incorruption and what is mortal will clothe itself with immortality" (1 Cor 15:53).

Conclusions

Creation is by nature mortal; only divine nature is immortal. This means that creation does not possess in its nature the power of eternal survival, of ever-being. Ever-being was not given to creation at the beginning; it is not a natural possession of creation but a supernatural grace to be granted at the end of creation's history.

Creation is endowed with a *dynamic movement* toward this end, i.e., toward ever-being. This movement, however, is *passive* (Maximus); it is not caused by nature itself but by an external factor. This factor is God and, at the same time, creation's union with him, that is, the ever-being which will be given at the end. It is this external factor, the end, that causes the dynamism of creation: *ever-being causes creation's being*; the end causes the history of creation in its entirety, i.e., from the very beginning to the very end of creation's being. It is by looking at the end that we can find the beginning

(Maximus). This is what it means that the dynamism of creation is "passive." *The eschaton acts upon the beginning and constitutes it*; history is moved by its end.

The end of creation that causes its history since its very beginning is, according to the Christian faith, not simply eternal being or union with God (*theosis*) but *incorporation into a certain person (anakephalaiosis)*. This person is the Logos, one person of the Trinity. The union of creation with him is the end for which the world was created (Maximus); this is the specific form that the ever-being of creation will take. Since the end causes the beginning and the process of creation's history, it follows that Christ is the person *for* whom (the end) and also *in* whom and *by* whom (the beginning) the world was created (Col 1:15–17). In other words, the Logos contains in himself all the *logoi* of creation before all ages, because he is the person that will recapitulate creation at the end of all ages. Eschatological recapitulation is identical with the pre-eternal will of the Creator, and it is to this eschatological destiny that creation owes its having come into being. The world was not created because God willed pre-eternally *simply* to create it (this would imply a protological approach to creation), but because he wanted it to be incorporated in his Son, in the end of times—*because of an eschatological reason*. A truly Christian doctrine of creation, therefore, cannot be expressed adequately in the statement "the world was created by God" or simply by "God created the world." God did not create simply a world but a *Christocentric world*, a world embodied in his Son. Speaking ontologically, there is no such entity called "creation" to which Christ is added logically afterwards. *The very definition of "creation" has to include Christ*: creation has a head, and its definition, its ontology, is not possible until its "recapitulation" in this head, Christ, at the end.

Patristic theology, building on St Paul, developed a Logo-centric view of creation very early on. The association of creation with the Logos was so close at the beginning that it took theology some time until it was clarified that the Logos was not part of creation. With the teaching of Nicaea I, the Logos was placed clearly on the level of the uncreated Trinity, but it is significant that this did not lead to a complete dissociation of the Logos doctrine from cosmology. While being by nature uncreated, the Logos continued to be present in creation sustaining it by his personal presence (Athanasius). Creation was still conceived as a Christocentric reality. The concept of creation included, by definition, the Logos, notwithstanding his uncreated nature. A Christless creation was inconceivable.

It was the merit of St Maximus the Confessor to develop this Christocentric cosmology in all its consequences. In a line of thought going back to St Irenaeus, Maximus saw creation as *history*, with a beginning, a process, and an end, and placed Christ not simply at its center but at the beginning, in the process, and at the end of its history. The dynamism of creation which Dionysius the Areopagite conceived in terms of space became in Maximus a movement through time and history toward an eschatological end. Christ guaranteed the being of creation through his Resurrection and its eschatological significance as the recapitulation of all in his person. Without this eschatological recapitulation, the beginning and the process of creation's history remain inconceivable. It is by looking at this end that we can reach the beginning of creation (St Maximus). It is because Christ recapitulates in himself the world eschatologically that he is the "head" of creation from the beginning and the center of creation which sustains it throughout its history.

The Christological approach to the doctrine of creation leads to an ontology which is at once personalist and eschatological. It is personalist because it shows that creation needs a personal presence, the incorporation in a *hypostasis*, in order to exist and overcome its natural mortality. Divine energies in themselves are nonexistent and inoperative without their "hypostasization" in a particular person and cannot sustain creation and secure its being, let alone its ever-being. This hypostasization of the divine energies applies to the involvement of all three persons of the holy Trinity, yet *with a specific role for each of them*: the Father initiates by his "good pleasure" (εὐδοκία) the hypostasization, the Son realizes it in his own hypostasis, and the Spirit perfects it by transcending the limitations of creaturehood and sanctifying it (Basil). Neither the Father nor the Spirit, however, *hypostasize* creation; it is only through the Son and his economy (Incarnation, recapitulation, etc.) that he performs this work. Creation secures its being and ever-being not simply through the presence of divine energies in it (in some form of panentheism) but by *becoming* the "body of Christ"—this must be stressed more than it is normally done even in Orthodox theology. Theosis is nothing but *Christopoiesis*, i.e., the realization of the body of Christ, the Church in her fullness. Theosis is an event of communion, not an individual's "experience" or "quality." It is an *ecclesial* reality in which the whole creation becomes a *Eucharist*, the body of Christ offered to the Father and eternally uniting creation with God.

This approach also leads to an eschatological ontology that involves *history*. Unlike the common operation of the three divine persons through their energies, the person of the Son is involved in creation in a specific way: *he becomes history* by taking upon himself not simply creation but the *history of creation*. This history has a beginning but also an end, a purpose and a destiny. Christ is the beginning of creation because he is its end: he fulfils in himself the pre-eternally-willed-by-God destiny of creation—its ever-being through its participation in the life of the immortal God by being recapitulated in Christ as his body. By taking upon himself creation in its history and making its ever-being evident already in his historical time through his Resurrection and the coming of the Spirit, Christ has given to creation the assurance of its ever-being in the future, the faith that mortality can be overcome and eternal life will prevail. This is the faith by which the Church walks in history (Heb 11:1), sustained and guided by the Holy Spirit, the "earnest" (2 Cor 1:22; Eph 1:14) of the eschatological survival of creation.

By accepting the Resurrection of Christ as the evidence already available now of the final overcoming of creation's mortality, the Church foretastes the eschata in history as an "already and not yet," as a "maranatha" (1 Cor 16:22), an invocation (*epiclesis*) of the coming of the One who has already come, Christ who has already brought immortality into history through his Resurrection and has thus initiated the resurrection of all creation in the future. By proclaiming the apostolic *kerygma* of the Resurrection through the preaching of the Word, by calling to repentance and to leading a life as if the final resurrection has already come (Col 3:1–9) (Christian ethics, according to Paul, draws its justification from eschatology), and by projecting those who have already experienced this in their lives (the saints) as witnesses of such a "proleptic" experience of the eschatological state of creation the Church exists within creation as a sign of the "new creation," of God's Kingdom.

This foretaste of the eschatological state of creation is to be found par excellence in the Church's celebration of the Eucharist. It is there that the eschatological recapitulation of creation as the body of *Christ* takes place in all its dimensions, vertical as well as horizontal, spiritual as well as material, personal and social, and, above all, as the foretaste of immortality and incorruption (Ignatius, Irenaeus), that is as creation's ever-being. Celebrated originally on Sunday, the day of Christ's Resurrection, with joy and gladness (Acts 2:46), the Eucharist feeds the historical life of the Church with the power of the future Kingdom, enabling her to carry the cross of creation's sufferings in history as her own and "transfusing" into the world the hope of a future free from evil and death. Thus "the Church lives in the Eucharist and by the Eucharist" (Florovsky) and becomes the sacrament "for the life of the world" (Schmemann).

All this presupposes the *kerygma* of Christ's Resurrection which, of course, the Church accepts as its foundation. But can this make any sense to those who are not members of the Christian community? Does the eschatological ontology, which results from the faith in Christ's Resurrection and a Christological doctrine of creation, have any meaning and relevance for humanity as a whole?

There are three areas of human life which we have discussed here as being affected by an eschatological ontology: the *ethical*, the *scientific*, and the *artistic*.

The ethical implications of eschatological ontology are extremely significant and extend beyond the subject of creation. With regard to this subject, the most important area affected by eschatological ontology, directly or indirectly, has to do with the present *ecological crisis*. As Moltmann in his *God in Creation* has so amply demonstrated, without a proper doctrine of creation, the ecological crisis cannot be tackled. This crisis is a result of the human being's attitude toward nature and the treatment of it as an "object" rather than as part of humanity's very being. In the perspective of a Christocentric doctrine of creation, such as the one expounded here, creation in all its aspects, material and spiritual, is inconceivable without a personal presence, divine *and* human, which makes it sacred and destined by the Creator to enjoy ever-being. The human being was created not in order to subject nature to humanity's interests but to act as a *priest* of creation, a "microcosm and mediator" (Maximus), and in a Christ-like manner, free it from the bondage of corruption (Rom 8:19–23) inherent in its nature. Eschatological ontology of this kind can increase human sensitivity toward all creation, along with respect for its integrity and responsibility for its fate.

With regard to science, the Christian doctrine of creation appears to raise a number of difficulties and problems. Physical science studies the laws of nature and seems to provide little room for personalistic approaches to cosmology, such as those required by a Christological doctrine of creation and eschatological ontology. And yet, the employment by modern physics of the language of *relationality* as a way of understanding the universe implicitly offers the possibility of an interpretation of the laws of the physical world with categories similar to those used in Trinitarian theology to describe personal relationships and may be called a *relational ontology*. This, of course, does not lead directly to a personalist view of creation, but it bears potential for further exploration.

With reference to eschatology in particular, attempts have been made to reach a convergence between theological and scientific views (by Pannenberg, Tipler, and others), but the gap still remains between the two sides. A great deal depends on whether scientists can agree on the question of the future of the universe and, consequently, whether they can talk at all about an eschatological ever-being of creation. From the patristic point of view we have presented here, which coincides with that of physical science, the *nature* of the universe is mortal, and this would suggest that it will naturally have an end. The overcoming of mortality can only come from a *personal* intervention from outside creation, which takes us away from a study of creation's nature and, therefore, away from science in the strict sense.

The Christian doctrine of creation and its eschatological aspect may be better expressed with the language of *art* rather than science. God creates as an artist rather than a scientist. Creation is traditionally described as *ktisis*, the building and ordering of something, and this makes art an appropriate hermeneutical tool for theology. Art, in its sense of creating something new and personal out of what is common and impersonal and not as simply copying nature or eliciting its qualities, resembles God's creative work in at least two ways: it is a *unique* work bearing the *personal* seal of the Creator, and it bears the *presence* of the Creator, albeit in the form of *absence*. There is, of course, a major difference between God and a human artist in that the former creates *ex nihilo* and the latter *ex vetere*. And yet, when we come to the idea of new creation, which is what eschatology is about, the resemblance is evident: God, too, brings about a new creation *ex vetere*, i.e., without destroying the old one.

From the point of view of eschatological ontology, art reveals nature's capacity for *transfiguration, transformation*, or *modification* and its "longing" for liberation from the futility and corruption to which it is subject. The artist grasps this and tries to create something eternal out of a temporal and perishable reality. Art reveals that creation in its historical existence lacks ever-being and perfection, and it is only by a *personal* intervention that the present world can reach eternal life.

"Creation groans and travails together [with us] in pain" in eager expectation "that it, too, may be liberated from the bondage of corruption in the glorious liberty of the children of God" (Rom 8:18–21). A Christian doctrine of creation is inconceivable without eschatology. The "blessed end" for which everything was created is nothing but the incorporation and recapitulation of all in Christ (St Maximus). All three persons of the Trinity are involved in the realization of this "end" through their uncreated energies, but it is only the Son that "hypostasizes" and "recapitulates" creation bringing it into the life of the Holy Trinity as *his body*. Theosis as creation's "participation in divine nature" (2 Pet 1:4) passes through this "body of Christ"; it is essentially eucharistic and ecclesial (cf. Col 1:18).

Excursus: **Historization of the Eschaton: The Significance of Iconic Ontology**

History must be eschatologized in order to acquire being: its events are subject to death unless they acquire a future; they are "being-unto-death." This eschatologization, however, does not lead to an identification of history with the eschata. The first Christians "experienced" the Kingdom while they were still waiting eagerly for its arrival. Oscar Cullmann coined the phrase "already and not yet".[149] We have described this in our Introduction as an "epiphany" and a "visit" of the future into the present, a "coming" which is "experienced" as an "expectation" and an "expectation" as something already "tasted" and present here and now.

But what sort of ontology does this imply? How can something "be" and at the same time "not be" there? The description of this ontology in terms of "paradox" does not lead us beyond the sheer statement of the problem. It does not say anything more than a statement of fact. We need an ontology different from the one provided by classical Greek thought. This is what we could call an *iconic ontology*.

Ontology has been associated with the mind and thought ever since its inception. If we regard the Presocratic philosophers as the initiators of the notion of *being*, the way to grasp being is no other than *thought*: "Thought and being are one and the same," wrote Parmenides. "Thought and that for which thought exists are one and the same," he continued.[150] And yet classical Greek thought was at the same time profoundly aesthetical. Its source and inspiration came from the observation of the world. For the ancient Greeks, seeing was believing. It is noteworthy that the term *idea*, which is so fundamental to ancient Greek philosophy, derives from the verb *to see* (the aorist of βλέπω, εἶδον, ἰδεῖν). Unlike Hebrew thought, which was based on hearing and, therefore, on oral transmission, the ancient Greeks associated truth with vision and observation of reality, particularly that of nature. Nature as *physis*—a reality dynamic and observable in its beauty and harmony as a manifestation of the *cosmos*—came to be regarded as almost identical with *ousia*, the ontological notion *par excellence*.

All this would lead to the conclusion that the idea of εἰκὼν is basically a Greek idea and a stranger to Hebrew and biblical thought. Such a conclusion would make sense in view of the prohibition of images and artistic representations of God in the Old Testament.

---

[149] See Oscar Cullmann, *Christ and Time*, trans. F. V. Filson (Philadelphia: Westminster Press, 1950), p. 146.

[150] Parmenides, *Frgm.* 5d,7.

And yet vision seems to play a central role in the Bible itself. We encounter it in the prophets, particularly in Isaiah, and in the later apocalyptic literature, notably in Daniel and in the New Testament in the book of the Apocalypse. It also seems to be central in the Gospel of St John and in Paul. Before ruling out the idea of *eikon* in Christian thought, we should try to understand how this idea is presented in the Bible and the early Christian writings and compare it with its classical Greek equivalent. This would help us appreciate the possibility as well as the content of what we may call an iconic ontology.

1. *Greek and Biblical Views of Eikon:*
A Comparative Examination

If we tried to compare the classical Greek with the Christian use of vision in its relation to truth, the following observations would have to be made:

1. For classical Greek thought, all visions of truth refer to an already existing reality, whereas the biblical and Christian understanding of *eikon* is always directed toward the future. For the Greeks, an *eikon* is always a *mimesis*, a copy of something that already exists, and for this reason, it is a *shadow* of the past, of something that has already existed in its perfection before it came to be depicted and represented. For the biblical and early Christian view, the *eikon* is a vision of the *eschata*, a foretaste of what is to come. Its truth does not derive from the past but from the future.

2. For classical Greek thought, an *eikon* can never acquire an ontological content in history. Transience and change cannot guarantee truth. A certain escape from history is always necessary in order for an *eikon* to relate to its truth. This escape from history takes place through the *mind*, a process leading to the identification of being with thought in the philosophy of the Presocratics, as we noted at the beginning, and in classical Greek thought in its entirety. Christian thought, on the contrary, attaches great significance to history. "The Word *has* become flesh and dwelt amongst us, and we have seen his glory," writes St John (1:14). The Resurrection of Christ is a historical reality, like his Incarnation, and this makes truth rooted deeply in history. It is not by an escape from history through the mind or otherwise that we can see the *eschata*, but in and through

history. *Eikon* signifies a representation of the eschatological reality with material taken from history, from *historical events*. In other words, *eikon*, in the Christian sense, is a representation of *events* rather than natural realities.

3. In classical Greek thought, the vision of truth is a matter of the individual's contemplation, whereas in Christianity, it is the experience of a *community*. Truth does not reveal itself except in the context of a community in the Christian experience—something that would sound strange to the ancient Greek mind. Moreover, what one sees in an *eikon*, the content of one's vision, is never an individual thing but a complex of interrelated beings. Seeing God means seeing the Trinity, the thrice Holy One in the vision of Isaiah (6:3), the Christian rendering of which was always related to the Holy Trinity. It also means seeing the Kingdom of God with the community of saints, as we note in the vision of Daniel or that of the Apocalypse.

These three characteristics, namely eschatology, history, and communion (or community) mark the difference between the classical Greek and the biblical and Christian understanding of *eikon* and can lead us to a definition of iconic ontology from a Christian theological perspective.

2. *Eikon and Being*

What does it mean to exist iconically? The question may sound artificial, but it entails fundamental ontological issues. Let us look at these in the light of Christian theology.

1. To exist iconically means, in the first place, to have a *face*, a *prosōpon*. Having a face—to recall Levinas—implies that your being is *other than* the one facing you, that you exist *vis-à-vis* (the root of this term is in itself significant) someone. This means that your being involves *communion and otherness* simultaneously. You are "other" because you are *seen* to be so by someone other than yourself. Should the other who sees you disappear, your being would cease to have a face because you wouldn't be confirmed as other; your iconic existence guarantees your otherness, that is, your being yourself and not someone or something else—in other words, your true ontology (if

ontology is understood as the assertion of being not in general but in the particularity of a concrete being).

This way of speaking about being is by no means foreign to patristic thought. We encounter it in patristic references to biblical texts which speak of the Son as the *eikon* of the Father (e.g., Col 1:15; Jn 1:18, 14:9; Rom 8:29; 2 Cor 4:4–5; Heb 1:3). The most striking of such patristic references is to be found in St Athanasius. It is worth quoting and commenting on it.

> [Without the Son,] the perfectness and fulness of the Father's *ousia* is depleted [or eliminated = ἀφαιρεῖται], and the error of the heresy is revealed even more if one remembers that the Son is the *eikon* and offspring of the Father, and his seal (χαρακτὴρ) and the truth (ἀλήθεια).... For if the Son did not exist before he was born, there was not always the truth in God. But it is not permitted to say this. For as long as the Father existed, truth was always in him, and this truth is none else but his Son who says "I am the Truth"; and as long as the hypostasis existed, immediately one must admit its character and *eikon*. For the *eikon* is not created from outside him, but he himself generates it, *in which seeing himself rejoices*, as the Son himself says: "It was me in whom he rejoiced" (Prov. 8:30). *When, therefore, was it that the Father did not see himself in his own eikon?* Was the *eikon* created out of nothing, and the Father was not rejoicing before the *eikon* was made? And how could the Creator see himself in a created and made substance? The *eikon* must be such as the Father of it is.[151]

The importance of this passage for our purpose here lies in the idea expressed so clearly in it that God the Father cannot exist without his *eikon*, and that it is in his *eikon* that he sees his truth (ἀλήθεια). Given that the Son is other than the Father, yet in unbreakable communion with him, the very being of God is conditioned by an iconic ontology. It is noteworthy that the verb *to see* plays such an ontological role in Athanasius' thought. Without the Son as the *eikon* in whom the Father sees himself, the Father's substance is depleted and his truth disappears. Truth and *eikon* coincide; they are not ontologically opposite to each other.

---

[151] Athanasius, *Contra Arianos* I, 20–21.

2. Now, if the Son is the *eikon* of the Father, does it follow that the Father is also the *eikon* of the Son? If we are left with the observations we made in the previous paragraph, we shall have to answer this question in the affirmative. Indeed, a depiction of the Trinity in the Rublev style, or a "persons in communion" Trinitarian theology, would suggest that every person is an *eikon* of the other as if there were no causality in God. Yet nowhere in the tradition is the Father called the *eikon* of the Son. This immediately introduces a differentiating nuance in the ontological significance of *eikon* in relation to truth. *Eikon* and truth are identical in substance, but the truth of the *eikon* is a *derived* truth. An *eikon* always presupposes a prototype, something or someone from whom it originates. Iconic existence is an ontologically dependent existence, an existence *caused* by a prototype. This causation does not have to be temporal or to imply a qualitative evaluation, something excluded in the case of God's being. Yet the very fact that you cannot reverse the iconic character of the Son and apply it also to the Father shows that iconic existence is inconceivable without some kind of *causation* or scale of existence (cf. Jn 14:28: "The Father is greater than I"). Athanasius, being preoccupied with the task of proving the Son's consubstantiality with the Father, did not engage in a discussion of this point. It was the Cappadocians that were called to do that. And they did that by introducing the concept of *cause* and by applying it to the *personal* existence of God and not to his substance. This means that iconic existence is a *personal existence* and is not applicable to substance. This is of capital importance, as we shall see immediately by looking briefly at the controversy concerning the sacred images or icons in the eighth and ninth centuries.

3. The theological discussions at the time of the Iconoclastic controversy do not concern us directly here except in so far as they touch upon the subject of iconic ontology. Indeed, this subject was not left out of the discussions. We can find interesting material in authors such as St John of Damascus and, particularly, Theodore the Studite. St John of Damascus defines *eikon* as identical, in all respects, with the archetype with a certain difference which, in the case of the Trinity, he specifies as referring to causation.

The *eikon* is not in all respects identical with the archetype. The Son is the living *eikon* ... of the invisible God, carrying in himself the whole Father, and being identical with him in all respects *except his being caused* ... For the Father is not from the Son but the Son is from the Father, since it is from him, albeit not after him, that he has his being (τὸ εἶναι).[152]

St Theodore the Studite is even more explicit and instructive concerning the attachment of the notion of *eikon* to personhood and not to substance.

Of everyone presented in *eikon* (εἰκονιζομένου) *it is not the nature but the hypostasis that is imaged.* For how can nature be imaged if it is not seen in a hypostasis? ... Therefore, Christ is describable according to his hypostasis, although he is indescribable in his divinity.[153]

This allows Theodore to state: "The *eikon* of Christ is not something else (ἄλλο) than Christ, in spite of the difference of substance (οὐκ ἄλλο τί ἐστιν ἡ Χριστοῦ εἰκών, ἢ Χριστός, παρὰ τὸ τῆς οὐσίας δηλαδὴ διάφορον)."[154] This he relates to the "face" as characteristic of the person:

How can you not observe the identity of veneration between Christ and his *eikon*[?] ... For it is known to all that none in someone else's face (ὄψιν), for example of Thomas, may behold another one's face (ὄψιν), for example, Luke's.... If that is true, whosoever has seen the *eikon* of Christ, he has seen in it Christ.[155]

Theodore's point is extremely profound: unless we are able to distinguish clearly between person and nature we cannot work out an iconic ontology. Equally, if we are able to distinguish between these two, we are obliged to arrive at such an ontology. This is so because, as Theodore states elsewhere, "the relationship between the archetype and its image is according to being (κατὰ τὸ εἶναι). Hence the one is not separated from the other except by the difference of substance."[156]

---

[152] John of Damascus, *De Imag.* 1.9 (PG 94:1240).
[153] Theodore the Studite, *Antirrheticus* III, 1.33 (PG 99:405).
[154] Theodore the Studite, *Antirrheticus* III, 2.10 (PG 99:425).
[155] Ibid.
[156] Theodore the Studite, *Antirrheticus* III, 2.9 (PG 99:424).

If we leave aside the problem of the veneration of images which may present difficulties to some of us, Theodore's argument can illustrate well the ontological content of *eikon*. Following this argument, we must conclude that if there is truth in iconic existence and we are not talking about fantasy, although *eikon* and truth are not to be fully identified, this can make sense *only if personal existence is not totally dependent on natural existence.* Is it conceivable that we can exist as persons without existing at the same time as natures?

By raising this question, we touch upon the most profound paradox of our existence as persons. Person and nature do not coincide harmoniously in human existence, as they do in God's being. Unlike God, we are preceded by nature, as we are born in accordance with its laws given to us and including, among other restrictions to our freedom, the bondage of mortality. Personhood finds these laws of nature to be provocative to its freedom, particularly if freedom is expressed and realized as love. We do not want those whom we love to be separated from us by the laws of nature, be it space and time or, finally, death. Only those who do not truly love somehow manage to reconcile themselves with the laws of nature. Throughout all ages, the human being strives to surpass and overcome nature's restrictions on its relations of love. Is this mere wishful thinking on man's part, or is it possible to speak of this tendency of the human being in terms of ontology? The answer to this question is not unrelated to what we call here iconic ontology.

If the *eikon* is to be defined as a personal presence without natural presence, the question arises whether there can be such a presence at all. If ontology is to be based on a Heideggerian "being-unto-death," it is hardly possible to work out an ontology on that basis. If, however, we are prepared to accept that there is in our existence such a thing as "presence-in-absence," then we shall come very close to an iconic ontology. I have tried to develop the theme of "presence-in-absence" elsewhere,[157] and I can only repeat here the conclusion that if there is any reality and truth in such things as creativity and art (in their genuine sense), it is only through an ontology of "presence-in-absence" that this can be comprehended. If the artist is in any sense

---

[157] Cf. my *The Meaning of Being Human* (Los Angeles: Sebastian Press. 2021).

at all present in his or her creation—a creation bearing their personal character and identity—it is only through his or her absence that this is realized. If there is no such presence at all, then the logical positivists and the empiricists have won the day in philosophy, and we can only attach reality and truth to what nature presents us as given data. The choice is ours, but our existence will remain to a large extent totally inexplicable if we limit its truth to what nature presents us with. We are not pure or mere nature, or else we are not human beings. If there is such a thing as an ontology of personhood, then there must also be a personal presence that does not depend on nature, and which, for this reason, is realized in the form of absence. I take Theodore the Studite's ontology of the icon as moving along such lines as these. If the icon involves a presence of hypostasis without the presence of nature, then we are talking, it seems to me, of a "presence-in-absence" ontology. Iconic ontology must be understood in that spirit.

4. By following this line of thought, we come close to another aspect of iconic ontology, namely the *eschatological* nature of the *eikon* to which we referred earlier. The attachment of truth to the future can only make sense if the person frees itself from nature, albeit, as a rule, by paying a cost. The ancient Greeks had no place in their philosophy for the idea of hope. This was consequent upon their ontology which was based on the past and which saw everything in existence as being caused by a preexisting reality almost by necessity. On the contrary, the Bible insisted that there is truth in the future and that it is this that "causes" whatever is true in time and history. The letter to the Hebrews (11:1) contains the extraordinary statement that "faith is the subsistence (ὑπόστασις = reality) of things hoped for." This points to an eschatological ontology which cannot be explained if nature, with its given laws, forms the basis of our concept of truth. It is again only if we employ the idea of personhood that we can make sense of this biblical statement. This is why the whole idea is described as "faith." Faith is nothing but the freedom of the person to accept and assert as true that which is not verified by the senses ("acceptance of things not seen"), i.e., which is not naturally present.

One could understand this faith as a reality which is expected to come but has not yet come. Such an understanding would rule out the possibility of an iconic ontology. There would be no room in this case for a presence of the future, not even in the form of absence. The present, in this case, would bear a relationship with the expected future only *psychologically*, not ontologically. Faith would be, in this case, a psychological experience, a confidence and trust that God's promises will be fulfilled in the future. No need in such a case to represent the future or depict it in any way; the entire present is filled with the psychological expectation of the future.

Such a replacement of ontology by psychology makes it difficult to fill the present with reality and leaves us with the psychological experiences of the individual as the only truth we possess in the present. Since we cannot exist only by psychology—which is also always vulnerable to the accusation of subjectivism—we seek the content by which to fill the present in what we have inherited from the past, such as the institutions transmitted to us through history, or the "word of God" that we have inherited again from the past in the form of Scripture. We thus employ, albeit unconsciously, the Greek ontology based on the past, which the Bible has rejected. Iconic ontology remains, in this case, a mystery and a paradox.

Iconic ontology means precisely the filling of the present with reality borrowed or drawn from the future. If this is not to remain a mere psychological experience of the individual, it will have to have certain characteristics which will protect it from falling into subjectivism. These would include:

(a) *Artistic creativity.* This is essential in order to fill with eschatological meaning the present world, including the natural world in which we exist in the present. Iconic ontology requires a creativity like this through which the eschata will open up the present world to what the world will be finally in the Kingdom. The artist, in this case, will apply the vision of the Kingdom to all aspects of our present-day life, using matter as a means of transforming the world through the entrance of the last days into history. This kind of art cannot be a faithful reproduction of past realities, even if it be realities of sacred history. The historical events have to be somehow "eschatologized," or transformed in the light of the Kingdom. It is only in this way that they can acquire the characteristics of iconic ontology.

(b) *The context of community.* Iconic ontology is by definition an *ecclesial* matter. This is because it is meant to fill the present with eschatological realities, which, again by definition, are communal in character. This would affect artistic creativity by making it *liturgical* in both form and matter. It will also lead to ecclesial structures, ministries, and forms of Church life, above all sacramental life, which will be thoroughly marked with iconic ontology.

Chapter Three

ESCHATOLOGY AND THE FALL

I. Fall from What?

The traditional presentation of the doctrine of the fall is markedly protological. It presupposes an original state of perfection from which the human being deviated, "falling" to a lower kind of existence dominated by moral and natural evil, such as sin, suffering, decay, and death. The Bible appears, at first sight, to offer support to this view, since according to the story of creation, after creating the world, God looked at it and found it to be "very good" (Gen 1:31). Everything was perfect at the beginning. The human being existed in a state of moral and natural perfection in "paradise," which it lost owing to its disobedience to God's commandment.

The view of an ideal and perfect original state of the world and the human being was not unknown to the ancient world outside the Bible; in fact, it was predominant in it. Hesiod in his *Works and Days*[1] provided the myth of a Golden Age to which later Greek and Latin poets would return again and again, and which Plato would use extensively in his *Politics*.[2] According to Plato, in the original state of the world, the gods reigned over the entire cosmos, the climate of the earth was always temperate, men lived on fruit, and there were no men or women or children because they were all reborn from the earth. Orphism speaks of a primordial Eros or *Protogonos* or *Phanes* (light) whom the Neoplatonist Proclus calls the god of the beginning of things and, at the same time, of the race of gold (cf. Hesiod), creation and the golden age of happiness coinciding. In Orphism, evil is the legacy of the event of Dionysus' murder by the Titans when the human soul experienced the brutal descent into a

---

[1] *Works and Days*, trans. A.E. Stallings (London: Penguin Books, 2018), line 109ff.
[2] Plato, *Politics* 271C–272.

body and its imprisonment in it. This is the original sin of the fall of humankind.[3] It is this idea of the fall of the soul that lies behind the anthropology of Plato, the Neoplatonists, and Origen. Gnosticism also extensively used the idea of the fall, although, unlike Genesis, it placed it at the same time, or even before, the creation of the world.[4]

The idea that human beings experienced at the beginning of their existence a "golden age" or a "paradise," in which there was no suffering or evil of any kind, appears to be incompatible with the scientific findings of our time.[5] The appearance of *homo sapiens* took place in the midst and as a consequence of a fierce struggle of survival among the various species, involving them in suffering and death. Death, both as a result of killing and a matter of senescence, was already there when the human being appeared; it was not introduced at the fall.

Commentators of the Old Testament in the past used to take an apologetic attitude by dismissing as insignificant and "without scientific ground" the view of natural historians that the original state of creation was not free from suffering and evil. Commenting on the creation narrative of Genesis, they would insist that "the fact which now prevails universally in nature and the order of the world, the violent and often painful destruction of life, is not a primary law of nature ... but entered the world along with death at the fall of man, and became a necessity of nature through the curse of sin."[6] More recent biblical scholarship, however, has presented the biblical narrative of creation and the fall in a way that does not necessitate a conflict with scientific findings. The following observations by recent scholarship are of particular importance:

[3] See Paul Ricoeur, *La symbolique du mal* (Paris: Aubier, 1960), pp. 264–279.
[4] H. Jonas, *The Gnostic Religion* (Boston: Beacon Press, 1963).
[5] "In modern times the whole concept of the Fall has often been rejected as inconsistent with the facts of man's development known to science, especially with evolution." *The Oxford Dictionary of the Christian Church* (Oxford: Oxford University Press, 1997), p. 597. Likewise, John Polkinghorne, *Reason and Reality* (London: S.P.C.K., 1991), p. 72 and A. Peacocke, *Theology for a Scientific Age* (Minneapolis, MN: Fortress Press, 1993), pp. 222–223.
[6] C.F. Keil and F. Delitzch, *Commentary on the Old Testament*, vol. I (T&T Clark, 1866–1891; repr. 2001), p. 40f. More recently, F.A. Schaeffer, *Genesis in Space and Time* (Downers Grove, IL: InterVarsity Press, 1973), pp. 62, 64, and 95.

1. The narrative of Genesis 2–3 comprises a unity. One cannot reduce it to a "before" and an "after" the fall. Both parts of the narrative form together the "primordial event" which lies on the other side of history.[7] To split it into two parts and conclude that it speaks of an "original" and a post-fallen state is to distort its meaning and intention.

2. The idea of a "fall" as something passive, fateful, and transmissible to all of humanity appears only in the apocryphal book of 2 Esdras in the first century AD and, taken in this sense, it is absent from the story of Genesis. "The narrative of Genesis 2–3 does not speak of a fall."[8]

3. The original narrative of the fall reflects the conditions of the Jewish people when the Yahwist document was edited under the impact of the Babylonian exile. It "elevates to the level of exemplary and universal history the penitential experience of one particular people," and, therefore, "all later speculations about the supernatural perfection of Adam before the [f]all are advertitious interpretations that profoundly alter the original meaning; they tend to make Adam a superior being and so foreign to our own condition. Hence the confusion over the idea of the [f]all."[9]

4. It is noteworthy that the story of the fall never appears elsewhere in the Old Testament. It is also surprising to see how little Adam figures in the other books of the Old Testament. The Apocrypha, on the whole, do not seem to have a very exalted idea of the original state of Adam and Eve. It was the rabbinic tradition that developed a lofty view of original humanity. And when we come to the Gospels we are struck by the absence of any reference to the prefallen state of the human race. Only Paul seems to refer to Adam's disobedience (Rom 5:12–21), but his interest is not so much in the first as in the last Adam, Christ. Paul in this text exalts the state of grace offered in Christ far more and higher than the original state of Adam (Rom 5:15–17, 20–21). The intention and purpose behind this

[7] See Claus Westermann, *Genesis*, trans. J.-J. Scullion (Minneapolis, MN: Augsburg, 1984), pp. 20f.; 276f.

[8] Ibid., p. 276.

[9] Paul Ricoeur, "Evil," *Encyclopedia of Religion*, vol V, ed. Mircea Eliade (New York: MacMillan 1987), p. 202.

text, on which so much of the Augustinian theology of the fall was constructed, is eschatological rather that protological. Its aim is to speak of the last rather that the first Adam.

5. We must take into consideration the nuances that the expression "good" or "very good" bear in their Hebrew original, as these are pointed out by Claus Westermann in his Commentary on Genesis. "In any case," he writes, "'good' is not to be understood as indicating some fixed quality; the meaning is rather functional: 'good for....' The world that God created and devised as good is the world in which *history can begin and reach its goal and so fulfil the purpose of creation* [emphasis added] ... The Hebrew does not contemplate the sheer beauty of what exists prescinding from the function of what is contemplated."[10] This comment helps us to place the narrative of creation and the fall in an eschatological perspective; in declaring it to be "very good," God had in mind creation as it *will* be in the end rather than as it then was. God creates "complete" and "final" things.

6. Neither of the texts referring to death as a consequence of Adam and Eve's disobedience (Gen 2:17, 3:19) suggests necessarily that death did not exist before the disobedience. Both of them may be understood in the sense of a realization of what was already there due to creaturehood, which the human beings could have avoided if they had obeyed God. This would be supported also by the original mythology, which the biblical author must have had in mind and transformed[11] and whose central point is that humans were expelled from paradise precisely because they attempted to obtain immortality that only the gods enjoyed.

The patristic evidence seems to split in two directions, one attaching perfection to the beginning and the other to the end of the world's history.

To begin with, there is no reference to the fall in the Apostolic Fathers, the *Didache, I Clement*, Ignatius of Antioch, or the Letter of Barnabas. Even in *Hermas*, who speaks extensively about penance and the connection between sin and death,[12] the idea of the fall is

[10] Westermann, *Genesis*, p. 165f.
[11] See H. Gunkel, *Genesis*, trans. M.E. Biddle (Macon, GA: Mercer University Press, 1997), pp. 37–39.
[12] Hermas, *Pastor*, vis 1.18.

absent. This silence is noteworthy. It is with the Apologists that the subject of the fall reappears, but it is very instructive to note the perspective in which it is placed by them.

Justin mentions the disobedience of Adam and Eve,[13] but he uses the word "fall" (πτῶσις) only for the demons, symbolized by the serpent. The demons "fell," Adam and Eve "disobeyed," and all those who disobey God's commandments "are like Adam and Eve" (ἐξομοιούμενοι)—no inheritance or transmission of sin is implied. And what is more significant is that *the perspective is eschatological*: the disobedience of the first human being had no other result but the loss of the future *theosis* and immortality. Human beings were deprived not of what they already possessed but of what they would have obtained had they not disobeyed, namely *theosis* (θεοὶ γενέσθαι).

The same eschatological perspective with regard to the original state of humanity is encountered in the rest of the second century patristic authors. Tatian openly denies the immortality of the soul and makes its survival dependent on the operation of the Spirit,[14] while Theophilus of Antioch takes a middle position, teaching that human beings were created neither immortal nor mortal but capable of immortality and deification in the future, if they would keep the commandments.[15] Athenagoras joins Theophilus[16] in regarding the future resurrection as *the cause* of creation, reminding us of St Maximus' similar position:

> The cause of [humanity's] creation guarantees (πιστοῦται) the ever-lastingness [of it], while the ever-lastingness [guarantees] the resurrection, without which humanity could not persevere ... *The resurrection demonstrates the cause of creation* and the mind (γνώμην) of the Creator.[17]

This orientation toward the future final state of humanity marks also the entire teaching of St Irenaeus. For this father, human nature *per se* is nothing but animalhood. It is the Spirit that makes the human being truly human, and this is an eschatological gift:

[13] Justin, *Dial.* 124.
[14] Tatian, *Adv. Graec.* 13; cf. 7.
[15] Theophilus, *Ad Autol.* 2.27.
[16] Ibid., 2.14.
[17] Athenagoras, *De resur.* 13.

[T]he man is rendered spiritual and perfect because of the pouring of the Spirit, and this is he who was made in the image and likeness of God. But if the Spirit be wanting to the souls, he who is such is indeed an *animal nature*, and being left carnal, shall be an imperfect being.[18]

Adam in his fall is *typus futuris*. Irenaeus reads Genesis christologically and his anthropology is inseparable from the idea of *theosis*;[19] humanity cannot be seen as sinful except in the light of the One who is without sin.[20] Adam fell from the state of *theosis*, to which he was called, not from an original state, which for Irenaeus was that of a child whose perfection was to come later.[21] The perfect human being for Irenaeus is Christ, the last Adam.[22] Even the fall, including death, was seen by Irenaeus as part of the divine plan to lead Adam to maturity: God allowed that humanity should pass through all kinds of situations and that it should know death so *that it may come to the resurrection* from the dead, and understand by its experience from what evil it has been delivered.[23] The fall makes sense, therefore, only if placed in an eschatological perspective. For Irenaeus, "the Saviour does not exist because there are humans to be saved. On the contrary, there are humans to be saved because the Saviour preexists":[24]

This is also why Paul calls Adam himself *typus futuris*, the figure of him who must come (Rom 5:14): because the Logos, the Maker of the universe had formed beforehand for himself the future dispensation of the human race, connected with the Son of God; God having predestined that the first human being should be of an animal nature, with this view, that he might be saved by the spiritual one. For in as much as he had a preexistence as a saving being, it was necessary that what might be saved should also be

---

[18] Irenaeus, *Haer.* V, 6.1.

[19] See Ysabel de Andia, *Homo Vivens: Incorruptibilité et divinisation de l'homme selon Irénée de Lyon* (Paris: Études Augustiniennes, 1986), p. 110.

[20] Ibid., p. 118.

[21] Irenaeus, *Dem.* 12.

[22] Cf. J. Fantino, *La théologie d'Irénée* (Paris: Editions du Cerf, 1994), p. 360.

[23] Irenaeus, *Haer.* IV, 39.1 and elsewhere. Cf. Roger Berthouzoz, *Liberté et grâce suivant la théologie d'Irénée de Lyon* (Paris: Éditions Universitaires, 1980), pp. 234f.

[24] J. Fantino, *La théologie*, p. 362f.

called into existence, in order that the being who saves should not exist in vain.[25]

Therefore, the last Adam is the ontological cause of the first Adam!

This Irenaean perspective was to be fully recovered and developed further by St Maximus the Confessor in the seventh century. Meanwhile, patristic thought appears to oscillate between the idea of an original state of perfection from which humanity fell—an idea supported by an authority no less than that of Origen—and the view inherited from Irenaeus that Adam's original state was imperfect and it is only in the eschata that we should look for perfection.

The view that Adam was created imperfect was maintained by Clement of Alexandria[26] and strongly supported by Methodius of Olympus in the fourth century.[27] It was with St Athanasius that the stress was placed also on the divine qualities, such as supernatural knowledge, rationality, and even incorruption and immortality, with which the human being was endowed from the beginning, being created in God's image.[28] These divine qualities, however, did not belong to the *constitution* of humanity (i.e., they were not part of its nature) but remained ontologically qualities coming to it from outside.[29] The human being was in its natural constitution a creature (κτιστόν) and as such unable to reach perfection by itself. Corruption was part of human nature.[30] This is why, although Athanasius speaks of the human being as originally "perfect" (τέλειος), he regards the state granted to it in Christ as something "more" (μεῖζον) than the original state because of the Resurrection which abolished death and gave immortality.[31] The fall, therefore, was a return of humanity to its *natural state* and the original "perfection" was to be supplemented by something much higher in the person of Christ.

When we come to the Cappadocian fathers, the accent seems to fall on original perfection. St Basil describes the original state of hu-

[25] Irenaeus, *Haer.* IV, 39.1.
[26] Clement Alex., *Strom.* 6.12 (PG 9:317B); *Protr.* II (PG 8:228C).
[27] Methodius, *Symp.* 3.5 (PG 18:68B).
[28] Athanasius, *C. gent.* 2–3 (PG 25:5f).
[29] Athanasius, *C. Ar.* 2.68 (PG 26:292C).
[30] Athanasius, *De Inc.* 4.7 (PG 25:108D).
[31] Athanasius, *C. Ar.* 2.67 (P 26:289B).

manity in the most idyllic terms,[32] and the same is true of Gregory Nazianzen[33] and Gregory of Nyssa.[34] There are, however, certain nuances in their thought which are worth noticing. Basil, for example, speaks of immortality as a *promise* and a purpose—not a fact.[35] Gregory Nazianzen speaks of humanity as it came out of the hands of God as a mixture of perfection and imperfection owing to the fact that it was constituted as a combination of soul and body. He describes the human being as "an animal composed of both visible and invisible nature, earthly, heavenly, temporary, and immortal," an "animal capable of deification" (ζῷον θεούμενον), that is, subject to both the lowest and the highest kind of existence.[36] Gregory of Nyssa, on the other hand, who appears to be the exponent *par excellence* of the idea of the original perfection of humanity, attaches to his conception two conditions of particular importance: (a) that the original perfection lies outside history,[37] and (b) that the only way to conceive this original perfection is by looking at the Resurrection of Christ and the eschata.[38] The fall, therefore, is not one from an original historical state of humanity but from a state which, although in its ideal form is presented protologically (in a Platonist manner), in its existential content is identical with the eschata. It is only by looking at the end that we can tell what the beginning was like.

It is, as we have said, with St Maximus that we recover the Irenaean conception of the fall as a deviation not from an ideal original state of humanity but from its future, eschatological destiny. Maximus develops this idea in depth, offering invaluable material to a systematic theological discussion of the subject.

For Maximus, our homeland is not to be found in the beginning but in the end, not in our past but in our future:

---

[32] Basil, *Hom.* 9.6 (PG 31:344A–C). This state, however, did not last; the fall followed "soon" (ταχὺ) (ibid., D) due to "satiety" (κόρος) (Cf. Origen).

[33] Gregory Naz. *Or.* 45.7–8 (PG 36:632A).

[34] Gregory Nys. *Or. Cat.* 6 (PG 45:28A–29B).

[35] Basil, *Liturgy*, Prayer of the Anaphora: "Thou didst set him [man] in the garden of Eden and *promised* unto him immortal life in the keeping of thy commandments."

[36] Gregory Naz. *Or.* 45.7–8 (PG 36:632A).

[37] Gregory Nys. *De hom. opif.* 16f. (PG 44:177ff).

[38] Ibid., 17 (188–9). Cf. Hans Urs von Balthasar, *Présence et pensée* (Paris: Beauchesne, 1942), pp. 41–61; J. Daniélou, *Platonisme et théologie mystique* (Paris: Aubier, 1944), p. 56f.

In looking for his end, man meets his origin, which essentially stands at the same point as his end ... For he should not seek (ζητῆσαι) the beginning, as I have said, as something that lies behind him, but he should search for (ἐκζητῆσαι) the end which exists ahead of him, so that he may come to know through the end his lost origin, as he did not know the end from the beginning.[39]

As von Balthasar dramatically puts it: "For Maximus the bronze doors of the divine home are slammed remorselessly shut at the very start of our existence; there remains only the dimension of the future."[40]

The original state of our existence, whatever paradise that may have been,[41] cannot be described in terms of history, since Adam fell "as soon as he came to existence" (ἅμα τῷ εἶναι or ἅμα τῷ γενέσθαι).[42] This does not mean that our pre-fallen state is a "myth" in the sense of something untrue. Maximus everywhere asserts that the human being issued from the hands of God free from sin, corruption, and death[43]—this was the will of God implanted in the inalterable logos of human nature and as such could not but be true. Truth, however, and historical reality are not to be identified.[44] "Truth" is identical with the will of God, while "reality" is the factual situation with

---

[39] Maximus, *QThal.* 59 (PG 90:613D).

[40] H. Urs von Balthasar, *Cosmic Liturgy*, p. 187.

[41] ὅπως ποτ' ἄν ἦν ὁ παράδεισος οὗτος. Maximus, *QThal.* 64 (PG 90:696A). Cf. ibid., 257C. Also Gregory Naz., *Or.* 45.8 (PG 36:632C).

[42] Maximus, *QThal.* 59 and 61 (PG 90:613C and 628A). Also, *Amb.* 42 (PG 91:1321B). The Greek word ἅμα denotes immediacy to the point of simultaneity. Maximus himself uses it repeatedly in this sense, even in referring to the Holy Trinity and to anthropology. E.g., in *Amb.* 24 (PG 91:1264A): between the Father and the Son there is no interval; *QThal.* 40 (PG 90:369A): no distance between the divine will and the coming into being of creation; *Amb.* 42 (PG 91:132D): the time of the coming into being of the soul and the body is one and the same. This consistent use of the word ἅμα in the sense of simultaneity by St Maximus—as indeed by all ancient authors, as a look at any Greek Lexicon shows— makes it impossible to accept the view that "il fallait donc entendre ἅμα au sense non pas d'une simultanéité, mais d'un court laps de temps" (ἅμα should therefore be understood in a sense not of simultaneity but of a short lapse of time) (J.-C. Larchet, *La divinisation de l'home selon saint Maxime le Confesseur* [Paris: Éditions du Cerf, 1996], p. 187).

[43] E.g., *QThal.* 61 (PG 90:629A); *Amb.* 10 (PG 91:1156D); *Amb.* 42 (PG 91:1321A) and elsewhere.

[44] For a discussion of this, see chapter two above, Excursus: "Historization of the Eschaton".

which we are confronted in history. Our pre-fallen state cannot be conceived and described with post-fallen categories.[45]

How, then, can we "know" (that is, have gnosiological access) to our origin, the state in which we issued from the hands of God, of which St Maximus himself speaks, if not by means of historical, post-fallen categories such as historical reality, etc.? For St Maximus, as we have seen, there is only one way by which we can know our original state, and that is *by looking at our end*. The truth of our pre-fallen state can only be conceived and described "after the disobedience," by looking not backward but forward, to the "blessed end" for which we were created: *anthropological protology can be reached only via eschatology*. "Truth is the state of the future things."[46] As Fr Florovsky noted, "it is characteristic of St Maximus that ... he judges the 'beginning by the 'end'—teleologically', as he himself observes."[47]

---

[45] Students of St Maximus have been perplexed by his repeated statements about Adam's fall ἅμα τῷ γενέσθαι (as soon as he was created) and his references equally to the prelapsarian state of the human being. Some saw in this a contradiction. Balthasar (*Cosmic Liturgy*, p. 186f) finds here a departure of Maximus from the teaching of Gregory of Nyssa and an affinity with Scotus Eriugena "for whom creation and the fall are conceptually distinct but factually simultaneous" (p. 187). A. Vletsis (*Το Προπατορικό αμάρτημα στη θεολογία Μαξίμου του Ομολογητού* [*The Original Sin in the Theology of Maximos Confessor*], [Katerini: Tertios, 1996], pp. 244f) argues against a historical (in the astronomical kind of time) experience of a pre-fallen perfection by the human being and makes the interesting suggestion that we interpret "ἅμα τῷ γενέσθαι" of the fall in the way we understand Maximus' idea of the relation between γένεσις and κίνησις, namely as an ontological sequence in simultaneity (without an interval of time). In my view, we must distinguish between the *ontological* and the *existential* states of humanity. The former involves only divine action: God creates the human being as he wills by giving it a nature capable of turning toward its Creator (*QThal.* Prol.). The latter—the existentialist—requires also human response; it is at this point that the fall occurs: Adam made use of the ability given to him by God to *modify* his nature (= freedom) and turned its movement away from God as soon as he came to existence, without, however, being able to destroy its original *logos* (the will of the Creator). Thus, creation and the fall do not coincide ontologically; if they did, the latter would have destroyed or absorbed the former. By distinguishing between *logos* and *tropos* in human nature and attaching the former to God's inalterable will, Maximus safeguarded the ontological independence of creation from the fall. Creation *precedes* ontologically the fall—otherwise the human being would be a cocreator of itself with God. The fall *follows* creation *in the sense of a response to a call*. The sequence does not involve a time interval, in the postlapsarian division of time between "before" and "after."

[46] Dionysius Areop., *Scholia. de eccl. hier.* 3.2 (PG 4:137D). Cf. Maximus, *Amb.* 21 (PG 91:1253CD) and *Cap. theol.* I, 90 (PG 90:1120C).

[47] G. Florovsky, "St. Maximus the Confessor," *The Byzantine Fathers of the Sixth to Eighth Century* (Belmont, MA: Nordland Publishing Company, 1976), p. 226.

Now, our homeland is in the end, not only because it is there that we can find our true beginning—the way we issued from the hands of God—but also and mainly because the divine pre-eternal will—our beginning—included in itself a *purpose* (σκοπός), a movement toward an *end* much higher than the beginning.[48] This "blessed end" for which "we were predestined before the ages" is "to be in him [Christ] as members of his body."[49] *Our origin was conditioned eschatologically right from the start.* We were created not simply in order to be, but also in order to *become*, to pass through time and arrive at an end which surpasses in importance our beginning. Time and history are constitutive ingredients of the way we were meant to exist according to God's pre-eternal will. Moving toward a future is built into our beginning; it is not a result of a "fall" from a "paradise lost" to which by a cyclical movement we should return.[50]

This movement toward the end was "inscribed" in the very "reason" of our creation. According to St Maximus, the logoi of creation are not static but "leading to the end" (ἀπάγοντες πρὸς τὸ τέλος).[51] Even if the fall had not occurred, the mystery of Christ would have been realized in history,[52] because it was inscribed in the very purpose of creation. The fall could not and did not affect this pre-eternal will of the Creator; it only led to a change in the "mode" (τρόπος) of

[48] Maximus, *Amb.* 7 (PG 91:1097CD): what is above nature (= the end) is much higher than what is according to nature (=the beginning). (N. Constas wrongly renders in English ἀνώτερον as "different" (*Maximos the Confessor, On Difficulties in the Church Fathers: The Ambigua* Vol. I [Cambridge Massachusetts and London: Harvard University Press, 2014], p. 133). The "end" does not restore our "nature" but elevates us "above nature."

[49] Maximus, *Amb.* 7 (PG 91:1097AB). Note the strongly Christological character of the eschatological *theosis*.

[50] Cf. P.M. Blowers, *Exegesis and Spiritual Pedagogy in Maximus the Confessor: An Investigation of the Quaestiones ad Thalassium* (Notre Dame: University of Notre Dame Press, 1991), pp. 224–225: "Maximus disclaims a sheer ontological identification of ἀρχή and τέλος and the quasi-cyclical view of salvation history that it presupposes. Human life and the process of salvation take place on a continuous and linear field of movement from an *irretrievable* [original emphasis] beginning to an eschatological end." On the anti-Origenist character of this position of Maximus, see also P. Sherwood, *The Earlier Ambigua of St. Maximus the Confessor*, pp. 90–91;164–180.

[51] Maximus, *QThal.* 59 (PG 90:616A).

[52] This is a typical idea of St Maximus. See G. Florovsky, "*Cur Deus Homo?* The Motive of the Incarnation," *Creation and Redemption, Collected Works*, vol. III (Belmont, MA: Nordland Publishing Company, 1974), pp. 163–170.

its fulfillment,[53] adapted to the existential conditions of the post-lapsarian state.

II. Fall to What?

The consequences of the human fall were not simply or primarily moral; they were mainly and above all *ontological*. Presenting the position of the Greek fathers on this matter, Andrew Louth pertinently describes the fall as "the letting loose of corruption and death driving the whole created order towards nonbeing."[54] The fall affected the very being of humanity and of the whole creation. Having lost their eschatological orientation, all the gifts given to humanity at the primordial stage were distorted. Thus:

a) The "image of God" in humankind was distorted so as to fit Adam's claim that he was already God. The human being made itself the ultimate point of reference in existence, an already divinized being.[55] Thus, Adam turned the image of God into an image of himself. Since then, religion has taken the form of worshiping a god made in the image and likeness of the human being, as Ludwig Feuerbach observed,[56] and this has led to all sorts of "religious experiences" which in the final analysis are nothing but a means of satisfying psychological needs of the human being itself.

Following this, humanity distorted the concept of εἰκὼν by making it point not beyond itself but to itself. Just as the human being, having lost its eschatological orientation, made its protological state the ultimate point of ontological reference, the "image" became an expression of what was already there, the already-existing. Humanity became a slave to *reality*, and the real became identical with the "true."

b) A similar fate awaited the other ingredient of humanity's protological state, namely *nature*. By depriving human nature of its es-

---

[53] Maximus, *Amb.* 7 (PG 91:1097B-D).

[54] A. Louth, *Maximos the Confessor* (London: Routledge, 1996), p. 31.

[55] Maximus *Amb.* 10 (PG 91:1156C); *QThal.* 64 (PG 90:713A), etc. Cf. J.-C. Larchet, *La divinisation*, p. 193f.

[56] L. Feuerbach, *The Essence of Christianity*, trans. M. Evans (New York: Blanchard, 1855), *passim* and p. 173: God is the fulfillment of my wishes; all images and concepts of God are projections of human longing.

chatological orientation toward a transcendence of itself to the ὑπὲρ φύσιν, the human being gave to nature an ontological ultimacy that turned it into a "self-existent" and a master over all created existence. The deviation of nature from its eschatological direction made humanity a slave to nature. This sometimes led to worshipping nature, as in the case of idolatry and the pagan religions, while in all cases and as a universal predicament the laws of nature now dominated human existence beyond all hope of liberation.[57]

All this has brought about an upsetting of nature's relation with its own *logos* and its hypostatic character. The *logos* of nature, summed up in its various *logoi* of created things in the divine *Logos,* was according to St Maximus eschatological in its orientation. The fall did not affect the *logos* of nature because the *logoi* are identical with God's pre-eternal will that human freedom could not alter. The fall, therefore, did not touch the *logos* of nature but it did affect its *tropos,* the way nature exists. Thus, the fall introduced a mode of nature which was contrary to its *logos*: it turned nature away from its eschatological orientation, enslaving it to its own laws and, finally, its own limits. By being self-sufficient and ontologically ultimate, nature enslaved itself to itself and became a victim of its laws.

One of the fundamental laws of nature is to express the general, the catholic, the "universal" character of existence.[58] But the will and providence of the Creator wanted a world in which difference and diversity would be as ultimate ontologically as unity and catholicity.[59] For this reason, nature was created *hypostatic,* i.e., consisting of different entities related to each other in the same nature. This hypostatic diversity was intended by the Creator to be eschatological (i.e., to last forever), but the fall upset it by giving ontological ultimacy to nature, to the general (versus the particular) and its laws, leading to a conflict between the general (nature) and the particular

---

[57] In several places in his writings, St Maximus speaks clearly of the need to free the human being from nature in its postlapsarian state in which nature itself exists under the yoke of the law of corruption and death. E.g., *Ep.* 9 (PG 91:448C); *QThal.* 61 (PG 90:637A); ibid., 636A–C; 637Af; etc. See my "Person and Nature in the Theology of St. Maximus the Confessor," in *Knowing the Purpose*, pp. 85–113 (esp. 104f).

[58] This was established as a philosophical and theological principle by the Cappadocian fathers and is repeated by St Maximus (*Ep.* 15 [PG 91:545A]).

[59] See Maximus, *Amb.* 10 (PG 91:1188D).

(person). Death, to which we shall return below, is the most tragic expression of this result of the fall. Particular "hypostases" in fighting death constantly strive to survive their absorption by the laws of the general and universal, with the human being leading the chorus of protest as a kind of spokesman for the whole creation (and, perhaps, with a sense of "guilt."[60]) This basically ontological problem is experienced by the human being also at the social level of its life, where person and community find it difficult to coexist without conflicting with each other.[61]

c) Finally, the consequences of the fall relate profoundly and decisively to the notion of *being*. St Maximus places being at the protological state of creation given to humanity together with the "image" and nature. Just as the "image" was given in order to become eschatologically "similitude" and nature to become "above nature," being was meant to become finally *ever-being*, that is, everlasting in the future. The fall, however, stopped this movement toward the future ever-being and condemned creation to the state of "simply being" (ἀπλῶς εἶναι).[62]

But what sort of being was that? It was a being that had nonbeing in its background, having come out of nothing and, therefore, conditioned by the nothing from which it came, a being that had nonbeing in its nature and was constantly threatened by a return to it, as St Athanasius writes.[63] This kind of being is a paradoxical and absurd mixture of being and nonbeing, a "being-unto-death."

This paradoxical and absurd being continues to mark creation. It is the kind of being with which the animals perpetuate their species through procreation. It contains the element of pleasure (ἡδονή), which played a crucial role in tempting the first human being to choose it, but it is at the same time bound up with pain (ὀδύνη) and

---

[60] The idea of guilt, as developed by St Augustine, is not to be found in the Greek fathers, their approach to the fall being ontological rather than psychological. But if we think of the importance the Greek fathers attached to death as the transmissible consequence of the fall, we could speak implicitly of humanity's *responsibility* for the sovereignty of death in creation.

[61] See my *Communion and Otherness: Further Studies in Personhood and the Church*, ed. Paul McPartlan (London: T&T Clark, 2006), Introduction and Chapter 1.

[62] Maximus, *Amb.* 10 (PG 91:1116C).

[63] Athanasius, *De Inc.* 4 (PG 25:104B).

death. Thus, the law of death has prevailed over the human race, since all of Adam's descendants are born naturally in the same way that the rest of the animals had always been born since before the emergence of the human race.

Death, therefore, was not caused to appear by the fall. In fact, it was part of the nature of creaturehood: all creation was in its nature mortal, having come from nonbeing (Athanasius), and marked with mutability, τροπή (Gregory of Nyssa).[64] Created being (i.e., proto-logical being) was subject to mortality. But unlike the rest of the animals, the human being was provided with a certain power (δύνα-μιν τινα) to naturally desire God,[65] —with the possibility (the voca-tion) to turn the original being into ever-being (ὄντως εἶναι = im-mortality) in the future, to turn the "image" into the "similitude" by being united with the only immortal being, God. The disobedience to God's commandment automatically signified the rejection of uni-ty with God and, therefore, death of the human being. Death was not *imposed* on humanity by God, although the biblical language at this point may suggest that at first glance; it was freely *chosen,* albeit "ignorantly" (as St Maximus notes), by the human being. Adam and Eve chose being without ever-being and rejected the eschatological gift. They chose *reality* and subjected themselves to it.

Thus, there is in the drama of the fall an interplay of sin and death: the disobedience to God's commandment (sin) brought about the enslavement to death, but, at the same time, the choice of the state of animalhood (death) constituted the subject of disobedience itself. Humanity died because it sinned, and it also sinned because it died. Sin is not a moral problem; as it is tied up in death, it acquires ontological proportions. Through the perpetuation of death, sin also survives; in fact, it is fed by death. The fact of death causes division in being, and this leads to the fragmentation and dissolution of na-ture.[66] Death destroys communion and gives rise to individualism (φιλαυτία)—to entities conceivable in themselves.[67] Thus St Paul's

---

[64] See chapter two, "Eschatology and Creation."

[65] Maximus, *QThal.* 61 (PG 90:628A).

[66] Maximus, *QThal.* Prol. (PG 90:256B).

[67] Ibid. Note how Maximus makes the move from the natural to the personal level: because "human nature is divided into a thousand pieces [through the fall] we who all

words in Romans 5 verse 12 must be read as meaning "because of death (ἐφ᾽ ᾧ = θανάτῳ) all have sinned."[68]

This leads us to the consideration of what St Maximus regards as the quintessence of sin, namely self-love (φιλαυτία).[69] *Philautia* is identical with the fall because it expresses at the moral level the ontological movement toward the protological state of existence, the affirmation of what is already there, the *self*.[70] The eschatological orientation required from Adam an exodus from the self, because it called for faith both in another person (God's commandment) and in a *future* "reality," other than the protological one which was under the control of his senses. Loving the self was, for Adam, loving what was already there, the surest thing he possessed. Self-love is rooted deep in the ontological causes and consequences of the fall, and this is why it is so difficult to remove it from the human being. It can only be overcome by the death of this being.[71]

I have been arguing, predominantly on the basis of the theological insights of St Irenaeus and St Maximus, that the fall was the turn of humanity away from its eschatological orientation and toward its protological state. Although this position may not agree with the common one concerning the fall, it is supported in Greek patristic thought, particularly in the above mentioned writers, and would also spare theology from needing to apologize to scientific cosmology and anthropology for its doctrine of the fall (if, of course, it cared to do so, as I think it should).

There is, of course, a question to be answered, if the position argued here is to be accepted: did God create an imperfect world and an imperfect humanity?[72] How could the absolutely perfect being

---

share the same nature, mindlessly tear each other into shreds, like wild beasts." Sin and death are interwoven.

[68] This was how the Greek fathers, differing in this respect from St Augustine, interpreted the Pauline verse. See, J. Meyendorff, "Εφ᾽ ᾧ chez Cyrille d' Alexandrie et Théodoret," *Studia Patristica* 4 (1961) 157–161.

[69] All passions, according to St Maximus, derive from self-love. *Char.* II, 8 (PG 90: 985C). Cf. the expansion of this idea by St Photius, *Bibliotheca*, cod 192 (PG 103:637f).

[70] Making the self the object of love implies that the self is established ontologically as the protological "reality" *par excellence*.

[71] This is exactly what happened in the Incarnation.

[72] See below Appendix II to this chapter, A Note on Perfection.

bring about an imperfect creation? This is an old question, but those who would answer it by proposing a protological perfection of creation and humanity would do so by disregarding two fundamental aspects of the Christian doctrine of creation. The first has to do with the importance of *history*: if everything was perfect from the beginning, history would have been meaningless, or even a "fall" from perfection. The Irenaean doctrine that humanity had to *grow* to perfection, instead of being perfect from the start, invests time and history with a significance that was absolutely necessary not only to refute Gnosticism but also to be faithful to the biblical faith in its Judeo-Christian mentality.

The other aspect of the Christian doctrine of creation that must be taken into account when we speak of the creation of a perfect world and humanity is even more important: the perfection of creation and humanity is to be found in the *Incarnation of Christ*. It is only in Christ that the world acquires perfection, and this means that God created a world which was to *become* perfect in time and history, indeed in the *fullness* of time and consummation of history—in the *eschaton*. By creating the world *in* Christ and *for* Christ, God created a perfect world, indeed, as it befits the supremely perfect Being; but as the supremely *loving* Being that he also is, God entrusted the perfection of his creation to his *image* (i.e., to the human being), granting it the freedom, a divine attribute, to become his "fellow-worker" (1 Cor 3:9) in the realization of creation's glorious destiny. God reserved the world's perfection for the time when creation would be recapitulated in Christ, becoming the body of his only-begotten Son and sharing the Trinitarian life. The world's perfection belongs to the "blessed end" (according to Maximus) for which it was created, not to the beginning. Perfection is not a protological but an eschatological category. We need not worry, therefore, that we undermine the perfectness of God's creation by arguing that the fall enslaved creation to its protological state.

But there is another reason, too, why we must regard the original state of creation as "imperfect" and the fall as nothing but a "fall" to this protological "imperfectness": *it is the only way to understand the human responsibility for the immense catastrophic consequences of the fall for the whole of creation,* "the letting loose of corruption and death" for the whole cosmos. Was the human being so powerful as to bring about by its disobedience a corruption and death that were not there before? Could Adam have "created" corruption and death as a cosmic reality by his decision? If death was imposed as a punishment for Adam's sin, as the Augustinian tradition would claim, this must have been a condemnation of Adam to the death *already existing* in creation. In any case, it would be more proportionate to the capacities of humanity to attribute to it a *failure* (ἀστοχία) to fulfil its mission for creation's sake than an act of "destroying" what was already perfect. The sin of Adam must be seen more as a fault than as a crime.

That the first human being was confronted, upon its arrival, with a world in need of perfection is clearly reflected in the thought of St Maximus.[73] The human being was created with a cosmic mission, and that was to transcend and heal in itself certain fundamental divisions found in the very constitution of creation, threatening it with disintegration, corruption, and death. That these divisions were not introduced by the fall, but were part of the original protological creation, is evident from the fact that they preexisted humanity, since their healing was the very purpose of the creation of the human being. This healing was to come later and be finally realized in the *last* Adam, Christ, after the first Adam's failure or refusal to fulfil this mission in himself.

A study of these divisions shows clearly their protological character. The first of them mentioned by Maximus is the division between *created* and *uncreated* being. This is a fundamental presupposition for the doctrine of creation, which would be removed only in the eschata (the difference of *ousia* between God and creation remaining intact). The same is true of the divisions between *sensible* and *intelligible* creatures, *heaven* and *earth*, and *oikoumene* and *paradise*: they all constitute protological divisions to be transcended in the eschata. Finally, humanity itself was created originally as a division between male and female to be transcended in the Kingdom of God (Mt 22:30). Had the human being not "fallen," all these divisions would be turned eventually into differences and thus be healed.

---

[73] Maximus, *Amb.* 41 (PG 91:1305f).

Therefore, the cosmological and anthropological significance of Adam's fall lies in his refusal to transcend these protological divisions, thus "condemning" creation to be deprived of the movement from the protological to the eschatological state.

III. The Problem of Evil

If the fall is to be described as a fall "from the future," from the eschatological state of being and a condemnation to the "past," evil is a return to the ultimate "past" of creation, the *nihil* that lies behind creation's being. Evil can be thought of against the background of nonbeing; it is nonbeing itself.

The understanding of evil as nonbeing was commonplace in ancient Greek philosophy and in patristic thought. We encounter this idea in Plato, Aristotle, the Neoplatonists, Origen, the Greek fathers, Augustine, and Thomas Aquinas—to mention only the ancients. The explanation given is in most of the cases protological: evil cannot have substance, because being logically precedes nonbeing; it is a deviation from perfection, and perfection always precedes imperfection, just as illness—to borrow Aristotle's example—is a deviation from health which precedes sickness logically and ontologically.[74] Evil is, in this case, a deviation from the beginning, the original perfection.

Yet, in a doctrine of creation "out of nothing," like the Christian one, the idea of nonbeing appears to ontologically *precede* that of being. Evil in that case cannot be regarded as a deviation from the beginning. The perfection of creation is not to be found in the beginning but in the end. Evil is nonbeing because it is a deviation from the end, from *ever-being*.

This is exactly how St Maximus presents the matter:

Evil has neither been nor will be existing with its own nature; neither has it in any way a nature or hypostasis or power or energy in beings; it is not a quality or a quantity or a relation or a

---

[74] The same illustration is used by Dionysius the Areopagite to show that evil is nonbeing. See *De div. nom.* 4.20 (PG 3:720). Compare this with St Maximus' eschatological approach to evil below.

place or a time or a position or an operation or a movement or a habit (ἕξις) or a passion to be seen in any way in the nature of a certain being.... [I]t is neither a beginning, nor a middle, nor an end. But to put it in a form of definition, *evil is the deprivation [or lack] (ἔλλειψις) of the energy toward the end of the powers implanted in nature* (τῆς πρὸς τὸ τέλος τῶν ἐγκειμένων τῇ φύσει δυνάμεων ἐνεργείας ἐστὶν ἔλλειψις) and nothing else. Or, again, evil is the irrational (ἀλόγιστος) movement, by an erroneous judgement, of the natural powers *toward a direction other than the end* (ἐπ' ἄλλο παρὰ τὸ τέλος ἀλόγιστος κίνησις). And by end, I mean the cause of all beings which is naturally desired by all.... The first human being, therefore, having deprived (ἐλλείψας) *the movement of its natural powers of the energy toward the end* (τῆς πρὸς τὸ τέλος ἐνεργείας) was diseased (ἐνόσησεν) with the ignorance of its own cause.[75]

St Maximus' position could not have been clearer: evil is nonbeing because it is a movement away from being, not as it originally was but as it will be in the end; it is a deviation not from the beginning but from the eschatological purpose of creation. *Evil is nonbeing because it is a deviation not from being but from ever-being*, from true being (ὄντως εἶναι). As such, evil is a *lie*, a deception which presents being in its protological form (i.e., without ever-being) as if it were true being. The deceiver, Satan, is a "liar" (Jn 8:44), and Adam's fault is that he was "deceived" to accept this "lie" and be "diseased *with ignorance* (νοσήσας ἄγνοιαν) *of the [end]*."

If we follow this eschatological approach to the problem of evil, the question of *theodicy* that has preoccupied so much of theological thinking and never ceased to trouble the human soul must be placed on a new foundation. Theodicy aims at answering the question of origin: *why does evil exist?* It demands a rational coherence, namely how we can maintain the following three presuppositions at once: God is all powerful—God is absolutely good—evil exists. But, as Paul Ricoeur rightly observes, the problem of evil is not a rational but a deeply existential problem: even if we manage to give a satisfactory logical explanation to its origin, evil continues to be an enigma. The problem of evil is not so much one of mental curiosity as of *de-*

[75] Maximus, *QThal.* Prol. (PG 90:253AB). My emphasis.

sire; it provokes a cry, a "lamentation," and directs our concern to the *end* rather than the beginning.[76]

Put on such a basis, the problem of evil seems to have received the following three "replies" in the course of Christian theology:

1. *The Reply of Psychology*

This is offered particularly by St Augustine and revived in our time by Ricoeur. For the latter, "acting" and "feeling" constitute the only proper context to place the aporia of evil. Instead of speculating on the origin of evil, we should try to respond—not to offer a solution—to the aporia of evil by asking what is to be done against evil—by turning attention not to the origins but to the future. But he recognizes that this is not enough, as there is evil which is not inflicted by humans but by natural catastrophes, epidemics, or even aging and death. Thus, he believes that the question is no longer "why?" but "why me?" To this question he proposes:

a) *Mourning* in the sense of Sigmund Freud's essay "Mourning and Melancholia,"[77] where mourning is described as the loosening, one by one, of all the bonds that make us feel the loss of a beloved object as a loss of ourselves, making us free for new emotional investments. This mourning must be accompanied by a liberation of God himself from "wanting" this specific evil—or, for that matter, wanting us to be punished for our sins.

b) *Protest* against God for permitting this evil (cf. the Psalms) and impatience *for the coming of the Kingdom* to deliver us from evil. And,

c) *Faith in God in spite of evil*—an integration of the speculative aporia into the work of mourning.

2. *The Reply of Vindication*

This is offered mainly by Karl Barth and other Protestant theologians of our time in certain variations. Barth had accepted the dilemma caused by theodicy (how can we reconcile logically the state-

---

[76] P. Ricoeur, "Evil," pp. 206–207; *Evil: A Challenge to Philosophy and Theology*, trans. J. Bowden (London: Continuum, 2007).

[77] S. Freud, *The Complete Psychological Works*, vol. 14, trans. J. Strachey (London: Hogarth Press, 1957), pp. 243–258.

ment: God is good—God is almighty—evil exists), but he rejected
the logic of noncontradiction and systematic totalization that had
dominated all the attempts to solve the problem of theodicy, especially since Gottfried Leibniz and Georg Wilhelm Hegel. His position was inspired by the Kierkegaardian logic of paradox and started
from the presupposition that only a "broken" theology, which has
renounced systematic totalization, can engage in the task of thinking about evil. By "broken" Barth meant a theology which recognizes evil as a reality that cannot be reconciled with the goodness of
God and the goodness of creation and has to be *annihilated*. Evil is
"thinkable" only against the background of "nothingness" (*Nich-
tige*), and the only "logic" applicable to it is that of annihilation. This
is, according to Barth, what happened on the Cross, where nothingness was conquered by God through his annihilating himself on it.
It is only in this way that we "know" nothingness and can offer a
reply to the problem of evil.[78]

We find a similar approach to the problem in Moltmann, who
also speaks of the annihilation of nothingness on the Cross through
God's annihilation of himself.[79]

3. *The Ontological Reply*

Admirable as it is, St Augustine's profound analysis of human
will in relation to sin and evil, did not have its counterpart in Greek
patristic thought. This may have been entirely accidental due to the
fact that there was not an equivalent of Pelagius in the East. But it
could be also explained by the observation that the entire approach
to the fall was different in the East.

It is generally agreed that Adam's sin was approached by the
Greek fathers more philanthropically and sympathetically than it
was in the West. The reason for this is that in the East the fall was

[78] See K. Barth, *Church Dogmatics* III/3 (Edinburgh: T&T Clark, 1960), pp. 289–352.
[79] J. Moltmann, *God in Creation*, p. 93. Pannenberg (*Systematic Theology,* vol. 2, pp. 164f) prefers to omit theodicy from his perspective on the ground that we cannot *reason* why things are not better than they actually are; asking why God did not behave in a better way amounts to raising our reason above him and thus to destroying the very (bib- lical) concept of God. Pannenberg prefers to attribute evil to man's refusal to accept his finitude: the acceptance of our finitude including death, is the way to overcome evil (pp. 171ff).

seen as a cosmic catastrophe, and, although the human being was to blame, humanity itself was caught up in a situation beyond its control, suffering the consequences *together* with the rest of creation and as an organic part of it. Thus, there was no interest in what happened to the human being in its internal self. The problem that the fall brought to the surface was, in this case, not "bad conscience" or "guilt" but the prevalence of *death* in the whole of creation. The human being took the wrong direction away, not simply from God's will (like in Augustine), but from the end toward which the entire creation was to move, headed by humanity, in order to overcome the mortality inherent in its nature.

It is for this reason that the idea of *guilt* and its transmission to humanity plays no central role in the Greek patristic view of the fall.[80] The fall was seen rather as a transmission of the *law of death* from generation to generation—mortality was the problem. Death was transmitted as a *law of nature*[81] and against the will of humanity[82] (and all creatures). Even in a rare case in which St Maximus speaks of the transmission of sin from generation to generation, he connects it with the natural law of procreation,[83] which for him is identical with the transmission of death.[84] It is not guilt that is transmitted by the fall (which would be applicable only to humanity); it is death and mortality (a natural law) that human beings inherit from previous generations. This is why, while for the Augustinian tradition Baptism is required in order to free the human being from guilt, for the Greek fathers Baptism is needed in order to give the baptized the charisms of the Kingdom of God (among which immortality is, of course, prominent),[85]—to point him or her in the eschatological direction.

[80] J.N.D. Kelly, *Early Christian Doctrines*, rev. ed. (New York: Harper Collins, 1978), p. 350: "There is hardly a hint in the Greek Fathers that mankind as a whole shares in Adam's guilt, i.e., his culpability."
[81] Maximus, *QThal.* 61 (PG 90:632Df).
[82] Ibid., 636B: ἀναγκαίως καὶ μὴ βουλόμενοι.
[83] Maximus, *Quest. et dub.* 3 (PG 90:788AB).
[84] See above note 80.
[85] This was also stressed in the West by St Ambrose. See Kelly, *Early Christian Doctrines*, p. 356. However, for St Augustine, Baptism offers the removal of guilt (*reatus*) whereas for the Greek fathers it offers the future blessings of the Kingdom. Ibid., pp. 364, 373, and 430f.

All this means that evil is not an anthropological but a cosmological problem and cannot be solved by any human effort (e.g., ethics, repentance, etc.) but *only through a cosmic transformation* at the end of history. As St Athanasius would argue,[86] not even divine forgiveness, let alone human repentance, can undo the consequences of the fall, as these permeate the entire created order through corruption and death. Unless, therefore, there is an ontological transformation of creation as a whole, there is no solution to the problem of evil.

Such a transformation of creation can only take place through a restoration of the original movement of creation toward its eschatological *telos*, that is, through the fulfillment of humanity's role as the head of creation that would lead it to its eschatological destiny. A new Adam, therefore, would be required who would also be the "last Adam," the eschatological one. The only solution to the problem of evil would, thus, be the *Incarnation* in all its history, from Christ's birth to his Parousia.

In such an approach, it would not be sufficient, or even appropriate, to speak of the annihilation of evil simply on the Cross. For the problem is not how to condemn and annihilate evil as such, but how to replace the post-fallen order of creation with the one intended by God in the end. Barth's position implies that the eschata will bring nothing ontologically new with regard to the elimination of evil; the Resurrection and the Second Coming of Christ will only "reveal" the original goodness of God and of creation, which has already being restored on the Cross.[87] Barth seems to adopt a protological approach to creation as being in its very origin perfect even in the presence of death.[88] For the Eastern tradition, however, cre-

---

[86] Athanasius, *De Inc.* 7 (PG 25:108CD).

[87] Barth, *Church Dogmatics*, III/3, p. 366.

[88] If I understand Barth correctly, his view is that the original state of creation, including the presence of corruption and death, did not stand in need of improvement. Evil is tied up exclusively with human sin: "it [sin] is not merely attended and followed by the ills which are inseparably bound up with creaturely existence in virtue of the negative aspect of creation, but by the suffering of evil as something wholly anomalous which threatens and perils this existence ... Nor is it a mere matter of dying as the natural termination of life, but of death itself as the intolerable, life-destroying thing to which all suffering hastens as its goal, as the ultimate irruption and triumph of that alien power which annihilates creaturely existence" (ibid., p. 310). Thus, the only problem is human sin, which is "the concrete form of nothingness, because in sin it becomes man's own act,

ation is to *become* perfect with the Incarnation, and the overcoming of evil would require a *history* culminating in the eschata. Evil as a deviation from the end would have to be annihilated at the *end* of this history. It continues to be at work after the Cross, even after Christ's Resurrection. The solution to the problem of evil is a matter for the future; it will require a *judgement on history in its totality.*

IV. The Elimination of Evil

Christ came to eliminate the power of evil by removing it from existence. His miracles of healing the sick, forgiving the sinners, accepting the socially-marginalized and outcast, and especially casting out demons—all of these were visible manifestations of the fact that the elimination of evil occupied a central place in our Lord's mission. But it was above all the defeat of death through the Cross and Resurrection that dealt the decisive blow to evil, as it attacked its ontological target, the world's ever-being.

All these, however, were "assurances" of a *future* state which is still to come. The total and final elimination of evil will come with the establishment of God's Kingdom in the last days, at the end of history. Only Christ's Parousia, his Second Coming, will eliminate evil; all other attacks on evil during Christ's life, including his Cross and Resurrection, served as an "earnest," an *arrabon,* of this future state as an "already and not yet." The eschaton will not simply "reveal" the annihilation of evil that took place on the Cross; it will bring about this annihilation of which the Cross and the Resurrection assured us as the "first fruits" and, therefore, proof of an existence without death and evil. This must be so since the whole cre-

achievement and guilt (ibid.)." "The true nature of sin and nothingness [is] our repudiation of the goodness of God" (ibid., p. 368) and of *original creation*: "God in His goodness required no more of him [man] than his adherence to this goodness and man was free by nature to meet this demand" (ibid.). The contrast with St Maximus emerges at this point clearly and relates directly to eschatology. According to Maximus, God required of Adam and Eve not simply to adhere to the original goodness but to reach, together with and as the head of creation, a state of existence higher than the original goodness. Barth seems to lack this eschatological (and cosmological) perspective, locating his concept of evil exclusively in the threat of nothingness as an extinction of existence (in its original "goodness").

ation, and not only humanity, needs to be redeemed from the consequences of the fall and acquire an immortality which was not there at the beginning. The eschatological state, therefore, is the "truth" of all the New Testament realities,[89] the ontological "cause" of their existence.

This promise kept alive the eager expectation (ἀποκαραδοκία, Rom 8:19) of the eschata, the Parousia, in the consciousness of the primitive Church. The first ecclesial communities fervently awaited the coming of the Lord to "deliver us from evil," as they recited the Lord's prayer. The cry *maranatha* (1 Cor 15:22) dominated their prayers, and their eucharistic services were oriented toward the coming of the Kingdom to bring about the "new creation" where justice will prevail and "death will be no more" (Rev 21:4).

1. *The Judgement of Evil*

The elimination of evil in the eschata and the eschatological event when this would happen were connected in the Church's consciousness from the beginning with *judgement*. Christ's Parousia will eliminate evil by judging it. This was already part of the expectation of post-exilic Judaism, which Christ himself and the Church accepted and incorporated into the Christian faith from the beginning. Eschatology was associated with the *apocalyptic*.

The term "apocalyptic," as its Greek original indicates, implies that something is revealed, literally uncovered (ἀπό+καλύπτειν): although the meaning of judgement has prevailed as an essential aspect of apocalypticism, the notion of *revelation* should not pass unnoticed. It can in fact be regarded as an aspect of the idea of judgement itself, if the latter is placed in an ontological perspective.

Judeo-Christian apocalyptic, which is what concerns us here, refers to revelations concerning history and its consummation, more or less in the spirit of Hebrew prophecy, with an eschatology that includes judgement on those who persecute the people of God and, in certain cases, with cosmological elements, such as the destruction of the universe and its replacement by a new world (2 Pet). The book

---

[89] Maximus, *Schol. eccl. hier.* 3.2 (PG 4:137d). Cf. *Amb.* 21 (PG 91:1253CD) and *Cap. theol.* I, 90 (PG 90:1120C).

of Daniel, which was written in response to the persecution of the Jews by Antiochus Epiphanes that led to the Maccabean revolt (c. 168 BC), and the Apocalypse of St John (c. AD 95) found their way into the canonical Scriptures of the Church, while other writings of the same genre were not given scriptural status and authority.

Modern biblical scholarship has made apocalyptic the content and basis of the life, the teaching, even the identity, of Jesus as presented to us in the New Testament.[90] The identification of Jesus with the eschatological figure of the Son of Man in the book of Daniel, the acceptance of the expectation of the resurrection of the dead by the first Christian communities, the probable relation of Jesus' teaching with the faith of the Qumran communities, and, above all, the faith in the approaching establishment of the Kingdom of God which marked Christ's teaching and the expectations of the first Christian Church—all of these have brought to the surface the importance of the apocalyptic for the understanding of the Gospel and the essence of Christianity.

That Christ "will come again to judge the living and the dead" became part of the Church's creed and thus an indispensible ingredient of Christian theology. But the interpretation of this doctrine has not proved to be a simple matter. The language that has been traditionally employed and has sealed the faith of the ordinary faithful is adopted from juridical experience. The final judgement is conceived as something analogous to our forensic experience with a judge imposing penalties for the transgression of a certain law.

This kind of interpretation of the apocalyptic teaching of the Church has raised questions that theology must take seriously into account. In the first place, it appears to be too anthropomorphic to be applied to God.[91] It appears also to be questionable if we try to reconcile it with God's love: how can the God of love be so cruel to his creatures as to impose eternal suffering on them?[92]

In the face of such difficulties, the temptation arose to dismiss the judgmental aspect of eschatology altogether. But such a position

---

[90] Cf. B.C. Blackwell, J.K. Goodrich, and J. Maston, eds., *Paul and the Apocalyptic Imagination* (Minneapolis: Fortress, 2016).

[91] See S. Bulgakov, *The Bride of the Lamb*, p. 381f.

[92] See below, chapter four on Eschatology, Hell, and Final Judgement.

would leave us without any answer to the elimination of evil. If evil must be removed from existence as an unacceptable offence not simply to goodness but to being itself, its elimination emerges as a response to the deepest existential needs of humanity and creation as a whole. "Creation itself will be freed from the yoke of corruption" (Rom 8:21) and all that this entails, while the thirst for life and love, indeed, for being itself, is so deeply built into all creatures that any power opposing it appears to be the enemy of the Creator himself. The elimination of evil appears as an absolute ontological necessity when evil is considered as nonbeing, as nothingness itself. An acceptance of the eternal survival of evil would amount to a denial of being, a suicidal option for creation itself.

But if it is the ontological problem that must be tackled in eliminating evil, the hermeneutic of the doctrine of the last judgement must also be of an *ontological* character. What does it mean ontologically that evil is judged and eliminated?

2. *The Purification of History*

We have seen that for the Greek fathers, especially Irenaeus and Maximus, evil entered creation through deceit and ignorance. As nonbeing, evil "deceives" humanity by presenting it with the lie that being can coexist with nonbeing, or that nonbeing is true being. Evil as nonbeing exists "parasitically" on being and contaminates history by making it difficult, if not impossible, to dissociate being from nonbeing, truth from falsehood. By being not only "moral" but also "natural," evil contaminates the history of humanity and that of creation as a whole: all humans sin (Rom 3:12, 23), and all creatures suffer from corruption and death (Rom 8:20–22).

History, therefore, is contaminated with evil and requires purification. This is dramatically reflected in human consciousness, which constantly strives to separate good from evil, truth from falsehood, health from disease, life from death. Science, philosophy, and, above all, ethics testify to this strife.

Yet, the absolute separation of being from nonbeing, truth from falsehood, good from evil proves to be impossible in history. There seems to be an antinomical structure in the very constitution of reality,[93] which must have its ontological roots in the fact that creation has come out of nothing and is permeated by nothingness.[94] The purification of history from evil requires a transformation of created existence in its totality, which no human effort can achieve. Such a purification cannot come from within creation and history. It can only be the result of the "swallowing up of mortality by life" (2 Cor 5:4) in the final resurrection. It can only be part of the end of history.

By abolishing mortality, and consequently the threat of a return to nonbeing, the eschatological resurrection will automatically signify the judgement of evil, through the "unconcealment (ἀποκάλυ-ψις)" or "revelation" of whatever in the course of history had "deceived" us as "being," although it was in truth nonbeing, and led us—and the world—away from true being, God, and from ever-being, the purpose or end for which the world was created. *The eschatological judgement will, thus, be identical with the resurrection itself* (Jn 5:29); the abolishment of death which contaminated the being of creation will automatically reveal which events or "realities" of history deserve eternal survival as corresponding to the "end" for which the world was created, and therefore embodying the truth of being, and which of them were deviations from this end and, therefore, evil or nonbeing.

Such an identification of the final judgement with the resurrection itself enables us to view the doctrine of the last judgement ontologically rather than juridically. This ontological hermeneutic of the doctrine of the eschata relieves it of the anthropomorphic characteristics with which it is commonly presented and makes it unnecessary to dismiss the last judgement as incompatible with God's goodness. By the very act of abolishing death through the general resurrection, God *reveals* the true being that was obscured by its co-

---

[93] See below Appendix I to this chapter: Slaves of Reality.

[94] See Maximus, *Amb.* 41 (PG 91:1312B): "All creation is a unity that comes together through the cooperation of its parts and draws inward on itself through the totality of its being—governed by a single, simple, in itself definite, and unchangeable idea: that it comes from nothing. In this concept, all of creation can be understood as a single, identical, and undifferentiated idea: namely, *that it has nothing as the basis of its being.*" (v. Balthasar's trans., *Cosmic Liturgy*, p. 151). Here St Maximus repeats St Athanasius' idea that creation has nonbeing as its very nature (*De Inc.* 4 [PG 25:104B]).

existence with nonbeing, death and evil in the course of history. Thus, the last judgement throws light (Jn 3:19–21) on what is now obscure in history, reveals the most hidden secrets of human hearts (Rom 2:16; 1 Cor 4:5; cf. Mk 4:22; Lk 8:17) and the ambiguities of historical existence, and annihilates evil by revealing its "nothingness" while depriving it of its parasitic coexistence with being. Through the very act of resurrection and the abolishment of death, the last judgement becomes κρίσις in the double meaning of the term: *discernment* or *separation*, and *condemnation*.

The identification of the last judgement with the resurrection also enables us to see this judgement as a *cosmic* event. The human being and other creatures endowed with freedom will be "judged" for the use of their freedom in the direction of nonbeing, for their conscious rebellion against the will of God, their *sin*. Yet, evil is broader than sin, as it applies to the whole of creation and not only to free beings. The last judgement must be seen not as a *vindictive* but as a *healing* act of God, a purification of the entire creation from evil. The presentation of the last judgement mainly as a condemnation of sin and an act of punishment overlooks the cosmic dimensions of evil and the *restorative* and *reconciliatory* character of the eschatological act of God. The ontological hermeneutic leads us to the association of the last judgement with the eschatological event that affects ontologically the whole of creation, the resurrection as the liberation from the "last enemy" of creation, from that which allows nonbeing to contaminate the world's being.

Finally, the identification of the last judgement with the general resurrection enables us to underline the *Christological* character of this eschatological act of God. Evil will be "judged," "condemned," and eliminated *only by Christ* (Jn 5:22, 27), by *God himself in and through humanity* (1 Cor 15:21). If evil was identified exclusively with sin, the Cross of Christ would probably be the crucial point of the Incarnation in which evil is annihilated. This is, as we have seen, the position taken by Karl Barth. But if we extend evil beyond humanity to the whole of creation and approach it as an ontological problem connected fundamentally with nonbeing and death, it will be the *risen* Christ that will emerge as the judge and conqueror of evil. Thus, in the Bible as well as in the patristic tradition the eschatological judge is identified with Christ not in his humiliation but *in his glory*. "When the Son of Man comes *in his glory* ... there he will sit on *the throne of his glory*" to judge (Mt 25:31f.). The dominion over all "powers" and the judgement of the world are given to Christ in connection with his Resurrection (Mt 28:18; cf. Acts 10:42 and 17:31) and, according to Paul, the subjection of all evil powers to Christ and ultimately to the Father is inseparably linked with the abolishment of death (1 Cor 15:52–57): the risen Christ as the "leader" (ἀπαρχὴ) of the universal resurrection subjects under his feet all evil powers including, above all, the "enemy" *par excellence*, death (1 Cor 15:23–26).

The biblical idea that the judgement of evil will not be the work of the crucified but of the risen and glorified Christ survives in the patristic period. St Justin states this explicitly by contrasting the two comings of the Messiah predicted in the Old Testament, the one in humiliation and the other in glory, while identifying the first one with the Incarnation and the second with the Parousia.[95] The idea found its way into the early creeds with that of Nicaea-Constantinople stressing the faith that Christ will come again *in glory* (μετὰ δόξης) "to judge the quick and the dead." It has thus become a fundamental article of the Orthodox faith, that the Parousia, the resurrection, and the final judgement form an unbreakable unity.

That this unity (Parousia-resurrection-judgement) constitutes a *single event* and not three successive stages of the divine eschatological act, as it is usually presented, is not to be found explicitly in tradition where the anthropomorphic language seems to have prevailed. It is, however, implicit in the faith that the resurrection, both of Christ and at the eschata, implies the rise of a body—and by extension of material creation as a whole—*freed and healed from* death, sickness, infirmity, deformity, etc.[96] This means that in the very event of the general resurrection evil is eliminated from creation, that is, *"condemned"* to *annihilation*. If the forensic language is replaced with an ontological one, evil is shown to be nonbeing only if put *sub specie resurrectionis*: "if Christ was not risen, you are still in your sins" (1 Cor 15:18). It is the *last* act of God that frees creation from evil.

[95] Justin, *I Apol.* 52; *Dial.* 14, 31, 32, 34 (PG 6:404Df.; 505C; 540Bf.; 541Df.; 545Df.).
[96] See Gregory Nys., *De anima et resur.* (PG 46:148Cf).

Appendix I:
Slaves of Reality

The fall is not simply an "event" of the past; it is a permanent condition of human existence. It is not accidental that human thought has always felt overpowered by the fatal necessity that imposes on creation the law of corruption and death, wondering how this "fate" came about, who or what caused it. Biblical faith rejects any suggestion that God was responsible for the law of corruption and death which permeates creation, or that this "fate" is ontologically inherent in creation itself. This "disease" of creation could have been avoided had the human being obeyed the Creator's commandment not to eat from a certain "tree" which bore "the fruit of knowledge of good and evil" (Gen 2:16). It is in this disobedience to the Creator's will that we must seek the cause of humanity's subjection to the law of corruption and death. But how does eschatology relate to this disobedience and the way we experience the fall in our existence?

We have insisted throughout this book that, notwithstanding the manifold interpretations of the fall and its implications for our existence, any endeavor in hermeneutics will have to take into account eschatology. Looked at from the eschatological perspective, the essence of the fall is the deviation of the human being from the purpose (the "end"), the destiny inscribed in the very "reason" (the *logos*) of its creation. Adam, the first human being, received a "call"— in fact it was this call that brought him into existence as other than the rest of creation[97]—to lead not only humanity but the whole of creation to a "blessed end," which would include the abolition of evil, corruption, and death, to a state of participation in the bliss and the glory of God himself—to *theosis*. This was put before Adam as a *future*, an eschatological destination which would have to pass through time and history, that is, through the exercise of human freedom. The human being was created as a forward-looking creature; eschatology was built into its ontology.

Adam's fall lies in his refusal to perform this mission. Instead of looking and moving forward, he chose to cling to what was already there, to nature, and, above all, to himself, to his senses, to what St Maximus calls τὰ αἰσθητά. Either out of fear or out of ignorance—

---

[97] See my *Communion and Otherness*, p. 41f.

or, most importantly, self-love (φιλαυτία)—the first human being from its beginning (ἄμα τῷ γενέσθαι) preferred to hold fast to what was *given* rather than to what was *promised*, to the certainty of *reality* which could be controlled by its senses, instead of embarking on a journey in faith, to the future. Adam preferred to be god as soon as he was created rather than wait for an eschatological *theosis*.[98]

The essence of Adam's sin—and of that of his descendants—lies, therefore, in the crisis of his *faith*: "everything that is not of faith is sin" (Rom 14:23). Faith is not simply the obedience to the word of God; it is, concretely, the consent to accept *God's future promises*, which ends up replacing the protological reality, which is controllable by our senses, with a "subsistence (ὑπόστασις) of things hoped for, the assurance (ἔλεγχος) of things not seen" (Heb 11:1). Abraham, the biblical example of faith *par excellence*, did not show his faith only in his obedience to God's order to sacrifice his son but also, according to the Christian interpretation given in the Letter to the Hebrews, in following the divine call to "go out to a place which he should later receive for inheritance, and he went out, not knowing where he went" (Heb 11:8). All of chapter eleven of the Letter to the Hebrews speaks of faith in terms of God's promises (ἐπαγγελίαι). Faith makes no sense without eschatology.

The fall did not erode the eschatological orientation of the human being altogether. The human being still wants to look forward, to hope, to progress, to develop, to foresee. The future continues to be a fundamental dimension of human existence. But it is no longer a future in the eschatological sense of faith. This is so not only in the case of sheer atheistic humanism[99] in which the future has nothing to do with obedience to a divine promise. It is also evident in every teleology in which the Omega point is a derivation from the Alpha point (as, for example, in Teilhard de Chardin and others), whenever the future is caused by the past instead of being the cause of it. Thus every "rational" future planning is based on given data, with

---

[98] According to St Irenaeus, Adam's sin consisted in *hastiness*, i.e., in the attempt to bypass or annihilate time and history (cf. Appendix to this chapter). J. P. Manoussakis, *The Ethics of Time*, p. 60, commenting on a passage from Kafka puts it very well: "The first man sinned insofar as he wanted to achieve *without waiting* [original emphasis] what was promised to him anyway but in due time."

[99] E. Bloch and K. Marx can serve as typical examples of this kind of eschatology.

the help of which all risks are minimized or eliminated. In our fallen condition, the human being fears risks and seeks assurance in what is already there, even when looking into the future. The future in all of our "fallen" teleologies is dependent essentially on the past.

This dependence of the future on the past also jeopardizes faith in theology. The predominance of "reality," of what is already there, obliges faith to be "apologetical" to reason, if it is to make "sense" to our minds. This attitude to faith has dominated theology in modern times, particularly since the Enlightenment, although its roots go back to medieval Scholasticism. Faith must somehow reconcile itself with reason if it is to be accepted in our fallen condition. Otherwise, a crisis erupts between the two, a Kierkegaardian "either/or," pushing faith to the realm of the irrational. Protestant theology inspired by the principle of *sola fide* has made a remarkable attempt, especially in its Barthian version, to overcome this apologetic type of faith by rejecting the scholastic *analogia entis* and giving to the word of God absolute priority over human reason.[100] Yet this was, regrettably, done with no reference to eschatology and its ontological significance, limiting faith to the individual's experience, without opening it up to our historical existence and our relation to the destiny of the "other" and of creation as a whole.

"Whatever is not of faith is sin," and "the wages of sin are death" (Rom 6:23). The refusal to look forward, the subjection of eschatology to protology, which is the essence of the fall, may have given us security in accommodating us to reality, but at the same time it condemned us—and creation—to the "real," the given, the past. The *"adequatio"* of our intellect with *"res"* has made reality a necessary condition of our existence. This introduced *necessity* into ontology, which our fallen existence accepts only reluctantly, if it does not revolt against it completely. This is the case primarily with regard to *death*.

If we put aside the forensic interpretation of the relation of sin to death (death as a "punishment" for disobedience), death is "the wages" of sin not because it is a result of it (death existed in creation before sin) but because sin (the fall) has subjected us to death and

---

[100] See my "Sola Fide: A Hermeneutical Approach", in eds. C. Chalamet, K. Delikonstantis, J. Getcha and E. Parmentier, *Theological Anthropology, 500 Years After Martin Luther: Orthodox and Protestant Perspectives* (Leiden & Boston: Brill, 2021), pp. 3-16.

made it dominate creation forever as part of "reality," owing to our progenitor's refusal to lead the world to a future free of death. By failing the test of faith, by not fulfilling the eschatological call, the human being "bought" (ὀψώνια) death as part of the "real" to which it chose freely to subject itself.

At this point, a reference again to St Maximus may be helpful. In interpreting the story of the two trees in paradise, Maximus explains the fall in ontological (not juridical or moral) terms: "the tree of life is certainly a maker of life; the tree not of life evidently is a maker of death. For that which does not make life for not being called tree of life, clearly would make death."[101] By eating from the tree of knowledge of good and evil, Adam chose death instead of life. Why did this tree produce death? Why did Adam die by eating from it?

Maximus defines the tree of good and evil precisely as that which we would call "reality": "if anyone should want to say that the tree of knowledge of good and evil was creation as it appears before us, he would not be wrong; for essentially this is what naturally (φυσικῶς) communicates to its participants joy and pain."[102] This means that, for St Maximus, death was already there, as part of the reality confronting Adam at his creation: it was there in the way the animals, to which he likened himself in all respects,[103] were perpetuating their lives. By choosing to subject himself to what was controllable by his senses (the αἰσθητά), i.e., to reality, Adam subjected himself to the death which was part of this reality: his sin "bought" him death.

Now, the "tree" from which Adam ate ("creation as it appears before us") contained not only evil but also good, not only death but also life. The reality to which Adam chose to subject himself was *antinomical* in its very nature. According to the Fathers, such as St Gregory of Nyssa, this was provided by God at the moment of our creation so that the fall, which was foreseen by him, would not lead to the disappearance of the human race. Death was intermingled with life in the same way that evil coexisted with good in the tree of disobedience. The fall did not destroy humanity—or creation. We continue to exist, albeit as mortal, as "being-unto-death."

---

[101] Maximus, *QThal.* 43 (PG 90:412B).
[102] Ibid., 257C.
[103] Ibid., 253C. Cf. Ibid., 269A (ἡ τῶν ἀλόγων ζώων ὁμοίωσις).

This antinomical existence reveals itself at the ontological level in the way we come into being, in *sexuality*. In the minds of many people, the fall has been associated with the sexual act, and Christian tradition has often tended to attach particular seriousness to sins relating to sexual activity. The New Testament and patristic eschatology exclude marriage and sexual reproduction from the Kingdom of God.[104] This is due to the association of sexuality with death which will be abolished in the eschata.

Sexuality, therefore, is at once good and evil: it is good because it reproduces life, and it is evil in that it does so by bringing forth mortal beings. "Between 'fear of death' and 'slavery to sensual desire through love for life', the circle is inescapably closed; the perpetuation of life, for which man strives, is in fact a perpetuation of death."[105]

Because "death dwells potentially in all coming-to-be, as a judgement on nature,"[106] all life is a mixture of desire and pain[107] and, in the final analysis, of being and nonbeing. Existence is antinomical at the ontological as well as at the psychological level: pleasure is mixed with pain, and "passions" (πάθη) are capable of serving and expressing both evil and good. "Even quarrelsome and unreliable people are moved by shadowy images of a love for peace; for they are driven by their passions, and in trying ignorantly to satisfy them, they believe they are moving toward peace."[108] In this respect, sexuality, too, involving as it does desire for union, is not just a means for perpetuating biological life but also a movement toward communion:

> Man seeks to have access to something good, to find the possibility of union, in the tender love of a comrade in mortality; and even if this love is itself open to corruption, still it is a distant, weak echo of the love of God and embraces a phantom only because of the good ... Through the very form of unity and love, man already possesses a shadowy share of the good.[109]

---

[104] Mt 22:30; Lk 20:24, 35. Athanasius, *Exp. Psalm*, 50.7 (PG 27:240CD); Gregory Nys., *De hom. opif* 16–18 (PG 44:177ff); John Chrysostom, *De virg.* 14 (PG 48:543ff); Maximus, *Quest. et. dub.* 3 (PG 90:788AB)., etc.

[105] Von Balthasar, *Cosmic Liturgy*, p. 198.

[106] Ibid., p. 198f.

[107] Maximus, *QThal.* Prol. (PG 90:256D).

[108] Maximus, *Schol. de div. nom.* (by John of Skythopolis?) (PG 4:397D).

[109] Ibid., 281AC. Cf. v. Balthasar, *Cosmic Liturgy*, p. 200.

The notion of πάθος contains and expresses, in a dramatic way, the antinomical character of our existence: with the same impulses rooted in our nature, we move simultaneously toward God (to life, love, etc.) and away from him (to death, selfishness, etc.).[110] Our entanglement in this dialectic constitutes the tragedy of our "fall."

The antinomical structure of reality vividly expresses itself also at the social level. The reality into which Adam "fell" included not only the "self" but also the "other," and its antinomical structure also affected the relationship between the two. The members of the first human couple felt, as soon as they ate from the forbidden "tree," the need to resort into "privacy" from one another as if they were strangers having something to hide from each other (Gen 3:7). Unity and communion would have, from then on, to coexist with privacy and individuality, making the relationship of the One and the Many a constant and unresolvable problem in our existence, the most painful antinomy in human social life. The other became our "hell" and our "original sin," and it was but an inevitable consequence of this fear of the other that Cain killed his brother, as early as the dawn of human history. Ever since, human ethics has (rightly so) found the act of homicide repulsive, but it can do little to attack its roots which lie deep in the antinomical structure of reality, the tension between the one and the many, the fear of the other, to which we are subjected by the fall. Just as death and life are vehicles of each other in our coming to be, in the same way antagonism with each other (whether in a "civilized" or a "brutal" form) constitutes the canvas on which our social relations are interwoven. The vicious circle of this antinomy can only be broken if the "self" dies for the other, but that would require a love as "kenotic" as that of Christ.

The consequences of the enslavement of the human being in the antinomical structure of reality—the choice of the given instead of the promised—through the eating from the "tree of the knowledge of good and evil" are dramatically present in the exercise of our *freedom*. In the fallen state of existence, human freedom is constrained by the choice of *given* possibilities, which are derived from the antinomical structure of existence. This kind of freedom shows that there

[110] Maximus, *QThal.* 1 (PG 90:269B).

are always limits to what we can choose and that any attempt to exceed these limits will cost us our very existence. The ancient Greeks called such an attempt *hybris*— audacity and boldness exceeding one's assigned limits—an offence punished severely by the gods.

Freedom, therefore, in our fallen existence is restricted and constrained by necessity. This is the utmost antinomy, a contradiction in terms, which we are called to accept as "truth." How can we reconcile freedom and necessity making them exist side by side as parts of "reality"? The answer is this: in the same way that we reconcile evil and good, death and life, nonbeing and being—as a "logic" which we must accept if we are to remain "sane" and avoid being put in an asylum.

Lev Shestov, in a remarkably penetrating survey of Western philosophy from its inception in classical Greece to modern times, has shown how philosophical thought—and science—has enslaved *knowledge* in the prison of necessary and indisputable universal truths, causal laws and unalterable empirical facts. For a thinker like Baruch Spinoza, God himself has no power to transcend the necessary structures that express even his own being. Rene Descartes, as well as Leibniz, Kant, and Hegel—all of them follow essentially the same line of thought. All these philosophers—and all of us—think that freedom is the freedom to choose between good and evil. But "do not," Shestov asks, "[n]ecessity and the capacity for choosing between good and evil testify, not to our freedom—as Spinoza and Hegel thought and all of us also think—but to our enslavement, to our loss of freedom? The free being possesses the sovereign right to give names to all things, and they will bear the names that he confers on them. The free man might not have authorized evil to enter into the world, but now must be content with 'choosing' between the evil that is not subordinated to him and the good that is likewise no longer in his power."[111]

Nietzsche longed to escape from the domination of the "eternal truths," but, according to Shestov, did not entirely succeed.[112] It is in Kierkegaard and, above all, in Fyodor Dostoevsky that freedom

---

[111] L. Shestov, *Athens and Jerusalem*, trans. B. Martin (Athens, OH: Ohio University Press, 1966), p. 148.

[112] Ibid., p. 182.

emerges as an absolute category, as a revolt against all forms of the given and the universal. Kierkegaard attacks Hegel for his submission of freedom to the necessity of the universal, and yet, Shestov observes, in dealing with faith Kierkegaard admits that one is a (free) individual only if he first submits himself to the universal and has become a man, an individual, through the universal.[113] This is why, in dealing with the ethical and its relation to freedom, Kierkegaard could only go so far as to speak of the "suspension" of ethics and not of its abolition.[114]

Dostoevsky, on the other hand, dealt the most merciless attack on the necessary laws of reason which constrain human freedom and make it subject to the power of universal causal principles and unalterable empirical facts. In his *Notes from the Underground*, he passionately protests against such a constraint on human freedom:

> But, good Lord, what do I care about the laws of nature and arithmetic if I have my reasons for disliking them, including the one about two and two making four! Of course, I won't be able to breach this wall with my head if I'm not strong enough. But I don't have to accept a stone wall just because it's there and I don't have the strength to breach it.[115]

Shestov makes no use of eschatology in his dealing with the fall. His approach is protological: the world was created by God in a perfect state, and Adam fell from this perfection by making use of the power of knowledge. Knowledge *per se* is, for Shestov, the essence of the fall.[116] He radically opposes reason and knowledge to faith, thus distancing himself, not only from Greek philosophy but also, implicitly, from patristic thought. In an eschatological approach to the fall,

---

[113] Ibid., p. 214.

[114] L. Shestov (Chestov), *Kierkegaard et la philosophie existentielle* (Paris: Vrin, 1948), pp. 63–79.

[115] F. M. Dostoevsky, *Notes from the Underground*, trans. A.R. MacAndrew (New York: Signet Classics, 1961), p. 99.

[116] L. Shestov (Chestov), *Kierkegaard et la philosophie existentielle*, p. 13: "From the moment human beings became *scientes*, that is with knowledge, sin came into being, sin and evil. This is what the Bible said." This position brought Shestov into conflict with his close friend N. Berdyaev. See N. Berdyaev, "L' idée fondamentale de la philosophie de Leon Chestov," "Preface" to L. Chestov, *Spéculation et Révélation*, French trans. S. Luneau (Lausanne: L'age d'homme, 1981), pp. 7–10.

however, the existential problem of the fall is not knowledge as such but the subjection of human reason to the knowledge *of good and evil*, to "reality," to the antinomical state of creation which was given to the human being with the call to "heal" and transcend its antinomies in the end. The "tree of life" (i.e., of life eternal or eschatological), from which Adam refused to eat, was also a tree of knowledge (John 8:28,32; 14:7,20; 16:3 etc.), not, however, of the world as it was when Adam was created (and as it still is because this was the tree from which he ate) but as it will be when it is freed from the antinomies of good and evil, of life and death in the eschata. The knowledge which Adam obtained by eating from the forbidden tree was the knowledge of the "real" world with its existential antinomies.

∴

Reality is not our true "home," and this is evident from the fact that, in spite of our reason's efforts to accommodate us in it, we constantly strive to escape from its domain. This is evident not only in the extreme cases of nihilism and the irrational, which we tend to exorcise from our life; it is to be found in acceptable areas that we regard as "culture" and "civilization," all of which entail some form of transcendence or modification of the "given" and the "real." Our social and political life is full of attempts to "correct" and "reform" the given by transforming the already existent into a new "reality" in an endless process of "revolutions." Science is doing the same thing to nature, even to the point of violating its given laws in our time. Art, in all its forms, aims at the transformation of reality, sometimes even by deforming it and altering its structure. We do not feel "at home" with the reality into which we have "fallen."

Despite all our efforts, however, to transform and transcend reality, the chains of Prometheus still bind him. There is something in reality which continues to bother us and from which we are unable to escape: the basic antinomies of our existence, those of good and evil, life and death, being and nonbeing, the fruit of the tree the human being chose to eat "as soon as it came to existence."[117] These require now an intervention from outside (from "above"), a death of the old and a resurrection into a new, eternal life offered to the world

[117] Maximus, *QThal.* 61 (PG 90:628AB).

in Christ and promised in the Kingdom. Only faith in the eschata can liberate us from the bondage of reality.

Meanwhile, thanks to the antinomical structure of reality, the fall has not resulted in catastrophe but only in tragedy. Even death possesses a dimension of the good, in that it does not allow evil to be immortal.[118] The fall has not delivered creation and humanity to the Devil; owing to the antinomical structure of reality, evil is bound up with good, and this prevents creation—and humanity—from being ontologically evil:

> For that which is not deprived of the good (τοῦ καλοῦ) but has partially coexisted with that which is deprived of the good (τοῦ ἀγαθοῦ), makes something participate fully in the good. For evil is not the partial but the total deprivation of the good. And it is not the partially but the fully deprived of the good that neither was, nor is, nor will be, nor can be.[119]

Still, the human being is not satisfied with this kind of antinomical existence. This is the greatest proof that we are ontologically constituted by eschatology. The existential experience of the fall and its tragic character show that our true home is not in *statu viae* but *in statu patriae*,[120] in the future, when evil and death will be abolished and the antinomies of our existence will be replaced by a pure "Yes" to God, by an eternal "Amen!" (cf. 2 Cor 1:20).

Appendix II:
A Note on Perfection

Objections may be raised to the thesis of the previous chapter that Adam fell to a preexisting state of creation in which corruption, death, and natural "evil" were already present and did not appear as a result of the fall. Would this thesis not imply that God created a

---

[118] This is a patristic idea. St Gregory Palamas exalts the love, wisdom, and mercy of God shown in the fact that he uses the original mortality of our nature in order to grant us something much higher, namely immortality (*The One Hundred and Fifty Chapters*, ch. 54., ed. R.E. Sinkewicz [Toronto: Pontifical Institute of Mediaeval Studies, 1988]). See also Appendix II to this chapter: A Note on Perfection, note 128.

[119] Maximus(?), *Schol. de div. nom.* 4.20 (PG 4:281B). This is a faithful expansion of the ideas stated in the Areopagetic writings (PG 3:784ff).

[120] To use the terminology of St Augustine, *Evang. Joannis tract.* CXXIV. 3C (PL 35:19f).

deficient world, that creation is in its nature "evil," and that God is in some sense the author of this unsatisfactory "reality" to which we have fallen?

We have already proposed that in an eschatological ontology truth lies in the end, not in the beginning. A "fact" which is complete and finished in the past falls into nonexistence unless it is confirmed ontologically as "true" in the end: it is in the end that we can find the beginning (according to St Maximus). Applied to the idea or "fact" of creation, this will mean that the world which issued from the hands of God was ontologically perfect *only in its totality which includes its end*. God does not create incomplete things, and whatever he creates corresponds fully to his will. What kind of world did God will to create?

According to the theological cosmology of the New Testament, God created the world "by," "in," and "for" Christ (Col 1:15f.) This Christological approach to cosmology is developed and nuanced by St Maximus in an eschatological perspective according to which creation has an "end" (τέλος), a final destination, in which it is to be "recapitulated" in Christ and participate in God's life. It is *this* kind of creation in its totality, including its "end," that issued from the hands of the Creator as *his will*.

When we ask, therefore, whether God created a perfect world, we should have in mind not the beginning but the end of creation. The world's perfection lies in its "end." Perfection is not a protological but an eschatological state. This means that creation was endowed with a dynamic movement toward an end, a becoming, a "history." The scheme proposed by St Maximus to express this is well-known: γένεσις—κίνησις—στάσις (coming into being—motion—rest).[121] Against Origen and the Platonic tradition, perfection (rest) belongs not to the beginning but to the end which is reached only through a movement. History, therefore, is crucial, indeed indispensable, as the way to perfection; it is part of the very definition of creation. Creation is historical in its very nature. This movement is not an evolvement from some original perfection. The Maximinian notion of motion draws its meaning, its *raison d'être*, from its final

[121] *Amb.* 7 (PG 91:1073B).

destination, its end. It is because of this that history is capable of hosting the eschaton in its course, as is shown in the Incarnation.

Like St Irenaeus and other ancient writers,[122] therefore, we should not be afraid to speak of an "imperfect" creation at the beginning. Even St Maximus describes the original state of creation as lacking perfection, since it involved divisions that had to be healed and transcended in Christ.[123] The nature itself of creation had to be lifted "above nature," and the "image of God" given to humanity at the beginning had to become "similitude" in the end. According to St Basil, too, immortality was given to Adam as a promise, not as an original state,[124] and it is not accidental that the Fathers speak of the work of "perfecting" creation which belongs, according to them,[125] to the Holy Spirit, who is identified with the coming of the Kingdom.[126] Creation did need perfection, and this is no scandal to the mind which conceives creation as receiving its fullness, even its definition, from its end.

A "scandal" *may* arise for some if the original "deficiencies" of creation are meant to involve such negative things as corruption, death, suffering, that which we call "natural evil": if these things belonged to the original state of creation (before the human fall) are they not to be attributed to the will and the work of the Creator? The whole Christian tradition would reject the view that God is the author of evil. The argument is based usually on protological thinking: God created a perfect world at the beginning, and whatever belongs to "natural evil" (corruption, death, suffering, etc.) must be blamed on the fall (of angels and humans). We have discussed the difficulties that such a position entails—not least for the relation of theology to science. What would the answer be if we employed an eschatological rather than a protological ontology?

If we borrow the definition of evil from St Maximus the Confessor, the argument will have to be based on eschatology. According to St Maximus, evil is "the deprivation (ἔλλειψις) of the energy to-

[122] See chapter three, "Eschatology and the Fall."
[123] Ibid.
[124] Ibid. The same is true also of St Gregory Palamas. See note 128 below.
[125] See chapter two, "Eschatology and Creation."
[126] Ibid.

ward the end of the powers implanted in nature ... the irrational
movement ... of the natural powers toward a direction other than the
end."[127] Therefore, whatever is a deviation not from the beginning
but from the end is evil. Evil is contrary to the will of God because
the will of God coincides with the end for which he created the world,
and evil contradicts this end or deviates from it.

Placed in this eschatological perspective, the original "deficiencies" of creation, including mortality and all the "side effects" of createdness, can be classified as "evil" only if they do not partake of the
movement toward the eschatological end, *if they hinder their eschatological transcendence and claim or acquire ultimate ontological significance.* If, on the contrary, they serve the movement toward the
end, these "deficiencies" (mortality, pain, decay, etc.) can be even
used by God as a pedagogical means on the way to the "blessed end"
which will bring about their abolition.[128] This is shown in a dramatic way in the Incarnation in which Christ defeats death, the creaturely "deficiency" *par excellence*, by undergoing it. The martyrs of
the Church follow the same path, having the eschatological vision as
their motivation.

The original "deficiencies" of creation, therefore, including death,
are not "evil" if they serve the movement of creation toward the
"blessed end" (*which will transcend or abolish them*). If they do not
follow the eschatological course, they become evil like everything
that deviates from the movement to the end, according to St Maximus' definition of evil.

By refusing to fulfill his mission to lead creation to the end, which
would "perfect" creation, Adam through his fall "stabilized" its original "imperfections" allowing them to acquire permanence. This made
death reign over nature and become a permanent partner of being
(being-unto-death) in an antinomical structure of the world's exis-

[127] Maximus, *QThal.* Pref. (PG 90:253AB). See above chapter three, "Eschatology and the Fall."

[128] St Gregory Palamas states clearly that mortality lies "in the very root of our [hu-man] race" even before death appeared (through the fall). But he regards this as a blessing of God's wisdom and love because "had it not been for that we would not have obtained really [in Christ] the first-fruits of immortality.... [O]ur nature would not have been en-throned at the right hand of heavenly majesty." (*The One Hundred and Fifty Chapters*, ch. 54.)

tence. It is in this sense that the fall can be considered as the "cause" of death and evil. Death was already there before the fall, but it was the fall that stopped the movement toward its final abolition making it, thus, a permanent "reality," "on account of which all have sinned" (Rom 5:12).

Τέλος (end) and τέλειον (perfect) share the same root in the Greek language. In Christian (biblical and patristic) ontology, with its dynamic association with time and history as constitutive elements of creation, perfection can only be conceived eschatologically, as a gift of him who "perfects" the work of creation by bringing the last days into history, God the Holy Spirit.

Accustomed as we are to a protological way of thinking, we may wonder why God did not create a perfect world at the beginning instead of putting its perfection in the end. In fact, many great thinkers in the course of history have found it more appropriate to conceive perfection as belonging to the beginning rather than the end. Ancient Greek philosophy has had many followers in history, also from the area of theological thought, who operated on such a principle. However appealing it may be to our common logic, such an assumption entails very serious consequences for our existence. A perfect creation at the beginning would impose on human beings a fateful necessity (which happened in ancient Greek thought), leaving little room for our freedom. By making creation move toward perfection (i.e., by granting it a history) and calling us to lead this process in freedom, God elevated humanity to the highest point of dignity in the whole universe. This, of course, involved a risk for creation, as the fall has so tragically shown. But risk is inevitable where there is freedom and love. And God places freedom—a quality of his own being—so high that even in restoring, after the fall, the movement to the eschatological perfection through the Incarnation he sought the assent of human freedom which was given in the person of the *Theotokos*. Might this not be the reason behind the delay of the Parousia, too?[129]

---

[129] For some very interesting suggestions on this topic see C.M. Hays, *et. al.*, *When the Son of Man Didn't Come: A Constructive Proposal on the Delay of the Parousia* (Minneapolis, MN: Fortress Press, 2016).

Chapter Four

ESCHATOLOGY, HELL, AND FINAL JUDGEMENT

Introduction

The problem of the eschaton is usually approached from a *jurid-ical* viewpoint, as the time of *judgement*. In the scene of Christ's Second Coming presented by St Matthew's gospel (Mt 25:31–46), Christ judges the world ("the nations") and divides it into two groups, "at his right hand" those who inherit "the kingdom prepared from the foundation of the world" and pass over "into eternal life," and "at the left" those are condemned "to the eternal fire" or "to eternal punishment." When this scene is combined with other similar references in the gospels (e.g., Mt 8:12, 13:42, 22:13, 24:51, 25:30; Lk 13:28), the juridical approach to the eschaton is completed. At the end of time, when Christ comes to establish his Kingdom, of which "there will be no end," humanity will experience for all eternity either an unceasing joy and blessedness or an endless agony.

This juridical understanding of the eschaton undeniably has depth and also, perhaps, an exclusively *psychological* character. What is presupposed is a God who punishes and, at the same time, a human experience analogous, if not quite identical, to that to which human beings are exposed in this life: retribution, pain, groaning, a "grinding of teeth." All these, if taken literally, presuppose a human body in its present form, which is compatible neither with the concept of the soul separated from the body after death, the so-called "intermediate state," nor with the state of bodies after the resurrection, when death will be no more and bodies will not be subject to decay. The psychology of pain is inevitably bound up with mortality, with our mortal bodies. It is a projection of historical experience to the eschaton, an understanding in terms of mortality of a mode of existence that is, however, happening *after* the abolition of death.

This juridical and psychological approach has overlain another more basic and fundamental view of the Last Judgement which refers to the *being* itself of humanity and of the world.[1] When we refer to the eschaton, to heaven and hell, we have in our minds as a rule certain "feelings"—either pleasant or unpleasant—as if the purpose for which God included the eschaton in his "economy" was confined to, or centered upon, our having pleasant or unpleasant feelings about what we call "beatitude," rather than upon whether *we should exist or not exist in a true manner.* The expression "eternal life" thus loses its ontological content and acquires what is, in essence, a meaning that is purely psychological. We forget that the synonym of "eternal life" is "true life," that is to say, life which does not self-destruct (and so, is a lie) on account of death, as is the case today with our biological life. Heaven and hell must be connected with ontological categories. Only then do they acquire their full meaning.

We encounter an ontological approach of this kind in St Maximus the Confessor. As with previous subjects, we shall take him as our point of departure and comment on him in the course of setting out our argument and theological reflection. If we wish to learn from the Fathers, we cannot just repeat their words; we must reflect on them.[2]

I. Judgement and Existence

Therefore the *logoi* of all things that exist in essence and will exist in essence, or that have come into being, or will come into being, or are apparent, or will be apparent, preexist in a stable manner in God. It is by virtue of these that all things are and have

---

[1] Eschatology, as Sergius Bulgakov notes in *L'Épouse de l'Agneau*, trans. C. Andronikof (Lausanne: L'Âge d'Homme, 1984), p. 292ff., and *The Bride of the Lamb*, p. 349ff) even the eschatology of Orthodox dogmatics has been shaped under Roman Catholic influence and is marked by two dangerous tendencies: (a) a *rationalism* that tends to transpose rational schemata taken from historical experience; and (b) an *anthropomorphism* that unhesitatingly transfers to God juridical categories belonging to the penal code. Thus, in my opinion, it is absolutely necessary for theology "to carry out an *ontological* exegesis of the relevant texts [relating to eschatology]."

[2] A theologian who does not reflect on the words of the Fathers but simply repeats them is rather like students who repeat what they have learnt parrot-fashion. No teacher would want such students; why should the Fathers want them?

come into being and persist forever, by their own *logoi* in accordance with God's purpose, approaching by a natural movement and assuredly being held in existence, in accordance with the quality and quantity of the movement and balance of deliberate choice, receiving either well-being through virtue and the direct movement that follows the *logos* by which it exists, or ill-being through wickedness and the movement that is contrary to the *logos* by which it exists, and, to put it briefly, according to the possession or loss of their power by nature to participate in him who is by nature utterly imparticipable, and simply grants himself to all, the worthy and the unworthy, wholly by grace through infinite goodness, and will create the permanence of ever-being just as each has disposed himself to be and is. In their case, the proportionate participation or nonparticipation in him who is being in the proper sense is an intensification and increase of the retribution suffered by those who are not able to participate, and the pleasure enjoyed by those who are able to participate.[3]

It becomes apparent from the study of this passage of St Maximus that the final judgement of the eschaton has a deeper ontological content and is not a juridical or psychological matter. What is judged at the eschaton is "participation" or "nonparticipation" in *being* in its *threefold form*, which occupies a central position in Maximus' thinking, that is to say, *being in the proper sense, well-being* and *ever-being*.[4] Eternal punishment (τιμωρία in Maximus, translated above as "retribution") is constituted by "non-participation" in *being*, in *well-being* and in *ever-being*, just as conversely eternal life is constituted by "participation" in being in its three forms. In the final analysis the judgement at the eschaton is a matter of participation or not by grace in the same God who "is by nature utterly imparticipable," and who alone is that which is truly *being* and *well-being* and *ever-being*.[5] "Nonparticipation" in this threefold being is equivalent to the separation of humankind from God.[6] This is hell represented in ontological categories.

[3] Maximus, *Amb.* 42 (PG 91:1329AB).

[4] Maximus, *Amb.* 10 (PG 91:1116B).

[5] Maximus, *Amb.* 65 (PG 91:1392D): "as of [God] alone, who is properly and truly being and ever-being and well-being." Cf. Maximus, *Carit.* 3.25 (PG 90:1024C).

[6] Maximus, *Ep.* 1 (PG 91:389A). Cf. Gregory of Nazianzus, *Or.* 16.9 (PG 35:945C).

The question that arises is what precisely this "nonparticipation" in this threefold being can mean and the "retribution" that is entailed by it. Does it imply a falling away from being, that is to say, complete nonexistence? St Maximus' reply to this question is not absolutely clear. In one passage, the impression is given that *well-being*, which depends on our own freedom and effort (whereas *being* and *ever-being* are divine gifts), also determines our participation in the other two forms of being (*being* in the proper sense and *ever-being*): if *well-being*, which depends on our own "gnomic will" and "motion," does not exist, so as to be able to unite the other two terms (*being* in the proper sense and *ever-being*), then "the appellation [of being] is rendered useless to them [to the other two terms]."[7] If there are people who do not participate in well-being, by reason of the way in which they have exercised their freedom, the reference both to being and to ever-being "is rendered useless to them."[8] So, does hell signify nonexistence?

Although such a conclusion could be drawn from this particular passage, other texts of St Maximus give a different impression. Without accepting the restoration of all (the ἀποκατάστασις τῶν πάντων), Maximus teaches that at the eschaton human nature will be restored and completed in its entirety: "in the future age, the works of sin will proceed into nonexistence, since nature receives its own powers in a sound state."[9] We shall then have "the restoration of the whole of nature in the Resurrection ... to incorruption and immortality,"[10] and, as a consequence, "the soul's distorted faculties will, through the prolongation of the ages, put away the memories of evil stored up

---

[7] Maximus, *Amb.* 10 (PG 91:1116B).

[8] Dumitru Staniloae misinterprets this passage, in my opinion, when he writes: "If the good is not realized in the context of our freedom, existence as a primary gift is no longer presented as a good" (Introduction and notes to Φιλοσοφικὰ καὶ Θεολογικὰ Ἐρωτήματα... τοῦ ἁγίου Μαξίμου τοῦ Ὁμολογητοῦ [Philosophical and Theological Questions of St Maximus the Confessor], "Epi tas Pēgas" series [Athens, 1978], p. 263). Here the point at issue is not the "good," but "being" itself: "for in so far as it is being it is also well-being and ever-being." The subject-matter of the two end terms is not the good but being itself.

[9] Maximus, *QThal.* 73 (PG 90:848A).

[10] Maximus, *QThal.* 13 (PG 90:796B). Note the connection of incorruptibility and immortality with the eschaton.

in them[11]... and will thus receive its faculties by knowledge of, not participation in, the good things, and will be restored to its original state and shown to be the guiltless creator of sin."[12]

So according to St Maximus, there will be at the eschaton a natural existence and immortality, as a restoration of nature, which is not a participation in being, well-being, and ever-being (or in God). This constitutes the different way in which Maximus understands the restoration of all in comparison with Origen, or even Gregory of Nyssa.[13] By distinguishing existence as *participation* in *true* being[14] from the general restoration of nature, Maximus does not leave any room for the restoration of the devil and of those who have chosen his part, which is not the case with Origen and Gregory of Nyssa. There is no doubt at all in St Maximus' mind that hell will exist.[15] But in the passage just cited, Maximus does not seem to accept the prevailing psychological view that in hell the soul with "remember" its sins and suffer. The restoration of nature in its entirety on account of the Resurrection (up to this point he agrees with the idea of the

---

[11] In this passage, Maximus seems to reject the understanding that at the eschaton the soul "remembers" its sins. The restoration of nature in its entirety on account of the general resurrection entails, according to Maximus, that evil will not exist even as a memory, since the sinner's soul will shed "the memories of evil deposited within it."

[12] Maximus, *QThal.* 13 (PG 90:796BC).

[13] E. Michaud maintained that Maximus accepts the idea of a universal restoration ("S. Maxime le Confesseur et l'Apocatastase," *Revue Internationale de Théologie* 10 [1992] 257–72). The same view is held by V. Grumel (*Dictionnaire de Théologie Catholique* 10 [1928], 457). H.U. von Balthasar, however, thinks that hell for St Maximus is simply "a threat alone, which finally will remain unrealized" (*Kosmische Liturgie* [Einsideln: Johannes Verlag, 1988], pp. 275–8). A. Louth also thinks that "Maximus similarly accepts the hope of the salvation of all" ("Eastern Orthodox Eschatology," in *The Oxford Handbook of Eschatology*, ed. J. L. Walls [Oxford: Oxford University Press, 2008], p. 245). The opposite opinion is expressed by P. Sherwood (*The Earlier Ambigua of St Maximus the Confessor*, p. 205ff).

[14] St Maximus clearly distinguishes "simply being" (ἁπλῶς εἶναι) from "truly being" (ὄντως εἶναι). The latter is identified with "ever-being" (ἀεὶ εἶναι), that is to say, with that which will be bestowed at the eschaton (i.e., ὄντως εἶναι, the eschatological version of ever-being): "so that hence for them *simply being* is *to be*, and *truly being* is what they will receive at some time as an addition" (future tense, i.e., at the eschaton) (*Amb.* 10 [PG 91:1116C]). This passage has special significance for eschatological ontology: a being that is not an eternal being is not truly a being but proves in the end to be nonbeing (*mē on*).

[15] See, among many other passages, Maximus, *Ascet.* 27–39 (PG 90:932–48); *Carit.* I, 56, 57 and II, 34 (PG 90:972BC and 996B); *Ep.* 1/4/8/24 (PG 91:338–9/416–17/612), etc.

apocatastasis) implies that evil will not exist even as a memory in the sinner's soul, which at the eschaton will shed "the memories of evil stored up in it." This is a rejection of the psychological interpretation of hell as the survival of the consciousness (the "memory") of evil deeds. For St Maximus, as for other Fathers, evil has no hypostasis,[16] no ontological content, and consequently cannot survive at the eschaton even as a memory. The eschaton is the survival of being, not of nonbeing, which is what evil is.

What, then, constitutes the hell that St Maximus believes in? In some of his early works written at the beginning of his monastic career, such as *On the Ascetical Life*, several of his letters, and the *Chapters on Love*,[17] we come across phrases from St Maximus that describe hell in psychological terms, even in terms precisely opposite to those we have already noted. As he moves toward his more mature works, such as the *Questions to Thalassius* and the *Ambigua*, we notice the following:

(a) A reserve with regard to the content of hell which only the Judge can know: "What is to be believed about our dread judgement only the just Judge knows."[18] The question is put to him: "What are the eternal bonds? And what is the nether darkness where [the demons] are held? And what should be believed about the judgement of the great day?" He avoids replying without reserve, saying in a moderate tone that the apostles (the reference is to 2 Pet 2:4 and Jude 6) had direct access to the Logos, whereas for him there are many impediments to "approaching the Logos." For this reason, despite the fact that he attempts some kind of answer, he concludes that "only the just Judge" knows precisely what will happen to the demons and those who follow them in their lives "on the dread day of judgement."[19]

(b) An avoidance of the psychological account of the content of hell and a preference for ontological language. Thus, to the question

---

[16] See *Scholia on Dionysius the Areopagite* (PG 4:304D).
[17] Dated to around 626 AD.
[18] Maximus, *QThal.* 11 (PG 90:293A).
[19] The same "agnosticism" is also expressed by John Damascene with regard to the eternal fire, which is not like the fire familiar to us, "but as God knows" (*De fide orth.* 27 [PG 94:1228A].)

itself about what the darkness (ζόφος) of hell consists in, he replies: "the utter and complete ignorance of divine grace, by which ... they are deprived of the blessed and all-luminous transmission of unfading light, having wasted all the intellectual power naturally given to them on nonbeing."[20]

Thus St Maximus connects hell with the free choice of nonbeing already in this life. That is why Hades is described as "perdition" for "those who have by their free disposition given subsistence to nonbeing within themselves," which is to say, that for those who have freely (κατὰ διάθεσιν) given subsistence to nonbeing, hell is "perdition" (ἀπώλεια).[21] Thus hell will be nothing other than "relative alienation from God," which has as its eternal "accuser" the "attitude that gives subsistence to nonbeing."[22] Expressing precisely the same understanding, the scholiast of the works of Dionysius the Areopagite who bears the name of Maximus (actually, John of Scythopolis) identifies those who "aim at evil" with those who "aim at nonbeing."[23]

II. Hell and Freedom

If the desire for evil is a desire for what is nonbeing and hell is "nonparticipation" in "ever-being and well-being," are those who have freely chosen evil and have "hypostasized" it in their lives condemned to nonexistence? If so, how is hell to be explained as a state that is eternal and unending? If hell is a consequence of the free choice of beings endowed with free will, and not a choice of God, exactly as emphasized by all the Fathers (that is to say, if in condemning to hell God does nothing other than respect our freedom), then those who have freely chosen nonbeing (evil) while still alive should be condemned precisely to that which they have freely chosen—to nonbeing, to nonexistence, and not to an eternal state that may be described as torment and pain. Does the ontological interpretation of hell perhaps refute its eternity? How can these two interpretations logically coexist? How is it possible for us to preserve the ontological approach

---

[20] Maximus, *QThal.* (PG 90:293A).
[21] Maximus, *Amb.* 20 (PG 91:1237B).
[22] Maximus, *Amb.* 21 (PG 91:1252B).
[23] *Scholia on Dionysius the Areopagite* (PG 4:293B). See also below, p. 227ff.

without obliterating it and replacing it with the juridical and psychological interpretation, which also includes, as we have said, besides
other things, the danger of anthropomorphism?[24]

To these questions St Maximus does not furnish a ready-made
answer. But he does provide us with the presuppositions by which
we can give some kind of answer with the help of patristic theology
as a whole and the Church's tradition.

We saw earlier that not only for St Maximus but also for St Gregory of Nyssa we shall have at the eschaton a full restoration of nature
in the form that God wanted or predetermined when he brought it
into existence (in its "*logos*"). But whereas for Gregory of Nyssa this
signified that at the eschaton, in view of the fact that God will be "all
in all" (1 Cor 15:28), all things and all people will participate in God
and in his good things,[25] Maximus regards such an inference as "cata-
chrestic" (illegitimate) on the part of Gregory of Nyssa[26] and proposes the following thesis: at the eschatological resurrection, we shall
have a full restoration of nature and consequently also of the faculties of the soul, which will shed "the memories of evil that have been
inserted into it" and will find itself in the end with God, "who has
no limiting boundary." At this point, Maximus introduces a distinction between those who at this meeting with God will simply have
a "knowledge" (ἐπίγνωσις) of the good things (and of God)[27] and
those who will have a "participation" (μέθεξις) in the good things.[28]

With regard to participation, we have already seen that for Maximus this is about sharing in ever-being and well-being by those who
have freely (προαιρετικῶς) chosen it, and with regard to nonparticipation (ἀμεθεξία), it is about "ill-being" (φεῦ εἶναι), the content of
which Maximus does not describe but restricts himself to contrasting with "well-being" (εὖ εἶναι): the Judge will assign it appropriately

[24] See above, note 1.
[25] Gregory of Nyssa, *On then the Son Himself* (1 Cor 15:28) (PG 44:1316D); *On the Soul and Resurrection* (PG 46:104B).
[26] "And indeed Gregory of Nyssa has argued catachrestically in his own discourses" (Maximus, *QThal.* 13 [PG 90:796B]).
[27] In the theology of St Maximus, "the good" and "God" are closely linked and some-times used interchangeably. See *Scholia on Dionysius the Areopagite* (PG 4:288A).
[28] "by knowledge, not by participation" (Maximus, *QThal.* 13 [PG 90:796B]).

– 224 –

to all who are not "receptive" (χωρητοί) to well-being since they have
been disposed against it and have not sought it during their lives.[29]

What is of particular interest, however, is the distinction that
Maximus makes between the "participation" in and the simple
"knowledge" of God and the eternal good things,[30] which those who
are bereft of well-being and will find themselves included in ill-being
will possess. The meaning of the term ἐπίγνωσις (translated here as
"knowledge") is not easy to define with any precision. But St Maximus himself comes to our aid, for he uses this distinction as a key
concept in his gnoseology:

> For the principle of the knowledge of divine things is twofold.
> On the one hand it is relative, since it lies only in speech and
> thoughts, and is the absence of a real perception of what is known
> through experience. It is by this that we are governed in our pres-
> ent life. On the other hand, in the true and proper sense, it lies
> only in actual experience apart from speech and thoughts and
> provides the whole perception of what is known by grace through
> participation. It is from this that we receive the deification that
> transcends nature at the end of time.[31]

Consequently, St Maximus' contrast between the term ἐπίγνωσις ("knowledge") and the term μέθεξις ("participation") signifies
that we are dealing with a state in which God and ever-being and
well-being are "known" but are not experienced, and not shared in
experientially. We could therefore define hell as the state in which
God and ever-being and well-being are *known* (ἐπιγιγνώσκονται)
without being "participated" in on account of their free rejection.
That is to say, those who find themselves confronted with an eternal
state in which something (or somebody) exists in which they do not
participate, because they have freely rejected it, experience hell.

This state appears to be somewhat abstract, but it can become
very clear and specific. Christ's Resurrection and the eschatological

---

[29] Maximus, *Amb.* 65 (PG 91:1392D). God never gives us what we do not want: "we
do not find [at the eschaton] what we have not sought for" (*Ep* 1. [PG 91:388B]).
[30] It is interesting that Bulgakov, who never refers to St Maximus in any of his works,
does not make this distinction, with the result that he writes: "la vie éternelle est donné
à tous" (*L'Épouse de l'Agneau*, p. 354; cf. *The Bride of the Lamb*, pp. 450–2).
[31] Maximus, *QThal.* 60 (PG 90:621CD).

resurrection linked with it entail the absolute affirmation of being (of ever-being and truly-being). All the Greek fathers of the Church, from Irenaeus[32] to Maximus and the Orthodox tradition as a whole, have linked the resurrection to incorruption and immortality. Maximus is clear: only by the resurrection is immortality and ever-being given.[33] Immortality, consequently, for Maximus does not exist for created being "by nature," but only "by grace."

If, then, the general resurrection will restore nature to ever-being, which also constitutes the *logos* for which it was created, then all who have freely chosen to live and exist in opposition to "the *logos* of nature," which is ever-being, will find themselves at the eschaton confronted with that in which they do not wish to participate: with ever-being. This "knowledge" of the eternal affirmation and confirmation of ever-being, in which they did not ever wish to participate, will prove for them to be "ill-being," or hell, for as long as ever-being, which the resurrection has guaranteed, exists—that is to say, eternally.

The question, however, arises: will there be anybody who will not want ever-being and will have freely chosen nonbeing? If hell only refers to such a category of human being, then very few will find themselves in it. But is this inference certain?

III. Being and the Demonic

Hell is "the eternal fire prepared for the devil and his angels" (Mt 25:41; cf. Rev 20:10, 2 Pet 2:4, and Jude 6). In order to understand hell, it is necessary for us to examine the meaning of the "demonic." It is not by chance that even St Maximus in referring to hell writes that

---

[32] Irenaeus, *Haer.* IV, 39.4.

[33] Maximus, *Amb.* 42 (PG 91:1325BC): "as a result of the resurrection, by which we are refashioned by grace with regard to ever-being." (PG 91:1348D): "through the great and general resurrection by which humankind is born into immortality." Ever-being *is not a natural property*: "nor does it in any way exist in beings naturally as a faculty" (*Amb.* 65 [PG 91:1392B]). In consequence, even the soul's immortality, according to Maximus, should not be considered as "existing entirely by nature," but only *by grace*, and indeed "as a result of the resurrection, by which we are refashioned *by grace* with regard to ever-being" (*Amb.* 42 [PG 91:1325B]). See also *QThal.* 13 (PG 90:796B): "the restoration to incorruptibility and immortality of the whole of nature at the resurrection."

"the most pitiable thing of all," which gives him pain just to think about, is "the assimilation to the devil and wicked demons that endures forever."[34]

The demonic in the Bible is linked with rebellion against God (Jude 6) and, by extension, against his will. From this there has also emerged the ontological dimension of the demonic. The devil has "the power of death" (Heb 2:14) and "was a murderer from the beginning" (Jn 8:44). The demonic is directly opposed not only to God but also to each of his creatures. And it seeks not only the misfortune of God's creatures but also their annihilation. The devil fights against well-being, but he is also against being itself and, of course, against ever-being.

Hell, then, which essentially is destined for the demons and the demonic—and this must not be forgotten—must be linked first and foremost with the rejection of the existent, the war against being, and with the choice and desire for nonbeing. That is why the Fathers identify evil with nonbeing, and those who pursue evil with those who pursue nonbeing. This rejection of being, of existence itself, which is the supreme will of God, the Creator of all things, may be directed toward three targets: *toward the being of God, toward the being of anything else, or even toward the being of oneself.* Dostoevsky gives a vivid description of this state in *The Possessed.* It is worth giving some attention to this description, because it is closely connected with our theme.

As Dostoevsky himself allows us to see from Luke's account of the healing of the Gerasene demoniac (Lk 8:32–6), which he sets at the head of this work, the demonic with which the novel deals has to do with existential problems, not with the moral order. Just as the demons of the gospel passage did not "calm down" until they had finally led the herd of swine to their death (by suicide), so too the final goal of anything demonic is nothing other than the annihilation of the existent (of God, humankind, and the creation in its entirety) with the ultimate aim of replacing God's will with its own will. The demonic is thus shown to be a matter of ontology, not of ethics.

---

[34] Maximus, *Ep.* 1 (PG 91:389A).

In Dostoyevsky's work, Kirillov wants to prove that God does not exist and that he himself is god (with a direct reference to the demons and the first human couple), not by rational arguments but by his existence itself. If God exists, he says to his interlocutor Pyotr, then his will always prevails, and I can do nothing against his will. If he does not exist, then my own will prevails, and I can do nothing but express it as "my own will." The greater truth, he adds, is that God does not exist. Human beings have invented God because they are afraid to realize that they are masters of their own existence.

But, according to Kirillov, how else can one demonstrate more persuasively that one is master of one's own existence than by the fact that one can make it whatever one wants and even annihilate it? He says that whoever wishes to acquire absolute freedom must be bold enough to put an end to his existence. This is the supreme boundary of freedom. This is the whole of it; there is nothing beyond this. Whoever dares to commit suicide becomes God. Anyone can do this and thus put an end to the existence of God, and then absolutely nothing will exist.

Kirillov's words lead us to the essence of the demonic, to evil as "nonbeing," to the free choice of death as absolute nonexistence.[35] Such a choice has its point of departure, paradoxically, in the desire to assert oneself, in self-love: when love of oneself becomes the highest goal, something that is expressed as one's own will in its absolute form, then the very existence of the self destroys itself together with the destruction of the existence of the other and of the supreme Other, namely God. Our own wills becomes demonic when we choose our own will in opposition to the will of the other, especially with the ultimate aim of annihilating it. This happens in the case of *hatred* and in every attempt to annihilate the Other, physically or morally, in order to promote ourselves.[36]

This ontological and not simple ethical or psychological concept of hatred, according to which hatred is not just a feeling but a drive toward the annihilation of the other, makes Maximus link hatred with the demonic and surmise that "of all hells the most hellish and

---

[35] Cf. *Scholia on Dionysius the Areopagite* (PG 4:293B).
[36] A typical example is vehement criticism, which is common among us.

severe is to live forever with those who hate," even "without torments."[37] In other words, even if hell is defined in nonpsychological terms ("without torments"), simply to be among those who hate for all eternity (on account of the free choices made in this life) constitutes the *ne plus ultra* of hell. This, together with separation from God and the "separation of the lover from the beloved," to which we shall refer in greater detail below, constitutes for St Maximus the quintessence of hell.

This linking of hatred with hell is not without reference to the saint's personal life itself. As Hans Urs von Balthasar writes,[38] and as Fr Dumitru Staniloae repeats, "within the cramped monasteries in which [Maximus] lives, the waves of jealousy and calumny mount high, as anyone with eyes to see can easily discern in the *Chapters on Love*. To all these [Maximus] responds always only with love, a love which has really distanced itself from every impassioned state and has immersed him in the freedom of a universal goodness that imitates God."[39] It is well-known that Maximus was condemned by the Orthodox, as his *Life* tells us, as a heretic (an "Origenist").[40] What he writes during his years in a monastery to counter slander is extremely edifying for all of us: whether anyone slanders his faith or his manner of life only prayer for the slanderer—give neither a defense nor testimony, nothing else.[41] What St Maximus fears is that "in being unable to bear the distress, we imitate the slanderers,"[42] and this is because it is by these means that the demons succeed in their aim,[43] which is to draw us into a state of hatred, that is, into hell.

---

[37] Maximus, *Ep.* 1 (PG 91:389B).
[38] Von Balthasar, *Cosmic Liturgy: The Universe According to Maximus the Confessor*, trans. B.E. Daley (San Francisco: Ignatius Press, 2003), p. 30.
[39] Dumitru Staniloae, "Introduction" to the Μυσταγωγία τοῦ ἁγίου Μαξίμου τοῦ Ὁμολογητοῦ (Mystagogia of St. Maximus the Confessor), in the series Epi tas Pēgas 1 (1973), p. 15.
[40] *Record of the Trial* 5 (PG 90:120A).
[41] Maximus, *Carit.* 4.88 (PG 90:1069B): "There is no greater pain for the soul than slander, whether someone slanders one's faith or one's manner of life. And no one is able to ignore it unless, like Susanna, he has his eyes only on God, who alone can rescue from danger, as he rescued her, and can give people assurance, as he did with her, and console the soul with hope."
[42] Maximus, *Carit.* 4.87 (PG 90:1069B).
[43] Ibid.

All this may be interpreted "morally" or "psychologically," but for St Maximus it is linked organically with "ever-being and well- (or ill-) being." Calumny for Maximus is always demonic. Its aim is the devaluation and extermination of the other so that he or she ceases to have a "hypostasis"—a form of murder in the absence of the courage or power to physically destroy. If we approach it from this ontological perspective, we can understand why at the eschaton the eternal *existence*, on account of the resurrection, of him or her whom in this life we hated would be for us an eternal hell.

IV. Hell as the Presence of the Other

By abolishing death, Christ's Resurrection proved that the annihilation of the other, on whom the demonic has its sights, is in the end a lie: as long as death is abolished, however much we desire the annihilation of the other, this desire will remain, in the end, unfulfilled. How can you kill when death does not exist? The demonic has deceived us, giving us the impression that we can deliver ourselves from the presence of the other. This deceit became possible on account of the fact that death has not yet been erased. At the eschaton, however, when the "last enemy" will be abolished, the desire for the annihilation of the other will be unfulfillable. At that time, the other will really be "my hell," to recall the words of Jean-Paul Sartre: his existence will "torment" me for all eternity.

It is in this spirit that we should understand what the Lord says in St John's Gospel (8:44) when he describes the devil as a "murderer," adding that the devil "does not stand in the truth, because there is no truth in him. When he lies, he speaks according to his own nature, for he is a liar." The devil's lie is linked to his characteristic as a "murderer," and what Jesus says in the following dialogue with the Jews (Jn 8:51ff) testifies that the abolition of death is the critical point. The devil's "lie" and deceit is that anyone can forever annihilate someone whom he hates. Thus, what John writes in his First Epistle (3:14–15) acquires its meaning: "All who hate a brother or sister are murderers, and you know that murderers do not have eternal life abiding in them," because "whoever does not love abides in death"— these are ontological categories.

We encounter this ontological interpretation of the demonic "lie," precisely as analyzed here, in the *Scholia on Dionysius the Areopagite* attributed to St Maximus. Here is the text:

How those who pursue nonbeing are those who pursue evil is to be read as follows. God is being and transcends beings. And therefore the truth is being. It is therefore reasonable to say that the opposite to truth is falsehood and not even being. It is therefore absolutely outside God. It is not even an image (εἰκών) of truth. For it has nothing good from God. *But because it persuades some people that it is actually something*, it will be a dark and obscure image (εἴδωλον) of things that are beings in any way whatsoever.[44] On which account, it is also an image (εἴδωλον) in its operation and a lie in its operation, that is to say, it is truly and really a lie. Hence it is nonbeing in its operation, for it does not exist and is truly nonbeing. Therefore just as in the case of things that exist falsely, and exist as the whole of this falsehood, when the falsehood is destroyed, the whole essence of the matter is destroyed, and thus he who loves falsehood, like the demons, loves nonbeing, and does not stand in the real, that is, in the truth, as the Truth itself says (Jn 8:44). The demons, then, as Jesus says, being liars and fathers of lies, do not even exist and *pursue nonbeing when they pursue the evil of falsehood*.[45]

In this text, we have the linking of the demonic with the false in its ontological, not its ethical, sense. "[H]e who loves falsehood, like the demons, loves nonbeing, and does not stand in the real, that is, in the truth" (the reference is clearly to Jn 8:44). But how is the falsehood of nonbeing linked with the eschaton and ultimately with hell?

---

[44] It is especially interesting to note how Byzantine ecclesiastical art, clearly inspired by patristic theology, depicts the demons. See the perceptive comments of Stamatis Skliris (*In the Mirror: A Collection of Iconographic Essays and Illustrations* [Los Angeles: Sebastian Press, 2007], p. 24ff): "There are indeed some instances in which some figures are depicted unlighted in the icons, namely the demons. In their case their failure to participate in light entails their shrinkage [diminution in size]. That is to say, there are creatures which partake in light and are full, and there are other creatures that do not partake in it and so shrink, that is to say, they are shown in the icon as if tending toward nothingness." In Western art, the demons are represented as hideous (a psychological aesthetic approach), whereas in the East they are without form, dark and shrunken (an ontological approach). In the same work, see also pp. 28 and 100.

[45] *Scholia on Dionysius the Areopagite* (PG 4:293BC).

The eschaton is connected with the "general resurrection," which, as an offspring of the Resurrection of Christ (1 Cor 15:12), will confirm definitively the victory of life over death, of ever-being and truly-being over nonbeing. Thus at the eschaton, those who chose in their lives to strive for, or simply desire, the annihilation and nonexistence of someone else, and have died without repentance, will find themselves confronted with the impossibility of fulfilling this desire of theirs. Likewise, those who in their lives have not forgiven their enemy will be obliged to "forgive" (συν-χωρεῖν) them (the etymological meaning in Greek is to "make space for" them), that is to say, to coexist with them eternally in the same "space." This is an endless hell which they themselves have freely chosen, "not a punishment imposed by God, but a punishment which we ourselves have brought on ourselves."[46] Just like the rich man in the parable (Lk 16:20ff.), they will experience as an endless agony the "chasm" which in their lives they freely allowed to separate them from the other, from their own Lazarus.[47]

Thus our free choice not to share the same space with others—not only our good things, but also our personal existential mode, our coexistence with them—will prove at the eschaton to be the choice of a "lie," since this choice will have no possibility of finding satisfaction and realization. If we have based the whole mode of our existence on this choice, as happens, for example, in the case of hatred, then the impossibility of its fulfilment will be equivalent to the loss of our own hypostasis, to our nonbeing as a "mode of existence," since we shall be unable to give hypostasis to our (negative) relation with others, on which we founded the whole of our earthly existence. The mode by which we decided in this life to hypostasize our nature will necessarily meet with death, and thus our nature, which will be restored by the general resurrection, will "attempt" eternally to hypostasize itself in a manner which is no longer attainable. (As long as death existed, we could have drawn personal hypostasis by rejecting the other—physically or morally—something that is no longer possible once the existence of the other remains eternally in-

---

[46] John Damascene, *Against the Manichaeans* 75 (PG 94:1569C).
[47] What is said about "the least of these brothers and sisters" in Mt 25 should be interpreted in this ontological spirit.

vulnerable on account of the victory over death through the Resurrection.) This unattainable attempt to hypostasize our nature through a relationship with others, which will be impossible to bring to completion, is described psychologically as pain and groaning because it is only in this way that its negativity can be conveyed, yet in essence it is an ontological matter, since it concerns not feelings but the mode of the realization of our being.

Hell, consequently, may be described both as "death" and as "perdition,"[48] something that at first sight seems to conflict with its description as "pain." In fact, only an ontological approach could explain the use of the terms "death" and "perdition" for the expression of the content of hell. The terms "death" and "perdition" refer to nonexistence, whereas pain is unintelligible in the context of nonexistence. Faced with this difficulty, many resort to giving a metaphorical sense to the terms "death" and "perdition." But the fact that hell is also associated by the Fathers with the concept of "nonbeing" obliges us to reject the metaphorical interpretation. "Separation from God is death," according to St Irenaeus[49] and the rest of the Fathers, who also describe hell as separation from God.

The free choice of human beings to hypostasize themselves by drawing their personal mode of existence from the rejection of the other, remaining as it does eternally impossible of achievement on account of the general resurrection, would entail a "metaphysical suicide," to borrow a phrase from Georges Florovsky of eternal memory, which, on account of the survival and restoration of nature by the general resurrection (of the just and unjust), would nevertheless not lead to complete nonexistence.[50] As St Maximus writes,[51] what is sought for in this life is that people should be reconciled with God and with all their fellow human beings, so that a conflict between the "gnomic will," that is, personal freedom, and "nature" might be avoided. It is precisely this conflict that is described as hell: the "gno-

---

[48] Maximus, *Amb.* 20 (PG 91:1237B).

[49] Irenaeus, *Haer.* V, 27.2.

[50] "The possibility of metaphysical suicide is open to her. But the power of self-annihilation is not given" (G. Florovsky, "Creation and Creaturehood," *Creation and Redemption, Collected Works*, vol. III, p. 49).

[51] Maximus, *Or. Dom.* (PG 90:901C).

mic will" (personal freedom) "divides" nature, and nature "by the gnomic will rebels against itself." This constitutes an *ontological rebellion*, a conflict between being and freedom, a kind of existence that hates existence without, however, being able to destroy it.

The purification of the human being from the "remembrance" of evil, the complete "forgetfulness of evil or injury" (ἀμνησικακία) thus becomes the highest ascetical goal. We should therefore not be surprised by the words of St Anastasius the Sinaite (d. 700), a faithful follower of the same tradition as St Maximus, when he writes:

If you wish to learn that the worst sin of all is the darkness of the remembrance of injury, listen. Every sin is committed in a brief space of time and is quickly brought to completion. For example, if one fornicates, and after this becomes conscious of the gravity of the sin, one passes to acknowledgement of it. But the remembrance of injury keeps the passion burning ceaselessly... Wherefore, once the remembrance of injury is planted, nothing is of any use, neither fasting, nor prayer, nor tears, nor confession, nor entreaty, nor virginity, nor almsgiving, nor any other good thing. For the remembrance of injury against a brother dissolves everything.[52]

And to the above he adds something that many would find offensive:

I often hear many people saying: "Alas, how can I be saved? I have not the strength to fast, I cannot make myself keep vigils, I am unable to maintain a state of virginity, I cannot bear to withdraw from the world. How then can I be saved?" How? I will tell you. Pardon others and you will be pardoned yourself. Forgive others and you will be forgiven yourself. See in this a short path to salvation. Now I will tell you a second way. Which one is that? Do not judge, it says, so that you may not be judged (Mt 7:1). See in this yet another way without fasting, and keeping vigils, and laboring. So do not judge your brother, even if you see him sinning with your own eyes.[53]

This insistence of both Maximus and Anastasius on freeing the human being from the remembrance of injury, and indeed on its substitution for serious ascetic labors and virtues, is due to the *onto-*

---

[52] Anastasius the Sinaite, *Discourse on the holy Synaxis* (PG 89:844BC).
[53] Ibid., 845A.

logical character which the remembrance of injury possesses. St Anastasius regards the remembrance of injury (or bearing of a grudge) as more serious than the other sins because "it keeps the passion burning ceaselessly." St Maximus expresses the same thought when, in more philosophical language, he urges its avoidance because the remembrance of injury "is imprinted" on the mind and, by cutting up nature by the gnomic will, it creates divisions among people and separates them. The remembrance of injury, consequently, is the attempt through the memory to give "hypostasis" to evil, which from the *ontological viewpoint* has no hypostasis, is nonbeing.[54] If this is transposed into eternity "from the present aeon to the life that does not age," that is to say, to the time when evil will be proved completely and forever to be "nonbeing," then the henceforth eternal conflict between the "gnomic will" and "nature" will signify eternal "hell" for the bearer of the "gnomic will."

V. The Eternity of Hell

The problem of the eternity of hell arose very early in theological thought for two principal reasons and on two different levels. One reason is connected with the *juridical* understanding of divine judgement and the other with the *ontological* questions which are provoked by the idea of an eternal hell. More specifically, the idea of a "punishing" God may be compatible with the concept of justice, but it raises questions with regard to the *love* of God: how can the love of God bear to see one of his creatures being tormented forever? On the ontological level, moreover, the question is unavoidable: does not an eternal hell signify the limitless perpetuation of evil, its eternal "existence," even if in the form of torment? Would not this conflict with the identification of evil with "nonbeing," which we have encountered in all the fathers of the Church, and indeed in St Maximus, whose thinking we have set out above?

We shall attempt to analyze the problem of the eternity of hell on these two levels, the juridical and the ontological, after first glancing at the history of the question.

---

[54] Maximus, *Or. Dom.* (PG 90:904A).

I. The juridical approach to the matter of the Last Judgement provoked questions in the patristic period as early as the time of Origen and reached a peak in the reaction to it by the Antiochene theologians of the fourth and fifth centuries, such as Diodore of Tarsus (d. before 394) and Theodore of Mopsuestia (d. 428). Origen regarded it as unthinkable that Christ, who suffered for our sins, would continue to suffer eternally,[55] whereas Theodore of Mopsuestia, in his *Against those who say that human beings fell by nature and not by will*,[56] appears to embrace the idea of the final restoration of all. It was, however, Isaac the Syrian, or Isaac of Nineveh (seventh century), who on the basis of the concept of God's love developed the idea of the apocatastasis and transmitted it to the East. His works, chiefly the one entitled *Second Part*, which was discovered recently and translated from Syriac into English by Sebastian Brock, discuss the temporary character of the torments of hell (citing the views of Diodore of Tarsus and Theodore of Mopsuestia), after which the restoration of all will prevail. These views do not correspond with the edition of Isaac's *Ascetica* published by Nikiphoros Theotokis (in Leipzig in 1770), which was based on the translation made by the monks Patrikios and Abraham of the Lavra of St Sabbas in the ninth century. Theotokis places Isaac in the sixth century,[57] thus giving leverage to the distinction between Isaac of the seventh century (who, apart from his views on the apocatastasis and his references to Diodore of Tarsus and Theodore of Mopsuestia, appears to have belonged to the Nestorians of the Persian Gulf area) and St Isaac the Syrian, or Isaac of Nineveh, who was known to the Orthodox fathers (Peter of Damascus, Symeon the New Theologian, Gregory of Sinai, etc.).

According to the *Second Part of the Ascetic Works* (attributed to the seventh-century Isaac), the idea of love conflicts with that of retribution and punishment.[58] That is why ultimately "the demons will not remain in their demonic state, nor will the sinners remain in

---

[55] Origen, *Hom. Lev.* 7.2 (PG 12:478B).

[56] See Photius, *Bibliotheca* (PG 103:513ff).

[57] See Isaac the Syrian, Τὰ εὑρεθέντα Ἀσκητικά (The Extant Ascetica), ed. I. Spetieris (Athens, 2005), p. ι'.

[58] Hilarion Alfeyev, *Prepodobnyi Isaak Sirin*, seventh ed. (St. Petersburg, 2013); Greek trans. Ἅγιος Ἰσαὰκ ὁ Σύρος (Athens, 2005), p. 359.

their sins. On the contrary, [God] will bring them to a unified state of perfection in relation to his own existence, to a state in which the holy angels now are, in the perfection of love and in a mind without passion."[59]

These theses have been echoed by modern theologians of chiefly the Russian tradition, who seem to be sympathetic to the idea of a final restoration, such as Sergius Bulgakov, Nikolai Berdyaev, Olivier Clément, Kallistos Ware, and Hilarion Alfeyev. In all these cases, including that of Bulgakov whose treatment also considers the ontological question, the reception of the idea of the apocatastasis is based chiefly on the way in which the love of God is conceived: how is it possible for faith in the love of God to be reconciled with the eternity of hell?

2. Apart from the argument about divine love, the idea of the eternity of hell also raises questions, as we have noted, on the level of ontology. Given the position of the Fathers that evil has no onticity, that it is "nonbeing" (μὴ ὄν), the perpetuation of hell is judged by certain ancient ecclesiastical authors as irrational and therefore to be rejected. We encounter this thesis chiefly in Origen and Gregory of Nyssa.

Citing specific biblical passages, and indeed 1 Corinthians 15:28, according to which at the eschaton all people and all things will be made subject to God, who will thus be "all in all," these authors conclude that sinners too, including the devil, will share in God and, consequently, will be saved. For Origen, this thesis constitutes a corollary, or part, of his theory of the "unity" (ἕνας) of rational beings, a "unity" which existed in the beginning, was followed by the fall of souls and their enclosure in bodies, and must logically return and be "restored" at the eschaton. The critical point of this theory lies in the philosophical principle that the beginning and the end must coincide (a Platonic cyclical concept).

Gregory of Nyssa agrees with Origen's opinion on the restoration of all, but without accepting the preexistence of souls or the linking of the fall with the body and the elimination of the body at the eschaton, thus following Methodius of Olympus.[60] The chief

---

[59] Part II, *Hom.* 40, cited by Hilarion Alfeyev, Ἅγιος Ἰσαὰκ ὁ Σύρος, p. 363.
[60] See E. Moutsoulas, Γρηγόριος Νύσσης (Gregory of Nyssa) (Athens: Apostoliki Diakonia, 1997), p. 454.

weight of Gregory's arguments in favor of the idea of the apocatastasis lies in *ontology*. In battling against Manichaeism, he wants to ensure by every means the uncoupling of evil from ontology, "for it is necessary in every way and wholly to detach evil from being and, as has already been said, that which is truly nonbeing is entirely without existence."[61] For precisely this reason, Gregory accepts the apocatastasis in order not to give an ontological content to evil: "It seems to me that the passage teaches the complete annihilation of evil.[62] For if God will be in all beings, evil manifestly will not be in them. For if anyone were to suppose that it was in them, how could we continue to maintain that God is all in all? For the exclusion of that one thing makes the inclusiveness deficient. But he who will be all in all will not be in that which does not truly exist."[63] St Gregory consequently approaches the eschaton with an *ontological argument* (not a juridical or psychological one). The question that is posed is a vital one: Does not an eternal hell entail the eternal existence of evil? Theology cannot ignore this question.

The Church has officially rejected the idea of the restoration of all as a false opinion and error. Whenever there has been a synodical condemnation, and especially one by an Ecumenical Council, the reception of the condemned opinion constitutes a heresy.[64] The Fifth Ecumenical Council (553 AD), following the theology of the emperor Justinian, condemned, among other things, the Origenian teachings concerning the apocatastasis, and adopted as its own of the fifteen canons against Origen of the Home Synod of Constantinople of 543.[65] Consequently, the responses to the questions that are given by ecclesiastical writers relating to the eternity of hell, both on the

[61] Gregory of Nyssa, *De an. et res.* (PG 46:101).

[62] The reference is to Eph 4:6.

[63] Gregory of Nyssa, *De an. et res.* (PG 46:104–5).

[64] In the climate of theological confusion and decadence in which we live today, the terms "heresy" and "heretical" are used for any theological disagreement, independently of whether such disagreement concerns synodical decisions or, indeed, decisions of an Ecumenical Council. This reflects a recent symptom of obscurantism, foreign to the tradition of our Church, which makes theological dialogue, even among Orthodox, difficult if not impossible.

[65] See I. Karmiris, *Dogmatica et Symbolica Monumenta Orthodoxae Catholicae Ecclesiae*, vol. 1 (Graz: Akademische Druck-u. Verlagsanstalt, 1968), p. 180ff.

ground of divine love and on the ontological level, cannot ignore the decisions of the Fifth Ecumenical Council with regard to this matter. But why has there been this insistence of the Church on the condemnation of the idea of the apocatastasis?

Both the argument based on divine love and the argument from the theory of evil as nonbeing come into conflict with the fundamental and inviolable principle of *freedom* when they are deployed against the eternity of hell. Thus, the question which the appeal to divine love raises is not, as is often assumed, whether the love of God conflicts with his justice (how is it possible for a just God to leave evil unpunished?),[66] but *whether it is possible for love not to respect freedom.* Can real love exist without freedom? If free beings, such as humans or demons, do not freely wish to participate in God, would it be an act of love on his part to deprive them of the freedom to reject this choice *for ever*? Neither Origen nor Gregory of Nyssa, despite the fact that they are not ignorant of the gift of freedom to rational beings, keeps this seriously in view when they maintain the restoration of all.[67] That is not something, however, that can be said of Maximus.

Referring to the first book of Corinthians 15:28, Maximus differs both from Origen and from Gregory of Nyssa when he writes: "And this is perhaps the subjection about which the divine Apostle spoke when he says that the Son will subject to the Father [at the eschaton] *those who freely accept being subjected,* with which and through which the last enemy, death, will be abolished as being dependent on us, *that is, on our free will.*"[68] And Maximus goes on to examine the theme of freedom and emphasize that at the eschaton the coincidence of our own will with that of God will be set forth and revealed in its fullness, so that what will prevail in the end is only His own will, a situation that will apply to the "worthy," that is, to those who, according to the example of Christ in Gethsemane, have arrived at "not what I want but what You want."[69] Deification, then, as the final

[66] It is interesting that St Maximus, at least so far as we know, does not seem to use this argument at all.

[67] J. C. Larchet points out a lack of coherence in Gregory of Nyssa's thought: "on peut se demander ... si cette position est bien cohérente" (*La divinisation de l'homme selon saint Maxime le Confesseur* [Paris: Cerf, 1996], p. 662).

[68] Maximus, *Amb.* 7 (PG 91:1076A).

[69] Maximus, *Amb.* 7 (PG 91:1076B).

"subjection" of all to God, necessarily presupposes our free will, something which does not permit the idea of the deification also of those
who did not freely wish to identify their own will with that of God.

3. But what is the meaning of "eternity" when we are referring
to the eschaton, according to which "time will be no more" (Rev
10:6)? Can we speak of *duration* when we are referring to the eternity of the eschaton?

Bulgakov's thesis that the eternity of the eschaton must be identified with God's eternity and is consequently incompatible with the
concept of duration raises the problem of the eternity both of the
Kingdom and of hell: if in some manner we do not introduce the
concept of *duration* into the idea of eternity, how do we understand
the phrase "of his kingdom there will be no end" (Lk 1:33), or the expressions "unaging" (ἀγήρως), by which the state of the eschaton is
described in patristic literature?

The concept of "duration" (διάρκεια) is doubtlessly linked to
that of "chronicity." Duration is a concept borrowed from mathe-
matics and suggests the extension of time to infinity. "Ever-being"
has an element of chronicity: "always, now, and forever and unto the
ages of ages."[70] For this reason Maximus, also attributes a beginning,
a middle, and an end, not only to time but also to the term "aeon"
(αἰών),[71] precisely because like time, the aeon has a "beginning of being." Where a beginning exists, motion follows, and motion has an
end—not a stop, but an objective, a goal. Consequently, we cannot
identify the eternity of the creature completely with the eternity of
God, which has no beginning. Humankind, as Maximus emphasizes, has received "ever-being" from God, "even though not without
a beginning yet without an end."[72]

The difference between divine and human eternity consists precisely in that the former has never had a beginning, whereas the latter came forth from nothing and "began" at some point, inaugurat-
ing time as movement toward some "end," even if the end is endless.
At the eschaton, however, will the human being cease to be a creature? Will the deification of the human being mean that his or her

---

[70]   Cf. Rom 1:25 and Phil 4:20.
[71]   Maximus, *Cap. theol.* I, 5 (PG 90:1085A).
[72]   Maximus, *Carit.* III, 25 (PG 90:1024C).

nature has not come into existence from nothing, that is to say, that he or she has passed from a created being to an uncreated being?

Maximus understands the "end" (τέλος) as "cessation" (στάσις) in God. But this "cessation" is described as "ever-moving" (ἀεικίνη-τος).[73] In the tradition of the Cappadocians, the human being, "in all the endless eternity of the aeon," "travels toward the infinite," moving "from beginning to beginning,"[74] never feeling "satiety" (κόρος) but with an enduring and ever-increasing appetite for God. According, also, to St Maximus, "what the knowledge of God brings about by virtue, *once perfected, again moves* toward increase. *For their ends have become the beginnings of other things.*"[75]

Eternity, consequently, is timeless or "beyond time," but only with regard to the property of time to divide beings and create an "interval" between them, that is to say, decay and death.[76] Apart from change and decay and death, however, time has also another property, that of *motion.* Thanks to this property created beings move not only with regard to the connection and relationship they have among themselves, but also with regard to their eschatological "end." For this reason, created time, in contrast to Platonism and Gnosticism, is not regarded in the Christian faith as something "evil" and therefore to be abolished but, on the contrary, as a constituent property of created being. Every creature by definition moves,[77] and this constitutes a gift willed by the Creator, not a curse that must be expunged at the eschaton.

In the degree, therefore, that eternity includes motion, it does not come into complete opposition to chronicity.[78] What differentiates these two concepts (time and eternity) at the eschaton is that, in historical reality, time is experienced as motion that collides with "interval" (divisibility), whereas at the eschaton motion is "ever-mov-

---

[73] See the excellent study of V. Mpetsakos, Στάσις Ἀεικίνητος (Ever-Moving Repose), (Athens: Armos, 2006).

[74] See Gregory of Nyssa, *Homily on the Song of Songs* 8 (PG 44:941C).

[75] Maximus, *Chapters on Theology and Economy* 55 (PG 90:1096C).

[76] See Basil the Great's definition of time as "the dimension that is coextensive with the constitution of the world" (*Against Eunomius* I, 21 [PG 29:560B]).

[77] Maximus, *Amb.* 23 (PG 91:1257CD).

[78] Bulgakov (*L'Épouse de l'Agneau*, 352) overlooks the dimension of motion in the concept of time and defines it only in categories of change, becoming, decay, and death.

ing" because, on account of the unity of all things, there is no "interval."[79] Thus eternity becomes an "endless" and "unaging" aeon, conserving its double signification both as a concept that expresses chronological duration and as endless and eternal existence: "for what time is to those subject to it, the aeon is to those who are eternal."[80]

There is therefore no question of contrasting, as Bulgakov does, the concept of eternity with that of duration. Eternity (αἰωνιότης) must not be confused with everlastingness (ἀϊδιότης), which is a characteristic belonging exclusively to the uncreated.[81] At the eschaton, the creature will be "deified," participating "by grace" in the everlastingness of God, but will not lose its property of createdness (this, in any case, is implied by the phrase "by grace"). This should not be forgotten when the phrase, "a human being without beginning and without end" by deification is under discussion.[82] St Maximus himself emphasizes that the human being as a creature receives ever-being from God, *although not in a manner without beginning*, yet nevertheless in a manner without end."[83] The eternity of God as everlasting has neither beginning nor duration, but the eternity of the creature has a beginning and moves eternally not only "in God" but also *toward* God.[84]

In accordance with these fundamental presuppositions there will be at the eschaton an enduring and endless motion either *toward* God (and at the same time *in* God) or *away from* God (despite the fact that God will be "all in all"). This second case describes hell, in which, although nature will be restored to its original *logos*, which is

---

[79] See St Maximus the Confessor, *Myst.* (PG 91:677A).

[80] John Damascene, *De fide orth.* 2.1 (PG 94:861B).

[81] See Basil, *Against Eunomius* II, 17 (PG 29:608D).

[82] As for example, P. Christou, "Άνθρωπος ἄναρχος, ἀτελεύτητος" (Beginningless and Endless Man), *Kleronomia* 12 (1980) 251–81.

[83] Maximus, *Centuries on Love* III, 25 (PG 90:1024C).

[84] The "toward" (*pros*) preserves the imparticipability of the created in the divine essence (*Scholia* [PG 4:404AB]). See the important comments of V. Mpetsakos (*Στάσις Ἀεικίνητος*, 233): "A *stationary motion* (στάσιμος κίνησις), which is at the same time an ever-moving cessation (στάσις ἀεικίνητος), presupposes apart from it the Other within which it takes place: the motion turns toward God and is stationary within Him. And the cessation is ever-moving, because it is not exhausted within its own boundaries, but turns away from it."

the union of created and uncreated in the person of the Son and Logos without their natural identification (see the Definition of Chalcedon), free will that has been set permanently against God and his will, will "rebel" against the union and will be borne away from God, with an ontological upheaval as a consequence (the one that we have mentioned above, person against nature, that is, an unfulfillable drive toward nonexistence, nothingness, death, and perdition).

This drive of the will away from God and against the "*logos* of nature*,*" that is to say, the rejection of the mystery of Christ, cannot be healed by force. As the ever-memorable Georges Florovsky observes, "nature is healed and becomes healthy only through the power of all-invigorating divine love, and hence it would be possible for us to speak of the 'force of grace.'... But the human will cannot be healed by force, since the entire meaning of the healing of the will lies in the fact that it constitutes a "turning," an active turning toward God."[85] And this is precisely because, as he observes elsewhere, "the will possesses an uncritical narrow-mindedness and obstinacy ... the sin that even at the restoration of all persists obstinately will remain unhealed. Conversely, the sin that is repented of will be forgiven 'in one hour.'"[86]

The will's drive either toward God or against his will begins and is made definitive in this life. This is because the eternity of the eschaton does not afford the possibility of *turning back* and *rectifying*, which is something only offered by historical time. The abolition of death by the Resurrection also abolishes chronicity as "διάστημα," "interval" (past, present, future), rendering repentance impossible in the eschaton.[87] At that point, the initiative lies only with the mercy of God. It is to God's mercy that the Church commends the souls of the deceased, knowing that they themselves can no longer repent, invoking their original turning to God in their Baptism and also something even more important: the relationship which they have

---

[85] Florovsky, Ἀνατομία προβλημάτων πίστεως (Anatomy of the Problems of Faith), trans. M. Kalamatas (Thessaloniki: Regopoulos), p. 90.

[86] Florovsky, Ἀνατομία προβλημάτων πίστεως, p. 197.

[87] "No repetition or return is possible, since no 'empty' time exists, nor 'endless' astronomical time, nor the revolution of the heavens" (Florovsky, Ἀνατομία προβλημάτων πίστεως, p. 194).

developed in this life with other members of the Church, especially with the saints who loved them and continue to do so and do not cease to pray for them. For this reason, the Church offers the divine Eucharist for them as the highest propitiatory sacrifice for their sins, invoking their relationship to this Mystery that they had developed in this life, believing that the love of him who has loved them until death will find, at the hour of Judgement, within the earthly fragments of their lives even a dim and weak turning toward God and his will.[88] Thus the Church intervenes between the justice and the love of God to annul any historical determinism which would make the eschaton the slave of our historical time.

VI. Eschatology and Ecclesia

"Try to come together more frequently to give thanks and glory to God. For when you meet frequently for the same purpose, the powers of Satan are abolished, and his destruction is dissolved."[89]

Eschatology without ecclesiology is demonic. To discuss the eternal fate of a human being in isolation from his or her relationship with others is as if we are attributing to Satan the absolute and final authority in existence, because the essence of the demonic is self-love, individualism, and division. When we hear "individual salvation" being discussed, we must be very much on our guard. Nobody is saved on their own. Indeed, the more one is anxious about one's own salvation alone, the more one distances oneself from it and submits to the "powers of Satan." Hell, according to St Maximus, in its most extreme and terrifying form ("of all punishments the most punitive and terrible"), is to "be separated from the one who loves and is loved."[90]

---

[88] Cf. Maximus, *QThal.* 10 (PG 90:792Cff): "Those who have achieved the perfection of love for God, and have exalted the soul's wing through the virtues in accordance with the Apostle, will be caught up in the clouds, and will not come to judgement. Those who have not achieved complete perfection but have acquired sins along with good deeds, these will come to the tribunal of judgement, and there through an examination of their good and bad deeds as if in a fire, if the balance tips away from their good deeds, they will be condemned to hell."

[89] Ignatius of Antioch, *Letter to the Ephesians,* 13.

[90] Maximus, *Ep.* 1 (PG 91:389B).

The Church exists precisely in order that the powers of Satan should be abolished, and this is achieved, according to St Ignatius, not by an individualistic purification but by coming "together more frequently to give thanks to God." However much human beings are cleansed of their passions, they do not escape what is "of all punishments the most punitive and terrible" if they do not avoid being "separated from the one who loves and is loved."

Unfortunately, even the divine Eucharist has to a large degree lost the content that constitutes it, which is *Synaxis* ("coming together"), that is to say, the transcendence of individualism and the attaining of unity. Today many go to the Divine Liturgy not to encounter the other and be united with them but to encounter God as individuals, as if they could not do this in their own homes. Nowadays, indeed, with the transmission of the Divine Liturgy on radio and television, this distortion of the meaning of the Divine Liturgy is formally endorsed with the blessing of the pastoral Church itself.

The Divine Eucharist, however, as the manifestation and realization of the Church itself,[91] exists precisely as *the supreme antidote to hell*[92]—not because it strengthens us by divine grace or energy as *individuals*, but precisely because it transforms us from individuals into *persons*. It links our personal salvation with that of others and reminds us, in this way, that no one is saved on his or her own—that the surest path to hell is our isolation from the others.

Extra ecclesiam nulla salus. In the life of the Church, this axiom was translated into practice by participation in the Divine Eucharist. Those who cut themselves off (or are cut off by the Church itself) from eucharistic communion are deprived of the "communion of the saints," within which alone they can hope to be saved.

It is consequently not without meaning that the Church fights against hell by praying for the souls of its deceased members, chiefly and supremely at the Divine Eucharist. Since ancient times (from the time of the apostles, according to Chrysostom), as we are assured by authors such as Tertullian,[93] Cyril of Jerusalem, Chrysostom, and

[91] Nicholas Cabasilas, *Interpretation of the Divine Liturgy* 38 (PG 150:425C–453A).
[92] Ignatius, *Letter to the Ephesians* 17.1; 20.2. Cf. Irenaeus, *Haer.* III, 19.1; IV, 38.4.
[93] Tertullian, *De corona* 3 and *De monogamia* 10 (PL 2:992).

others, the Church believed and continues to believe that by offering the Eucharist on behalf of the dead, "the greatest profit will accrue to the souls on whose behalf the supplication of the holy and most dread sacrifice is offered."[94] St Cyril of Jerusalem replies, thus, to the question of whether it is possible for sinners to escape hell after their death, using the example of some men condemned by the emperor, on whose behalf those connected with them intervened, "having weaved a wreath":[95] "In the same manner we too offer supplications to God on behalf of the deceased, *even if they are sinners*. We do not weave a wreath but offer Christ slain for our sins, the lover of humankind, as an expiation on their behalf and on ours."[96] In the same spirit, St John Chrysostom (characteristically adding *almsgiving*, that is to say, love, to the supplications offered on behalf of the dead) writes: "*Even if he* [the deceased] *is unworthy*,[97] God will be importuned by us. If he saved others through Paul and *through others spares others*, how will he not do the same through us?"[98]

These words of the Fathers and the uninterrupted tradition of the Church of memorial services witness that the Church, especially through the Divine Eucharist,[99] intervenes decisively in the logical sequence "sin = hell," inserting love between these two dimensions, a love for others ("through others he spares others") in the ecclesial-eucharistic community, with him "who takes away the sins of the world" (Jn 1:29) at its head, the "atoning sacrifice for our sins" (1 Jn 4:10). The sin of human beings does not bind God's mercy, just as the Church's prayer also does not bind God. Hell will always remain a mystery to human logic, hidden deeply in the mercy and freedom of God. None of us can erase it completely in the name of divine love,

---

[94] Cyril of Jerusalem, *Catechetical Lectures* 5 (PG 33:1116–17).

[95] The wreaths we lay at funerals probably go back to this custom.

[96] Cyril, *Catechetical Lectures* 5 (PG 33:1116–17).

[97] This unworthiness includes the sinner having lived "in wantonness, licentiousness, covetousness, sin, with the devil."

[98] John Chrysostom, *On the Acts of the Apostles* 21 (PG 60:169).

[99] The novel practice of conducting holy memorial services (and episcopal ones at that) outside the Divine Liturgy cuts them off from their eucharistic environment, which gives them their meaning. (Fortunately, at the Ecumenical Patriarchate it is still regarded as inconceivable to hold an episcopal memorial service without the bishop serving the Liturgy.)

adopting variants of the "apocatastasis," but equally none of us can predict God's judgement. According to St Anastasius the Sinaite, "he who judges before the coming of Christ is Antichrist, because he appropriates Christ's role."[100] It is not by chance that the same Church Father, St John Chrysostom, who insists on the need to cultivate the fear of hell within the faithful[101] is the one who, as we have seen, also emphasizes the prayer of the Church and almsgiving as antidotes to hell. The Church by its nature fights against hell, not only by its teaching but chiefly by prayer and the love of its members, ceaselessly beseeching the mercy of God, into the ocean of which it "casts the soul's despair," believing that his compassion "will be victorious [over sins] in limitless measure,"[102] not only of the living but also of the dead. In this manner the Church, without underestimating the seriousness of hell and encouraging complacency, averts despair and its destructive consequences for the spiritual health of its members.

But what is the ontological basis upon which all this rests? How can the sins of a human being and the punishment that they entail be affected by the Church's prayer and God's mercy? With a purely juridical approach, the reply to this question would be that God, as absolute judge, has the power, the "authority" as legislator, also to pronounce the remission of sins. If things were as simple as that, then what point is there to the Church's mediation, the Eucharist, and so on? The fact that *only* by this path is there hope for the remission of sins must lead us to another explanation beyond the juridical.

There are three basic ontological principles by which the Church's memorial services on behalf of the dead can be understood:

1. *The Ontology of the Person*

Existence cannot be understood in terms of atomic individuality. The concept of the "individual" is the greatest ontological myth that the human intellect has conceived as a consequence of our fall. Nothing in existence can be understood without a relation with something else. This is equally true for existence after death. The

---

[100] Anastasius the Sinaite, *Discourse on the holy Synaxis* (PG 89:846B).
[101] See, for example, John Chrysostom, *On II Thessalonians* 3 (PG 62:478); *On the Psalms* 11 (PG 55:146).
[102] Kneeling Prayers for Pentecost.

dead are not cut off from the relations which have defined their historical existence—on the contrary, these relations will finally judge their eternal future. The Church regards its members who have departed from this life as being in an existential relationship with it. That is why it commemorates them by name and places the "portion" for each of them, along with "portions" for the living, on the sacred Paten and finally in the Holy Chalice.

This ontological relationship between the "living" and the "dead" cannot but extend to the eschaton the reciprocal prayer and concern of each member for the other. If hell, according to St Maximus, is for "the lover to be separated from the beloved," the Church by its memorial services, and especially by the Divine Liturgy, endeavors to avert this separation, calling upon the intervention of divine mercy. The memorial services, consequently, independently of their result and benefit, constitute an existential need for the Church, dictated by its very ontology.

2. *The Ontology of Love*

The concept of the person—and, by extension, of love—in the Church passes indispensably by the Cross. The Cross of Christ reveals an ontological principle that is recognized for the first time: persons are not only linked existentially among themselves, but also mutually coinhere in such a way that one receives and "lifts up" the existence of the other in all its forms, including, sinfulness. This "kenotic" love in its highest sacrificial form is found in the Cross of Christ. Here the "One" takes upon himself the sins of the "others" and becomes a "propitiation" before God. Sin ceases in this way to be a nondetachable element of personal identity, as it was in ancient Greek tragedy, as it is "remitted" from the sinner, since it was shifted from the sinner to the sinless one, and consequently the former ceases to bear responsibility for it.

It is therefore not by chance that the Church, as we have said, from the beginning linked memorial services for the dead with the Divine Eucharist, where precisely Christ is offered as "a ransom for many" (Mt 20:28), as "his body, given for us," and as "the blood poured out for you" or "for many" (Mt 26:28; Mk 14:24; Lk 22:30), specifically "for the forgiveness of sins" (Mt 26:28).

This eucharistic ontology, in accordance with which the bond of love is so strong and indissoluble that the sin of the one can be "taken away" and assumed voluntarily by the other, in order not to break the existential unity and communion of the "lover with the beloved," is transferred by the Cross of Christ to the life of the Church's saints. Moses' prayer to God is characteristic: "Forgive them this sin. But if not, blot me out too from this book of yours, which you have written" (Ex 32:32). Shocking words: either with my people to heaven, or without them I too in hell! These words remind one of the saying of the Apostle Paul: "I could wish that I myself were accursed and cut off from Christ for the sake of my own people, my kindred according to the flesh" (Rom 9:3). One finds the same spirit in the desert ascetics, who pray that the demon that torments their brother should pass over to themselves, something which God permits and the monk gladly bears.[103]

It is to this "kenotic" principle that the Church owes its faith in the mediation of the saints and the power of the memorial services, which are in essence only an extension of the commemoration of the departed in the holy Anaphora. The "logic" of the memorial services flows from the ontology of the Eucharist and is not intelligible without it.

3. The Ontology of Mercy

There is much discussion in the dogmatic handbooks about the "benefit" and efficacy of the memorial services: is it possible through the celebration of memorial services to avert the punishment of a sinner? Rational thought stumbles over this question and is often led by the power that such thought exercises to the thesis that the benefit of the memorial services is "restricted"[104] and cannot be extend-

---

[103] The stories of the desert ascetics are full of similar instances. St Barsanuphius (*Epist.* 72–3) writes that "the perfect" are able to take upon themselves all the transgressions of the others, but the weaker only half of them. See my *Communion and Otherness*, p. 82ff.

[104] Thus, for example, P. Trembelas, Δογματικὴ τῆς Ὀρθοδόξου Καθολικῆς Ἐκκλησίας (Dogmatics of the Orthodox Catholic Church), vol. 3 (Athens: Sotir Brotherhood, 1979), 411 ff. French trans., P. Trembélas, *Dogmatique de l'Église orthodoxe catholique*, vol. 3, trans. P. Dumont (Chevetogne: Éditions de Chevetogne/Paris: Desclée de Brouwer, 1968), Book VI, chapter 3.

ed to serious sins. Not only, as we have seen, do Church fathers such as Cyril of Jerusalem and John Chrysostom not appear to accept such a distinction or restriction, the practice and tradition of the Church has never excepted those who have sinned gravely from the holy memorial services. Only those who have been cut off from the Church's communion through a synodical decision by "anathema" or "excommunication," as heretics or for any other reason, are not commemorated in the Divine Eucharist and, by extension, in the holy memorial services.

The practice of memorial services is a challenge to rational thought precisely because, by the concept of mercy and the kenotic ontology of the Cross, it cuts across and shatters the logical causality linking sin and punishment. This causality prevailed in antiquity, as is set out in ancient Greek tragedy, but the ontology of love, which Christianity brought, removes it by introducing the concept of *mercy*. Sin entails punishment, and "the wages of sin is death" (Rom 6:23). Despite this, God "has mercy on whomsoever he chooses" (Rom 9:18), and the Church has never ceased to proclaim that the mercy of God can "overcome an immeasurable multitude [of sins]."

The breaking of the logical causal connection between sin and punishment by the intervention of the concept of mercy takes place through the introduction of *freedom* into ontology: between cause and effect there intervenes personal freedom, which transforms natural causality into personal causality. As was the case with the creation of the world from nothing, which was due to the *will* (of God), so too in all personal causality can freedom remove logical necessity and lead to a causality different from that which is "imposed" (of necessity) by "correct reasoning."

The ontology of mercy consequently constitutes a combination of *love* and *freedom*. This means that in the causality of sin–punishment freedom is inserted both from the side of God and from the side of humankind. Thus, when we seek God's mercy, we are suggesting that God *can* break the logic of this causality, only, however, *if he wants to*—the seeking of mercy from God does not prejudge the result, and the Memorial Services do not *necessarily* have the result that we desire. Given, however, that also from the side of human beings the exercise of their freedom is always presupposed, God's mercy cannot but always go to meet the human will—that is to say, what is needed is the *repentance* (μετάνοια) of human beings, even in the simple form of the seeking of mercy, as in the case of the Publican. God does not impose his mercy on those who do not want it.[105]

At this point it is especially important to bear in mind that *the Second Coming of Christ has not yet occurred*, so we should not judge those who have departed from this life in the rejection of his mercy. The words of Anastasius the Sinaite already cited guide us once again: "He who judges before the coming of Christ is Antichrist, because he appropriates Christ's role ... For many ... are judged to be sinners by us, but by God they are justified."[106] The Church conducts the holy memorial services for all its members who have fallen asleep, regardless of the degree of their sinfulness, not restricting God from "having mercy on whom he wishes," and in anxious expectation that all its members will come together and be united again as one Body of Christ, so that "the separation of the lover from the beloved" will be avoided in his eternal Kingdom.

All within the Church's space, most especially its Saints, accord- ing to the model of "the one and only Holy One," feel themselves so united ontologically with the sinners that their heart "burns"[107] for them, to the degree that they are ready themselves to go to hell in their place. The will, however, of God's free creatures is sometimes so obstinate that it does not want on any account to be inserted into the "communion of the saints," whatever the punishment might be. Since the will cannot be forced, the "restoration of all" in any of its forms cannot necessarily prevail. Hell must remain forever—alas!— a real choice for free existence.

---

[105] Maximus, *Ep.* 1 (PG 91:388B).
[106] Anastasius, *Discourse on the holy Synaxis* (PG 89:845BC).
[107] Isaac the Syrian, *Τὰ εὑρεθέντα Ἀσκητικά* (The Extant Ascetica), p. 306.

Chapter Five

ESCHATOLOGY AND LITURGICAL TIME

Introduction

Theology and the Church often give the impression that, during the course of the centuries, they have lost sight of the significance of the new dimensions brought into human and, indeed, cosmic existence through the experience of the Liturgy. As a result, they have deprived the Gospel of its existential relevance. Liturgical experience has become a separate compartment in the lives of Christians, something taking place on Sunday or at some other special time without bringing any new and decisive insights into ordinary everyday experience. Similarly, in theological work, all matters pertaining to liturgical experience are usually left outside the domain of dogmatic theology, as if systematic theology could be done without any consideration of the liturgical experience of the Church.

That all this deviates from the original Gospel is clearly seen in the fact that, in the early Church, liturgy and theology were so closely connected that scholars still find it difficult to disentangle one from the other, both in the New Testament[1] and in early patristic writings. Without the Church's liturgical experience, we would not have the New Testament (certainly not in its actual content and form), and patristic theology would be, as I am afraid it is in fact for many students of the Fathers, an exercise in philosophical or intellectual and philological debate, with no clear implications for our existence in the world. It is, therefore, imperative, if we want to understand what the Bible and the Fathers really intended to say in their theology and to make all this relevant for us, to recover this primitive link between theology and liturgy by establishing the existential significance which joins them together.

[1] See C.F.D. Moule, *The Birth of the New Testament* (London: A. & C. Black, 1981). Also, E. La Verdiere, *The Eucharist in the New Testament and the Early Church* (Collegeville, MN: Liturgical Press, 1996).

With this concern in mind, I intend to raise two basic questions. In the first place, I should like to ask if liturgical time differs fundamentally from what we may call non-liturgical, ordinary time. Secondly, if there is a difference between these two kinds or ways of understanding time, how do they relate to each other and in what way does liturgical time affect ordinary existence in time?

I. Time as an Existential Problem

What do we mean when we use the word "time"? We certainly do not mean in theology the conventional time with the help of which we arrange our appointments and organize our work. Neither do I wish to use here the word "time" in a purely conceptual sense, as if one could speak of time as *such*, a sort of entity to which one could attach being and existence ("time is this or that"), regardless of the concrete beings to which it is related. Our concern here is with time as *it affects existence*. It is the existential significance of time that we are interested in.

The word "existential," however, calls for immediate qualification. Under the influence of modern existentialist philosophies, which in this respect go back to St Augustine, the concept of time has been associated mainly with what man experiences psychologically as time. Augustine seems to have been the first to deduce time from the self-interpretation of presence, as a study of Book XI, chapters 13–29 of the *Confessions* shows. Friedrich Schelling, Pascal, Kierkegaard, Heidegger, in addition to most of Romanticism seem to have followed this line to its conclusion by sharply distinguishing between humanity's "internal" time and the time in which the world around it moves, the "external" time.[2]

This understanding of time, valid as it may be to some extent, introduces a dichotomy between the human being and nature that makes it difficult for biblical and patristic notions of being to be accommodated. We shall, of course, discuss the personal dimensions of time, but we should not make it look as if personal time is *another* time and not the time in which natural events take place. Instead

[2] See A. Darlap, "Time," in *Sacramentum Mundi*, vol. VI, p. 259.

of trying to distinguish two kinds of time, the personal and the natural, we shall try to see how these two relate to each other as two dimensions of one and the same time. In this approach, "existential" means in fact "ontological," in the broad and general sense which comprises everything that can be said to *be*, to have a particular identity, a place in existence. In our concern, therefore, with the existential significance of time, we must try to work out an approach that will make room for creation as a whole and not only for humanity's experience of time, as if only the human being existed in the world or as if time would not really have existed if there was no human being to experience it.[3] Our sense of existential time here includes, all under the same rubric of "time," the cosmic and natural repercussions of time such as the life and death, growth and decay, and being and nonbeing of everything that *is*. Only such an understanding of time as a notion applicable to both person and nature can do justice to the Christian liturgy which claimed from the beginning to affect being as a whole—not just the psychological experience of the human soul, as we have often been led to believe through the various forms of pietism both in the East and in the West.

How then does time affect being as a whole, and in what way does it constitute a problem that liturgical time addresses?

If we try to approach patristic theology with these concerns in mind, we shall realize that throughout the patristic era, in the East as well as in the West, the notion of time was linked inseparably with creation. Augustine stated clearly for the first time that time as a concept is introduced automatically with creation and cannot be applied outside it.[4] Such a view seems to lie behind the mainstream thought of the Greek fathers, too.[5] The main important conclusion following from this is that time must not be associated either with God's being *in itself* or with the fall of man. Time is neither God's context of existence in an ultimate sense nor the outcome of the fall and sin. In what way, then, can it be said that time constitutes a prob-

---

[3] The human being, according to the Christian faith, was brought into existence after the rest of the material world. Therefore, time does not appear with the creation of the human being; it appeared with the creation of the world (Augustine).

[4] Augustine, *Conf.* XI, 9–13; cf. H. Chadwick, *St. Augustine: Confessions*, p. 227f.

[5] E.g., Basil, *C. Eunom.* 1.21 (PG 29:560B).

lem of existence? If the fall is not the necessary context and condition of time, then is it true to say that time, in an ultimate sense, constitutes a problem for being?

Here we must make an observation in order to clarify the position we are going to take in this study. We often tend to think of the fall as having introduced something *new* to creation. Under the influence of Augustine, for example, we tend to understand death as a penalty imposed by God because of the human being's disobedience to his law. This juridical imagery carries with it the false assumption that a new thing called "death" was now added, so to say, to creation through the fall. Death then becomes a problem for existence only as long as sin exists, and the ultimate ontological connections between death and being are thus obscured. If we, however, follow the approach which seems to have been the mainstream of the Greek fathers, we must understand the fall as doing nothing more than unveiling, uncovering, and realizing what was already there as a possibility inherent in creation, namely death. Death is a problem which ultimately goes back to creation. Creatures die because they are creatures[6] which have had a beginning. The fall made them unable to overcome their creaturely limitation and achieve the immortality for which they were created.[7]

This introduces us to the problem of time. If we dissociate time ultimately from the fall and attach it to creation, the first thing we must do is to see how it can be at one and the same time a positive and a negative thing, how time can constitute being, the being of creation—since without time creation would simply not be—and how it can equally constitute a problem for being, since without time neither the fall nor death could be realized. What is it that makes time such an ambiguous and paradoxical factor in creation? Only if we can somehow answer this question, can we go on to consider in what ways liturgical time constitutes a redeemed time for existence.

---

[6] I.e., because of their *nature*, which is mortal. See Athanasius, *De Inc.* 4 (PG 25:104B–C): "For the transgression of the commandment turned them back to the state *in accordance with their nature*, so that just as they had come into being out of nonbeing, so were they now deservedly returning through corruption to nonbeing again.... Man is mortal *by nature*, since he is made out of nothing."

[7] See my *Being as Communion: Studies in Personhood and the Church* (Crestwood, NY: St Vladimir's Seminary Press, 1985), p. 101f.

In an attempt to consider this matter, let us begin with Aristotle's classical definition of time. In his *Physics*, he calls it "the enumeration of movement according to the *earlier* and the *later*."[8] For Aristotle, the objective, natural time, the time of physics, which is his starting point, meets the time of the measuring subject, the time of human consciousness, precisely at the point at which the transience (or *ekstasis*, as he calls it)[9] takes place from the *earlier* to the *later*. This transience produces, objectively speaking, a change, a contingency (a *metabole*, in Aristotle's terms),[10] which consciousness measures as time.

Now, the existential problem arises precisely at this point. What is the link between the *earlier* and the *later* which enables us to grasp the transience and thus measure it as time? Aristotle, who regards this "in between" as crucial for the measuring of time, refers to it with two words which seem to be contradictory: the word νῦν (now) and the word οὐθὲν (nothing). Without the *now*, time collapses into nothing, as it is no longer measurable.[11] But since everything moves from the earlier to the later, this "now" represents no ontological ground in itself, as it can contain no beings (οὐθέν).[12]

All this may sound too speculative, but in fact it is a way to introduce ourselves to the problem of time as patristic theology saw it in relation to creation. In order to understand this, let us consider how ambiguous and paradoxical time is for everything that exists in the world, including ourselves. Like space (which in this respect is a correlative of time), time accounts for the particular identities of beings. Had it not been for space and time, I would not be able to distinguish myself from my parents. The space—and the time—that is between them and me secures my identity, my very being as myself. And yet, paradoxically enough, this very space and time which unites

---

[8] Aristotle, *Phys.* IV 10–11, 218a 30ff.

[9] Ibid., IV 13, 222b 16.

[10] Ibid., IV 14, 222b 30, 31.

[11] "Time cannot exist and is unthinkable apart from the 'now,' and the 'now' is a kind of middle-point, uniting as it does in itself both a beginning and an end, a beginning of future time and an end of past time" (Aristotle, *Phys.* VIII 251b 19f). "The 'now' measures time, insofar as time involves the 'before and after'" (ibid., 219b 12).

[12] "Nothing can be in motion in a 'now'" (Aristotle, *Phys.* VI 3, 234a 24). Equally, however, "nothing can be at rest in a 'now' either" (ibid., 35f).

me with them and guarantees my identity constitutes my separation from them and my transience into nonbeing. The very thing that brings about my being takes it away. My "now," this crucial "in between" the "before" and the "after," is my *nothing*, my nonbeing.[13] And since my being depends on time, on this "in between" for my continuity, the transformation of this *nothing* into a *now* with an ontological content, which would prevent it from involving *nothing*, is the crux of the matter of the particular's survival.

Before we discuss the ways in which this problem could be tackled, let us apply it to creation as a whole, in order to grasp its ultimate ontological implications, to which patristic theology seems to be extremely sensitive. The attachment of the notion of time to that of creation by the Fathers appears to be an inseparable part of their doctrine of creation *out of nothing* (*ex nihilo*): creation and time and creation-out-of-nothing seem, in the final analysis, to be one and the same thing. If created existence is left to itself, the "now" which brings about continuity is inevitably realized as nothing. Like you and me and every physical body existing in time, the world as a whole *which can only exist in time* realizes its existence in and through the crucial "in between," the "now" which, as we have seen, is its "nothing." To say, therefore, that the world was created together with time and to say that it was created out of nothing amounts to the same thing. Since the world not only in its particular bodies but also taken as a whole (as one particular "being") can be measured and identified as itself (i.e., not confused with something else, for example, God) *only against the background of nothing*, what gives the world its self-identity, its being in time, is inevitably realized as "nothing." By insisting on these two doctrines, namely that time and creation are correlative notions and that the world was created out of nothing, the Fathers ruled out any possibility of solving the problem of time by understanding the "in between" factor which sustains the world's being in time as an *eternal now*.[14] The world has no eternal now of its own; its

---

[13] Aristotle puts his finger on this paradox when he writes precisely that owing to the "now," time is both continuous and divided: "Time, then, is both made continuous by the 'now' and divided by it" (*Phys.* IV, 220a). It is this division of time that makes time an existential problem for the person.

[14] *In this respect* the Greek fathers appear to be rather Aristotelian than Platonic.

existence in time is through the intermediary of nothing, the intermediary of death. This is what it means to be a creature.

It is at this point that time becomes not only a problem but also a challenge: a problem, that is, that cannot be left unsolved. It is, also, at this point that the *personal dimension* of time emerges as a crucial one. The fact that beings come and go, live and die (that is, pass through the intermediary of "nothing") seems to present no existential problem as long as through their death and disappearance other identities arise in a cosmic or biological circle of being.[15] Thus, beings die but being goes on. The world's being is taken for granted. Such a thought is often used as a consolation for death. And yet this sort of escape from the problem leaves unsatisfied everyone who would find a particular identity, a certain being so dear and dearly loved as to be indispensable and irreplaceable.[16] This is what is meant by person: a being so deeply loved as to be unique and irreplaceable, just as the divine Persons, who are the "model" of true personhood, are. Death, even if it involves the transformation of a certain being into another being, thus appearing to be acceptable to nature, is unacceptable to a person who is so bound up with this being in love as to find intolerable the loss of its identity. This makes the Fathers, particularly St Maximus the Confessor, understand the whole creation as needing a loving relationship between the human being, as the head of creation, and God in order to avoid the problem of death inherent in the nature of creation in time—a relationship which the Fathers see in the Person of the Son in whom the world was made and who, in his Incarnation, sums it up and incorporates it in this relationship.[17] As long, therefore, as God has a personal relationship—not just a

[15] For Aristotle, for example, time is no problem from the existential point of view, since time is a numbering not of any movement but of the continuous movement which always is (*Phys.* VIII 1, 215b 13, 25): ἀεὶ χρόνος ἐστὶν (there is always time) on the basis of the "now" in which nothing moves. This makes the circle by which the movement of the sphere is measured and which measures it of decisive existential importance: all human affairs are a circle like all natural generations (*Phys.* IV 223b 11–28). Cf. J. Chevalier, *Histoire de la Pensée* I. *La pensée antique* (Paris: Flammarion, 1955), p. 333.

[16] Cf. my *Communion and Otherness*, chapter 6, "Human Capacity and Human Incapacity."

[17] E.g., Maximus, *Amb.* 5 (PG 91:1057C). See, for a more detailed discussion, my *Communion and Otherness*, pp. 22–32, esp. n. 51.

natural one—with the world through the love of his Son, God cannot tolerate the disappearance of the world, just as any true person
who so loves a certain being that he regards it as unique and irreplaceable would want this being to exist forever.[18]

This problem was not raised for the first time by Christianity,
but it was only Christianity that insisted on attaching a certain condition to its solution, namely the condition that time should be respected and maintained as constitutive of beings. In the Platonic
dialogues, and particularly in the *Symposium*, the personal dimension
of time is central to the discussion of the problem of Eros: the lover
finds it intolerable that time will take away from him his beloved or
diminish the love existing between them. This erotic motive is as biblical and patristic as anything can be, but the transformation of the
"in between" of time from a "now" that involves "nothing" to a "now"
of real presence takes place in Platonism as an "ever" (ἀεί), which is
outside and beyond time. It is on the level of the extratemporal world
of ideas, through the love of the eternal and unchangeable beauty and
good, that the two lovers are called to find the solution to the problem of time in Platonism.[19] In this solution, it does not really matter
in the end whether their bodily identities will disappear through
death; their eternal souls—which could even be reincarnated into
other temporal identities—will secure the survival of the eternal
good which was, after all, the ultimate concern behind their eros.[20]

---

[18] Shakespeare's *Sonnets* are full of this fight with Time for the sake of the beloved one:

"And all in war with Time for love of you,
As he takes from you, I engraft you new" (XV)
"When I have seen by Time's felt hand defac'd,
The rich-proud cost of outworn buried age,
When sometime lofty towers I see down-res'd,
and brass eternal, slave to mortal rage; ...
When I have seen much interchange of state,
Or state itself confounded to decay;
Ruin hath taught me thus to ruminate—
That time will come to take my love away.
This thought is as a death, which cannot choose
But weep to have that which it fears to lose." (LXIV)

[19] Plato, *Phaedros* 252e.

[20] As it is put in Plato's *Symposium* (210e–211b), love (eros) should be directed in such a way as to move from a concrete beautiful body to the beauty of all beautiful bodies and

Thus the person is deprived of an ontology of its own and love ceases to be constitutive of concrete beings. Concrete beings, if they are loved for what they are and as they are when the relationship is established, are spatiotemporal beings. Unless space and time survive together with these identities, the person who loves them cannot be happy. This means that if you love a human being so much as to want its identity to be eternal, you cannot help but also wish that the spatiotemporal context, which has formed the identity of this person, be saved too, so as to make the person what it was when you loved it by giving it its identity. This means not only that unless there is resurrection of *bodies* there is no solution to the temporal dimension of time, but also that unless the spatiotemporal world as a whole (which has brought about the beings we love) somehow survives in the end, no eternity is possible for human persons. If the person is taken seriously as an ontological notion, eternity is not and cannot be for creation simply the survival of souls. Eternity cannot be an alternative to time; time is its condition.

II. Toward a Liturgical Conception of Time

Let us now consider the importance of liturgical time for all of this. How does liturgical time relate to the problem of time as we have described it here—namely, how does liturgical time transform or claim to transform the "in between" of time from a "now" of *nothing* into a *now* of *presence*?

Here, immediately, there come to mind certain conceptions of liturgical time that need to be rejected. What I have in mind is especially the Platonizing mystical interpretations of liturgical time which seem to take us out of time into an extratemporal eternal "now." These tendencies can take various forms. They can take the

finally to that "which exists eternally and is not subject either to birth, or to perdition, or to increase, or to decrease; which is not beautiful in a certain way and ugly in another, neither beautiful today and not tomorrow...but exists in itself, self-sufficiently, by itself, one in form, eternal, in which all participate in such a way that by their birth and disappearance it suffers neither growth nor decreasing or anything at all." It is clear from this that the problem of time with reference to love is solved by Platonic thinking through an escape from temporal existence in an eternal "ever" (ἀεί) and, most significantly, through a sacrifice of the concrete and particular for the sake of the general, the idea.

form of a symbolism which would suggest that what takes place in the liturgy is an image and a reflection of something higher taking place outside time. Such tendencies are to be found in the theology of Clement of Alexandria,[21] Origen[22] (though not so much in connection with the liturgy as with history as a whole), in his follower Eusebius of Caesaria,[23] and to some extent in Dionysius the Areopagite.[24] In all these cases, the (liturgical) symbols are images of something extratemporal and thus ways of transforming the "in between" of time into an eternal now. Another way of doing essentially the same thing is in fact much commoner to us than we suspect. It is the psychological way, namely the rejection of symbolism and the resort to imagination. Every time we close our eyes in prayer so that the spatiotemporal conditions may not disturb us, we imply such a kind of liturgical time.[25]

There are also opposite tendencies which nevertheless amount to the same thing. I have in mind the concern for preserving time and history in the liturgy to such an extent that the events of salvation history, certain events that took place in the history of Israel and in the time of Jesus, become the ultimate point of reference for liturgical time. Here the worshiper is called to connect himself with the *past* and find in it the *now* of his existence.[26] In this *anamnetic* time, the ultimate danger is not so much escaping from time as being en-

[21] Clement, *Protr.* 9 (PG 8:196C): Ἡ σήμερον γὰρ ἀΐδιος αἰὼν (or αἰώνος) ἐστὶν εἰκὼν (For today is an image of the eternal age); *Str.* 1.2 (PG 8:709B).

[22] Origen, *In Jo.* 13.59 (PG 14:512B); 10.16 (PG 14:333B); 13.64 (PG 14:521C).

[23] Eusebius of Caesaria, *Hist. Eccl.* 10.4.25 (PG 20:860A): ὥσπερ ἀρχετύποις χρώμενος παραδείγματος τούτων τὰς εἰκόνας ὡς ἔνι μάλιστα δυνατόν, εἰς τὸν ὁμοιότατον δημιουργῶν ἀπειργάσατο (using the archetypes as a model of these, he wrought their images, creating the closest likeness in the highest degree possible).

[24] Dionysius Areop., *Eccl. Hier.* 2.3.2 (PG 3:396C); 4.3.4 (PG 3:477B); 3.3.1 (PG 3:428A).

[25] This is a tendency observable in Western Christianity, particularly among Protestants of the Puritan or pietistic tradition which has reduced artistic representation in places of worship to a minimum. It is also a tendency in certain modern Orthodox circles influenced by a pietistic mentality, who worship in the Church by looking into books of worship or hiding in dark corners as if the artistic representation around them were an obstacle to their "spiritual" contemplation and prayer.

[26] Such a tendency lies behind the theology of the Eucharist as the *anamnesis* of a past event, particularly that of the Cross, and all the discussions concerning the question of whether the Eucharist is a repetition of Christ's sacrifice or not.

slaved by it, that is, denying it its redemption. This enslavement in the past is also, as we shall see, a basically Greek attitude to time that Christianity confronted with a radically alternative view expressed mainly in the liturgy. Let us now consider this in some detail.

The Christian attitude to the problem of time took shape gradually in the theology of the Fathers as Christianity acquired its own self-consciousness vis-à-vis the Greek culture and contemporary Judaism which rejected Christ. In the ancient Greek world, the solution to the existential problem of time was sought, as we have seen, along the lines of an atemporal eternity. This meant that a single event in history is in its particularity something insignificant. The idea that such an event could introduce a new decisive factor is basically foreign to the ancient Greek world. The greatest criticism that Celsus could make of Christianity was its novelty. It is noteworthy that Christians were at first disconcerted by these criticisms and succumbed to the temptation of Hellenic thought. Origen, for example, accepted that the spiritual creation had existed in its perfection from the beginning and, no doubt, was coeternal with the Logos.[27] This creation had fallen, and the role of Christ was not to bring about something new, but to re-establish what already existed previously in perfection. The events of history introduce nothing new. It would have been better if nothing had ever occurred and if everything had remained in the original state of immobility. Likewise, for Eusebius, Christ did not bring a new message but came to reestablish in its purity the original religion of humanity, which Judaism had provisionally replaced.

This typically Greek idea that perfection is what always existed at the beginning carries with it serious existential implications, which become apparent in ancient Greek tragedy. In ancient Greek culture, the past—the original past, that which the gods held in their hands—determined the course of history both universal and personal. Oedipus did not acquire a name or an identity through what he did, but he was given his name and his identity by the gods. Only by a return to what was eternally and originally meaningful could history acquire meaning.

[27] Origen, *De Princ.* I, 4.3 (J. Behr, Origen, *On First Principles*, I [Oxford: Oxford University Press, 2017], p. 84).

The Church's discussion with the Jews, on the other hand, brought out another problem, namely that of the relation between various single events, which gives time its continuity. By attaching ultimate significance to certain single events in the past, Judaism made these events binding forever. The Temple, the sacrifices of the Old Testament: to what extent were they binding for Christians? Here the dilemma was either to affirm these events as good and hence to make them binding or to say that they were never good and reject them. The Church and ancient thought in general had no tools by which to work out a concept of time capable of saying that an event was both good and rejectable or replaceable. This is to be seen in the fact that Christian thinkers such as Justin and Pseudo-Barnabas were forced to say that the Old Testament institutions were never good in themselves and that their sense was always spiritual, while their liberal practice was either sinful (Barnabas) or due to the hardness of the Jewish heart (Justin).[28]

It was not, in fact, until Irenaeus and his contemporary, Melito of Sardis,[29] that patristic theology did work out a theoretical solution to this problem by introducing the idea of *kairos*: the single events of salvation history are all God's acts and therefore good, but God is not bound by the past. He is free to act anew, and what He does replaces the past by new events without condemning it.[30] Thus, a particular event represents a moment of *freedom*. Here time liberates existence from the past. The past is not binding, precisely because there is a future event which gives to the past its meaning. The past must be ready to sacrifice itself, like John the Baptist, by bowing be-

---

[28] Cf. J. Daniélou, *Message évangélique et culture hellénistique* (Tournai: Desclée, 1961), p. 183ff.

[29] Ibid., p. 185: "[sa] (Justin's) théologie de l'Ancien Testament reste négative. C'est Irénée qui le premier montre le fondement dernier de la relation des deux Testaments en élaborant une théologie de l'histoire..." See also his "Figure et évènement chez Meliton de Sardes," in *Neotestamenta et patristica, eine Freudesgabe ... Oscar Cullmann zu seinem 60. Geburtstag überreicht* (Leiden : E.J. Brill, 1962), p. 282–92.

[30] The idea of *kairos* is particularly stressed by Melito of Sardis, *Homily on the Pacha*, passim and 6.17–18. The relevant passage is worth quoting: "Everything has its own time (καιρός). The figure (τύπος) has its proper time, the reality (ὕλη) has its own. The first Pascha [that of the Jews] was already "most honorable," yet only because in it the mystery of Christ was signified. With the arrival of the reality [Christ], *the Jewish Pascha is confirmed and honoured and at the same time replaced*" (5.30–35).

fore the new event in order to receive from it its meaning (Jn 3:30: "He must increase, and I must decrease"). Thus, in the words of Gregory of Nyssa, time "goes from beginnings to beginnings by means of beginnings which have no end."[31]

This view, however, leaves open some questions which are fundamental and to which only liturgical theology could offer the answer. If the various events, by constituting new beginnings, can be conceived like drops of rain in the ocean of time, how do they succeed in maintaining their continuity? By what means does one single event relate to its successor or predecessor without being subject to negation by the "nothing" of the "in between" factor that relates the anterior to its posterior in time, and without creating a causality or a *continuum* of potentiality in the Aristotelian sense mentioned above? How, in other words, did Christianity manage to replace the "nothing" of the "now" without abolishing time? Here the role of liturgical time seems to have been decisive.

Liturgical time was born out of the experience of the Resurrection of Jesus.[32] During the Resurrection appearances and the meals shared with Christ, the disciples experienced a sense of time that was bound to affect the entire existence of the early Church. What were the characteristics of this time?

In the first place, it was a liberation of time from its bondage to the past and from historical or natural causality. The events of the past (for example, the Old Testament Passover meal) with regard to the Eucharist, did not play a *causative* role. By being "figures" (τύπος or σκιά), these events received their truth from the future event to which they pointed. Secondly, the time of the Resurrection was a time that had spatiotemporal structure, i.e., time as it relates to space. The body of the Resurrection could enter through closed doors (Jn 20:19, 26) thus proving that space too was liberated from its divisive nature that leads to death. Thirdly, the Resurrection was a *final* event. Nothing could be expected anymore. It was a future binding upon the past. Finally, however, it was a future which bound by not binding, in that it did not automatically transform the single events of

---

[31] Gregory of Nyssa, *Hom. Cant.* 8 (PG 44:941C).
[32] Cf. O. Cullmann, *Early Christian Worship*, p. 15ff.

the past into eschatological realities. This was the deeper significance of the *Spirit* as a notion attached to the Resurrection from the beginning (Rom 8:11).

It is important to note that we can do no justice to Resurrection time without Pneumatology. The risen Christ brought the future into history through the Holy Spirit, which means through the reality of freedom. Each single event of the past is thus not destroyed but instead freely (i.e., in the Spirit) made "spiritual." The Old Testament events, for example, become, in Paul's terms, spiritual events[33] in the community of the Church and particularly in its liturgical life. The time of the Church marks the time of a future which will have to be *freely* realized. The Resurrection is a spiritual event in the sense that its future is accessible to the world as a free gift, *freely* accepted and *freely* realized in the Spirit. Thus, the delay in the Parousia and the interval of the time of the Church are understood as the intervention of the future between the "before" and the "after," as the "in between" which liberates us from the past by opening it up into the future. The time of the Church is the time of the *free* realization of the eschaton.

The interception of the future between the "before" and "after" of single events was made evident in the perpetuation of the post-Resurrection meals—that is, in the Eucharist and through it in all liturgical and sacramental life. Let us consider briefly the conceptual framework which was created as a result of this situation, before examining some of its main existential implications.

The new concept of time that was introduced with the post-Resurrection liturgy is expressed with the help of certain key terms to be found in the liturgical language of the patristic period. The most significant of these terms are σκιά (shadow), τύπος (type or figure), and, above all, εἰκών (this is untranslatable, but it is close to the idea of image). A study of the interrelation between these terms as they are used in patristic sacramental theology reveals the basic characteristics of liturgical time.

These terms have, of course, various meanings in the vocabulary of the Fathers, but in their liturgical application they are concepts more or less relating to liturgical time. Σκιά is used mainly for Old

---

[33] E.g., 1 Cor 10:1–4. Cf. 1 Pet 3:20–21.

Testament realities which prefigure those of the New Testament.[34] This is important. It indicates that the past is the shadow of the future—not *vice-versa, as the ancient world would normally suppose.* The image implied in σκιὰ is that of a figure coming toward us and lit from behind it, so that its shadow comes first. When the figure itself arrives, its shadow is naturally abolished, though not negated, for the arrival of the figure proved that it was a *true* shadow and not a false one. The abolition of the past has meant its affirmation, *which would not have been possible but for its abolition by the arrival of the future.*[35]

The term τύπος, on the other hand, seems to be applied equally to the old and to the new.[36] It signifies the link between the two without an evaluative connotation. It was the merit of the late Cardinal Jean Daniélou[37] to have pointed for the first time to the crucial importance of typology both in biblical exegesis and in the liturgy. The deeper significance of typology lies in its role as the expression of the unity and continuity and therefore of the intelligibility of history through single events. But it fails to indicate which of these events are the ultimately significant ones. Typology does not take into account all the problems raised by the notion of time.

It is mainly the idea of εἰκὼν that seems to be the most meaningful for our subject. Apart from its general use, the application of this term to the concept of time and history is revealing. There are applications of it in the mainstream of patristic thought. The first use of εἰκὼν, as signifying the image of a reality that is lower than the truth or reality, is used more or less in the same sense as shadow. In this sense, it is applied equally to the Old Testament realities which are called εἰκόνες. We find this use in Origen,[38] in Clement of Alexan-

---

[34] Thus, Methodius of Olympus, *Symp.* 9.9 (PG 18:180C); Athanasius, *C. Ar.* 2.8 (PG 26:161C); Basil, *De Spir.* 31 (PG 32:121B); Chrysostom, *Hom. In 1 Cor.* 7.4 (PG 61:59); Maximus, *Scol.* 3.3.3 (PG 4:137D), and others.

[35] See Melito of Sardis, note 30 above.

[36] Maximus, *Amb.* 37 (PG 91:1296C): "Everything considered by us now to be truth is a τύπος"; Chrysostom, *Hom. In 2 Cor* 4.13: "τύπος is not the opposite of truth but bears affinity to it (συγγενὲς)" (PG 51:285).

[37] J. Daniélou, *The Bible and the Liturgy* (Notre Dame, IN: Notre Dame University Press, 1956).

[38] Origen, *In Joann.* 10.16 (PG 14:333B).

dria,³⁹ and also in Eusebius,⁴⁰ where it serves as the basis for rejecting the representation of Christ in images.⁴¹ In Dionysius the Areopagite, the pair archetype-εἰκὼν is common and is used in spatial rather than temporal terms.⁴² The second use of the term is to be found mainly in the non-Alexandrian tradition. Here εἰκὼν is sharply contrasted to σκιά and is used strictly for New Testament realities. We find this in Methodius of Olympus⁴³ and John of Damascus.⁴⁴ The third and most interesting application of this term is to be found in Maximus the Confessor, who reflects the stream of Greek patristic thought beginning with Irenaeus, passing through Athanasius and the Cappadocians. In an important scholion on Dionysius attributed to Maximus, he writes: "the things of the Old Testament are shadow (σκιά); those of the New Testament are εἰκὼν; and those of the future state are truth (ἀλήθεια)."⁴⁵

Here we are faced with a concept of time that is, strictly speaking, *liturgical*. Maximus in fact applies this understanding of time throughout his *Mystagogia*, his interpretation of the Eucharist. What happens in the liturgy is not to be understood in spatial categories, as is the case with Dionysius, but rather in spatiotemporal ones. The liturgy is a movement of the *kosmos* to its eschatological πέρας (end).⁴⁶ The truth lies in the eschaton, but it has its εἰκὼν in history through the liturgy. This εἰκὼν is not a shadow or simply a τύπος; it is reality, as real as the presence of Christ in the New Testament itself. Yet it is a reality not in itself but in relation to what is finally to come. Thus, liturgical time is the time of the εἰκὼν of the eschaton. It is not the reflection of an archetypical time or state. It is time, but time carrying the final goal, the πέρας of creation.⁴⁷ In the liturgy, we have time.

³⁹ Clement, *Strom.* 4.22 (PG 8:1352B).

⁴⁰ Eusebius, *Hist. eccl.* 1.3.4 (PG 20: 69B).

⁴¹ See G. Florovsky, "Origen, Eusebius and the Iconoclastic Controversy," in *Church History* 19 (1950) 77–96.

⁴² E.g. Dionysius Areop., *Eccl. Hier.* 5.5 (PG 3:505B); 2.3. Theoria 2 (397C), etc.

⁴³ Methodius of Olympus, *Symp.* 5.7 (PG 18:1096).

⁴⁴ John of Damascus, *De Imag.* 1.15 (PG 94:1244D), where the application of εἰκὼν to Old Testament realities is clearly rejected.

⁴⁵ *Scholia on Dionysius the Areopagite* 3.3.2 (PG 4:137D).

⁴⁶ Maximus, *Myst.* 2 (PG 91:669A–D).

⁴⁷ The *eikon* carries with it and in it the reality of the truth which is to come. This real-

The world moves; it does not stand still. It moves, however, toward its proper end, which is eternal life, not death. The incarnate and risen Christ has shown that space and time can be turned into vehicles of presence. In liturgical time, the "in between" the earlier and the later is therefore neither nothing nor the eternal and atemporal now; it is an "unending time," what St Basil calls the *aeon*.⁴⁸ The Greek fathers taking up the biblical philosophy of history, took up the term αἰὼν and applied it to the liturgy. What intervenes between the before and after in the liturgy is the αἰὼν, the future αἰὼν, which is an unending αἰὼν. Liturgical time is thus a time εἰς τοὺς αἰῶνας τῶν αἰώνων,⁴⁹ a time without death.⁵⁰ Liturgy, therefore, takes place in the time redeemed by the intrusion of the future into the "now," which becomes in this way a *kairos*, a moment in time filled with ontological significance as it draws its content from the eschatological truth.⁵¹

ity is in a sense already here; he that will come has already come and is present in the liturgy, albeit in an historical form, i.e., in a different substance (in the form of the celebrant as the "icon of Christ" or in that of the venerated *eikon* which depicts Christ in iconography). The "type" differs from the *eikon* in that it does not contain ontologically the truth it points to. Typology and eikonology should not be taken to mean the same thing.

⁴⁸ Basil, *Hom. Hex.* 2.8 (PG 29:59B–C): "The property of the αἰὼν is to return on itself and never to end."

⁴⁹ Cf. the exclamation of the celebrant, as he removes the eucharistic gifts from the altar at the end of the liturgy: "Always, now and forever and to the ages of ages (εἰς τοὺς αἰώνας τῶν αἰώνων)."

⁵⁰ St Basil and the other two Cappadocian saints, Gregory Nazianzen and Gregory of Nyssa stress this in particular, as they discuss the theme of the "eighth day" in connection with the Resurrection and the Sunday Eucharist. See the excellent presentation of the "Eighth Day" in J. Daniélou, *The Bible and the Liturgy*, pp. 262–275. The "eighth day" is the future age which is beyond the cosmic week (seven days). It is a day or time without succession or division into the Aristotelian "before" and "after." It is this "unending aeon" *that enters into the course of historical time at the celebration of the Eucharist, especially on Sunday, the day of the Resurrection, and forms the existential ground upon which we experience redeemed liturgical time. It is important to understand the "eighth day" not in the sense of Origen's contrast between the historical and the intelligible or "spiritual"* (see Origen, *In Joann.* 1, 10, 18) i.e., in a Platonic way, but rather in Irenaeus' typology of an historical event prefiguring another historical or temporal reality. On the contrast between Origen and Irenaeus with regard to this matter, see O. Cullmann, *Christ and Time*, p. 56f. H. de Lubac seems to defend Origen's position (*Exégèse Médiévale* II [Paris: Aubier, 1959], p. 629f). St Basil's notion of the eighth day as *aeon* becomes crucial in this respect.

⁵¹ This approach was more common in the East which conceived the "eighth day" as something *outside* the cycle of the week, whereas the "Western tradition, more realistic

III. The Liturgy as the "Unending Age"

Belief in the redemption of time through the "intrusion" of the eschaton into history is expressed *par excellence* in the eucharistic liturgy. The Divine Liturgy is an image of the Kingdom of God, an image of the last times. There is nothing so clear as this, at least in the Orthodox liturgy. Our liturgy begins with the invocation of the Kingdom, continues with the representation of it, and ends with our participation in the Supper of the Kingdom, our union and communion with the life of God in Trinity.

Strangely, our theology in recent years has not given appropriate weight to the eschatological dimension of the Eucharist. The principal interest of contemporary theology appears to lie in the relationship of the Eucharist less with the last things than with the past, with the Last Supper and with Golgotha. Perhaps we have yet another serious influence from the "Babylonian captivity" on Orthodox theology, to quote the ever-memorable Fr Alexander Schmemann.[52] Western theology, both Roman Catholic and Protestant, has indeed focused its attention on the relationship between the Eucharist and Golgotha, because, in the West, culminating in the theology of Anselm, the quintessence of the divine economy is to be found in Christ's sacrifice on the Cross. Everything flows from this; everything leads up to it. The Kingdom is something that has to do only with the end of history, not with its present. Typically, for Western theology as a whole, the Resurrection of Christ is nothing more than a confirmation of the saving work of the Cross. The essential part has

and historically-minded, sought to find in the week a key of the succession of the ages" (J. Daniélou, *The Bible and the Liturgy*, p. 275). This remains true up to now. Eschatology in Western theology normally means the last phase in a linear *Heilsgeschichte*, whereas in the Orthodox Church, following the Greek fathers, it is understood as a *new* creation entering the biological-historical-linear time of the seven-day period and renewing it. Hence the observation of the late Cardinal Yves Congar remains always valid: "[L' orthodoxie] suit beaucoup plus l' idée, très présente chez les Pères et dans la liturgie, d' une 'phanie' d' une manifestation des réalités célestes, invisibles, sur la terre. Il s'ensuit une conception principalement sacramentelle et iconologique de l'Église," In *Le Concile et les Conciles*, ed. B. Botte et. al. (Paris: Éditions du Cerf, Éditions de Chevetogne, 1960), p. 287.

[52] In his book, *The Eucharist* (Crestwood, NY: St Vladimir's Seminary Press, 1988), Fr Alexander Schmemann develops the eschatological character of the Eucharist and is sharply critical of academic theology in relation also to other aspects of its eucharistic theology. His criticisms deserve particular attention.

already been accomplished in the sacrifice on the Cross.[53] Besides, for Western Christians the crucial and constitutive moment of the Eucharist is the repetition of the "words of institution" of the Mystery—"Take eat, this is my body"—and not the invocation of the Holy Spirit, whose presence is necessarily linked with the coming of the "last days" (Acts 2:18).

Thus, the question which has for centuries dominated the dispute between Roman Catholics and Protestants in the West is whether or not the Eucharist is a repetition of the sacrifice on Golgotha—not whether it is an image of the last times. Orthodox theology also became embroiled in the same question, particularly from the seventeenth century onwards (the Orthodox confessions of Peter of Mogila, Cyril Loukaris, Dositheus of Jerusalem, and others), with the result that the connection of the Eucharist with the last times, with the Kingdom of God, was overlooked.

1. *The Biblical Evidence*

Proving the eschatological character of the Divine Eucharist in the New Testament would not require much effort. The description of the Last Supper in the Gospels already orientates us toward the Kingdom of God. The Twelve partake of the Supper as a foreshadowing of the new Israel, and for this reason the Evangelist Luke places within the narrative of the Last Supper the words of Christ to the Twelve: "As my Father appointed a *kingdom* for me, so do I appoint for you that you may eat and drink at my table *in my kingdom* and sit on thrones judging the twelve tribes of Israel" (Lk 22:29–30). As we shall see later, this passage is very important in the origin and shaping of the various functions in the Eucharist, and in the Church more generally. For the moment, we note the fact that the Last Supper was an *eschatological* event, inextricably bound up with the Kingdom of God. This is why, in the course of the Supper, Christ refers

[53] Characteristically, the Roman Catholic theologian Maurice de la Taille is quite clear in his monumental work, *Mysterium Fidei de Augustissimo Corporis et Sanguinis Christi Sacrificio atque Sacramento* (Paris, 1921), p. 581: the *res tantum*, i.e., the ultimate meaning of the Eucharist and all the sacraments is our union with the sacrifice of Christ on the Cross. Cf. P. McPartlan, *The Eucharist Makes the Church. Henri de Lubac and John Zizioulas in Dialogue* (Edinburgh: T&T Clark, 1993), p. 218. Compare this with St Maximus the Confessor, below.

to the Kingdom explicitly and with particular intensity of feeling: "I have earnestly desired to eat this Passover with you before I suffer; for I tell you I shall never eat it again until it is fulfilled *in the kingdom of God ...* for I tell you that from now on I shall not drink of the fruit of the vine *until the kingdom of God comes*" (Lk 22:15–16, 18, and parallels).

In the context of the strongly eschatological character which the Last Supper has in the Gospels, Christ's commandment to his disciples, "Do this in memory of me," cannot be unrelated to the Kingdom of God. As has already been observed by well-known biblical theologians (J. Jeremias[54] and others), the "remembrance" of which the Lord speaks is most likely to refer to the remembrance of Christ before the throne of God in the Kingdom which is to come. In other words, the eucharistic remembrance is in fact a remembrance, a foreshadowing, a foretaste, and a "fore-gift" (an ἀρραβὼν) of Christ's future Kingdom. As we shall see below, the Divine Liturgy of St John Chrysostom which is celebrated in the Orthodox Church expresses this with clarity. The remembrance, then, of the Last Supper, and by extension of the Eucharist, is a remembrance of past events, placed in the light of a future "event," (i.e., of the Kingdom of God)[55] as the culmination and fulfilment of the whole history of salvation.

The most significant point, however, in confirmation of the eschatological character of the Eucharist is the fact that the roots of the Eucharist are to be found historically not only in the Last Supper but are to be interpreted through the experience of Christ's appear-

---

[54] In his classic work, *The Eucharistic Words of Jesus*, trans. N. Perrin (London: SCM Press, 1966).

[55] The phrase "Kingdom of heaven" should not be understood as some kind of static state above the earth (a kind of Platonic notional of ideal reality). It is quite simply a paraphrase of the expression "kingdom of God," since the phrase "the heavens" paraphrases the word "God," which the Jewish Christians avoided using out of reverence (cf. St Matthew's Gospel, where the phrase occurs 31 times—see J. Jeremias, *New Testament Theology*, p. 97). This observation has been thought necessary because in the thinking of the faithful, the phrase "Kingdom of heaven" is very often translated as "heavenly Kingdom," i.e., in spatial and often Platonic contrast with whatever exists and is done on earth. In the New Testament, as J. Jeremias observes (*op. cit.*, p. 102), "the Kingdom is always and everywhere understood in eschatological terms. It signifies the time of salvation, the consummation of the world, the restoration of broken communion between God and man."

ances during the forty days after the Resurrection. During these appearances, we have the breaking of bread and the risen Christ eating with his disciples (Lk 24; Jn 21). The prevailing atmosphere is one of joy, since the Resurrection has demonstrated God's victory over his enemies, which is the dawning of Christ's Kingdom in history. It is not accidental that in Acts, Luke stresses that the early Church celebrated the Eucharist "with glad hearts" (Acts 2:46). Only the Resurrection and the Parousia could justify, or rather necessitate, such an atmosphere of rejoicing.

This eschatological orientation of the Eucharist is also evident in the first eucharistic communities. The Aramaic expression *"Maranatha"* (1 Cor 16:22), which is unquestionably a liturgical-eucharistic term, is eschatological in content (meaning, the Lord is near, or is coming, or will come). When the Apostle Paul repeats the eucharistic words of the Lord (1 Cor 11:23–26), he adds a reference to the Second Coming ("until he comes").[56] The Revelation of John, which is basically a eucharistic text and seems to have had an influence on the shaping of the Orthodox Liturgy, does not only consider the Eucharist as an image of the Kingdom, something that takes place before the Throne of God and the Lamb; it also ends with an emphatic reference to the expectation of the last times: "The Spirit and the Bride say, 'Come.' And let him who hears say, 'Come.'... Amen. Come, Lord Jesus!" (Rev 22:17, 20).

This vivid expectation of the last times has disappeared from our eucharistic consciousness. Yet if the Book of Revelation is inaccessible for various reasons to the members of our eucharistic assemblies, there is another text which is not only at the heart of the Divine Liturgy but on the lips of all believers within the Liturgy and outside it, which ought to remind us strongly of this expectation. It is *the Lord's Prayer.*

---

[56] The meaning of this passage is: "we proclaim the death of the Lord looking with joy for His coming" (J. Moffat, *The First Epistle of Paul to the Corinthians* [New York and London: Harper, 1954], p. 169). Cf. Acts 2:46: "in gladness." The earlier theory of H. Lietzmann (*The Mass and the Lord's Supper* [Leiden: E.J. Brill, 1953–1979]), that the Eucharist was celebrated in the Pauline Churches in an atmosphere of sadness as a remembrance of Christ's death, but in an atmosphere of joy in the Church of Jerusalem, is shown to be wrong. In each case, the Eucharist was celebrated in an atmosphere of joy and gladness because of its connections with the Kingdom.

This prayer has now lost both its eschatological and its eucharistic character in our minds. And yet we must not forget that this prayer was not only eschatological from the beginning but also formed the center and the core of all the ancient Liturgies: it is not impossible, indeed, that its historical roots were eucharistic. In this prayer, there are two prominent references to the last times[57] which usually escape us. One is the petition, "hallowed be Thy Name, Thy Kingdom come," which reminds us of the "Maranatha" and "Come Lord" of the first eucharistic liturgies. The second, and more important, is the petition, "Give us this day our daily (ἐπιούσιον) bread." Exegetes have been unable to agree on the meaning of these words.[58] There is, however, plenty of evidence leading to the conclusion that the "bread" we ask for in this prayer is not the ordinary bread we eat every day, which is the way we usually understand it, but the Bread of the Eucharist, which is ἐπιούσιος in the sense that it is "of that which is coming" or "to come"—in other words, of the Kingdom which is to come. However much this phrase in the Lord's Prayer solicits differing interpretations, the position in the Divine Liturgy which this prayer has occupied with notable consistency from earliest times—*immediately before Holy Communion*—is evidence that, at least in the mind of the early Church, the petition for *epiousios* bread refers not to the bread we eat every day, but to the meal and the nourishment of the Kingdom.[59] This is "the bread which comes down from heaven," in other words, the flesh or body of the Son of Man (Jn 6:34), who, it should be noted, is also an eschatological fig-

---

[57] It is probable that petitions, such as "forgive us our trespasses" and "lead us not into temptation" also have an eschatological meaning. Cf. R.E. Brown, "The Pater Noster as an Eschatological Prayer," *Theological Studies* 22 (1961) 171–208.

[58] The question hinges on whether the term *epiousios* comes from *epeinai* or *epousia*, in which case it would mean "essential for our existence," or from *epienai*, which would mean "coming" or "of the day which is to come." The antithesis in the text between *epiousios* and "this day" and the evidence of ancient sources in both East and West both point to the second of these two meanings. But even if it is talking about the bread we eat every day, as E. Lohmeyer points out *("Our Father,"* p. 157), all Jesus' references to bread and meals have an eschatological meaning.

[59] It is noteworthy that the Lord's prayer was recited in the Liturgy only by the faithful and not by the catechumens. Cf. J.-J. von Allmen, *Essai sur les Repas du Seigneur* (Neuchâtel, Paris: Delachaux et Niestlé, 1966), p. 81f.

ure. In the Eucharist, we ask *today* for the bread of *tomorrow*, the future or "coming" bread of the Kingdom.

One could add many other elements from Scripture which bear witness to the eschatological character of the Eucharist and its connection with the Kingdom of God. But where we find this connection expounded in depth and established in the consciousness of the Church is in the theology of the Greek fathers and the eucharistic liturgies of the ancient Church, which continue to be in use today.

2. *The Kingdom Which is to Come—the Cause and Archetype of the Eucharist*

Amidst the wealth of patristic evidence for a connection between the Eucharist and the Kingdom, we may single out one truly important passage from St Maximus the Confessor which, so far as we know, has not yet received the attention it deserves in theology. This passage indicates not only the unbreakable connection between the Eucharist and the Kingdom, but also *the radical overturning of the ancient Greek notion of causality*. Apart from anything else, this demonstrates how unjust and far from reality is the prevalent notion that Maximus was influenced by ancient Greek philosophy, both Platonic and Aristotelian. We shall set out this passage in its entirety, so that we can go on to comment on it in relation to our theme. In his *Scholia* on Dionysius the Areopagite's work, *On the Church Hierarchy*, Maximus writes:

> [The Areopagite] calls "images (εἰκόνες) of what is true" the rites that are now performed in the synaxis … For these things are symbols, not the truth…

> *From the effects.* That is, from what is accomplished visibly to the things that are unseen and secret, which are the causes and archetypes of things perceptible. For those things are called causes which in no way owe the cause of their being to anything else. Or from the effects to the causes, that is, from the perceptible symbols to what is noetic and spiritual. Or from the imperfect to the more perfect, from the type to the image, and from the image to the truth. For the things of the Old Testament are the

shadow; those of the New Testament are the image (εἰκών). The truth (ἀλήθεια) is the state of things to come".[60]

In this passage, St Maximus interprets in his own way the concept of the Eucharist as *image* and *symbol* in relation to the concept of *causality*. What takes place in the Divine Eucharist is an "image" and "symbol" of what is "true." Reading this passage up to a certain point, one seems to be moving in an atmosphere of Platonism. The things "accomplished visibly" are images and symbols of the "unseen" and "secret": perceptible symbols are images of what is "noetic and spiritual." In accordance with the Platonic view, the perceptible and visible world is an image of a stable and eternal world which, being noetic and spiritual, is the truth, the true world. In consequence, one would say that what is accomplished in the Divine Liturgy is an image and reflection of the heavenly Liturgy which is accomplished eternally, and which is the "archetype" of the earthly Eucharist. That would indeed be a typically Platonic understanding of the Eucharist.

But Maximus has a surprise in store for us at the end of this passage. The Divine Eucharist is for him an image of the true Eucharist which is nothing other than *"the state of things to come."* The truth "of what is now accomplished in the synaxis" is to be found not in a Platonic type of ideal reality but in a "reality of the future," in the Kingdom which is to come: the crucial element which overturns the Platonic relationship between archetype and image is the *category of time*. To get from the image to the prototype we do not have to go outside time, but we certainly have to pass through the expectation of an "event" or state which lies in the future. This changes the whole mentality from a Platonic to a biblical one. For while it is impossible in Platonic thought to pass from the image to the archetype through time, as if the archetype were to be found at the end of history, in the biblical understanding, it is essential. In the biblical understanding, as in that of St Maximus, what is represented in the Eucharist is *what is to come, he who comes*, and the *Kingdom* which he will establish.

This passage is also important because it poses the problem of *causality*, thus also overturning Aristotelian notions of "entelechy."

---

[60] PG 4:137. Many of the *Scholia* are attributed also to John of Skythopolis (middle of the sixth century). This particular one must belong to St Maximus himself, as its content is confirmed by Maximus' *Amb.* 21 (PG 91:1253CD).

Causes, says Maximus, are those which do not in any way owe their cause to anything else. In ancient Greek and Western thought, as in common sense, a cause is logically but also chronologically prior to its effect. In the thought of St Maximus, however, the further back we go in time, the further we get away from the archetype, from the cause: the Old Testament is "shadow," the New Testament is "image," and the "state of things to come" is truth. In other words, the archetype, the cause of "what is accomplished in the synaxis," lies in the future. *The Eucharist is the result of the kingdom which is to come.* The Kingdom which is to come, a future event ("the state of things to come"), being the *cause* of the Eucharist gives it its true *being*.

This is what comes out of a careful reading of Maximus. Later on, we shall look at its existential significance—because this is what concerns theology in the final analysis, not the historical or philosophical curiosity in which theologians often expend all their energies. For the time being, we note that the biblical connection between Eucharist and Kingdom, far from losing its force in the patristic period, was securely established on an ontological basis: the Eucharist is not simply connected with the Kingdom which is to come; it draws from it its being and its truth. Liturgical practice formed, and continues to form, the language in which the Church expresses this thesis.

3. *Liturgical Practice*

We usually think of the order (the *rubric*) of a liturgical service as something secondary and unimportant. And it is indeed true that our Liturgy has come to be loaded down with a whole lot of secondary symbolism and aesthetic decorations, but this does not mean that every rite in the Liturgy is unrelated to its essence. Liturgiologists, who are usually historians of liturgy with no theological or ecclesiological interests, do not enlighten us as to the theological content of the rites and the differences between the essential and inessential parts. Thus, our clergy, especially, but also the laity either consider every aspect of the order of the service equally important and keep it religiously, or—and this is dangerous—they abbreviate, leave things out, change the order of these rites, etc., destroying the "image" of the Kingdom that the Liturgy is meant to be. Thus, we end up losing the representation of the last times in our Liturgy, either because we have overloaded it with rites which do not express the coming of the Kingdom or because we remove or mix up fundamental elements of the Liturgy and thus dangerously distort its eschatological character.

a) The Gathering "In One Place"

One of the basic elements of the coming of the last days is the gathering of the scattered people of God—and by extension of all mankind—"in one place" around the person of the Messiah, in order for the judgement of the world to take place and the Kingdom of God to prevail. In St Matthew's Gospel, the Kingdom of God is likened to "a net which was thrown into the sea and *gathered* fish of every kind" (Mt 13:47), while in the description of the Parousia of the Son of Man we read yet more clearly that on that day of the last times "before him will be *gathered* all the nations" (Mt 25:32). In John, again, the purpose of Christ's passion and, by extension, of the whole work of salvation is considered to be not only the salvation of Israel, "but to *gather into* one the children of God who are scattered abroad" (Jn 11:52).[61]

It is not incidental, therefore, that the Eucharist as image of the Kingdom is very clearly described as a "gathering" (σύναξις) or gathering "in one place" (ἐπὶ τὸ αυτό: 1 Cor 16:23, or ἐν ἐκκλησίᾳ: 1 Cor 11:18). In the sixth chapter of St John's Gospel, in a passage which is clearly talking about the Eucharist, after the multitude has eaten its fill, Jesus commands the fragments left over to be "gathered up," which is considered as a sign that he is "he who is to come" (Jn 6:12–14). The *Didache* gives us the most explicit description of the Eucharist as an image of the eschatological gathering of the scattered children of God, the Church: "Even as this broken bread was scattered over the hills, and was gathered together and became one, so let thy Church be gathered together from the ends of the earth into thy kingdom."[62]

Indeed, what has become of this strong eschatological sense of the eucharistic gathering over the course of time? In the time of Ig-

---

[61] Cf. J. Jeremias, *New Testament Theology.*
[62] *Didache* 9.4.

natius, it clearly still survives,[63] and, as we have seen, in Maximus in the seventh century the Eucharist is consistently called "synaxis" and considered an image of "the state of things to come." But little by little, the sense of the gathering of "the whole Church" in one place (1 Cor 14:23; Rom 16:23) recedes, as does the eschatological character of the gathering. In the Roman Catholic West, things deteriorated even further with the introduction and spread of the private mass, which the priest can celebrate on his own. But in the Orthodox Church too, even if celebration of the Liturgy is not permitted without the presence of laity, it often happens that the laity are absent or "symbolically" present in insignificant numbers. As it is now celebrated, our Eucharist is now anything but an image of the eschatological gathering "in one place." Indeed, with the proliferation of eucharistic gatherings in parishes, chapels, monasteries, etc., and with the bishop absent as head of the gathering of the "whole Church" because the dioceses are geographically too large, the term "gathering" has lost its meaning. We should call it now the dispersal of the faithful, rather than their gathering "in one place."

b) Passage Through the Ascetic and Baptismal Experience

The coming of the Kingdom of God has no meaning unless the people of God have first passed through the "catharsis" of the trials, sorrows, and death of the Christ. The Messiah himself has had to pass through these things in order to bring the Kingdom, and the people of God must do the same. A passage in Luke (22:28) is significant here: those who pass through the "trials" of Jesus are the ones to be given the privilege of eating and drinking at his table in his Kingdom. The entrance into the Kingdom is through the "narrow gate" and "strait way" of "endurance," which in the first centuries meant, in practice, endurance of persecutions (the Epistle to the Hebrews lays particular emphasis on this) and, later on, meant the period of penitence and fasting which had to precede Baptism. (Great

---

[63] For a detailed discussion, see my *The Unity of the Church in the Divine Eucharist and the Bishop in the First Three Centuries* (in Greek), (Athens: n.p., 1965, 2nd ed. Athens: Gregori, 1990); English translation: *Eucharist, Bishop, Church: The Unity of the Church in the Divine Eucharist and the Bishop During the First Three Centuries* (Brookline, MA: Holy Cross Orthodox Press, 2001), esp. p. 87ff.

Lent, with its strict fast and its prohibition of the celebration of the Eucharist except on Saturdays and Sundays, is an indicative vestige of this, since Baptism was initially performed on Easter day.) In liturgical action, this was all experienced in Baptism, which already in the New Testament is linked with sacrifice and martyrdom (Mk 10:39; Lk 12:50), as also with death (Rom 6:4; Col 2:12), exactly as happened to Christ. The Areopagitic writings, the Cappadocians, and Maximus all speak of a stage of "those being purified," which is identified liturgically with the catechumens who are preparing for "illumination" (i.e., Baptism), who enter the rank of those "made perfect" upon receiving chrismation and the Eucharist. (These ranks clearly refer to those participating in the sacraments of Baptism, Chrismation, and the Eucharist and not simply to the monks, at least in St Maximus.)[64]

Thus, the eucharistic gathering, as an image of the last times, certainly should involve *only the baptized*. In this sense, we are talking about a *closed community* which comes together with "the doors being shut" (Jn 20:19, cf. the exclamation, "The doors! The doors!" in the Orthodox liturgy and the ancient *disciplina arcana*). The eucharistic gathering should never be a means and instrument of mission, because in the last times, which it represents, there will be no mission; anyway, *mission presupposes dispersal not a gathering "in one place."* Consequently, it is contrary to the nature of the Eucharist as image of the Kingdom to broadcast it over television or radio, whether for pastoral reasons or for the purpose of mission. In the Eucharist, we either participate "gathered in one place" or do not participate at all. Participation at a distance has no meaning. As for those who are sick or unable to come to the gathering, the Church's very ancient practice is to bring them the fruit of the gathering (Holy Communion, antidoron, etc.) by the "acolytes" in the early Church or by priests and deacons later.

c) The Eucharist as a Movement and Progression

With the weakening of the temporal dimension of the Eucharist as icon of the Kingdom *which is to come*, there has also been a gradual loss of the sense that in the Divine Eucharist there is a *movement*

---

[64] See for example, Maximus, *Scholia in eccl. hier.* 6 (PG 4:168–169).

"toward the End": the journey of the world, in Maximus' phrase, toward the Kingdom and the coming of the Kingdom to the world.[65]

From this point of view, it is interesting to look at the interpretations of the entrance in liturgical sources from the period when the entrance was a real entrance of the clergy and the people, headed by the bishop, into the church and the altar. These interpretations are dominated by a typology which has the entry of the bishop as an image of Christ's first coming to earth in the flesh, with a clear description of the progression to the eschaton. In the seventh century, as St Maximus demonstrates,[66] this early typology still survives. For him, the bishop's entry into the church to celebrate the Eucharist is an image of the Lord's first coming to earth, and everything that follows leads directly to the eschatological setting of the Kingdom: the sacred readings, and in particular the Gospel, represent "the end of the world," after which "the bishop comes down from the throne" for the judgement, with the dismissal of the catechumens and the closing of the doors. From that moment on, Maximus continues, everything takes place before the throne of God in his Kingdom. "The entry of the holy and venerable mysteries [clearly the so-called "Great Entrance"] is the beginning and prelude [...] to the new teaching about God's economy towards us which will be imparted in heaven."[67] (Note again the future tense, which distances us from a Platonic type of correspondence between the heavenly and the earthly.) "For God the Word [Logos] says, I will not drink any more of the fruit of the vine until that day when I shall drink it new with you in my Father's Kingdom."[68] The kiss of the peace also has an eschatological

---

[65] This has come about with the complete disappearance of the dimension of *entrance* within the Eucharist. The so-called "entrances" (great and little) which have been preserved in the Orthodox Liturgy are in fact circles made by the celebrant when he "enters" into the altar where he was before. Since the "prothesis" and "skevophylakion" ceased to exist as special annexes of the church building, the clergy have entered into the altar to put on their vestments and to do the "proskomide." But then what is the point of the so-called "little entrance"? In fact, it has no point, since the Eucharist has (probably under the influence of the works of Dionysius Areopagite) ceased to signify the *journey* to the Kingdom or the coming of the Kingdom, and become a static reflection and representation of it that takes place in space without reference to time.

[66] See Maximus, *Myst.* 8–9 (PG 91:688Bff).

[67] Maximus, *Myst.* 16 (PG 91:693C).

[68] Maximus, *Myst.* 16 (PG 91:693CD).

meaning, indicating "the concord that will prevail [again, a reference to future time] amongst all at the time when the ineffable good things which are to come are revealed."[69] Even the Creed, despite its historical content, leads us to the future: "The confession by everyone of the divine Creed points forward to the mystical thanksgiving *which will be rendered in the age to come* for the most marvelous principles and ways of God's most wise toward us, by which we have been saved."[70] The hymn "Holy, Holy, Holy" also leads us spiritually to the *future* state: "It indicates the union and equality in honor with the bodiless spiritual powers which *will be manifest in the future.*"[71] The Our Father also represents the future adoption in which all the saints shall be called and shall be sons of God through the grace which *will come* upon them.

There exists, then, a continuous progression within the Eucharist; a progression which, according to Maximus at least (things change somewhat in later Byzantine commentators on the Liturgy), literally *moves us along* and sets us in the Kingdom which is to come. Everything in the Liturgy moves forward: nothing is static. The symbolism in the Liturgy is not that of a parable or allegory. It is the symbolism of an icon as that is understood by the fathers of the Church, meaning participation in the *ontological content* of the prototype. And the prototype in this case, as can be seen in the passages of St Maximus just quoted, is the Kingdom which is to come, and our ultimate reconciliation and union with God and one another when we are incorporated into Christ.[72]

d) The Sacrifice of the Paschal Lamb

The Divine Eucharist is a *sacrifice*. The tradition in both East and West lays great stress on this aspect of the Eucharist.[73] This sac-

---

[69] Maximus, *Myst.* 17 (PG 91:694D–696A).

[70] Maximus, *Myst.* 18 (PG 91:696AB).

[71] Maximus, *Myst.* 19 (PG 91:696B).

[72] From all this, one understands that the abolition of the entrances into the Church building or the Altar is a great liturgical loss. It is true, certainly, that the church architecture which now prevails does not permit the priests to make a real entrance as they did in the ancient Church. The bishops, however, are able to make an entrance, and it is a shame that they no longer do it, clearly because they do not appreciate its significance.

[73] So, for instance, Cyril of Jerusalem (*Catechesis* 23.8, 9), Gregory of Nazianzus (*Orations* 2.95 and 4.52), Cyril of Alexandria (*On the Mystical Supper*, PG 77:1028), and John

rifice is none other than the death on the Cross of Christ, whose body and blood are offered "for many" (Mk 14:24, Mt 26:28); in other words, they have the effect of deliverance from sins, which are "forgiven" thanks to this sacrifice and the "communion" of the "many" in it, which is the fount of "eternal life."

This sacrificial aspect of the Divine Eucharist is indisputable both in biblical consciousness and theology, in the Fathers and the Liturgy. However, the point that we often tend to overlook or underestimate is *the connection and relationship between this sacrificial character of the Eucharist and the coming of the Kingdom of God, the "last times."* The Eucharist is indisputably the very sacrifice of the Lord upon the Cross. But there is a close relationship of this sacrifice with the coming of the Kingdom.

This is of vital importance for theology and, also, for the way in which we as believers experience this great mystery of the Church.

All the indications from the story of the Last Supper, handed down to us by the Gospels and the Apostle Paul, testify that with the words "this is my body" and "this is my blood," Christ was referring to himself as the Paschal Lamb (cf. 1 Cor 5:7f., "for Christ our paschal lamb has been sacrificed for us"). This identification of Christ with the paschal lamb was so widespread in the early Church that it was repeated without elucidation, not only by the Apostle Paul but also by other texts from the apostolic age, such as the first book of Peter (1:19), Revelation (5:6, 12, and 12:11), St John's Gospel (1:29, 36), and others. So, it is not by chance that in the language of the Church's liturgy, the portion of the eucharistic bread which is changed into the Body of Christ at the Divine Eucharist came to be called "the Lamb (ὁ Ἀμνός)."

The sacrifice of the paschal lamb has its roots in the exodus of Israel from Egypt, as described in the Book of Exodus (12:6). In the case of the Last Supper, however, it is clear that we have not merely a remembrance and repetition of the sacrifice of the lamb in Exodus, such as took place at every celebration of the Jewish Passover, but the sacrifice of the *perfect, eschatological Paschal Lamb.* This is borne out

Chrysostom (*On the Epistle to the Hebrews* 17.3), as well as the Divine Liturgies of St John Chrysostom and St Basil the Great which are celebrated in the Orthodox Church, call the Eucharist a *sacrifice* which is "unbloody," "reasonable," etc.

by many elements in the story of the Last Supper in the Gospels and also by the liturgical practice of the early Church. Let us refer to some of these as examples.

We have already underlined, at the beginning of this study, the fact that the Lord clearly links the Last Supper with the Kingdom of God, according to the account given us by the Gospels. What we must note here is the connection of the sacrifice to which Christ refers there with the *new covenant*. It has already been observed by biblical scholars that the term "Covenant" should be regarded as equivalent to the term "Kingdom of heaven."[74] The sacrifice of Christ as the Paschal Lamb is the fulfilment of the eschatological purpose of the sacrifice both of the original paschal lamb in Exodus and of all the subsequent sacrifices performed by the Jews in imitation of the sacrifice of that lamb. So, when Christ says at the Last Supper, and the Church repeats in the course of the Eucharist, that "this is my blood, the blood of the new covenant," our thoughts are directed toward the coming and establishment of the Kingdom of God, and not simply toward an event which took place in the past. The sacrifice of the Lord upon the Cross cannot be isolated from its eschatological significance. Remission of sins is itself linked in the New Testament with the coming of the Kingdom (Mt 6:12; Lk 11:4; Jn 20:23, for example), and this surely applies especially to the remission of sins which stems from the sacrifice of Christ as the Paschal Lamb.

Things are even clearer in the book of Revelation, which without a doubt contains elements or fragments of the ancient eucharistic liturgy.[75] In this book, the description of Christ as the Lamb occurs repeatedly and, without any doubt, in connection with the paschal lamb of Exodus 12:6. The eschatological significance that Revelation gives to the Lamb comes across clearly from the following remarks, which are of profound significance.

---

[74] See J. Behm, διαθήκη, in G. Kittel, *Theological Dictionary of the New Testament*, vol. II, 1964, pp. 106–134.

[75] See P. Prigent, *Apocalypse et Liturgie* (Neuchâtel, Paris: Delachaux et Niestlé, 1964). On the influence of this book on the Orthodox Liturgy, see P. Bratsiotis, "L'Apocalypse de saint Jean dans le culte de l'Église grecque orthodoxe," *Revue d'Histoire et de Philosophie religieuse* 42 (1962) 116–121.

1) The "lamb that was slain" has the authority to open the book with seven seals, with the meaning of this book's contents revealed only at the end of history.

2) The sacrifice of the Lamb concerns not only the people of Israel, but peoples "from every tribe and tongue and nation" (Rev 5:9).

The universal character of this salvation suggests the end of history and the dawning of the "day of the Lord" (1 Cor 1:8; 1 Thess 5:2). It is characteristic that the Apostle Paul, who awaits the Second Coming of Christ imminently, regards as its "first fruits" the return of the gentiles and their grafting into the trunk of Israel (2 Thess 2:3).

The fact that the blood of the lamb is shed "for all" also refers us to the "servant" of God in the book of Isaiah (chapters 52 and 53) who "bore the sin of many and was given up for their sins" (53:2, Septuagint), but who also in the last times *will bring together the scattered Israel* and will be "a light to the nations, that my salvation may reach to the end of the earth" (48:6), because "many nations will wonder at him ... for they that have been told of him shall see, and they that have not heard shall understand" (52:15, Septuagint).

3) In particular, we should note the connection in the book of Revelation between the Lamb that was slain and the "new song," the "alleluia" which is repeated three times by a great multitude and by the whole of creation ("like the sound of many waters") in the context of the marriage of the Lamb and the worship of him (19:8).

The fact that this "alleluia" is an eschatological hymn is made clear by the reason given for it in the text itself, "For the Lord our God the Almighty reigns" (19:6): in other words, the Kingdom of God has been established. This is also why, despite the fact that the Lamb has been slain, the prevailing tone is one of *joy*: "let us rejoice and be glad" (19:7), recalling the "in gladness" of Acts (2:46) in connection with the celebration of the Eucharist by the first Christians.

These observations take on even greater interest if this hymn is connected with the Last Supper itself. The Gospels note (Mt 26:30; Mk 14:26) that immediately after the Supper and the words of Christ, which connect it with the Kingdom, "when [Christ and his disciples] *had sung a hymn*, they went out to the Mount of Olives." As expert scholars indicate, this refers to the *hallel* which followed the Jewish paschal meal, in other words the singing of psalms 114–118

(113–117) antiphonally, with one of the group reading the text aloud while the others (cf. the "multitude" or the "people" in Revelation) would respond with "alleluia" after the middle of each verse. Already in Christ's time, these psalms had an eschatological-messianic meaning for the Jews. The verses which end psalm 118 (117)—"This is the day which the Lord has made; let us rejoice and be glad in it"—are clearly eschatological. Since "this day" for us is the day of Resurrection, the final verses of that psalm—"Blessed is he that comes in the name of the Lord ... The Lord is God and has appeared unto us,"—have for the Christians, too, the same eschatological character.

In conclusion, the Last Super and the Lamb slain for our salvation cannot be understood without reference to the "last day," the "day of the Lord," the Parousia, and the establishment of the Kingdom of God. In the words of St Cyril of Alexandria,[76] the Eucharist is not simply "the performance of the dread sacrifice" but "the gift of immortality and a pledge of life without end."

This conclusion is reinforced and confirmed by another observation: the ancient Church never celebrated its Mystical Supper, the Divine Eucharist, on the same day as the Lord's death, but *after* it. It is known from history that Christians in Asia Minor in the second century celebrated Easter on the fourteenth of Nissan, the same day as the Jewish Passover. It is significant, however, that they did not celebrate the Eucharist except at dawn the next day, in other words, after the Jews' paschal meal, during which the Christians fasted. The fact that even today the Orthodox Church, following the ancient tradition, waits for the Jewish Passover to pass and only then celebrates its own Passover (Easter) is not simply due, as is often thought, to an anti-Jewish stance on its part; apart from anything else, it is due to the fact that the Passover of the Church, which is associated with joy and gladness, cannot precede the moment in time at which, historically, the Last Supper took place and the crucifixion followed. This time is a time of fasting, while Easter is a time of festivity.

Have we ever seriously thought about why the Church dissociated not only its Passover but also its Eucharist from fasting and linked it with the radiance of the Resurrection? It is significant, as

---

[76] Cyril Alex., *Hom. on the mystical Supper* (PG 77:1028f).

we noted earlier, that celebration of the Eucharist on fast days was forbidden in the Church. (The exception of the Exaltation of the Cross and the commemoration of the Forerunner does not negate the rule.) This has been confined, of course, to the period of Great Lent,[77] but the sense remains: the Eucharist is an eschatological event and cannot be other than festive, joyful, and radiant. Its sacrificial character is transformed into the joy of the Resurrection, which means eschatological joy. In Christ there is no such thing as sacrifice without deliverance, and deliverance means not just remission of personal sins, but the ultimate transfiguration of the world, the overcoming of corruption and death. This is what we celebrate when we perform the Eucharist: a sacrifice on the Cross which takes its meaning from the Resurrection, as the first realization in history of the Kingdom which is to come.

e) A Festival of the Resurrection

The most eloquent proof of the eschatological character of the Eucharist and its identification with the foretaste of the Kingdom of God is the fact that from the beginning it has been associated with Sunday, as the most appropriate day for its celebration. We referred above to the Quartodecimans in Asia Minor in the second century who celebrated Easter on the fourteenth of the month of Nissan. This, of course, involved celebration of the Eucharist on a day other than Sunday, at least on Easter day. As is well known, this custom gave rise to the paschal controversy which threatened to divide the early Church because, apart from anything else, it created variations in the time of fasting in places such as Rome, where Easter was celebrated on Sunday by the local Church and not according to the practice of the Quartodecimans, who came from Asia Minor and were living in Rome in the second century. But it was not long before this custom gave way, and the celebration of Easter and performance of the Eucharist on Sunday became general. Evidence for the connection of the Eucharist with Sunday could start with the Acts of the Apostles (20:7) and the First Epistle to the Corinthians (16:2) and

---

[77] According to the testimony of the ancient historians such as Socrates (in his *Church History* 5.22 [PG 67:676A]), in the early Church, at least in Alexandria, the Eucharist was not celebrated on *any* fast day throughout the year, and not just during Lent.

proceed to the Revelation (1:10), the *Didache* (14:1), and Justin (*First Apology* 67), who is clear on this question.

But why Sunday? What led the Church to this practice? What is the deeper theological meaning of this practice?

Sunday is the day of the *Resurrection* of Christ. The Christians regarded it thus from the beginning[78] on the basis of the biblical evidence that the Resurrection took place "on the first day of the week" (Mk 16:2; cf. Mt 28:1 and Lk 24:1). The meaning that they gave to the Resurrection of Christ from the beginning was very profound, and was necessarily carried over both to Sunday and to the Eucharist which was celebrated on that day. It is worth noting some of the fundamental aspects of this meaning in order to understand better the relationship between Eucharist and Kingdom.

As the day of Resurrection, Sunday is the *eighth day*. The reason is that the "new creation" begins on this day, when "our Christ appeared risen from the dead, it being forever, however, the first in terms of its significance. For Christ, being the firstborn of all creation, again became the chief of another race, that which is regenerated by him."[79] St Basil the Great throws light on the eschatological character of the "eight day," when he writes the following:

> Thus, we all look to the East at our prayers, but few of us know that we are seeking our old country, Paradise, which God planted in Edem in the East. *We pray standing on the first day of the week*, but we do not all know the reason. *On the day of the Resurrection,* we remind ourselves of the grace given to us by standing at prayer, *not only because we are risen with Christ and are bound to seek those things which are above, but because that day seems to us in some sense an image of the age which we expect.* Therefore, though it is the beginning of days, it is not called by Moses "first" but "one" ... as though the same day often recurred. Now "one" and "eight" are the same, in itself distinctly indicating that day which is really "one" and truly "eight" ... *the state which follows after this present time, the day which knows no end or evening, and*

---

[78] See, for example, Ignatius, *Magnesians* 9; *Epistle of Barnabas* 15.8ff.; Justin, *First Apology* 67, *Dialogue* 41 and 138; Tertullian, *On prayer* 23; Eusebius, *Church History* III. 27.5; *Apostolic Constitutions* II.59, V.20,19, etc.

[79] Justin, *Dialogue* 138 (PG 6:793B).

no successor, that age which does not end or grow old. Of necessity, then, *the Church teaches her own foster-children to offer their prayers on that day standing, in order that through the constant reminder of the endless life* we may not neglect to make provision for our removal thither. Moreover, all of Pentecost is a reminder of the resurrection expected in the age to come. For that one and first day, if seven times multiplied by seven, completes the seven weeks of the holy Pentecost.... And so it is a likeness of eternity.... *On this day* the rules of the Church have educated us *to prefer the upright attitude of prayer, for by their plain reminder they, as it were, make our mind to dwell no longer in the present but in the future.*"[80]

We have quoted this lengthy passage in its entirety because it gives us, quite clearly, the eschatological meaning of Sunday and of the Eucharist which is celebrated on that day. We note in particular that, for St Basil, the avoidance of kneeling on Sunday[81] is necessitated not only by the fact that it is the day of the Resurrection but also by *the expectation of the age to come,* so that our minds are made to dwell "no longer in the present but in the future." This strong impetus toward *what is to come,* not simply toward what is above, brings the dimension of *time* into eschatology and recalls what we have said above in commenting on the relevant passages of St Maximus: the eschatology of the Divine Liturgy, like that of Sunday, is not a Platonic type of representation of the heavenly state, but a *movement and progression* toward and a *foretaste* of the future. Maximus and Basil concur on this point.

It is noteworthy, again, that St Basil refers to praying toward the East. For the East was not only the place of the original paradise but also the direction from which the Lord is expected to appear at his Second Coming. As St John of Damascus says, summarizing the

---

[80] Basil, *De Spir.* 27.66 (PG 32:189f), trans. B. Jackson, *A Select Library of Nicene and Post-Nicene Fathers of the Christian Church,* vol. VIII (Edinburgh: T&T Clark; Grand Rapids, MI: W.B. Eerdmans, repr. 1996), p. 42 (lightly adapted). The emphasis is mine.

[81] The prohibition of kneeling on Sunday goes back to ancient times, as Irenaeus testifies in his lost work *On the Pascha.* See fragment 6 in the series *Library of the Greek Fathers,* published by the Apostoliki Diakonia, vol.5, p. 174.

reasons for praying toward the East[82]: there are many reasons, and they include the future coming of the Son of Man from the East according to the Gospel passage (Mt 24:27), "as the lightning comes from the East and shines as far as the West, so will be the coming of the Son of Man."

After quoting this passage, the Damascene concludes, "waiting for him with longing, we worship toward the East": in other words, because we are awaiting Christ's final coming in glory, we pray facing East.

This resurrectional and eschatological character of the Eucharist, has another consequence, too: during the Eucharist, the Church *is bathed in light and adored with all available splendor.* A Eucharist in dimly-lit churches, ostensibly for the sake of devout concentration, is antithetical to its very nature. It was characteristic of the Byzantine churches, with that of St Sophia of Constantinople as their model, to be decorated in gold and painted with bright colors precisely in order to depict, by artistic means, the splendor of the Kingdom—an indication that in celebrating the Eucharist we look to the last times, to the future.

Unfortunately, the pietism which has crept into our consciousness and our worship has misled us into the mistaken idea that richness in vestments and in the decoration of churches is a bad thing. Just one simple observation shows how alien this idea is to the Orthodox tradition: the richest and most splendid vestments in our Church are to be found in our monasteries, and particularly on the Holy Mountain, the most important and authoritative monastic center for Orthodoxy. Why, then, does a genuine Orthodox monk— who according to the sayings of the Fathers should wear a shoddy and threadbare *rason* and that he should hang it outside his cell door in the certainty that no one would be tempted to steal it—why during the Liturgy does this same man, as celebrant, put on the most splendid vestments, without being scandalized or scandalizing anyone else? Quite simply, because the eschatological character of the Eucharist remains vivid in his consciousness: in the Eucharist, we move within the space of the age to come, of the Kingdom. There we

---

[82] John Damascene, *De fide orth.* 4.12 (PG 94:1136B).

experience "the day which knows no end or evening, and no successor, that age which does not end or grow old," in the words of St Basil.[83] We do not have the right to turn the Eucharist into an opportunity to show off our humility, or a means to psychological experiences of compunction. Besides, "he who offers," the real celebrant, is Christ, and indeed the risen Christ as he will come "*in his glory*," and those who celebrate the Liturgy are nothing more than icons of this eschatological Christ. And, of course, "the honor paid to the icon passes to the prototype,"[84] which indicates that in celebrating the Eucharist we look to the last times, to the future.

How resolutely the Church refused to link the Eucharist with sorrow and compunction is shown by the fact that even on the days when the martyrs are commemorated, when she recalls their death, the Divine Eucharist is offered with the same splendor as on Sundays. It is known that from the first centuries it became the practice to celebrate the Eucharist on the feast days of martyrs, and subsequently of all the saints. What is often overlooked is the fact that from the beginning, the martyrdom of the saints was seen not just as a repetition of Christ's sacrifice on the Cross, but as a *revelation of the glory of his Kingdom*. Already the description of the martyrdom of Stephen in the Acts of the Apostles (7:55ff.) makes clear the eschatological character that the Church recognizes in it: "he gazed into heaven and saw the glory of God, and Jesus standing on the right hand of God; and he said, 'Behold, I see the heavens opened, and the Son of Man standing at the right hand of God.'" (The reference to the "Son of Man," who is considered an eschatological figure in Scripture, is characteristic.) The same goes for the "Acts"—the martyrologies—of all the martyrs of the early Church.[85] The celebration

[83] Basil, *De Spir.* 27.66 (PG 32:192B).

[84] Basil, *De Spir.* 18.45 (PG 32:149C).

[85] A moving passage, and one that reveals the eschatological character both of martyrdom and of Eucharist, is the following extract from the martyrdom of Saint Agathonike, published by Harnack (*Die Akten des Karpus, des Papylus und der Agathonike*, Texte und Untersuchungen, III, 3/4, 1888, pp. 451f): "A certain Agathonike was standing beside them [during the martyrdom of Papylus and Carpus]; and seeing the glory of the Lord which Carpus said that he saw and contemplating the heavenly invitation, at once she lifted up her voice: 'For me too is this supper [*ariston*, or "dinner"] prepared. And I too must eat my share of this glorious meal.'" The association between martyrdom and the Eucharist is clear, as is the eschatological character of both.

of the Eucharist on saint's days cannot be separated from the eschatological character of the Eucharist, and for that reason are always celebrated with particular splendor and involve the lifting of the fast.

f) Remembrance (ἀνάμνησις) of the Future

The Eucharist is a remembrance *(ἀνάμνησις)*. But what is meant by "remembrance"? In psychology, remembrance means recalling the past. The basis for this meaning is Platonic and, in general, ancient Greek. For Plato, in particular, all truth is stored up in the soul. Nothing new can happen "under the sun," as the saying goes. Truth (ἀ-λήθεια) is an escape from forgetfulness (λήθη), a manifestation of what *already exists*. For this reason, the teacher does not do more than to prompt the pupil to remember once again what he already knows, to extract the truth from him (Socrates' method of acting as "midwife").

This understanding is also based on common sense. None of us can comprehend what it means to "remember the future." This is because time, in our experience since the fall, is *fragmentary* and is inevitably divided into past, present, and future, in a sequence which cannot naturally be reversed because of death, which has established itself with the fall of man. Thus, the future naturally comes after the past and present, making it meaningless to "remember" it.

But what happens in a time freed from this fragmentation because death has been abolished? In such a case, the future is not separated from the past and the present. If indeed the future is that which gives meaning both to the past and to the present, it is then transformed into a source from which both equally draw their substance. The future acquires "substance" (Heb 11:1) and can be "anticipated" so as to become part of our memory. Thus, it is possible to talk about remembrance of the future.

The fact that this is precisely what happens in the Divine Eucharist is as evident to the careful student of the Eucharist as it is unknown to those who approach it without an awareness of its eschatological character. Let us take a closer look at this subject.

The Anaphoras of the Divine Liturgy, still in use in the Orthodox Church, both that of St John Chrysostom and that of St Basil, include the following phrase which is a stumbling block for common sense: "remembering then this saving commandment, the Cross, the tomb, the Resurrection on the third day, the Ascension into heaven, the sitting at the right hand *and the second and glorious coming again,* offering to thee thine own of thine own, we hymn thee."

To remember past events (the Cross, the Resurrection, etc.) is "natural." But to "remember" something that has not yet happened (the Second Coming) cannot be explained unless it is transferred to an existential plane on which the fragmentation and necessary sequence of the three elements of time (past, present, and future) have been healed. This is precisely what happens in the Kingdom of God. In this Kingdom, everything is not turned into "present"—that would be a typically Platonic deliverance from death—but into the "future age which does not end or grow old," as St Basil calls the Kingdom (which, being the state that ultimately prevails, the "truth" in the words of Maximus the Confessor, is logically prior, since it is this that gives "substance" and meaning to both past and present). The "end" constitutes the "reason" for which both the past and the present "subsist," according to St Maximus,[86] and in consequence the "future age which does not end" becomes not an effect, as happens in time as we know it after the fall, but the *cause* of all past and present events.[87] Consequently, remembrance of this "endless" future is not only possible but also ontologically definitive in the realm of the Eucharist as icon of the Kingdom. This is attested both in the Gospel descriptions of the Last Supper and in the liturgy of the Church.

In the description of the Last Supper in Luke (22:20), a prominent place belongs to the Lord's words to his disciples, which are repeated by St Paul (1 Cor 11:24–25) and by eucharistic liturgies throughout the ages: *"Do this in remembrance of me."* According to our common, protological logic, bounded as it is by our experience of time since the fall (as described above), the meaning of this phrase would

---

[86] Maximus, *QThal.* 60 (PG 90:621AB).

[87] This matter had already been raised in the second century AD in connection with the annulment by the New Testament of certain provisions of the Mosaic Law (circumcision, sacrifices, etc.). The answer given by St Irenaeus remains the basis for Maximus' thinking: a future event (the coming of Christ) can annul an event in the past (e.g., the sacrifices of the Old Testament), not because the latter was evil and had to disappear, but because it existed solely for the sake of the future event, which gives it meaning and substance.

be: "*Do this in order to remember me.*" The question, however, is whether the Lord was interested in perpetuating his memory in the minds of his disciples (or of human beings generally) through the celebration of the Eucharist or whether he wanted, through the celebration of the Eucharist by his disciples (and by the Church), to link the Eucharist with the eternal memory of God in the Kingdom which he would establish.

This question has generated much debate among biblical theologians since J. Jeremias, in the work referred to earlier,[88] refuted the first of the above views with serious arguments and supported the second one, to the point of formulating the extreme position that Christ gave the commandment that the Eucharist should be celebrated in order that God should remember him (as Messiah) at the Second Coming. We shall not concern ourselves with this discussion, which is anyway not immediately relevant to our theme in all its aspects. What interests us is whether the remembrance of Christ at the Eucharist is a psychological, human remembrance of an event in the past or whether it is linked with the future, with the Kingdom, and that not just psychologically but *ontologically*.

If we want to use St Paul as our interpreter for the phrase "in remembrance of me," we shall be led without a doubt to the conclusion that the eucharistic remembrance is *orientated toward the second coming*. The explanation Paul gives for the phrase, "in remembrance of me," is that ("for") in the Eucharist, "you proclaim the Lord's death until he comes" (1 Cor 11:26). As Jeremias notes, "until he comes" is used repeatedly in the New Testament in reference to the last times (Rom 11:25; 1 Cor 15:25; Lk 21:24), and its meaning in this particular case is that in the Eucharist, the Lord's death is not proclaimed as an event of the past, but *in the perspective of the second coming*.[89] This explains the connection of the Eucharist with the very early Aramaic liturgical exclamation "*maranatha*," which Paul knows (1 Cor 16:23) and the significance of which we have already mentioned.

At the Eucharist, consequently, we place the events and persons of the past and the present within the context of the Kingdom which will come, and not simply psychologically (through a movement of

[88] Jeremias, *The Eucharistic Words of Jesus.*
[89] Jeremias, *The Eucharistic Words of Jesus*, p. 253.

our imagination toward the future) but *ontologically—with the purpose of giving these events and persons substance, so that they are not destroyed (by time and death) and live eternally.* This eternal survival of events and beings *cannot be secured by placing them in human memory.* Human memory comes and goes, because it is a created memory. When we pray as the Church that someone's memory may be eternal, we do not mean that this person should live on in our own human memory, because this would have little meaning since human memory, being created, passes away. We mean that this person lives on in the eternal *"memory" of God.* Only what exists in the thought of God really exists. When God pronounces the terrible words, "I do not know you" (Mt 25:12), the consequences are not psychological but ontological; so also, when he says, "I will remember their sins no more" (Heb 8:12, 10:17), the consequences are of ontological significance (total erasure from existence) for those particular sins. Conversely, when God "remembers" something or someone, he is not operating psychologically—it is meaningless, anyway, to introduce psychology into God's being—but is performing an ontological action whereby that particular being is existentially affirmed.[90]

This relates directly to the eucharistic Liturgy. A basic and essential element in any eucharistic Liturgy is the *commemoration*: there is no such thing as a Eucharist which does not commemorate, in one way or another, events (principally the creation of the world and the events of Christ's life on earth) and also names. What is the meaning of this commemoration in the Eucharist?

As our Liturgy has developed, it is difficult to make out the meaning of the commemoration of names. There are three principal points at which names are commemorated in the Orthodox Liturgy today. One is the "Proskomide," which is when the faithful hand over their gifts (their loaves of bread) to the celebrants (priests and deacons) *before* the Divine Liturgy so that the Eucharist can be prepared from them. For practical reasons, this point has come to be the

[90] The words "Remember me, O Lord, when Thou comest in Thy Kingdom," which we have been repeating in the Church since the time of the thief at the right hand of the Crucified, bear witness that the *kingdom* is the space in which our being is secured, by reason of the fact that God commemorates us, and not merely human beings (Remember, O Lord...).

preeminent moment for names to be commemorated, when the particles for those commemorated are cut out, to be placed on the paten beside the Lamb, and finally put into the chalice with it. The whole service as it is now performed is devoid of obvious reference to the Kingdom which is to come, and its symbolic references are mainly to the sacrifice of Christ on the Cross. This practice of particles was introduced gradually, beginning in the eighth century, but does not form part of the eucharistic Anaphora which, as the offering and sacrifice of the *eschatological* Lamb, takes place later in the Liturgy.

The other moment at which names are today commemorated is at the Great Entrance, principally when a bishop is celebrating. The fact that a celebrant bishop commemorates names at this time, when he receives the gifts of the people from the priests and deacons, should be connected with the fact that the bishop is not present during the preparation of the gifts (the Proskomide), since he comes into the Church only at the Little Entrance. Thus, this commemoration of names, too, should not be considered as the proper eucharistic commemoration. It is nevertheless worthy of note that the commemoration of names at this point makes a clear reference to the kingdom: "May the Lord God remember in his Kingdom."

There thus remains the third moment of commemoration, which is also the moment of eucharistic "remembrance" *par excellence*: this is the moment of the *Anaphora*. It is a real misfortune that the commemoration of names has ceased to take place at that time and has been shifted almost exclusively to the "Proskomide" for practical reasons: the entire *theological* meaning of this act is thereby destroyed. What is this meaning? If we go back again to the Church fathers, we shall find some valuable information in Cyril of Jerusalem. Interpreting the eucharistic Anaphora, St Cyril regards it *in its totality* as a *commemoration* (remembrance). In the prayer of the Anaphora, which begins immediately after, "Let us give thanks to the Lord," and the people's response, "It is meet and right," "*we commemorate*," he says, "heaven and earth and sea ... *and all creation, rational and nonrational* ... angels, archangels ...," in other words, God's creation, which through this commemoration participates in a certain way in the Mystery of the Eucharist. After the invocation of the Holy Spirit and the change of the elements into the Body and

Blood of Christ, "upon that sacrifice of propitiation" we commemorate first the living ("churches, kings, armies, the sick, and, in a word, all who are in need of help") and then those who have fallen asleep, "patriarchs, prophets, apostles, martyrs, ... bishops, and, *in a word, all who have fallen asleep before us*, believing that it will be of the greatest advantage to the souls for whom the prayer is offered *when the holy most awful Sacrifice is set forth.*"[91]

From these words and from what St Cyril writes in continuation, it follows that *the commemoration both of the living and of those who have fallen asleep is organically connected with and takes its meaning from* "the holy and the most awful Sacrifice *which is set forth,*"— the Sacrifice which is being offered up to God *at that moment. That,* in consequence, is the moment for commemoration of the living and the dead which brings "the greatest advantage" to them. This is because then, at the holy Anaphora of the Sacrifice, those who are commemorated are placed before God "for an eternal memorial"; thanks to the sacrifice of the Lamb, they are not only forgiven but also receive "eternal life," in other words, true existence. To the question, "what does it profit a soul that departs this world with sins, or without sins, if it is commemorated during the offering?" (in other words, the perpetual rationalistic question which makes the freedom of divine grace —and the power of the Eucharist, which it disparages as a supposedly "magical" act—subject to the laws of "fact"), St Cyril gives the categorical answer: we "believe" unshakably that through the Eucharist we "propitiate our God who loves mankind on behalf of them [i.e., those who are commemorated] and of ourselves," even if they are sinners, because "we offer Christ who was slain for our sins."[92]

At this point, we come to the matter of the diptychs and the ultimate fate of this essential element in the Eucharist. The problem of the historical appearance and shaping of the diptychs will not concern us here.[93] We shall simply make some remarks of a general nature which throw light on the subject of our study.

---

[91] Cyril of Jerusalem, *Mystagogic Caechesis* 5.5–8 (PG 33:1113A13–1116B5). The emphasis is mine.

[92] Cyril of Jerusalem, *Mystagogic Caechesis* 5.10 (PG 33:1116B8–1117A13).

[93] The most thorough study on this subject has been written by the well-known liturgical scholar, Robert Taft, *A History of the Liturgy of St John Chrysostom*, vol. 4, *The Diptychs* (Rome: Pontificium Institutum Studiorum Orientalium, 1991).

It has become the practice today for the so-called "diptychs" to be recited only when heads of autocephalous Churches are celebrating or when a bishop is celebrating at a great feast. This restriction encourages the disuse, with the passage of time, of a very essential element in the Eucharist. In the early Church, the diptychs had a central place and importance in the Divine Liturgy, as Chrysostom[94] and Maximus,[95] among others, testify. As can be deduced from the case of Chrysostom's exile, at least Constantinople, Alexandria, and Antioch recited the diptychs in the Anaphora, immediately after the Epiclesis. This place that they had in the Liturgy is clear evidence that the diptychs did not only have the very important purpose of showing mutual recognition and communion between the Churches (as shown by the incident of removing Chrysostom's name from them); they also formed an organic part of the eucharistic commemoration to which we referred above. Clearly, since the first of these two reasons prevailed (proclamation of the unity and communion of the various local Churches), it was finally considered sufficient for the diptychs to contain bishops only and to be read only when heads of autocephalous Churches were celebrating. Yet the second reason, the commemoration of bishops, kings, and faithful people, living and departed, is equally important. The eucharistic Anaphora, as we have seen (as described by Cyril of Jerusalem above), requires this commemoration by its very nature.

There are two categories of faithful that are commemorated after the Epiclesis and the consecration. One category is those who have fallen asleep, which begins with, "especially for our most holy … Lady," and the other is that of the living, which begins with, "Among the first remember, O Lord, our archbishop."[96] What we have, clearly, is a form of diptychs at a point in the Liturgy that would also be best and preeminent place for the eucharistic commemoration. That is when the names should be commemorated or at least some of them, such as the names of those for whom a memorial Lit-

---

[94] Chrysostom, *Hom. on Acts 21.4* (PG 60:170).

[95] Maximus, *Relatio Motionis* 5 C (PG 90:117CD).

[96] The reading of diptychs of the departed only is mentioned in the Areopagitic writings, but, as we have seen, the evidence for diptychs of the living as well is ancient. Cf. also Maximus the Confessor, *Scholia* (PG 4:145).

urgy is being celebrated, and, if the names are many, there should be a general reference to those who have been commemorated during the Prothesis. All these things are not mere formal rules: they underline that the "remembrance" of Christ in the Eucharist includes within it all the saints and members of the Church, the *communio sanctorum*, on whose behalf this "reasonable worship" is offered.

The commemoration of the departed in the liturgies of Basil and Chrysostom begins with "especially for our most holy … Lady"[97] and includes the recognized saints along with all the faithful. The fact that the Eucharist is also offered *on behalf of* the Mother of God, the Forerunner, and the saint of the day, as well as "for all those who have fallen asleep in faith, ancestors, fathers, patriarchs, prophets, apostles, preachers, evangelists, martyrs," etc., demonstrates that *all the saints* stand in need of the Eucharist and have to be incorporated into it. The question has already been asked by St John Chrysostom:[98] why do we offer the sacrifice on behalf of the martyrs since they are already saints? Despite the fact that they are saints, we make commemoration *on their behalf,* he replies, because the Lord is present at that moment, and it is a great honor for them to be commemorated at that time. The important point in this case is that, in the body of the Eucharist, the sacrificed and risen body of the "new creation," the Church with her Eucharist, places together the saints and the sinners on behalf of whom—saints and sinners alike—she offers the Sacrifice. In the first case it is to honor them and to show that the saints too are only saved as members of his body, and in the other case, it is for them to seek their salvation, always by means of the communion of all in the one body of Christ.

The commemoration of the living, on the other hand, begins with the phrase ,"Among the first …," in other words, with the local bishop in the first place. He is the head of the living, as the Mother of God is of the departed. Even if there are members of the Church holier than the bishop, they are not commemorated "among the first" because the body of the local Church has only one head: the bishop.

---

[97] According to Taft (*The Diptychs*, p. 118), this was introduced by St Gennadios of Constantinople (AD 458-471) and formed the beginning of the exclamation of the diptychs of the departed.

[98] Chrysostom, *Hom. on Acts* 5 (PG 60:170).

The living are saved only in union with their bishop, and apart from him, they have no relationship with the body of Christ, which is offered "for eternal life." Anyone who does not commemorate his bishop at this time in the Eucharist cuts himself off from the roll of the living. For this reason, a Eucharist which is not celebrated in the name of the local bishop, or of another bishop to whom he has yielded presidency, is without salvific significance for those who perform it.

In all we have said in the above paragraph, we want to stress that: (a) the Eucharist is the supreme commemoration of the living and the departed; (b) the subject of this "commemorating," that is, the one who does the remembering, is not simply a human being but God himself ("Remember, O Lord ..."); (c) this remembrance is not psychological but ontological in its significance (it is concerned with transcending death and with substantive, true "eternal being" in Christ); and (d) this commemoration stems from the passion of the Christ and his sacrifice on the Cross[99] but refers to and is fulfilled in the Kingdom of Christ which is to come ("Remember me Lord, when thou comest in thy Kingdom"). Thus, the eucharistic remembrance becomes also a remembrance of the future, of the "second and glorious coming again."

We are truly alive only to the degree that God will remember us and will ultimately give us "substance" (*hypostasis*) in the Kingdom of his Son. The Eucharist, by transferring us to this Kingdom, offers us the sacrifice of Christ "unto remission of sins" and also "unto eternal life"—in other words, as "eternal being and well-being,"[100] our hypostatic-personal being in the "age which does not end and grow old."[101]

g) The Structure of the Church's "Institution"

The Eucharist is not only an icon of the kingdom but also a revelation of the Church itself, and this is because the Church is not confined exclusively to the period between Christ's earthy life and the Second Coming but preexisted, being linked with the pre-eter-

---

[99] In reality, it contains and sums up the whole history of salvation, the divine economy. Cf. Theodore the Studite, *Antirrheticus* I (PG 99:340).
[100] Maximus, *Carit.* III, 23–25 (PG 90:1024).
[101] Basil, *De Spir.* 27.66 (PG 33:192B3–4).

nal will of God concerning the course and outcome of the divine economy, and will extend "unto ages of ages" as the Kingdom of God.[102] The Church is a many-sided mystery, and its definition—if it is not impossible to define—is itself many-sided and complex. A "definition" which refers us not to intellectual conceptions but to actual experience is the well-known one given by Nicholas Cabasilas: "The Church is made known in the mysteries."[103] If one can ever see (not "define") the Church, it will only be in the Divine Eucharist: "if anyone is able to see the Church of Christ ... he will see nothing other than this body of the Lord's only ... It is therefore in no way unfitting that the Church should be made known here through the mysteries."[104] According to Cabasilas, there exist between Church and Eucharist not an "analogy of likeness" but an "identity of reality" (ibid.). This allows him to write that the Church is changed into Eucharist (Cabasilas, ibid.) or in the phrase of Florovsky and Karmiris: "the Eucharist makes/constitutes the Church."[105]

As Fr Florovsky writes, however, "*sacramental* [communion/ community] means nothing less than eschatological [communion/ community]." In constituting the Church, the Eucharist reveals it as the *communion and community of the last times*, since "the Church bears in general an eschatological character and lives continuously in the "last hour."[106]

Now, the Church is a community with a particular *structure*. It is not simply a "community of faith and hearts." But from where does the Church derive its structure? Since it is in its structure an escha-

---

[102] The Church "comes into being in this life and takes its beginning from here but is perfected in the future, when we attain to that day" (Nicholas Cabasilas, *On the Life of Christ* 1–4 [PG 150:493, 501]).

[103] Nicholas Cabasilas, *Interp. of the Sacred Liturgy* 38 (PG 150:452C13–14).

[104] Nicholas Cabasilas, *Interpr. of the Sacred Liturgy* 38 (PG 150:452C–453A).

[105] G. Florovsky: "the sacraments constitute the Church" ("The Church: Her Nature and Task," in the collection *The Universal Church in God's Design* [World Council of Churches, 1948], p. 47). In 1938, de Lubac endorsed the principle that "the sacraments make the Church," the "sacrament of sacraments" being the Eucharist (*Catholicism* [Ignatius Press,1988], pp. 87–89). Cf. H. de Lubac, *Corpus Mysticum: The Eucharist and the Church in the Middle Ages*, trans. G. Simmonds (London: SCM Press, 2006), pp. 88–89; also P. McPartlan, *The Eucharist makes the Church. Henri de Lubac and John Zizioulas in dialogue.*

[106] Florovsky, "The Church: Her Nature and Task," p. 54.

tological community, how is its structure connected with the Kingdom of God?

As has happened with the Eucharist itself, so also with the institutions of the Church has the entire effort of academic theology focused on showing how the Church's various institutions and ministries are or are not connected with the early life and teaching of Christ and his apostles (or, indeed, with tradition). Very little effort has been put into showing how these institutions and ministries relate to the Church's eschatological perspective, and yet the fact that these ministries stemmed and continued to stem from the Eucharist[107] demonstrates that it is impossible for them not to be closely connected with the eschatological community of which the Eucharist is an image.

But what relation can the Kingdom of God have with *"structure"*? The concept of structure has been given a bad name not only by pietism, which puts all the emphasis on what is within man or his ethical behavior, but also by modern philosophy and thought, which tends to regard any structure as an alienation of the person and his freedom. If, however, we do not give "structure" the legal character of an authority imposed from without but connect it with the *otherness of personal relationships*, then it becomes a different matter. In the Kingdom of God, *otherness of relationships* will exist, and this creates the variety and hierarchy of ministries.

To be more specific: on the evidence of scripture and patristic writings, the eschatological community (the Kingdom of God) will include the following basic elements, which constitute otherness of relationships and, in this sense, a structure which is existential in character:[108]

(a) A *gathering* (*synaxis*) of the scattered people of God and, by extension, a uniting "in one place" of the world which was fragmented by corruption and death. As we have already seen, this gathering forms an essential element in the last times, in the Kingdom of God.

(b) A gathering *centered on the person of Christ*, who on the one hand embodies the very presence of God in the world as "the image

---

[107] For more detail, see my *Eucharist, Bishop, Church.*
[108] For more detail see my *Being as Communion*, pp. 172–187.

of the invisible God" (Col 1:15) and on the other incorporates and unites "the many" in his person as the "Servant of the Lord" and the eschatological "Son of Man," or as the "firstborn of all creation ... firstborn of the dead," as "the head of the body, which is the Church" (Col 1:15–20).

(c) A gathering centered on Christ who, however, *is surrounded* by the *"Twelve" (the apostles)*, who will "sit upon twelve thrones judging the twelve tribes of Israel" (Mt 19:28; Lk 18:31).

In consequence, the Kingdom of God, the eschatological community, will be a *gathering* of the "people of God" and the "many" in which, however, there will be an otherness of relationships determined by the difference between the three elements, at least, to which we have referred: the people (or "the many" or even "all things"), Christ, and the apostles. Without these elements, the eschatological community and, by extension, the Kingdom of God is inconceivable. The Kingdom is not simply an interior experience of "hearts,"[109] but a unity of all in the person of Christ as the apostles have made him known to us, not as each individual would like him to be or imagines him.[110] Furthermore, within the people or the "many" there will be a variety of gifts, because it is not conceivable that everyone should be levelled out in the Kingdom of God. The variety and multiplicity which does not break up the unity of the body but holds it together (1 Cor 12) will assuredly be a characteristic of the Kingdom as it is of the Church.

All these things are "imaged" by the Divine Eucharist as an image of the Kingdom. Thus the following observations take on an especial significance:

(a) All ordinations to the basic structural ministries of the Church (layman, deacon, priest, and bishop) necessarily take place within

[109] The Lord's saying "The Kingdom of God is among/within you [*entos hymon*]" (Lk 17:21) means, as is evident from the context: the Kingdom of God is in your midst (obviously with the presence of Christ himself), not in your inner selves, as it is often understood.

[110] It should be noted that in the last times "many false Christs will arise" (Mt 24:24; Mk 13:22), and therefore the witness and judgment of the genuine apostles is of decisive significance not only historically, but also eschatologically. The Church—and the Kingdom of which she is an *eikon*—is "apostolic" not only in the historical but also in the eschatological sense of apostolicity. Cf. my *Being as Communion*, p. 172f.

the Divine Eucharist. Baptism and Chrismation are the "ordination" of lay people, because "lay" does not mean unordained, as is commonly thought, but denotes someone who through Baptism and Chrismation is a regular member of the eucharistic gathering with all the rights and obligations that this entails. These two mysteries were united with the Eucharist in the early Church and were unthinkable apart from it, as with ordinations.

(b) These ordinations have been regarded even from the time of Ignatius of Antioch as involving ministries which "image" the elements which, as we have seen, "construct" the eschatological community: the "multitude" (i.e., the people in a gathering), the throne of God which is occupied by the bishop, and the apostles, represented by the presbyters, with the deacons as an intermediate ministry.

The conclusion that the Eucharist as an image of the last times— with precisely that property—provided and continues to provide the basic structure of the Church, without which, as St Ignatius says, "it cannot be Church."[111] These structural elements of the Church are essential and relate to its *being* (not merely its *well-being*), because they *touch upon its nature as an image of the Kingdom*. In other words, the disruption of this basic structure of the Church distorts the image of the Kingdom which the Church is meant to manifest in history.

Viewing the Church's ministries and institutions as an image of the Kingdom means that the institutions cannot be understood and cannot function except *in relationship* with one another. Since each institution and each ministry *forms a part of an image*, if one of these ministries isolates itself and exalts itself so as to say to the others, "I have no need of you" (1 Cor 12:21–24), the result is a *distortion of the whole image*. The image of the Kingdom is a unified one, and the ontology of the ministries requires interdependence and relationship between them, as St Paul emphasizes dramatically in the First Epistle to the Corinthians (chapter 12). It is not possible, for instance, for the bishop to exist without presbyters and the people, nor for the presbyters and people to exist without the bishop. This protects the Church both from episcopal "despotism" or "clericalism" and "Pres-

---

[111] Ignatius, *To Trall.* 3.1.

byterianism" and also from "laicism," aberrations which have come into being historically when the iconic-eschatological approach contained in eucharistic ecclesiology has given way and been replaced by an individualistic and legalistic ontology of the ministries. Proof of this is to be found in the fact that, in the Orthodox Church, *the Eucharist alone* has preserved the interdependence of the Church's ministries, theoretically at least, since it is forbidden to celebrate the Eucharist without a gathering of the people, without the people's "Amen,"[112] or without a priest or a bishop—even if it is only with the bishop's antimension and the commemoration of his name. None of this makes any sense outside the Eucharist, where every ministry (lay people and clergy) operates, without a gathering of the people around the bishop and the presbyters. It preserves and expresses in history the image of a world which will have transcended its death-bringing fragmentation and corruption, thanks to its union and incorporation into him who, according to the testimony of his apostles, has by his Cross and Resurrection united what was sundered, gathered his world "into one," and thus established his Kingdom.

h) Communion of the Holy Spirit

It is not by chance that, according to one of the hymns for Pentecost, the Holy Spirit is he who "holds together the whole institution of the Church." The thing that often escapes us is that, in the New Testament, the Spirit is given to men *after* Christ's Resurrection (Jn 7:39), precisely because his coming into the world signals *the coming of the "last days" into history* (Acts 2:17). It is no exaggeration to identify the Kingdom with the Holy Spirit: "Thy kingdom come: that is, the Holy Spirit."[113] So, the linking of the Holy Spirit with the structure of the Church suggests that both the "institution" of the

---

[112] What Cyril of Alexandria writes is characteristic (PG 74:893): the presence of the laypeople's "Amen" at the Eucharist is essential "in order that what seems to be lacking in the priests may be supplemented by the measure of the laity, and that God may as it were accept the small with the great as a unity of the Spirit." The "amen" is the sacred right of the laity, and it is wrong that it is usually exclaimed by the clergy during divine services. It goes right back to the first apostolic Churches (1 Cor 14:16) and to the first centuries (see Justin, *First Apology* 65).

[113] Maximus, *Or. Dom.* (PG 90:885B).

Church and the framework within which it becomes a reality, the eucharistic synaxis, derive their meaning from the Kingdom of God.

The Divine Eucharist is normally approached from a Christological point of view, while the Holy Spirit usually plays only a subsidiary role in eucharistic theology. The dispute over this question between the Orthodox and the Latins after the Schism is well known: is the invocation of the Spirit (the Epiclesis) an essential part of the Eucharist? The issue is above all *theological*, and its significance touches on the question which concerns us here.

If the Eucharist were simply a repetition of a past event, then one wonders why the action of the Last Supper is not copied exactly during the Liturgy: at the Last Supper, Christ blessed the bread and wine and then spoke the words, "Take, eat," while in the Liturgy, the order is reversed. It is obvious that in the Eucharist we are not copying a historical event. As Nicholas Cabasilas writes, the description of the Last Supper at the Eucharist—and the repetition of the Lord's words "Take, eat"—takes place "in the form of a narrative," while the work of transforming the Gifts requires the descent of the Holy Spirit.[114] The Holy Spirit, then, in his coming brings the "last days" into history (Acts 2:17). The presence of Christ in the Eucharist cannot exist outside this pneumatological and eschatological framework. The "real presence" of Christ in the Eucharist presupposes and entails the gathering "in one place" of the eschatological community which the Spirit holds together. Only within the framework of this gathering does the transformation of the elements into the body and blood of Christ take place.

This observation gives rise to an important conclusion: the Eucharist is a communion and partaking not only of the body and blood of Christ, but also of the *Holy Spirit*.[115] We partake of Christ but, at the same time, "in the communion of the Holy Spirit": "And

---

[114] Nicholas Cabasilas, *Interpr. of the Sacred Liturgy* 29–30 (PG 150:433B–437B).

[115] Characteristic is the phrase "The fullness of the cup of faith of the Holy Spirit" which the celebrant pronounces every time he places the portion of the Lamb in the Holy Chalice before Holy Communion. He repeats the same thing when he pours in the Zeon (warm water). During the discussions between Latins and Orthodox after the Schism, the latter regarded the Zeon as a serious point of disagreement, because its symbolism in Byzantium was connected with the Holy Spirit.

unite all of us who partake of the one bread and the one cup one to another *in the communion of the Holy Spirit,*" as the Liturgy of St Basil prays to the Father at the sacred moment of the Anaphora. The Spirit does not come down only "upon these gifts here set forth" but also "upon us" (the celebrants and the eucharistic gathering). Thus the "real presence" of Christ is broadened to include the head and the body in one unity in the Holy Spirit. The Eucharist as communion of the Holy Spirit becomes a "communion of the holy" in a double sense: communion in the holy things (*communio in sacris*) and the communion of saints (*communio sanctorum*), that is, of holy people.[116] The Eucharist thus becomes the *mystery of love.*

IV. Liturgical Time and Ordinary Existence

What kind of existential equipment do we possess that can help us grasp this liturgical kind of time? This is a difficult question, because our experience of time is still basically dominated by the present *aeon*, by the time of corruption and death. We cannot, therefore, identify liturgical time with time in general, the time of ordinary experience. The liturgy remains in this world an eschatological event, and as such its time does not coincide fully with the time of history. But this does not mean that the time of history is negated by the time of the liturgy; on the contrary, the latter aims at correcting the direction of the former so that the threat of nothing inherent in it may be overcome. Correcting the direction of something is not abolishing it. Direction is important because time "exists" not for itself but for creation; as we said at the beginning, it is not a concept in and of itself but a relational concept. Time does sustain creation, although it negates it, too. But the fact that it can also sustain it means that liturgical time, which precisely aims at sustaining creation, has something in common with ordinary time. What is this common element?

I referred earlier to the ambiguity of space and time as factors both uniting and separating beings. The Greek fathers thought that distance and separatedness (διάστημα) are the cause or even the es-

---

[116] On this double meaning of "communion of the holy," see the minutely detailed examination of patristic sources in W. Elert, *Eucharist and Church Fellowship in the First Four Centuries*, trans. N.E. Nagel (St Louis, MO: Concordia Publishing House, 1966).

sence of createdness and of death.[117] If we could only prevent time from separating and dividing beings, the problem of death would be solved. Thus, speaking of redeemed time means, in the end, not denying time but freeing it from its individualizing and dividing capacity. Here the concept of *communion* becomes identical with that of redeemed time.

The liturgy is not simply a movement in time; it is also an event of communion. The Spirit who brings the eschaton into history is *koinonia*. He redeems time by turning it from a divisive and individualizing factor into a uniting one. The Liturgy is based on the condition of Baptism, which itself introduces a concept of time the existential implications of which are significant. Baptism is a new birth, which means a new beginning in time, a new identity. Its existential significance lies in its contrast with the old biological birth. There, nature manages to play a trick on the person. As the person aims through love to bring forth new identities that would *be forever*, procreation through the erotic movement makes the person believe that such a true ontological identity is, in fact, established through biological birth: every parent, in being a person, treats his or her offspring as if it were an eternal being with whom he or she will be in communion forever. But time, which contributed to the appearance of this new identity, will prove that biological birth leads to death and separation. The Greek fathers who, like Gregory of Nyssa and especially Maximus the Confessor, attached biological birth to death,[118] were not anti-sexual ascetics but realistic observers of nature. Biological birth cannot be the hypostasis (i.e., the ontological ground) of personal being. Baptism is precisely the event which brings about new identities based on the "last Adam," born in the spirit and therefore an eschatological being and a being-in-communion.

As we observed earlier in connection with liturgical time, however, the new frees from the old only in order to affirm the old, not to destroy it. What Baptism does to the biological identity is to hy-

---

[117] Thus, Athanasius, *C. Arian.* 2.5 (PG 26:268C); Gregory of Nyssa, *C. Eunom.* 12 (PG 45:933B); ibid., 1064C.

[118] Gregory of Nyssa, *On the Creation of Man* 16–18 (PG 44:177f); Maximus, *Amb.* 42 (PG 91:1340C). Cf. *QThal.* 61 (PG 90:636).

postasize it in a different way, in the way that God is hypostasized. This is true personal existence in which a particular being affirms itself only in love and communion. The hypostases of God exist as different identities only because they are in unity and communion. Should they be divided or separated, they would cease to be. Baptism into Christ, by involving us in the very filial relationship of the Father and the Son as the basis of our new identity, corrects the course of the biological identity by attacking the very root of the problem: the old being affirms itself not in itself and by itself, but by being opened up to the other as to an infinite future.

This can be grasped better if we look at its concrete *ethical* consequences. One of the fundamental conditions attached to both the coming of the Kingdom and the Eucharist in the New Testament— the connection of the two is indeed noteworthy—is *forgiveness of sins.* Forgiveness is not just a matter of juridical or psychological significance; it has deep ontological implications and relates directly to the problem of time. What happens in forgiveness is a *liberation from the past.* The ancient Greek world, precisely because of its concept of time to which we have already referred, could not see how the past could be undone and its causal relation with whatever followed be broken. This is dramatically presented in classical Greek tragedy. Our common concept of history, which is also based on similar assumptions, implies that a fact is a fact and that its identity is rooted in the past. But forgiveness seeks to destroy this concept of facticity. The past does not create closed beings, or if it does, it does so by ultimately destroying them. Forgiveness is the removal of the existential ground of the old being from the past into the future. "How many times should we forgive, Lord? Seven or seventy?" No, "neither seven nor seventy, but seventy times seven" (Mt 18:22), that is, infinitely.[119] Now, we may think that all this is a matter of "internal time," of something taking place in the individual's soul with no ontological consequences, but the early Church in its liturgical experience certainly did not think so. For them, forgiveness, just like Baptism, meant that a new identity would emerge out of the death

[119] Cf. F.V. Filson, *The Gospel according to St Matthew* (Black's New Testament Commentaries, 1960), p. 203. The seventy times seven opens up numbering to infinity; it liberates numbers from individuation.

of the past, an identity which would be conceived as an identity which has a *future*.

This community, the Church, born itself of the Spirit, becomes thus, by its very existence, a witness to the new concept of time: a time which does not move from the earlier to the later, from the old to the new, not through the intermediary of *nothing*, which delineates and establishes necessary "phases" and "facts," but *through that of the future*, which liberates the past from the necessity of facticity. If there is such a community in time, then time is redeemed, or, at least, we now know because of it that it *can be redeemed*. Hence, the taste of love and forgiveness is the assurance that time can be redeemed, that we are not talking fantasy.

> Love never ends; as for prophesies, they will pass away; as for togues, they will cease; as for knowledge, it will pass away. For our knowledge is imperfect, and our prophesy is imperfect; but when the perfect comes, the imperfect will pass away ... So faith, hope, and love abide, these three; but the greatest of these is love (1 Cor 13:8–13).

The eschatological character of the Eucharist is essentially linked to the eschatological character of love, which is *the experiential quintessence of the Kingdom*. All asceticism and all cleansing from the passions is in essence a *precondition* for the Eucharist, because the Eucharist cannot be understood apart from love. Love is that which survives into the "age which does not end or grow old," when all the gifts which impress us today, such as knowledge, prophesy, etc., will pass away.[120]

Of all the forms of love, the most significant from the viewpoint both of the Eucharist and the last times is *love for our enemies*. This love is not simply a matter of ethics (imitation of Christ and obedience to his commandment) but has ontological content directly connected with the Eucharist and its eschatological character. St Maxi-

---

[120] A phenomenon worth noting, and particularly evident today, is the way people go running after impressive spiritual gifts such as foresight, clairvoyance, etc., and consider these the supreme indications of holiness and of the presence of the Holy Spirit. These people remind us of the Jews who "seek after a sign" in order to believe. But these gifts— which, much to St Paul's sorrow, the Corinthians of his time also considered the most important (see 1 Cor 12–13)—are much inferior to love because, as St Paul writes, unlike love they will not survive into the last times.

mus tries to show this in a profound analysis of the petition of the Lord's Prayer "forgive us our trespasses," which he connects with the previous petition, "give us this day our daily bread." The argument is complex, like the whole of his language, but the following points summarized from his interpretation of the Our Father deserve our attention:

The ontological character of love for our enemies resides in the fact that if remembrance of the wrongs our enemy has done us becomes "stamped on our mind," it *sunders* nature "according to the will (γνώμη)," because through remembrance of wrong one appears to be, and indeed is, "separated from some other man," while being oneself a man (i.e., sharing the same nature). Love for enemies, in consequence, is actually a union of the will (γνώμη) and the principle of nature ("the will being in union with the principle (λόγος) of nature"). Through this love, human nature ceases to rebel against itself because of the will, and this leads also to reconciliation with God, because "once the will is in union with the principle of nature, the free choice of those who have achieved this is not in a state of rebellion against God."[121]

If one does not forgive one's enemies, one submits to nature as it is in the "present age," in other words to division, to its "rebellion," and to death, and endangers its true being which the bread of the Eucharist offers to man as the bread of the "age to come," of the Kingdom: "For I think that by 'today' it means this age ... that bread which thou didst prepare for us in the beginning *that our nature might be immortal* do thou give us today, *while we are in the present time of mortality* ... that it may conquer death."[122] It is not, therefore, surprising that in certain patristic texts one finds interpretations of the Eucharist which place an almost excessive emphasis on forgiveness of enemies. St Athanasius of Sinai (†608?), for example, commenting on the Divine Liturgy (which like Maximus he calls simply

---

[121] Maximus, *Or. Dom.* (PG 90:901B–D). The argument is based on the principle of the unity of human nature: by separating ourselves from another human being through remembrance of the wrong it has done to us, we set our will against our nature which we have in common with our enemy. This amounts to an ontological conflict between nature and person.

[122] Maximus, *Or. Dom.* (PG 90:897Af).

the "Synaxis"), says this, among other things, about the petition "Forgive us our trespasses":

Therefore, I pray you, let us flee this wicked and unpardonable sin [of remembrance of wrong]. And if you want to learn that the darkening from remembrance of wrong is worse than any other sin, then listen. Every other sin takes a brief while to commit and is soon over, as when someone commits fornication, and afterwards realizes the enormity of his sin and comes to consciousness of it; but remembrance of wrong has a passion which never ceases to burn ... Where remembrance of wrong has put down roots, nothing is of any avail; not fasting, or tears, or confession, or supplication, or virginity, or alms, or any other good thing. For remembrance of wrong toward our brother destroys everything. I often hear many people saying, "Alas, how shall I be saved? I haven't the strength to fast; I don't know how to keep vigil; I can't live in virginity; I couldn't bear to leave the world—so how can I be saved? How? I will tell you how. Forgive and you will be forgiven;... here is a short cut to salvation. And I will show you another. What is that? Judge not, it says, and you will not be judged. So here is another path without fasting or vigil or labor.... He who judges before Christ's coming is Antichrist, because he abrogates the position that belongs to Christ.[123]

These, perhaps, "exaggerated" words of Anastasius, combined with those of Maximus about the same topic,[124] not only explain why the Church has from the beginning regarded reconciliation with our enemies as an inviolable precondition for participation in the Eucha-

---

[123] Anastasius the Sinaite, *Discourse on the holy Synaxis* (PG 89:844B–845B).

[124] It is profoundly striking what St Maximus writes about slander, both in matters of "life" and matters of "faith" (it seems that the saint endured both): "There is no pain of the soul that weighs more heavily than slander, whether one is slandered as to faith or as to life. And no one can scorn this except only the man who, like Susannah, looks to God who alone is able to rescue him from calamity as he did her, and tell people the truth as he did about her; he can also comfort his soul with hope. As he prays from his soul for the person who has slandered him, in that same measure God too reveals the truth to those who have been scandalized" (PG 90:1069). There is always a strong temptation to counterattack the slanderer so that "souls are not scandalized." Maximus does not seem to approve this approach: he runs the risk of people being scandalized so as to secure the love and forgiveness of the slanderer, leaving it to God to inform those who have been scandalized. How alien all this sounds to our modern mentality, even a modern "Christian" mentality!

rist (Mt 5:23), they also show us how firmly the Eucharist is existentially bound up with the Kingdom of God. The crucial point in all of this is that we have to encounter the other person not as he was yesterday or is today, but *as he will be in the future in the last times*, which means as a member of and our neighbor in the Kingdom. This is so because the *future* gives all things their true substance, their place in the Kingdom. And this is precisely what eludes our judgment, because the future belongs exclusively to God and to the other person's freedom.

Thus, the eschatological orientation of the Eucharist creates its own ethos: the *eucharistic* ethos, the ethos of forgiveness, which is not merely an inner state but is experienced as *communion* and *coexistence* in the same community *with the person who has hurt us*, in sharing a future which we do not control and which has no end, the "age which does not end or grow old." In order for the Eucharist to be "for forgiveness of sins and unto eternal life" for those who take part in it and receive Communion, it must also be for forgiveness on our part of the sins of others and "unto eternal life" *with them* in the gathering of the Kingdom.

Conclusions

1. Time is a constitutive element of created being. Everything that has had a beginning, having come out of nothing, exists in time. A timeless creation would amount to a contradiction in terms.

Time sustains creation by providing it with continuity. As it was observed by Aristotle, however, this continuity which is a movement "from the earlier to the later" is experienced and measured through the "now" (νῦν), which is empty of ontological significance, since nothing (οὐθὲν) moves or rests in it. Continuity in existence, thus, passes through discontinuity: the "now" both unites and divides time, splitting it into past, present, and future while uniting it through a process of "generation and corruption" (γένεσις καὶ φθορά).

This continuity in discontinuity was not an ontological problem for Aristotle since, in his view, nature in its "power and movement" (δύναμις καὶ κίνησις) guarantees the continuity forever for particular entities through the reproduction of their species. It acquires, however, tragic dimensions as soon as we attach absolute ontological significance to the particular: the survival of its species is no consolation for its disappearance. The division of time into past, present, and future becomes, in this case, an acute existential problem.

Christian anthropology, as expressed particularly in patristic thought, was forced to wrestle with this issue. Each particular human being possesses in the eyes of God an absolute uniqueness; its eternal survival forms part of the will of the Creator who implanted in it the desire of eternal being. The death of the particular person cannot be tolerated by the Christian faith. This is why the resurrection both of Christ and of all human beings is a fundamental part of the Gospel: "if Christ has not been risen ... your faith is vain" (1 Cor 15:14), and "if there is no resurrection of the dead, neither is Christ risen" (1 Cor 15, 13). Only if the resurrection somehow intervenes in the course of time can the particular survive and time be redeemed and healed from its existential ambiguity.

2. Liturgical time was born out of the experience of the appearances of the risen Christ.[125] The meals shared with him after the Resurrection placed the anamnesis of the Last Supper in an eschatological perspective. As the eucharistic liturgies, particularly in the East, from the ancient times until now testify, the anamnesis of the salvation events include the remembrance of the Resurrection and the future Second Coming. This is why the eucharist was from the beginning celebrated "with gladness of heart" (Acts 2:46), not with grief: by conquering death, Christ's resurrection brought with it the faith that time is redeemable from its existential ambiguity. The intervening between the past and the present "now," which is ontologically void since nothing (οὐθὲν) moves or rests in it and causes the interruption of the existential continuity of a particular being (by corruption and death), is filled with the risen Christ's presence through the intrusion of the eschaton into history. Time is, thus, capable of carrying in itself the "eighth day," the "age that does not grow old."[126] Liturgical time offers an *arrabon*, a taste of the eschatological "new creation" in which space and time are no longer bearers

[125] O. Cullmann, *Christ and Time*, trans. F.V. Filson (London: SCM Press, 1962).
[126] Basil, *De Spir.* 27.66 (PG 32:192AB).

of division, corruption, and death and, instead, become agents of unity and communion and, thus, of eternal life.

3. This experience of redeemed time is more than a matter of celebration and worship. It also contains an *ethical* dimension. Liturgical time was from the beginning an experience not of isolated individuals but of a community; it involved a relational way of existence. Already, in Baptism, one has to die as an individual and become a member of the community, while the forgiveness of his or her past sins demands an attitude of forgiveness to everyone's past in view of the eschatological future that God has prepared for all in the risen Christ. This, like Baptism itself, is an absolute condition for participation in the Eucharist (cf. Mt 6:11)—for experiencing the redemption of time through the foretaste of the communion with the risen Christ in the banquet of his Kingdom. The experience of liturgical time, thus, culminates in the practice of *love*, the only "virtue" that will survive in the eschaton (1 Cor 13:8), the quintessence of the Kingdom.

4. With the entrance of the last days into history through the appearances of the risen Lord and their subsequent celebration in the church's liturgy, *the past does not disappear*; it is, on the contrary, verified and confirmed by receiving ultimate meaning. The historical Last Supper, which would be a "passed" event destined to disappear like all past events, acquires eternal ontological status by becoming the eschatological meal of the Kingdom. It is, therefore, a gross mistake to consider eschatology as an alternative to history or to think that by stressing eschatology we deny or undermine the importance of history. On the contrary, the whole argument promoted here is that the entrance of the last days into history frees historical events from their deadly imprisonment in the division of historical time, between the "earlier" and the "later," and grants them existence "unto the ages of ages." Just as the Cross would have been a "passed" event had it not been verified and confirmed by the risen Christ who elevated it to the state of eternal glory (Jn 20-21), in the same way the "body and the blood" of the Last Supper would not be a reality *present here and now* without the entrance into history of the risen eschatological Lord.

5. The bearing of all this on *sacramental theology* is apparent. The long debate since the Middle Ages and the Reformation concerning Christ's real presence in the Eucharist and the question whether Christ's sacrifice on the Cross can be repeated presuppose a conception of time which is unredeemed from its divisive character. It is indeed impossible to logically relate what happens in each celebration of the Eucharist with what happened at the Last Supper and the Cross in the remote past, if time is still divided between the "earlier" and the "later," the past and the present. There must be something to fill the gap between these two periods of time so that the "now" of each eucharistic celebration may contain an event of the past making it present *hic et nunc*. The appearance of the risen Lord and the post-Resurrection meals that accompanied them did precisely that. Our eucharistic celebrations make the past events of the Cross and the Last Supper present here and now because it is the *risen* Christ that presides over them. The "real presence of Christ" in the Eucharist and the transformation of the bread and the wine into the sacrificed body and blood of Christ as an "offering" to God here and now are due to the presence of the *risen* Christ who brings the eschata into history. In the sacramental events, *the way to Calvary passes through the Resurrection*; the past acquires real existence through the future.

6. The entrance of the future into the present through the presence of the risen Lord was associated from the beginning with the work of the *Holy Spirit*. Christ's Resurrection itself was linked with the Holy Spirit (Rom 8:11), and the coming of the Spirit was regarded as an eschatological event (Acts 2:18). The role of the Holy Spirit was from the beginning to bring into history the experience of the Kingdom within historical time, to be the "earnest" (ἀρραβὼν) of the eschatological life by offering not only its assurance but also its foretaste, its experiential *prolepsis*: "no one can say that Jesus is the Lord [i.e., the eschatological King to whom everything will be subjected] except in the Holy Spirit" (1 Cor 12:3). Pneumatology is tied up with the proleptic experience of the eschatological state.

The Church's liturgical time, which emerged from the appearances of the risen Lord, was therefore "worship in the Spirit" (cf. Jn 4:23)—an experience *hic et nunc* of the future eschatological life. This is why the Holy Spirit in particular was designated as "life-giving" (ζωοποιὸν) in the New Testament (Jn 6:63; Rom 4:17; 1 Cor 15:45; 2 Cor 3:6; 1 Pet 3:18) and in the Creed of Nicea-Constantinople. Life and immortality, which are eschatological gifts, are given as an experience of the risen Christ's presence in the "now" of the liturgical and, particularly, eucharistic time of history. It was this experience that made St Ignatius and St Irenaeus speak of the Eucharist as "medicine of immortality, an antidote against death."[127]

Pneumatology, therefore, is a constitutive element of sacramental theology. This, together with the importance of eschatology, seems, unfortunately, to have faded into the background in the history of theology. The sacraments, which were originally regarded as granting the Holy Spirit and, thereby, entrance into the Kingdom, came to be eventually described as "means of grace," the concept of "grace" bearing almost no relation to eschatology.

The constitutive role of both pneumatology and eschatology in the celebration of the sacraments has survived in the East only in liturgical practice. This is evident in the fact that in the Eastern liturgies the *Epiclesis* of the Holy Spirit and the remembrance of the future Parousia come *before* the transformation of the eucharistic elements into the body and blood of Christ. (In the Western liturgies, the *Epiclesis* of the Spirit comes *after* the consecration, while the remembrance of the Parousia is absent.) This is a clear indication that, at least in the Eastern liturgical tradition, it is the coming of the future Kingdom into history through the descent of the Holy Spirit that brings about what we call a *sacrament*. A sacrament is primarily an *event* transforming time and history into carriers of eternal life.

Owing to its pneumatological and eschatological dimensions, the Eucharist acquired a central place in Christian worship. The first Christians continued for some time to worship in the Jewish temple, and this form of worship was pursued throughout the ages in services such as Matins, the Hours, and Vespers. But when it came to sacramental acts, such as Baptism, Chrismation, and Ordination, which involved the giving of the Holy Spirit and thereby the entrance of the eschatological Kingdom into history, their liturgical context was the Eucharist. For a liturgical act to be a sacrament, it

---

[127] Ignatius, *Eph.* 20:2.

must be somehow connected with the Eucharist. In fact for many centuries, up at least to the time of Nicholas Cabasilas in the fourteenth century, the term "sacrament" (μυστήριον) was used in the East exclusively for the Eucharist, precisely because it is in the Eucharist that the risen Christ, as in his post-Resurrection appearances, is present bringing in the Spirit the foretaste of the future Kingdom and the assurance of the liberation of the historical existence from mortality. It was only when this eschatological perspective faded into the background in Christian theology that the sacramental acts were numbered and detached from the Eucharist liturgically, the Eucharist itself being treated as one sacrament among others.

Thus, the Eucharist continued for many centuries to affirm and proclaim the truth that historical time can be redeemed of its mortality and historical events can survive eternally and acquire ultimate existential significance, provided that they become part of the Resurrection event which brought about the annihilation of death and the entrance of the last days into history. It is against this background that we must understand the introduction of the celebration of notable events of the history of salvation into the Christian calendar of feasts. It is well known—and quite significant—that originally the only feast of the Church was that of the Resurrection (celebrated on Sunday). But it is very significant, too, that when the celebration of other great events of the history of salvation such as Christ's Nativity and Baptism or the death of martyrs and saints became part of the liturgical calendar, their commemoration always involved the celebration of the Eucharist, the feast of Christ's Resurrection. No historical event can survive in the Church's memory unless it passes through the Resurrection, the remembrance of the future and its entrance into the "now" of historical time.

In liturgical time, eschatology meets history in order to save it from dying by becoming "passed." There is no higher confirmation of history than its eschatologization. Far from being an escape from time, the liturgy witnesses to its transformation into a carrier of "eternal life" and ultimate existential significance. The liturgy is "the sanctification of time."[128]

---

[128] Gregory Dix, *The Shape of the Liturgy* (London: Continuum, 2005), pp. 303–396.

Select Bibliography

Allmen, J.-J. von, *Essai sur les Repas du Seigneur* (Neuchâtel, Paris: Delachaux et Niestlé, 1966).

Andia, Y. de, *Homo vivens: Incorruptibilité et divinisation de l'homme selon Irénée de Lyon* (Paris: Études Augustiniennes, 1986).

Arendt, H., *The Life of the Mind*, vol. II, *Willing* (New York: Harcourt, Brace, Jovanovich, 1978).

Balthasar, H.U. von, *Cosmic Liturgy: The Universe According to Maximus the Confessor*, trans. B.E. Daley (San Francisco, CA: Ignatius Press, 2003).

Balthasar, H.U. von, *Présence et pensée* (Paris: Beauchesne, 1942).

Barrow, J.D. and F.J. Tipler, *The Anthropic Cosmological Principle* (Oxford: Oxford University Press, 1986).

Barth, K., *Church Dogmatics* III/3 (Edinburgh: T&T Clark, 1960).

Bauckham, R., *Jude, 2 Peter*. Word Biblical Commentary, vol. 50 (Waco, TX: Word Books, Publisher, 1983).

Bauckham, R., *The Theology of Jürgen Moltmann* (Edinburgh: T&T Clark, 1995).

Bergson, H., *The Creative Mind*, trans. M.L. Andison (New York: Philosophical Library, 1946).

Berthouzoz, R., *Liberté et grâce suivant la théologie d'Irénée de Lyon* (Paris: Éditions Universitaires, 1980).

Blowers, P.M., *Exegesis and Spiritual Pedagogy in Maximus the Confessor: An Investigation of the Quaestiones ad Thalassium* (Notre Dame, IN: University of Notre Dame Press, 1991).

Bratiotis, P., "L'Apocalypse de saint Jean dans le culte de l'Église grecque orthodoxe," *Revue d'Histoire et de Philosophie religieuse* 42 (1962) 116–121.

Brown, R.E., "The Pater Noster as an Eschatological Prayer," *Theological Studies* 22 (1961) 171–208.

Bulgakov, S., *The Bride of the Lamb*, trans. B. Jakim (Grand Rapids, MI: Eerdmans; Edinburgh: T&T Clark, 2002).

Büschel, F., "εἰμί, ὁ ὤν," in G. Kittel, *Theological Dictionary of the New Testament*, vol. II, trans. and ed. G.W. Bromiley (Grand Rapids, MI: Eerdmans, 1964), pp. 398–400.

Clément, O., *Byzance et le Christianisme* (Paris: Presses Universitaires de France, 1964).

Clément, O., *Orient–Occident: Deux passeurs, Vladimir Lossky et Paul Evdokimov* (Geneva: Labor et Fides, 1985).

Cobb, J.B., Jr., *Christ in a Pluralistic Age* (Philadelphia, PA: Westminster Press, 1975).

Cullmann, O., *Christ and Time*, trans. F.V. Filson (Philadelphia, PA: The Westminster Press, 1950).

Cullmann, O., *Early Christian Worship*, trans. A.S. Todd and J.B. Torrance (London: SCM Press, 1953).

Cullmann, O., *The Christology of the New Testament*, trans. S.C. Guthrie and C.A.M. Hall (London: SCM Press, 1959).

Daniélou, J., *Message évangélique et culture hellénistique* (Tournai: Desclée, 1961).

Daniélou, J., *Platonisme et théologie mystique* (Paris: Aubier, 1944).

Daniélou, J., *The Bible and the Liturgy* (Notre Dame, IN: Notre Dame University Press, 1956).

Darlap, A., "Time", in K. Rahner, ed., *Sacramentum Mundi: An Encyclopedia of Theology*, vol. VI (London: Burns & Oates, 1970).

Dix, G., *The Shape of the Liturgy* (London: Continuum, 2005).

Elert, W., *Eucharist and Church Fellowship in the First Four Centuries*, trans. N.E. Nagel (St Louis, MO: Concordia Publishing House, 1966).

Fantino, J., *La théologie d'Irénée* (Paris: Éditions du Cerf, 1994).

Florovsky, G., Ἀνατομία προβλημάτων πίστεως, trans. M. Kalamatas (Thessaloniki: Regopoulos).

Florovsky, G., *Christianity and Culture*, vol. II of *The Collected Works of Georges Florovsky* (Vaduz: Buchervertriebsabstalt, 1974).

Florovsky, G., "Cur Deus Homo? The Motive of the Incarnation," *Creation and Redemption*, vol. III of *The Collected Works of Georges Florovsky* (Belmont, MA: Nordland Publishing Company, 1974), pp. 163–170.

Florovsky, G., "Eschatology in the Patristic Age," in B. Gallaher and P. Ladouceur, eds, *The Patristic Witness of Georges Florovsky* (London: T&T Clark, 2019), pp. 311–324.

Florovsky, G., "*In Ligno Crucis*: The Church Fathers' Doctrine of Redemption", in B. Gallaher and P. Ladouceur, eds, *The Patristic Witness of Georges Florovsky* (London: T&T Clark, 2019), pp. 71–80.

Florovsky, G., "Preface to *In Ligno Crucis*", in B. Gallaher and P. Ladouceur, eds, *The Patristic Witness of Georges Florovsky* (London: T&T Clark, 2019), pp. 65–70.

Florovsky, G., "Redemption," *Creation and Redemption. The Collected Works of Georges Florovsky*, vol. III (Belmont, MA: Nordland Publishing Company, 1976), pp. 95–159, 280–309.

Florovsky, G., *The Byzantine Fathers of the Sixth to Eighth Century*, vol. IX of *The Collected Works of Georges Florovsky* (Belmont, MA: Nordland Publishing Company, 1976).

Florovsky, G., "The Lamb of God", in B. Gallaher and P. Ladouceur, eds, *The Patristic Witness of Georges Florovsky* (London: T&T Clark, 2019), pp. 81–94.

Florovsky, G., "The Last Things and the Last Events", *Creation and Redemption. The Collected Works of Georges Florovsky*, vol. III (Belmont, MA: Nordland Press, 1976), pp. 243–265, 317.

Florovsky, G., "The Predicament of the Christian Historian", in B. Gallaher and P. Ladouceur, eds, *The Patristic Witness of Georges Florovsky* (London: T&T Clark, 2019), pp. 193–220.

Gilson, É., *L'esprit de la philosophie médiéval* (Paris: J. Vrin, 1932).

Hays, C.M. *et al.*, eds., *When the Son of Man Didn't Come: A Constructive Proposal on the Delay of the Parousia* (Minneapolis, MN: Fortress Press, 2016).

Heidegger, M., *Being and Time*, trans. J. Macquarrie and E. Robinson (Oxford: Basil Blackwell, 1967).

Heidegger, M., *Der Begriff der Zeit* (Frankfurt: Vittorio Klostermann, 2004). Eng. trans. by I. Farin, *The Concept of Time: The First Draft of Being and Time* (London: Continuum, 2011).

Heidegger, M., *Identity and Difference*, trans. J. Stambaugh (New York: Harper & Row, 1969).

Hengel, M., *Judaism and Hellenism: Studies in their Encounter in Palestine during the Early Hellenistic Period* (London: SCM Press, 1974).

Jeremias, J., *The Eucharistic Words of Jesus*, trans. N. Perrin (London: SCM Press, 1966).

Jeremias, J., *New Testament Theology*, trans. J. Bowden (London: SCM Press, 1971).

Kelly, J.N.D., *Early Christian Doctrines*, rev. ed. (New York: Harper Collins, 1978).

Larchet, J.C., *La divinisation de l'homme selon saint Maxime le Confesseur* (Paris: Éditions du Cerf, 1996).

La Verdiere, E., *The Eucharist in the New Testament and the Early Church* (Collegeville, MN: Liturgical Press, 1996).

Levinas, E., *Ethique et Infini* (Paris: Fayard, 1982). Eng. trans. by R. Cohen, *Ethics and Infinity: Conversations with Philippe Nemo* (Pittsburgh, PA: Duquesne University Press, 1985).

Levinas, E., *God, Death and Time*, ed. J. Rolland, trans. B. Bergo (Stanford, CA: Stanford University Press, 2000).

Levinas, E., *Totalité et Infini* (The Hague: M. Nijhoff, 1971). Eng. trans. *Totality and Infinity: An Essay on Exteriority* (Dordrecht: Kluwer Academic Publisher, 1991).

Lison, J., *L'Esprit répandu: La pneumatologie de Grégoire Palamas* (Paris: Éditions du Cerf, 1994).

Lohmeyer, E., *Our Father: An Introduction to the Lord's Prayer*, trans. J. Bowden (London: Collins, 1965).

Lossky, V., *The Mystical Theology of the Eastern Church* (Cambridge: James Clarke & Co., 2005).

Lossky, V., *The Vision of God*, trans. Asheleigh Moorhouse (Leighton Buzzard, Bedfordshire: Faith Press, 1963).

Louth, A., *Maximos the Confessor* (London: Routledge, 1996).

Lubac, H. de, *Corpus Mysticum: The Eucharist and the Church in the Middle Ages*, trans. G. Simmonds (London: SCM Press, 2006).

MacIntyre, A., *After Virtue* (London: Duckworth, 1981).

MacIntyre, A., *A Short History of Ethics* (Notre Dame, IN: University of Notre Dame Press, 1998).

McIntyre, J., *The Christian Doctrine of History* (Edinburgh: Oliver and Boyde, 1957).

MacKinnon, D.M., "Death," in A. Flew and A. MacIntyre, eds, *New Essays in Philosophical Theology* (New York: Macmillan, 1955), pp. 261–266.

McPartlan, P., *The Eucharist Makes the Church. Henri de Lubac and John Zizioulas in Dialogue* (Edinburgh: T&T Clark, 1993).

Macquarrie, J., *Principles of Christian Theology* (London: SCM Press, 1977).

Mannheim, K., *Essays on the Sociology of Knowledge*, ed. P. Kecsmeti (London: Routledge and Kegan Paul, 1952).

Manoussakis, J.P., "The Anarchic Principle of Christian Eschatology in the Eucharistic Tradition of the Eastern Church," *Harvard Theological Review* 100:1 (2007) 29–46.

Manoussakis, J.P., *The Ethics of Time: A Phenomenology and Hermeneutics of Change* (London: Bloomsbury, 2017).

Manson, T.W., *The Teaching of Jesus* (Cambridge: Cambridge University Press, 1955).

Marcel, G., *"Tu ne mourras pas," Textes choisis et présentés par Anna Marcel* (Paris: Éditions Arfuyen, 2012).

Marion, J.-L., *Dieu sans l'être*, 4th edn (Paris: PUF, 2013). Eng. trans. from 2nd edn by T.A. Carlson, *God Without Being* (Chicago and London: University of Chicago Press, 2012).

Meyendorff, J., *Byzantine Theology* (New York: Fordham University Press, 1979).

Meyendorff, J., "Εφ' ᾧ chez Cyrille d'Alexandrie et Théodoret," *Studia Patristica* 5 (1961) 157–161.

Meyendorff, J., *The Byzantine Legacy in the Orthodox Church* (Crestwood, NY: St Vladimir's Seminary Press, 1982).

Michel, O., "μιμνήσκομαι," in G. Kittel, *Theological Dictionary of the New Testament*, vol. IV, trans. and ed. G.W. Bromiley (Grand Rapids, MI: Eerdmans, 1967), pp. 675–678.

Moltmann, J., *God in Creation: A New Theology of Creation and the Spirit of God*, trans. M. Kohl (Minneapolis, MN: Fortress Press, 1993).

Moltmann, J., "Hope and Confidence: A Conversation with Ernst Bloch," *Dialog* 7 (1968) 42–55.

Moltmann, J., *The Crucified God. The Cross of Christ as the Foundation and Criticism of Christian Theology* (Minneapolis, MN: Fortress Press, 1993).

Moltmann, J., *Theology of Hope: On the Ground and Implications of a Christian Eschatology*, trans. J.W. Leitch (London: SCM Press; New York: Harper, 1967).

Morse, C., *The Logic of Promise in Moltmann's Theology* (Philadelphia, PA: Fortress Press, 1979).

Moule, C.F.D., *The Birth of the New Testament* (London: A. & C. Black, 1981).

Mowinckel, S., *He That Cometh: The Messiah Concept in the Old Testament and Later Judaism*, trans. G.W. Anderson (Oxford: Basil Blackwell, 1956).

Mpetsakos, V., Στάσις Ἀεικίνητος (Athens: Armos, 2006).

O'Donovan, O., *Resurrection and Moral Order* (Grand Rapids, MI: Eerdmans Publishing, 1994).

Pannenberg, W., *Basic Questions in Theology*, vol. III (London: SCM Press, 1973).

Pannenberg, W., *Jesus–God and Man* (Philadelphia, PA: The Westminster Press, 1977).

Pannenberg, W., *Revelation as History* (with R. Rendtorff *et al.*) (London: Macmillan, 1969).

Pannenberg, W., *Systematic Theology*, trans. G.W. Bromiley, 3 vols (New York and London: T&T Clark International, 2004).

Pannenberg, W., "Theological Appropriation of Scientific Understandings. Response to Hefner, Wicken, Eaves, and Tipler," *Zygon: Journal of Religion and Science* 24 (1989) 255–271.

Pannenberg, W., "Theological Questions to Scientists," *Zygon: Journal of Religion and Science* 16 (1981) 65–77 (also in A.R. Peacock, ed., *The Sciences and Theology in the Twentieth Century* [Notre Dame, IN: University of Notre Dame Press, 1981]).

Papanikolaou, A., *Being With God: Trinity, Apophaticism, and Divine-Human Communion* (Notre Dame, IN: University of Notre Dame Press, 2006).

Papanikolaou, A., "Creation as Communion in Contemporary Orthodox Theology," in J. Chryssavgis and B.V. Folz, eds, *Toward an Ecology of Transfiguration: Orthodox Christian Perspectives on Environment, Nature and Creation* (New York: Fordham University Press, 2013), pp. 106–114, 426–427.

Papanikolaou, A., *The Mystical as Political: Democracy and Non-Radical Orthodoxy* (Notre Dame, IN: University of Notre Dame Press, 2012).

Polkinghorne, J. ed., *The Trinity and an Entangled World* (Grand Rapids, MI: Eerdmans, 2010).

Polkinghorne, J. and M. Welker, eds, *The End of the World and the Ends of God: Science and Theology on Eschatology* (Harrisburg, PA: Trinity Press, 2000).

Prigent, P., *Apocalypse et Liturgie* (Neuchâtel, Paris: Delachaux et Niestlé, 1964).

Rahner, K., *On the Theology of Death* (New York: Herder and Herder, 1961).

Rahner, K., "Theos in the New Testament," *Theological Investigations*, vol. I (London: Darton, Longman and Todd; New York: Seabury Press, 1974), pp. 125–130.

Rahner, K., *The Trinity*, trans. J. Donceel (New York: Seabury Press, 1970).

Ricoeur, P., *La symbolique du mal* (Paris: Aubier, 1960).

Riou, A., *Le monde et l'Église selon Maxime le Confesseur* (Paris: Beauchesne, 1973).

Rordorf, W., *Sunday: The History of the Day of Rest and Worship in the Early Centuries of the Christian Church* (London: SCM Press, 1968).

Ross, W.D., *Aristotle* (London: Methuen, 1959).

Russell, N., *The Doctrine of Deification in the Greek Patristic Tradition* (Oxford: Oxford University Press, 2004).

Russell, R., "Cosmology and Eschatology," in J.L. Walls, ed., *The Oxford Handbook of Eschatology* (Oxford: Oxford University Press, 2008), pp. 563–580.

Sartre, J.-P., *Essays in Existentialism*, ed. W. Baskin (London: Citadel, 1993).

Schmemann, A., *The Eucharist* (Crestwood, NY: St Vladimir's Seminary Press, 1988).

Schweitzer, A., *The Mystery of the Kingdom of God* (New York: Association Press, 1950).

Schweitzer, A., *The Quest of the Historical Jesus* (London: A. & C. Black, 1954).

Sherwood, P., *St. Maximus the Confessor. The Ascetic Life. The Four Centuries on Charity* (New York: Paulist Press, 1955).

Sherwood, P., *The Earlier Ambigua of St. Maximus the Confessor* (Rome: Pontificium Institutum S. Anselmi, 1955).

Shestov, L., *Athens and Jerusalem*, trans. B. Martin (Athens, OH: Ohio University Press, 1966).

Shestov, L., *Kiekegaard et la philosophie existentielle* (Paris: J. Vrin, 1948).

Sorabji, R., *Time, Creation and the Continuum* (London: Duckworth, 1983).

Swinburne, R., *The Resurrection of God Incarnate* (Oxford: Oxford University Press, 2003).

Taft, R., *A History of the Liturgy of St John Chrysostom*, vol. 4 *The Diptychs* (Rome: Pontificium Institutum Studiorum Orientalium, 1991).

Teilhard de Chardin, P., *The Vision of the Past*, trans. J.M. Cohen (London: Collins, 1966).

Thunberg, L., *Man and the Cosmos: The Vision of St Maximus the Confessor* (Crestwood, NY: St Vladimir's Seminary Press, 1985).

Thunberg, L., *Microcosm and Mediator: The Theological Anthropology of Maximus the Confessor* (Lund: C.W.K. Gleerup, 1965).

Tipler, F.J., *The Physics of Immortality: Modern Cosmology, God and the Resurrection of the Dead* (New York: Doubleday, 1994).

Torrance, A., *Human Perfection in Byzantine Theology* (Oxford: Oxford University Press, 2020).

Vletsis, A., *Το Προπατορικό αμάρτημα στη θεολογία Μαξίμου του Ομολογητού* (Katerini: Tertios, 1996).

Walls, J.L., ed., *The Oxford Handbook of Eschatology* (Oxford: Oxford University Press, 2008).

White, L.R., Jr., "The Historical Roots of our Ecological Crisis," *Science* 155 (1967) 1203 – 7.

Williams, R., *Christ the Heart of Creation* (London: Bloomsbury Continuum, 2018).

Yangazoglou, S., *Κοινωνία θεώσεως. Η σύνθεση χριστολογίας καὶ πνευματολογίας στὸ ἔργο τοῦ ἁγίου Γρηγορίου τοῦ Παλαμᾶ* (Athens: Domos, 2001).

Zilsel, E., "The Genesis of the Concept of Scientific Progress," *Journal of the History of Ideas* 6 (1945) 325–349.

Zizioulas, J., *Being as Communion: Studies in Personhood and the Church* (Crestwood, NY: St Vladimir's Seminary Press, 1985).

Zizioulas, J., *Communion and Otherness: Further Studies in Personhood and the Church*, ed. P. McPartlan (New York: T&T Clark, 2006).

Zizioulas, J., *Eucharist, Bishop, Church: The Unity of the Church in the Divine Eucharist and the Bishop During the First Three Centuries*, trans. E. Theokritoff (Brookline, MA: Holy Cross Orthodox Press, 2001).

Zizioulas, J., "Person and Nature in the Theology of St. Maximus the Confessor," in M. Vasiljević, ed., *Knowing the Purpose of Creation through the Resurrection: Proceedings of the Symposium on St Maximus the Confessor, Belgrade, October 18–21, 2012* (Los Angeles: Sebastian Press, 2013), pp. 85–113.

Zizioulas, J., "Sola Fide: A Hermeneutical Approach," in C. Chalamet *et al.* eds., *Theological Anthropology, 500 Years After Martin Luther: Orthodox and Protestant Perspectives* (Leiden and Boston: Brill, 2021), pp. 3–16.

Zizioulas, J., *The Eucharistic Communion and the World* (London: T&T Clark, 2011).

Zizioulas, J., *The Meaning of Being Human* (Los Angeles: Sebastian Press, 2021).

Index of Scriptural References

Index of Names

Christou P. 242

Chryssavgis J. 114, 139

Clement of Alexandria 48, 177, 262, 267

Clément O. 123, 237

Cobb Jr. J.B. 105

Cohen J.M. 106

Congar Y. 6, 7, 78, 270

Constas N. 181

Contopoulos G. 120

Cotsakis T. 120

Cullmann O. 12, 19, 73, 74, 77–79, 160, 265, 269, 314

Collingwood R.G. 30, 95, 109

Croce B. 30, 95

Cyril Loukaris 271

Cyril of Alexandria 133, 282, 286, 305

Cyril of Jerusalem 82, 245, 246, 250, 282, 296–298

Dahl N. A. 10

Daley B.E. 143, 229

Damascius 87

Daniel 161

Daniélou J. 178, 264, 267, 269, 270

Dante 113

Darlap A. 254

Darwin C. 23, 105

Delikonstantis K. 204

Delitzch F. 172

Descartes 93, 208

Diels H. 87

Dilthey W. 30, 31

Diodore of Tarsus 236

Dionysius the Areopagite 67, 98, 114, 124, 155, 180, 189, 223, 262, 268, 275, 281

Dionysus 171

Dix G. 318

Donceel J. 39, 69

Donovan Oliver O' 55

Dositheus of Jerusalem 271

Dostoevsky F. 21, 208, 209, 227, 228

Dumont P. 249

Duns Scotus 67, 94

Einstein A. 145

Elert W. 307

Eliade M. 173

Elliot T.S. 126

Eriugena Scotus 180

Evagrius 48, 98, 141

Eubank N. 151

Euripides 23

Eusebius of Caesaria 262, 263, 268, 288

Evans M. 182

Fantino J. 176

Feiner J. 2

Feuerbach L. 182

Florovsky G. 1, 4, 8, 17, 22, 26, 30, 33–35, 40, 42, 64, 81, 95, 97, 109, 157, 180, 181, 233, 243, 268, 301

Filson F.V. 73, 160, 309

Flew A. 83

Foltz B.V. 114, 139

Freud L. 94

Freud S. 191

Gallaher B. 1

Gadamer H.-G. 12, 31, 32

Garrigues J.-M. 129

Gilson E. 69

Gennadios of Constantinople 299

Getcha J. 204

Goethe 149

Goodrich J.K. 197

Gregory Nazianzen 21, 38, 65, 67, 70, 133, 177, 179, 219, 269, 282

Gregory of Nyssa 65, 82, 98, 121, 124, 151, 177, 185, 201, 205, 206, 221, 224, 237, 238, 239, 241, 265, 269, 308

Gregory of Sinai 236

Gregory Palamas 65, 70, 114, 123, 124, 134, 141, 211, 213, 214

Griffin D.R. 24

Grumel V. 221

Gunkel H. 174

Guthrie S.C. 77

Hall C.A.M. 77

Hänge A. 6

Hankey W.J. 69
Harmer J.R. 7, 13
Harnack A. von 2, 3, 291
Hauerwas S. 57
Haught J.F. 120
Hays C.M. 215
Hegel G. 192, 208, 209
Heinzer F. 129
Hengel M. 64, 84
Heraclitus 87
Hermas 46, 174
Herodotus 29
Heidegger M. 4, 25, 31–33, 36–39, 63, 69,
   104, 109, 254
Hesiod 23, 171
Hobbes T. 56
Homer 72
Hoskyn E. C. 1
Hume 44
Husserl 4

Ignatius of Antioch 13, 139, 157, 174, 244,
   245, 288, 304, 317
Ionescu E. 100
Irenaeus of Lyon 14, 19, 21, 29, 55, 76, 81,
   84, 91, 123, 124, 128, 129, 133, 135, 139, 155,
   157, 186
Isaac the Syrian 236, 251
Isaiah 161, 175–177, 198, 203, 213, 226, 233,
   245, 264, 268, 269, 289, 293, 317

Jackson B. 289
Jakim B. 84
Jeremias J. 7, 10, 76, 272, 278, 294
Jerome 82
John Chrysostom 6, 65, 66, 80, 140, 206,
   245, 246, 247, 250, 267, 272, 283, 292,
   298, 299
John Damascene [John of Damascus] 67,
   140, 164, 165, 222, 232, 242, 268, 289, 290
John Philoponus 91
John of Skythopolis 206, 223, 276
John the Baptist 264
Jonas H. 172
Justin 65, 123, 175, 201, 264, 288

Kafka F. 203
Kalamatas M. 243
Kant I. 44, 208
Karmiris J. 238, 301
Kattenbusch F. 78
Kaufmann W. 23, 95
Kearny R. 4
Kecskemeti P. 150
Keil C.F. 172
Kelly J.N.D. 70, 84, 193
Kirk G.S. 87
Kittel G. 9, 64, 284
Kierkegaard S. 13, 208, 209, 254

Lacoste J.-Y. 4
Ladouceur P. 1
Lamarche P. 132
Larchet J.-C. 179, 182, 239
Leibnitz G. 40, 70, 192, 208
Leontius of Cyprus 140
Leitch W., 3
Levinas E., 35–39, 41
Leon-Dufour X., 132
Lietzmann H. 273
Lightfoot J.B. 7, 13
Lison J. 123
Locke J. 56
Lohmeyer E. 72, 76, 274
Lossky V. 4, 5, 84, 113, 114, 137
Lot 90
Louth A. 182, 221
Lubac H. de 269, 301
Luneau S. 209
Lyotard J.-F., 149

MacAndrew A.R. 209
Macarius of Egypt 49, 98
Mackintosh H. R. 2
MacIntyre A. 44, 46, 74, 83
Mackinnon D. 83
Macquarrie J. 25, 120
Mannheim K. 150
Manoussakis J.P. 4, 94, 203
Manson T.W. 78

Index kindly produced by
Fr. Basil Gavrilović.

Biographical Note

John D. Zizioulas (1931–2023) was a modern theologian and former Metropolitan of Pergamon, in the Ecumenical Patriarchate of Constantinople.

He was born in Greece, January 10, 1931. He began his studies at the University of Thessaloniki, but received his undergraduate degree in theology from the University of Athens in 1955, where he also later received a degree of Doctor of Theology.

Metropolitan John's education included a period of study under the Eastern Orthodox theologian Father Georges Florovsky at Harvard Divinity School. He received his M.T.S. at Harvard in 1956 and was a Fellow at Dumbarton Oaks Center for Byzantine Studies. He received a doctorate in theology from the University of Athens in 1965. His doctoral thesis on the bishop in the early Church was published in English as *Eucharist, Bishop, Church: The Unity of the Church in the Divine Eucharist and the Bishop During the First Three Centuries* (Brookline, MA: Holy Cross Orthodox Press, 2001).

Somewhat later, he taught theology at the University of Edinburgh for a period, before becoming Professor of Systematic Theology at the University of Glasgow, where he held a personal chair in systematic theology for some fourteen years. In addition, he went on to be Visiting Professor at the University of Geneva, King's College London, and the Gregorian University, Rome. He was also a part-time professor at the University of Thessaloniki. Metropolitan John became a regular member of the Academy of Athens in 1993 and its president in 2002–2003.

He was consecrated as a bishop on June 22, 1986, and named Metropolitan of Pergamon. He has represented the Ecumenical Patriarchate on international Church bodies for many years. Metropolitan John was a member of the committees for dialogue with the Roman Catholic Church, and with the Anglican Church, and was Secretary of Faith and Order at the World Council of Churches in Geneva, where he gradually came to be recognized as one of the most influential Orthodox theologians of our times.

His ecumenical involvement has led him to publish a number of articles and studies in various periodicals. Some of his books are *L'Être ecclésial* (Paris: Labor et Fides, 1981), *Being as Communion: Studies in Personhood and the Church* (Crestwood, NY: St Vladimir's Seminary Press, 1985), *Communion and Otherness* (London: T&T Clark, 2006), *Lectures in Christian Dogmatics* (London: T&T Clark, 2009), *The One and the Many* (Los Angeles: Sebastian Press 2011), *The Eucharistic Communion and the World* (London: T&T Clark, 2011).

HERE ENDS THE BOOK, "REMEM-
BERING THE FUTURE: AN ESCHATO-
LOGICAL ONTOLOGY" BY JOHN D. ZI-
ZIOULAS, EDITED BY BISHOP MAXIM
VASILJEVIĆ AND PROLOGUED BY POPE
FRANCIS; THIS EDITION IS LIMITED
TO 2000 COPIES, IN THE CONTEMPO-
RARY CHRISTIAN THOUGHT SERIES,
NUMBER 81, PRINTED AT THE
BIROGRAF COMP IN BELGRADE,
SERBIA, REALIZED BY SEBASTIAN
PRESS IN LOS ANGELES, CA, AND
FINISHED ON THE 1TH DAY OF
OCTOBER IN THE YEAR OF THE LORD
2023.